D1594560

STRATEGIC CURRENCY INVESTING

TRADING AND HEDGING IN THE FOREIGN EXCHANGE MARKET

ANDREW W. GITLIN
EDITOR

PROBUS PUBLISHING COMPANY
Chicago, Illinois
Cambridge, England

This publication is designed to provide accurate and authoritative information in regard to the subject matter covered. It is sold with the understanding that the author and the publisher are not engaged in rendering legal, accounting, or other professional service.

Authorization to photocopy items for internal or personal use, or the internal or personal use of specific clients, is granted by PROBUS PUBLISHING COMPANY, provided that the U.S. $7.00 per page fee is paid directly to Copyright Clearance Center, 27 Congress Street, Salem, MA 01970, USA; Phone: 1-508-744-3350. For those organizations that have been granted a photocopy license by CCC, a separate system of payment has been arranged. The fee code for users of the Transactional Reporting Service is 1-55738-466-5/93/$00.00 + $7.00.

ISBN 1-55738-466-5

Printed in the United States of America

BB

1 2 3 4 5 6 7 8 9 0

Contents

In the News

Preface

Strategic Currency Investing is a discussion of the impact currencies have on investors and treasurers, and some of the many ways they can respond to such impact. The book is intended to assist professionals in choosing the appropriate currency management ideas for their individual needs. In this regard, readers will appreciate that the contributors to this book include practitioners in and professors of the art of currency management. As such, this book is a forum for current thinking presented by those most responsible for developing or implementing advances in currency management. The authors discuss a myriad of currency management strategies as well as techniques for implementation. Consider this book a convenient and concise opportunity to sample ideas and techniques from some of the most renowned currency professionals in the market today.

Reviewed in this book are the two basic reasons for engaging in active currency management. First, to hedge the risk resulting from exposure to foreign denominated assets or liabilities. Second, to generate investment returns by taking advantage of currency market opportunities. These two endeavors are intimately related. In fact, the tone of this book should cause one to draw a link between these activities. Investing in the currency market requires some ability or tool for predicting the expected behavior of currency prices. Bear in mind that at the heart of any active or dynamic currency hedging program (often called "overlay") is the need for having a view on currency price direction. Ultimately, both currency overlay and currency investment programs are driven by the same basic engine, which must perform well for the client to benefit.

The title of this book is meant to convey the need for corporate treasurers and institutional investors to actively confront the impact that the currency market may have on their financial results. The key word in the title is "strategic." It suggests that any approach to currencies must be planned, methodical, and managed as professionally as any other component of a portfolio or balance sheet. There are numerous ways treasurers and investors may approach currencies, including hiring external professionals or using in-house management. The book simply argues for actively reviewing the opportunities and risks that currencies generate, and taking appropriate action.

My opinions on these matters may be distilled to the following: First, do not minimize the complexity of this market. More than perhaps any financial instrument, currency prices incorporate the most complete range of global economic and political realities and expectations. To dismiss currencies as extraneous noise is to ignore some of the more potent information available in the global capital market arena. The management of currencies without innovative, experienced guidance, either in-house or through external professionals, is simply not prudent. Second, to dismiss the potential investment returns that can be generated from the currency market, on a reasonable risk adjusted basis, is to miss some significant opportunities.

Readers will come across a few *Wall Street Journal* articles throughout the book. I believe that these articles help illustrate that the currency market is perhaps the most dynamic, challenging and, frankly, exciting financial market on earth.

For those who are new to the currency market, the appendix provides an overview of how this market operates.

The authors represented in this book have contributed their chapters as a way to share with the reader their thinking about the currency market. As such, the opinions and ideas expressed are exclusively those of the authors and not those of the editor or of any companies with which the editor is affiliated.

I would like to express my appreciation to all the authors for the thoughtful work they have put into their submissions. A special thanks go to Nancy Allen, Andrew Kaplan and Rajiv Nanda for their invaluable assistance. Also, thanks to Probus Publishing, particularly Pamela van Giessen for her patience; Linda McLaughlin for her help; and Diana Andrews for, among other things, her design expertise.

Andrew W. Gitlin
AIG International Asset Management Inc.
Greenwich, Connecticut

About the Editor

Andrew W. Gitlin is President of AIG International Asset Management Inc. (AIGIAM), a company managing private global hedge funds. These hedge funds utilize a broad diversification strategy with substantial emphasis placed on innovative international investment opportunities as well as structured strategies employing derivative instruments. AIGIAM is majority-owned by AIG Trading Corporation (AIGTC), which engages in trading and market making activities in spot, forwards, options, swaps, and other derivatives in foreign exchange, energy, and metals. AIGTC is a wholly-owned subsidiary of American International Group, Inc., a leading diversified global insurance and financial services organization.

After earning a degree from Cornell University, Mr. Gitlin spent four years in investment management and venture capital. He went on to spend two years in foreign exchange trading and has spent the last four years as an international investment fund manager.

About the Contributors

Kevin Bailey joined Record Treasury Management Ltd. in 1988 and was appointed a Director of the firm in 1993. He is responsible for US client relations and marketing. He received a degree in Mathematics from Bristol University and a MSc in Statistics from London University.

Record Treasury Management Ltd. is a currency risk management company based in Europe.

Sheri Gorin Baker is Senior Vice President of KB Currency Advisors, Inc.

KB Currency Advisors, Inc., is a foreign exchange investment management and hedging/advisory firm located in Englewood Cliffs, New Jersey.

John F. O. Bilson is a vice president with Trading Development Corporation, a commodity trading advisor, located in Chicago.

David F. DeRosa is with the foreign exchange trading unit of the Swiss Bank Corporation. He received an A.B. in Economics and a Ph.D. in Finance from the

University of Chicago. He is the author of *Managing Foreign Exchange Risk* and *Options on Foreign Exchange,* both available from Probus Publishing.

Martha Eden is responsible for currency research and trading at The Hanseatic Group. She received an undergraduate degree in Economics from Vassar College.

The Hanseatic Group is an investment firm specializing in trading and hedging programs in the global markets using a technical system.

Anthony Foley graduated from Oxford University with a BA in Philosophy, Politics and Economics before earning a MSc in Economics from the London School of Economics. Mr. Foley first worked for Touche Remnant monitoring UK economic performance, then Salomon Brothers as an International Bond Strategist before joining Pareto Partners, where he is responsible for product development and enhancement.

Pareto Partners, located in London, is an investment advisor engaged exclusively in quantitative management of value-added currency, equity, fixed income, cash and tactical asset allocation strategies for institutional clients worldwide.

William Fung received a Ph.D. in Mathematics from London University and a Ph.D. in Finance from the University of Manchester. He taught for eight years in

England and the United States before joining Lehman Brothers and then Bankers Trust. Mr. Fung is a specialist in derivative products and the development of computerized trading models. He is currently Principal of Falcon Investment Management Corp.

Falcon Investment Management Corporation, an investment management company located in New Jersey, specializes in non-exchange traded instruments and derivatives on these instruments.

Gerry Grimes is a Director of Gandon Fund Management Limited, an associated person and a member of the Institute of Bankers. He worked for ten years in the Central Bank of Ireland in various investment management positions. Ultimately, as Chief Foreign Exchange Dealer, he was responsible for the currency allocation of the external reserves and the management of the Irish pound in the European Exchange Rate Mechanism. In April 1988 he joined Gandon.

Gandon Fund Management Limited is a Dublin-based investment management firm specializing in currency and financial futures trading.

Sanford J. Grossman is the Steinberg Trustee Professor of Finance at the Wharton School, University of Pennsylvania. From 1985 until 1989 he taught at Princeton University, where he held the position of John L. Weinberg Professor of Economics.

He has been an economist with the Board of Governors of the Federal Reserve System, and had also taught at Stanford University, the University of Pennsylvania, and the University of Chicago.

Quantitative Financial Strategies, Inc. (QFS) was founded by Dr. Sanford J. Grossman to develop financial investment models using his research discoveries in the field of quantitative finance.

David Hsieh is currently Associate Editor of the *Review of Futures Markets, Journal of International Financial Markets* and *Institutions & Money*. In addition, he has spent most of his career teaching Economics and Finance at the University of Chicago, Graduate School of Business, and Duke University, Fuque School of Business.

Eunan King is a Senior Economist with Gandon. He previously was Treasury Economist with Bank of Ireland Group Treasury and spent nine years in various economic departments in the Central Bank of Ireland.

Gandon Fund Management Limited is a Dublin-based investment management firm specializing in currency and financial futures trading.

James T. Kneafsey is President and Chief Hedging Strategist for the Cambridge Foreign Currency Hedging Program. Prior to founding Cambridge Financial Management, Mr. Kneafsey was a faculty member at M.I.T. He received a Ph.D. in Economics from Ohio State University, an M.A. in Economics from the University of Florida, and a B.S. in Mathematics from Loyola College.

Cambridge Financial Management, Inc., is a registered investment advisor providing foreign exchange hedging programs to institutional clients.

Andrew J. Krieger, a foreign currency and currency option trader and Managing Director of KB Currency Advisors, Inc., built his career at Salomon Brothers and then Bankers Trust.

KB Currency Advisors, Inc. is a foreign exchange investment management and hedging/advisory firm located in Englewood Cliffs, New Jersey.

Adrian F. Lee is a manager of the International Fixed Income and Currency Group in London, where he has been responsible for much of J. P. Morgan's currency management research. Mr. Lee earned an MA in Mathematical Economics and Statistics from Trinity College, Dublin, and an MBA in Finance & Actuarial Science from the Wharton School of Business.

J. P. Morgan Investment Management Inc., a wholly owned subsidiary of J. P. Morgan & Company, Inc., provides international asset management services to U. S. tax-exempt funds and international clients.

James Leitner received a Bachelors Degree in Economics from Yale, then went on to earn a Masters Degree in International Finance from Columbia University. Mr. Leitner has been trading in the foreign exchange and global interest rate markets for 15 years. In 1991, he established Falcon Investment Management Corporation with Mr. Fung.

Falcon Investment Management Corporation, an investment management company located in New Jersey, specializes in non-exchange traded instruments and derivatives on these instruments.

Richard M. Levich is a Professor of Finance and International Business at the Stern School of Business, New York University, as well as a Member of the National Bureau of Economic Research.

Anthony Minopoli is responsible for futures research at EAI. He joined EAI in 1987 as a member of the research department, where he concentrated his efforts in structured fixed-income products and derivative strategies.

Evaluation Associates, Inc. (EAI) is a consulting firm, located in Norwalk, Connecticut. EAI's work involves establishing investment policy and objectives, prescribing asset allocation, defining management structure, selecting and monitoring investment managers and providing performance evaluation.

Virginia R. Parker graduated with an AB Degree in Economics and

Political Science from Duke University. She joined Ferrell Capital in 1988 and works as Director of Research for Ferrell Capital Management. Her responsibilities include analysis of trading strategies using derivative instruments. Ms. Parker has developed two indices, the Ferrell FX Manager Universe and the Ferrell FX Index.

Ferrell Capital Management, based in Greenwich, Connecticut, specializes in designing and managing diversified investment portfolios for institutions and private investors.

Grant N. Smith joined Millburn in 1975 to do quantitative research in futures markets. He is currently Senior Vice President, Director of Research & Computer Support, and a principal of the firm.

Millburn Ridgefield Corporation is a registered investment advisor located in New York, specializing in interbank currencies and financial futures.

John R. Taylor, founder of FX Concepts, has been an active participant in foreign exchange for over 10 years. Prior to founding FX Concepts, Mr. Taylor worked in the foreign exchange areas of Citibank and Chemical Bank. He is a graduate of Princeton University.

FX Concepts is a foreign currency manager responsible for corporate, public pension and institutional and individual investor assets. The company has been in the FX business for over 10 years.

Lee R. Thomas is a Member of the Management Committee of Investcorp Bank E.C., Bahrain. He is responsible for managing the Proprietary Trading Department and a number of investment funds.

Ezra Zask is President of Ezra Zask Associates, Inc. He held previous positions with Mellon Bank, as Senior Vice President and Global FX Manager, and Manufacturers Hanover Trust, as Managing Director and European FX Manager, where he consulted widely with corporations, pension funds, and financial institutions on currency and interest rate risk management. In addition, he has also lectured and written extensively on financial risk management and was adjunct professor of finance at Carnegie-Mellon University.

In the News

Pound Crisis Shakes World Currency Markets

Douglas R. Sease
Staff Reporter, *The Wall Street Journal*
Reprinted from *The Wall Street Journal,* Sept. 28, 1992

On September 16, 1992, world currency markets were racked by some of the most turbulent trading in memory amid the chaos surrounding the apparent breakdown of Europe's Exchange Rate Mechanism.

"It was a crazy day," said Lawrence Weinman, manager of currency option sales at Societe Generale. All the assumptions that have sustained currency traders "were collapsing before their eyes."

Among the major European currencies, the mark was a big winner as traders bet that other currencies would be forced to devalue against the mark. The pound, on the other hand, was the big loser, plunging 2.7 percent against the mark after Britain decided to suspend its membership in the ERM, a step tantamount to devaluation.

But stock and bond markets fared far better as many traders and investors became convinced that the turmoil ultimately will result in sharply lower interest rates in Europe and renewed economic growth both in the U.S. and abroad.

"The pressure is so intense that we'll get to the promised land of lower interest rates pretty fast," said Richard Hoey, chief economist at Dreyfus Corp. "Defending indefensible exchange rates with intolerable interest rates clearly can't last."

The result was a mixed close for U.S. stocks, modest gains in stock prices in London, Paris, Zurich, and Amsterdam and equally modest declines in stock markets in Frankfurt, Stockholm, and Milan. Government bond markets showed similarly mixed results. Although U.S. Treasury bonds lost some ground, and British government bonds tumbled, German and French government bonds rallied sharply.

But the relative calm that descended over the stock and bond markets did nothing to smooth the frenzied action in currency markets. Traders on foreign exchange desks around the world were hard pressed to keep up with the rushing flow of news and rumors. The U.S. dollar benefited from a flight to safety as some traders sought refuge from the chaos of Europe, soaring 4.5 percent against the British pound and gaining 1.3 percent against the mark. But the focus was on the rapidly shifting relationships among Europe's various currencies.

Although the roots of the currency crisis lay in Germany's high interest rates, Britain took center stage. Stock, bond and currency traders arriving at their desks throughout Europe were confronted by a two-percentage-point increase in the Bank of England's minimum lending rate. The increase was aimed at bolstering the sickly British pound, but flopped, leaving the pound at the bottom of its trading band against the German mark as set by the European Monetary System.

Later in the day, the Bank of England took the extraordinary step of announcing a further planned increase of three points in the minimum lending rate, to 15 percent; that, too, failed to bolster the pound. The Bank of England later said it wouldn't implement the second rate increase. Instead, Britain announced it would suspend sterling from the ERM, effective September 17, 1992.

The European Community's Monetary Committee subsequently held an emergency meeting in Brussels. At the conclusion of the meeting, it was announced that Italy would abstain temporarily from intervention in the foreign-exchange market and that the Spanish peseta was being devalued 5 percent.

While the suspensions could result in the dissolution of the ERM, which links together 11 European currencies, analysts said a realignment is the more likely outcome. "If they did get rid of the ERM snake that has been killing everyone with high interest rates, it might not be the worst thing that could happen," said Peter Canelo, a market strategist at County NatWest in New York. "But I think instead this will force a necessary realignment of European currencies."

Analysts predicted that the ultimate result of the crisis would be lower interest rates in Europe as Germany's Bundesbank bows to the increasing international pressure to relax the high interest rates that have impeded European growth. Britain and other countries in the ERM have had to keep interest rates higher than they wished in order to defend their currencies' values.

"It appears that the foreign exchange markets are going to continue to fire salvos across the bow of German monetary policy, and that over time that's going to lead to lower rates in Germany," said Hugh Johnson, chief investment officer at First Albany Corp. "Frankly, the Germans have to be convinced to become better team players in the exchange markets."

The intensity of the currency crisis prompted some investors to retreat to the safety of dollar-denominated

FIGURE 1.1 A Tumultuous Week in World Financial Markets

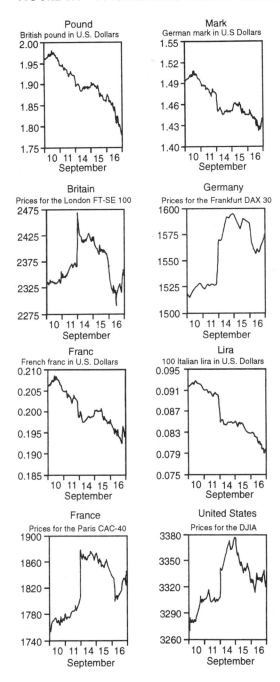

Pound
British pound in U.S. Dollars

Mark
German mark in U.S Dollars

Britain
Prices for the London FT-SE 100

Germany
Prices for the Frankfurt DAX 30

Franc
French franc in U.S. Dollars

Lira
100 Italian lira in U.S. Dollars

France
Prices for the Paris CAC-40

United States
Prices for the DJIA

investments, such as U.S. Treasury bills. Alan Brown, chief financial officer of Panagora Asset Management, which manages $650 million in three short-term global income funds, said he had raised the U.S. short-term holdings in the funds to between 50 percent and 60 percent from 30 percent.

"There are chaotic market conditions in a number of places, and there's really no place to hide" in Europe, he said. "In disorderly market conditions, the manager reserves the right to retreat back home."

Other money managers said they were sitting tight until the results of the vote in France on the Maastricht treaty that calls for greater European unity. The future of that treaty was already in doubt.

"Any investment decision made today has a half life of about 30 minutes," said Lawrence Marks, managing director of Harbor Capital Management, which oversees about $1.2 billion in pension money.

But even as conservative money managers were heading for safety, or at least delaying any major decisions, investors with a more speculative bent were selling safe but relatively low-yielding U.S. debt securities to gamble on making big killings in European notes and bonds if interest rates abroad fall rapidly. That selling of U.S. notes and bonds contributed to the modest decline in U.S. bond prices seen on September 16, 1992.

And then there were the joyous investors cashing in on earlier bets that the value of the pound, mark and Italian lira would decline. "I'm absolutely giddy," said Nicole Holmes, European fund manager for ARCO Investment Management, the investment arm of Atlantic Richfield. ARCO made an average 6 percent profit on currency contracts it purchased in the second week of September 1992 on the three currencies. "Now I have to figure out what I'm going to do for an encore tomorrow."

Many analysts said most U.S. investors aren't likely to be much affected by the turmoil abroad, and may even profit in the long run.

"This whole thing is a European problem, not a U.S. problem," said Joseph McAlinden, chief market strategist at Dillon Read. "They created it by setting up the ERM in the first place. The other countries in Europe basically turned over their economic policy to the Bundesbank, and I don't think that can endure."

2

Currency Trading:
A European Perspective

Eunan King, Gandon Fund Management Limited
Gerry Grimes, Gandon Fund Management Limited

OBJECTIVES OF THIS CHAPTER

The main objective of this chapter is to provide a background to what differentiates trading currencies in European markets from other centres. In order to achieve this, the background and structure of the European currency markets is explored in detail with emphasis on the players, main currencies and main centres. Later, particular time is spent on the development of the European Exchange Rate Mechanism and the path toward European Monetary Union. Given the recent turmoil in the European markets and the importance of this subject to the future of European currency trading, this general area embodies the main part of this study. Finally, a view of what the future may hold for currency trading in Europe is spelt out.

STRUCTURE OF THE EUROPEAN CURRENCY MARKETS

Unlike the other main centres for currency trading, i.e., North America and the Far East, Europe is quite unique in the number of centres that are actively involved in the currency markets. For example, Switzerland alone has three main centres, with currency traders in Zurich, Basle and Geneva all claiming dominance in Swiss currency trading.

With the move toward greater capital liberalisation through the 1980s, strong domestic foreign currency markets were often seen as a good indication of the strength of an individual country's currency. As a result of this, currency centres emerged that had no historical experience or reputation for currency trading. The development and liberalisation of the credit markets of these countries were often seen as dependent on a strong currency market and as a result trading in currencies was actively encouraged by central banks. Currency trading now takes place right across Europe from Athens to Dublin.

The secular move throughout the 1980s by banks toward treasury operations and the move toward a freer trade zone in Europe with the consequent need for foreign currency transactions were also dominant factors in the development of the European markets. Indeed, it is difficult now to think of a European bank that would not have an active treasury/currency operation to service the large foreign currency requirements of European business. According to estimates by the EC, businesses across the continent convert $7.7 trillion from one member currency to another each year. Conversion charges on this activity amount to $13 billion, around 1/2 percent of EC GDP.

As explained previously, currency trading operates in Europe from a myriad of centres. However, the main dealing centers for foreign currency are London, Frankfurt, Paris, Amsterdam, Dublin, Milan, Zurich, Madrid, Copenhagen, Stockholm, Brussels, Luxembourg, Basle, Geneva and Oslo. Although turnover figures for each centre are not readily available, preliminary results for a study being collated and organized by the Bank of International Settlements in Basle based on trading volumes in April 1992 show some interesting data. The following table sets out the main findings and sets out some European turnover data against the world's other major trading centres.

Average Daily Currency Turnover April 1992

	US $ BN		US $ BN
United States	192	London	303
Japan	128	Frankfurt	57
Hong Kong	61	Paris	37
Canada	22	Switzerland	68
New Zealand	5	Belgium	18
Australia	35	Sweden	23
		Norway	7
		Ireland	6
		Netherlands	23

The obvious conclusions to be drawn from these numbers are as follows:

- Treating "time zones" as centres, Europe is by far the biggest and most liquid currency market.
- London is the most dominant centre within Europe and indeed the world.

The reasons for Europe's dominance in this regard are manifold. The most relevant point is the fact that each European country has its own currency so that from a trade viewpoint there are large commercial currency transactions taking place in Europe each day. Furthermore, the European investment community would tend to be less insular than their U.S. or Japanese counterparts with a greater willingness to invest outside their base currencies, thus leading to large investment flows throughout Europe. Perversely, the move toward a more stable currency regime in Europe encouraged such investment flows and they now form a large part of currency trading in Europe. Finally, Europe and in particular, London, has always been home to the style of currency trading known as "spot trading." Spot traders tend to have a continuous presence in the global currency markets with most trading decisions being made on a short-term, intra-day basis. While the moves being sought may be smaller in nature, spot trading, because of its continuous nature, leads to larger volumes of trading and more liquid markets as traders tend to be willing to make markets more readily in order to trade off their own side of the spread.

A more detailed examination of the data for London taken from the Bank of England survey in April 1992 showed some interesting details on European currency trading. As London is by far the most dominant currency centre in Europe, it is believed that the detail of trading in London can be taken as fairly representative of overall European currency trading. However, it is fair to assume that the level of Stg-based trading in London exaggerates the overall weighting of sterling.

Currency Composition

The relative shares of total turnover of the main currencies traded are presented in Table 2.1.

TABLE 2.1

	Spot	Forwards	1992 Total*	Total
L/US$	7.3	11.2	19	27
US$/DM	13.5	8.5	23	22
US$/Yen	5.1	7.0	13	15
US$/Swiss Franc	2.7	2.9	6	10
US$/Canadian $	0.7	1.9	3	2
US$/Australian $	0.6	1.5	2	2
US$/Lira	0.5	0.8	1	2
US$/Other ERM Currencies*	2.2	6.1	8	N/A
US$/Other	0.9	2.4	3	7
L/DM	4.8	0.8	6	3
L/Other	0.7	0.8	1	1
DM/Yen	2.1	0.3	3	2
DM/Other ERM Currencies*	3.5	0.3	4	*
Other Cross-Currencies	2.6	0.7	3	3
ECU-Denominated	2.3	2.6	5	2

*Including options and futures business

Source: Bank of England

The most interesting number from the above table is the dominance of the U.S. dollar in European currency trading. The U.S. dollar is the base currency for 78 percent of all currency transactions thus reaffirming its importance as the world's most liquid reserve currency. (In New York trading, the U.S. dollar is also the most actively traded currency being involved in 89 percent of all transactions.)

This large use of the dollar suggests the extent of the investment/speculative nature of European trading as commercial activity in dollars would account for a far smaller portion of overall trading. Perhaps the most surprising number is that for inter ERM trading, which only accounts for 9 percent of total trading. In this regard it should be noted that April was a relatively tranquil month in the ERM and September 1992 would surely show a far higher portion of overall currency trading. Furthermore a large portion of inter ERM trading tends to take place in the domestic markets. For most European currencies the most relevant and widely used cross rate is for the Deutschemark and individual centres tend to be dominated by domestic currency/DM trading. For example, in 1992 French Franc/Deutschemark trading accounted for 23 percent of trading in the Paris currency market.

THE PLAYERS

Bank treasury operations are by far the most important participants in the European currency markets. Of the total turnover in foreign exchange in London during April 1992, 77 percent was conducted on an interbank basis whether domestic or cross border. Other financial institutions accounted for 14 percent and nonfinancial institutions only accounted for 9 percent of total turnover.

Currency trading is not readily identified as a separate asset class in Europe. Rather most participants see it as a speculative/hedging medium. The emergence of the managed account business in Europe and the wide use of currencies within this business should help develop the view of currencies as a separate asset class but at this point of time the theory and development of this subject would seem to be mainly emanating from the U.S., despite the role of Europe as the major centre for currency trading.

TIME ZONE

The European time zone is often perceived as the most important reason for the dominance of Europe as a currency centre. Most European trading desks come in towards the close of Tokyo trading and exit towards the middle of the New York trading day. (In fact it is commonly viewed that New York trading loses much of its liquidity when Europe goes home.) Our own belief is that Europe is not "lucky" to have a fortuitous time zone but that, rather, the other markets tend of trade off Europe with this being far more relevant to New York than Tokyo. Tokyo tends to operate on a "stand-alone" basis with the yen being the dominant currency traded. Our own view is that if global time zones were rearranged in such a way as to place the U.S. after Tokyo and before Europe as opposed to vice versa that this would not necessarily see a major swing of trading activity toward the U.S.

HISTORICAL BACKGROUND TO ERM/EMU

At a meeting of the leaders of the European Economic Community in the Hague in 1969 agreement was reached to the eventual establishment of an economic and monetary union in Europe. This agreement was long on objectives and very short on detail.

However, in 1972 the post-Bretton Woods fixed exchange rate system was abandoned and several European currencies established a semi-fixed exchange rate regime known as "the Snake." With hindsight it would seem that the technicalities of this system were deficient in many respects and it had little hope of survival and in fact sterling's participation in this system only lasted six weeks. The oil shock of the mid 1970s and the consequent effect on inflation rates in Europe did not provide a proper background for moves towards monetary union and the project was by and large put on hold whilst member countries grappled with their own domestic problems.

The most important event towards EMU took place by a resolution of the European Council in December 1978 when the European Exchange Rate (ERM) and European Currency Unit (ECU) were agreed. The objective of the system was to encourage monetary stability in Europe which would eventually lead to full monetary union. The system itself whilst highly technical in nature is essentially a semi-fixed exchange rate regime in substance not overtly dissimilar to the failed "Snake" system of the early 1970s. The belief was that through instilling external discipline on individual members' exchange rates that they would be encouraged to adopt domestic policies on both the fiscal and monetary side, which would produce convergence across Europe towards a low inflation/sound money economic system, perhaps typified by post-war Germany.

The early days of the ERM saw limited success. Many countries had extreme difficulties adjusting to a low inflationary environment and discipline and the system only held together through frequent realignments of the member currencies of the system (see Table 2.2). The absence of Sterling from the ERM throughout the 1980s was cited by many as a sign of the system's incompletion.

At a meeting in Luxembourg in December 1985 the EC leaders agreed the watershed Single European Act which reaffirmed their commitment towards full monetary union by December 1992. These objectives got a serious push from the Delors report published in April 1989 which recommended a 3 stage approach towards EMU. These three stages are presented in Table 2.3.

At a meeting of EC leaders in Madrid in June 1989 it was agreed that Stage 1 of Delors should commence on 1 July 1990. This meeting confirmed for the first time the British intention to join the

TABLE 2.2 Realignments of the ERM

Date	Currency: DM	DFl	FFr	BFr	IL	DKr	IR£	Spta
24.09.79	+2	—	—	—	—	−3	—	—
30.11.79	—	—	—	—	—	−5	—	—
05.10.81	+5.5	+5.5	−3	—	−6	—	—	—
22.02.82	—	—	—	−8.5	−3	−3	—	—
14.06.82	+4.25	+4.25	−5.75	—	−2.75	—	—	—
21.03.83	+5.5	+3.5	−2.5	+1.5	−2.5	+2.5	−3.5	—
22.07.85	+2	+2	+2	+2	−6	+2	+2	—
07.04.86	+3	+3	−3	+1	—	+1	—	—
04.08.86	—	—	—	—	—	—	−8	—
12.01.87	+3	+3	—	+2	—	—	—	—
08.01.90	—	—	—	—	−3.75	—	—	—
14.09.92	+3.5	+3.5	+3.5	+3.5	−3.5	+3.5	+3.5	+3.5
17.09.92	—	—	—	—	—	—	—	−5
23.11.92	—	—	—	—	—	—	—	−6
01.02.93	—	—	—	—	—	—	−10	—
14.05.93	—	—	—	—	—	—	—	−8

Expressed in percentage parity changes.

Source: Commission of the European Communities.

TABLE 2.3 The Planned Stages Towards EMU

Economic	Monetary
Stage 1	
• Completion of the internal market.	• Capital market liberalisation.
• Strengthened competition policy.	• Enhanced monetary and exchange rate coordination.
• Full implementation of the reform of the structural funds.	• Realignments possible, but infrequent.
• Enhanced coordination and surveillance.	• All EC currencies in the narrow-bank ERM.
• Budgetary adjustments in high debt/ deficit countries.	• Extended use of the ECU.
Stage 2	
• Evaluation and adaptation of Stage 1 policies.	• Establishment of EuroFed.
• Review of national macroeconomic adjustments.	• Possible narrowing of ERM bands.
Stage 3	
• Definitive budgetary coordination system.	• EuroFed in charge of monetary policy.
• Possible strengthening of structural and regional policies.	• Irrevocably fixed exchange rates or ECU as single currency.

Source: Commission of European Communities.

ERM following major differences on this issue between Prime Minister Thatcher and several of her leading cabinet ministers.

Throughout 1990 the move towards EMU gathered pace. In January the Italian Lira moved to the narrow 2.25 percent band. In May Belgium announced its intention to hold the Belgian Franc in a narrower 1 percent band against the Deutschemark and in October Sterling became a member of the ERM joining the Spanish peseta in the wider 6 percent band.

In 1991 and part of 1992 there was unprecedented convergence of inflation and interest rates around Europe with the growing belief by financial markets that EMU was both possible and imminent. This belief was best reflected in the convergence of bond yields across Europe (see Table 2.4).

FIXED VERSUS FLOATING EXCHANGE RATES

The key difference between European currencies and other currency blocs is the bias in favour of fixed/semi-fixed exchange rates. In this section we examine the main arguments in this debate.

The main differences between a fixed exchange rate and a floating rate policy are the channels through which economies adjust to changes in demand and supply. The range of policy instruments available to the authorities is different if a fixed exchange rate target is in place.

For example, in situations of excess demand generated by whatever means, a fixed exchange rate economy will tend to generate a balance of payments deficit as the excess demand is met partly by the importation of goods and the diversion of exports to the domestic market. This will tend to place upward pressure on domestic inflation and interest rates will be forced up to protect the currency. Government expenditure may need to be curtailed or taxes raised to help reduce the demand. In a fixed rate regime the main channels through which the excess demand is reduced must be interest rates and fiscal policy.

If a floating exchange rate policy is in operation, however, excess demand, which manifests itself in an increased balance of payments deficit, will be met with a fall in the value of the currency. This process helps curb demand by driving up the price, in domestic currency, both of the goods imported and of domestically produced goods as there will be "knock-on" effect on domestic wage costs from a rise in import prices.

In theory, at least, excess demand could be eliminated purely by a fall in the exchange rate, which would result in domestic prices rising to a level at which demand and supply were again in equilibrium. There need not in theory be any changes in domestic, monetary or fiscal policies where free floating is in place. Of course practice is different because a number of rigidities in economies can prevent smooth adjustment taking place.

The discussion on the merits of fixed versus floating have continued for many years. There are a lot of possible problems with both systems. There may be no such thing as a purely free floating currency. Markets may overshoot in one direction or another and thus not stabilise at the price level which eliminates the excess demand. Uncertainty is itself a factor which may lead to lower investment and output under a floating regime.

Among the problems with a fixed rate system are the risk that the level chosen to fix the rate is "wrong." The rate may be wrong in the sense that adherence to it may entail large cutbacks in output before the domestic costs and prices fall into line with those of the economies against which the currency is fixed. Domestic money and fiscal policies may not be correctly attuned to be consistent with a fixed rate objective.

Without entering further the discussion of the merits of the two alternatives it seems clear that the balance of the argument in Europe has come down in favour of fixed or at least fixed but adjustable exchange rates in the last twenty years. The wider world has not necessarily set its face against this view. Attempts to set ranges for the dollar against the Yen and Deutschemark have become less and less substantive since the ending of the Bretton Woods fixed rate regime in 1971.

The smaller European economies, which have more or less fixed their exchange rate to the largest currency block, the DM, have given up a degree of independence in policy making to the Bundesbank. Willingness to do so is a recognition that Germany has succeeded over the long term in achieving a lower inflation rate than most countries in the world. Small open economies with a fixed exchange rate to a larger currency bloc will over time tend to have similar inflation and interest rates. This is brought about partly by the influence of flows of traded goods which will tend to equalise price changes if not price levels in the two areas. Capital flows are also important in tending to equalise interest rates if there are no restrictions on such flows. The interest rate differential between a small economy and its major trading partner to which its currency is linked will reflect differences in liquidity in the respective money markets and a risk premium which reflects how credible the fixed currency link is. Credibility depends on correctly attuned money and fiscal policies and not on official statements of intent.

Ireland is perhaps the prime example of such small open economy. For over 100 years the Irish pound had a fixed no margins link with the U.K., Ireland's main trading partner. Ireland's interest rates were almost precisely the same as in the U.K. and inflation remained very close to U.K. levels. Since 1979 Ireland has linked its currency to a number of other European currencies in the European Monetary System (EMS).

For a period in the mid 1980s domestic fiscal policy in Ireland was not in keeping with a more or less fixed link to the DM and this culminated in a devaluation of the Irish Pound. However, since 1987, considerable adjustments to policy have been made. Ireland's inflation has fallen below that in Germany and Irish interest rates have converged close to German levels. During this same period U.K. interest rates diverged as much as 4 percent from Irish rates.

Implication of ERM for Currency Volatility

The range of movement for most currencies in ERM is fixed at +/- 2.25 percent around a central parity. Clearly this is much more stable than the dollar mark, which in the past two years could be said to have a +/- 10 percent range around DM 1.65 but with no formal agreement to stop either side of that range being breached. Volatility within the EMS is further reduced by the fact that some countries such as the Netherlands and Belgium fix their currencies much more closely to the DM than ERM limits require. Monthly volatility over substantial periods of time of ten ERM currencies has been less than half that of the major European currencies outside the system. The counterpart is that interest rates in most ERM countries have to respond almost exactly to German interest rate changes. This leads to the conclusion that the currency plays of most interest within EMS relate to high yielders, which tend to have 6 percent bands of fluctuation. In periods when the risks of realignment are judged to be low long positions in high yielding EMS currencies against low yielders can be profitable. Interest rates may be held high to achieve the necessary adjustments in the domestic economy to enable long run participation in EMS and entry to the narrow band. Thus the Peseta was attractive to hold because interest rates were high and the currency was at the top of its 6 percent ERM band.

When interest rates begin to rise in an already high yielding currency it should be seen as a danger sign for those holding the currency. The ERM requires central banks to defend their currencies using intervention and interest rates. If these and policy changes fail devaluation is the result.

A range of potential opportunities has been opened in the European currencies of non-EMS participants such as Switzerland and Sweden. The Finnish marku and the Swedish Krona established links with a view to eventual entry to the EEC but have since floated. At times of strain EMS caused by doubts about progress on EMU and dollar weakness, the Swiss Franc may outperform the DM.

The Dollar and ERM

Dollar volatility has important implications for EMS. Since efforts to stabilise the currency relationship between the U.S., Germany, and Japan have had limited success dollar depreciation can impose stresses on the EMS. This is because the DM is the largest reserve currency in the bloc and flows out of dollars will be skewed much more in favour of the DM than the French Franc or sterling. Efforts to reduce this effect have so far had little impact.

Generally, though, a fall in the dollar only brings realignment if there are already fundamental factors present which suggest it would be appropriate. A number of bouts of dollars weakness in the past two years have been successfully weathered by the ERM without realignment. This was because fundamental factors were not judged to have diverged sufficiently to warrant a currency adjustment.

MONETARY UNION—THE OUTLOOK

The Treaty

The Maastricht Treaty stated that to qualify for EMU the following convergence criteria should be met at the time of union:

(i) Price inflation within 1.5 percent of the three lowest countries' performance.

   (ii) The general government deficit should not exceed 3 percent of GDP.

  (iii) The ratio of government debt to GDP should be less than 60 percent.

  (iv) The currency should have been in the narrow band for the previous tax year with devaluing.

   (v) Long bond yields over the previous year should be within 2 percent of the average of the lowest three countries.

Table 2.4 sets out progress on these criteria at this stage.

It is clear that only France and Luxembourg meet all criteria while Greece and Portugal do not meet any. A "core" group of countries are more or less in the same category with inflation 4 percent or below, budget deficits close to 3 percent of GDP and debt to GDP ratios close to 60 percent of GDP or falling rapidly in that direction. This group includes Germany, France, Netherlands, Belgium, Denmark, and possibly Ireland. Even within this group however there is a wide variation in terms of deficit to GDP and debt to GDP ratios.

The Maastricht Treaty was negotiated as part of the planned progress towards monetary union which has been underway for some years. It ignored the impact of German unification on the other European economies and thus potentially on the path to

TABLE 2.4 EMU Convergence Criteria

	Latest inflation	10 yr Bond	Gov't Balance	Gov't Debt	ERM Band	Score (5 Max)
France	3.2	8.54	−2.0	36	2.25	5
Lux.	2.3	7.7	+1.7	8	2.25	5
Denmark	2.1	9.33	−1.3	63	2.25	4
Belgium	2.3	8.39	−6.5	129	2.25	3
Germany	4.8	7.47	−4.7	44	2.25	3
Ireland	3.6	10.05	−3.8	101	2.25	3
Netherlands	4.4	7.77	−4.8	78	2.25	2
U.K.	4.0	8.94	−3.8	43	6.00	2
Italy	5.6	12.90	−11.1	101	2.25	1
Spain	6.9	13.27	−3.8	45	6.00	1
Greece	17.8	23	−15.4	90	—	0
Portugal	8.0	17.00	−5.5	68	6.00	0
Max. Limit	3.7	9.65	−3.0	60	2.25	

EMU. The combination of loose fiscal policy and tight monetary policy which followed unification of Germany resulted in high real interest rates. This in turn supported the DM. Given the commitment made to EMU, other ERM countries were reluctant to devalue against the DM because it might endanger participation in monetary union. However, the rise in German demand lasted longer than many expected and the spillover effects in terms of activity outside Germany was confined to the Netherlands, Belgium, and to a lesser extent, France and the U.K.

Thus many countries had high real interest rates needed because their currencies were linked to the DM but little boost to economic growth as a result of the unification process. Eventually this has taken its toll in terms of the perceived political will to endure the fall in output and rise in unemployment.

The first crack in the EMU/no realignment story was the Danish failure to ratify the Maastricht Treaty. This led to doubts about whether EMU was politically as opposed to economically viable. The run up to the French vote on ratification led to renewed strains within ERM exacerbated to some extent by dollar weakness. Italy, the U.K., and Spain were consequently identified as currencies vulnerable on fundamental grounds. The Bundesbank apparently offered a deal to cut interest rates in return for devaluation of these currencies against the DM. This package would have been consistent with progress toward EMU since it would have enabled interest rates to fall and, given a satisfactory devaluation, differentials with Germany to narrow. However, these discussions led only to a devaluation of the Lira and a rather small cut in German interest rates. The lack of coherence which this evidenced led to increased rather than reduced pressures in ERM. Sterling and the Lira left the system and the Peseta devalued by 5 percent. Short term interest rates rose very sharply in some countries. The French Franc, despite relatively strong fundamentals, came under severe pressure. Confidence in progress towards EMU was seriously damaged. Bond yields diverged sharply again. See Table 2.5.

Despite a successful defence of the FF/DM parity interest rates remained high in France until after the elections. The Irish pund and Escudo devalued. At the time of writing the Franc and Danish Krone are again under pressure. Really the question is whether EMU has a future following the events of the summer and autumn of 1992.

TABLE 2.5   Interest Rate Movements Since June 1992 Change

	June	October	Change
10 Year Bonds			
U.S.	7.35	6.47	88
Japan	5.52	5.01	51
Germany	7.95	7.47	48
Netherlands	8.31	7.77	54
Belgium	8.79	8.39	40
France	8.51	8.54	−3
Denmark	8.67	9.33	−66
U.K.	8.96	8.94	2
Spain	10.92	13.27	235
Italy	11.01	12.90	189
3 Month Euro Deposits			
U.S.	3.94	3.375	57
Japan	4.63	3.94	−69
Germany	9.63	8.94	−69
Netherlands	9.44	8.71	−73
France	9.88	11.25	137
Denmark	10.00	12.00	200
U.K.	9.88	8.75	113
Italy	11.88	15.50	−362

EMU—The Future?

The events of mid 1992 highlighted the fact that lack of convergence imposes strains on a budding monetary union. Exchange controls had been greatly relaxed in the EEC. This was a weak situation for the system because freedom of capital movement without at least pooling of reserves or a unified central bank left individual countries' reserves vulnerable to large portfolio shifts combined with speculative sales.

Divergence of Germany's growth and fiscal position from many other ERM countries had posed a threat for the last three years. The competitive position of Italy, the U.K., and Spain were in question and in the case of Italy the direction of fiscal policy. This mix of fundamentals, virtual freedom of capital movements, and a large degree of political uncertainty engendered by Danish and French referenda served to bring an ERM crisis in September 1992.

The outlook now is still uncertain. It seems clear that ERM can't return to the same position as before the Danish vote with a high degree of convergence of bond yields accompanied by the assumption that realignment is a low risk. Neither can it be assumed that Maastricht for all 12 countries can be put back on track to occur before the year 2000. This is because convergence has not progressed sufficiently and with freedom of capital movement markets can ask serious questions about the political ability of the authorities to hold ERM together. Something must give because the new situation is unstable.

A return to widespread use of exchange controls is unattractive because it is going back from EMU and potentially damages growth potential in Europe. The authorities continue to move ahead with ratification of Maastricht in several countries. However, there are reasonably wide differences even among the core group and even wider gaps with the remaining countries. Therefore it would appear that if EMU is to happen it will have to be in a two tier format initially. The move by the first tier will need to be fairly rapid to avoid shocks to the system leading to forced realignments. Freedom of capital movement leaves the system vulnerable to this until the common currency is established. The second tier countries may join the union when it is clear they have converged sufficiently.

For the moment there are considerable difficulties in putting a two tier process in place. Maastricht dominates the political and institutional framework and dictates that agreement of all 12 countries is required. This is not likely to be forthcoming because it would involve political as well as economic losses for the prospective tier two countries. Bond yields would rise even more relative to the core group.

While it appears there is a lot of political capital invested in the notion of monetary union, the way forward is now very confused indeed. Ratification of Maastricht is now largely complete. However, in our view this does not provide a viable framework and a further crisis within the existing ERM may be needed to make it clear that the Maastricht framework should be abandoned in favour of some form of two tier approach.

This crisis if we are correct is likely to involve the French Franc, Danish Krone, and Belgian Franc.

SUMMARY

The evolution of European exchange rates has had a fixed rate ever since the break up of the Bretton Woods fixed regime in 1971. This implies that domestic interest rates and fiscal policy have to be adjusted to ensure the fixed exchange rate target is held, i.e., to ensure that the balance of payments position is sustainable. In economies with floating exchange rates, there is a greater freedom to gear policies to the domestic economy and by definition the exchange rate bears more responsibility for ensuring a sustainable balance of payments position.

Exchange rate volatility tends to be lower within Europe for long periods as a consequence of this approach. However, when pressure builds there tends to be very large interest rate movements often followed by relatively big realignments of currencies.

Currency trading in the European context is dependent on the perception of realignment risk. At times of low risk, it is profitable to hold high yield currencies. High yield currencies whose interest rates begin a renewed rise have to be regarded with suspicion. Only where the high yield and the currency have been fairly stable for some time should long currency positions be entertained. The September 1992 crisis, though sudden, still allowed sufficient time to liquidate long positions in high yielders since Italian, Spanish, and eventually U.K. interest rates rose rapidly before devaluation occurred.

Sharply rising interest rates in a semi fixed regime are thus the danger signal. The dangers in ERM are not yet over and we are unlikely to return to the situation pertaining before mid 1992. In our view Maastricht has to be largely abandoned and monetary union approached on a two tier basis. Otherwise, it will not be credible and there is sufficient freedom of capital movement to prevent non-credible approaches being implemented.

3

Currency Hedging

Anthony Minopoli
Evaluation Associates, Inc.

INTRODUCTION

As foreign-denominated assets become a larger portion of pension funds' asset mix, currency fluctuations present both a risk and an opportunity to plan sponsors. While many plan sponsors argue that currency's effect on total return is minimal, others contend that short-term volatility is large enough to warrant action, such as hedging.

Most plan sponsors are ill-equipped to make the many timing decisions involved in currency hedging. In fact, many international equity managers choose not to hedge because they lack the expertise to do so. If a plan chooses to hedge, perhaps the most prudent way to do so would be to hire currency overlay managers. These managers combine technical models and practical experience to achieve their hedging goals, thus reducing the volatility of foreign investments and potentially adding incremental value to the portfolio.

Investing in foreign equity and nondollar fixed income securities is a twofold investment: firstly, in the underlying asset itself and secondly, in the currency of the country where the asset is based. Considerable debate arises around the question of whether or not currencies should be treated as a separate asset class, but most agree that currencies' short-term volatility can have significant impact on the total return of nondollar denominated assets.

Currency has not always been such a volatile commodity. After World War II and prior to August 15, 1971, the Bretton Woods fixed exchange rate system was in place. Currency exchange rates were adjustable under Bretton Woods, but were static compared to the free-floating exchange rate system that exists today. The Bretton Woods system ended in 1971 when President Nixon suspended the right of foreign central banks to convert their U.S. dollars into gold. However, it was not until 1973 that the monetary authorities of the major industrial countries adopted the floating-rate system. The floating-rate system added additional risk to foreign equity and nondollar fixed-income securities investments as currency exchange rates became more volatile. Exchange rate volatility has had significant impact on the total return of nondollar denominated assets.

TO HEDGE OR NOT TO HEDGE

There are two schools of thought about the benefits of hedging foreign currency. In one school are those that take the long-term view and in the other are those that view the short term. Evidence exists to illustrate both views.

Those that take the long-term approach point to the statistics that illustrate that the net effect of currency on total investment returns is negligible in the long run. Some of the arguments that fall into this category are as follows:

- Since pension funds have a long investment time horizon, there is no need to manage currencies against short-term fluctuations.
- It is very difficult, if not impossible, to precisely forecast changes in foreign exchange rates over time.
- Hedging foreign exposure back to the U.S. dollar can raise the correlation among the international and domestic asset classes, thereby reducing the investment diversification sought by expanding into international markets.
- Currency management is complex and it requires experienced professionals and substantial resources in order to implement a hedging program.

The arguments supporting an ongoing hedging program focus on the short term rather than the long term. Tables 3.1 to 3.4 and Figure 3.1 show that currency has contributed substantially to

TABLE 3.1   MSCI EAFE Index U.S. $ vs. Local Currency

	U.S. $	Local Currency	Currency Effect
Annual			
1970	–10.51%	–10.51%	—
1971	31.22	20.63	8.78%
1972	37.60	37.67	–0.05
1973	–14.17	–20.43	7.87
1974	–22.19	–23.46	1.66
1975	37.13	45.91	–6.02
1976	3.76	5.32	–1.48
1977	19.45	5.54	13.18
1978	34.29	15.87	15.90
1979	6.16	11.07	–4.42
1980	24.42	19.83	3.83
1981	–1.01	12.20	–11.77
1982	–0.64	10.35	–9.96
1983	24.39	32.87	–6.01
1984	8.05	21.85	–11.33
1985	56.95	28.63	22.02
1986	70.26	43.14	18.95
1987	25.28	–1.78	27.55
1988	28.92	34.36	–4.05
1989	11.07	22.02	–8.97
1990	–22.93	–29.60	9.47
Annualized			
1970–1990	14.10	11.30	2.52

Over long periods, returns in U.S. and local currency have been similar,
indicating currency fluctuations are neutral over the long term.

total return for shorter time periods. Proponents of currency hedging offer the following arguments:

- Any nondollar investment is inherently an investment in foreign currency, therefore currency management is part of any international investment.
- The short-term exchange rate volatility offers opportunity to add incremental value to a portfolio's total return. Selective and active hedging can be planned to take advantage of the cyclical nature of currency fluctuations.
- Although hedging foreign exposure back to the U.S. dollar raises correlations, the increases are so slight that the reduction in diversification can be overcome by improved returns (see Table 3.5).

TABLE 3.2   MSCI EAFE Index U.S. $ vs. Local Currency

5 Years Ending	U.S. $	Local Currency	Currency Effect
1974	1.53%	–1.97%	3.58%
1975	10.58	8.09	2.30
1976	5.51	5.20	0.29
1977	2.57	–0.25	2.82
1978	12.17	7.54	4.31
1979	19.36	15.86	3.03
1980	17.06	11.38	5.10
1981	15.97	12.80	2.81
1982	11.77	13.81	–1.79
1983	10.07	16.97	–5.89
1984	10.46	19.16	–7.29
1985	15.72	20.86	–4.25
1986	28.97	26.89	1.64
1987	35.09	23.97	8.97
1988	36.06	24.25	9.51
1989	36.82	24.28	10.09
1990	18.68	10.17	7.72
Periods Ending 12/90			
20 Years	15.49	12.54	2.62
15 Years	17.17	14.06	2.73
10 Years	17.22	15.43	1.55
5 Years	18.68	10.17	7.72

TABLE 3.3   Salomon Brothers Non-U.S. Bond Index Hedged vs. Unhedged

Annual	Hedged	Unhedged	Currency Effect
1978	18.50%	3.39%	14.61%
1979	–4.98	–0.31	–4.68
1980	13.69	7.55	5.71
1981	–4.62	7.91	11.61
1982	11.89	23.42	9.34
1983	4.37	9.63	–4.80
1984	–2.02	11.20	–11.89
1985	37.19	11.03	23.56
1986	33.94	12.58	18.97
1987	36.13	8.73	25.20
1988	2.97	8.05	–4.70
1989	–4.52	1.87	–6.27
1990	14.10	2.83	10.96
Annualized			
1978-1990	11.08	8.15	2.71

TABLE 3.4   Salomon Brothers Non-U.S. Bond Index Hedged vs. Unhedged

5 Years Ending	Hedged	Unhedged	Currency Effect
1982	6.44%	8.10%	−1.54%
1983	3.77	9.38	−5.13
1984	4.41	11.79	−6.60
1985	8.41	12.51	−3.64
1986	16.02	13.47	2.25
1987	20.66	10.63	9.07
1988	20.34	10.31	9.09
1989	19.72	8.39	10.45
1990	15.39	6.74	8.10
Periods Ending 12/90			
13 Years	11.08	8.15	2.71
10 Years	11.84	9.59	2.05
5 Years	15.39	6.74	8.10

- Transaction costs may be minimized by using the forward markets rather than the options markets.
- The complexity of the currency market is being challenged by a growing number of investment professionals that have an increasing base of knowledge and experience. More participants and the increased availability of information make the foreign exchange markets less risky.

FIGURE 3.1   Historical Risk/Return Profile: Hedged and Unhedged Global Bond and Equity Markets, 12/31/77–12/31/90

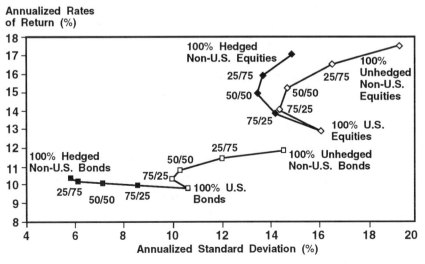

TABLE 3.5   Correlations Report

	World Bond $	World Bond Local	Capital World Index	Local World Index	S&P 500	LB Gov't Corp.
World Bond $	1.00					
World Bond Local	0.90	1.00				
Capital World Index	0.50	0.46	1.00			
Local World Index	0.27	0.36	0.94	1.00		
S&P 500	0.29	0.36	0.86	0.91	1.00	
LB Gov't/Corp.	0.83	0.96	0.38	0.31	0.35	1.00

HEDGE STRATEGIES

Plan sponsors may choose between three currency hedging strategies: permanently unhedged, permanently hedged, or actively hedged.

Plan sponsors who choose to be permanently unhedged typically take a passive view of currency and subscribe to the concept that the long-term net effect of currency fluctuations in international investing is zero. During periods of stable exchange rates, this strategy offers diversification through the currency above and beyond that of adding a foreign asset to a U.S. investor's portfolio. In periods of declining dollar value, U.S. investors will find this strategy attractive. As the U.S. dollar declines, the translation of a foreign investment into U.S. dollars benefits from a weaker dollar. This adds incremental return to the total return of the foreign assets. Conversely, as the dollar appreciates, foreign investment total returns are impacted negatively by a strong U.S. dollar.

Plan sponsors who choose a fully hedged strategy may take positions in the forward or futures market in order to fix the exchange value of currencies at a future date. The use of this strategy can eliminate the currency risk in a given portfolio. However, by hedging the entire portfolio, an investor cannot take advantage of currency movements to add value to the portfolio, because the forward exchange rate between two markets usually is represented by the interest rate differential between two markets.

An actively hedged portfolio potentially can combine the best features of the two more passive strategies. An effectively managed portfolio can add value in stable or falling U.S. dollar environments. For example, by selectively hedging through forwards, futures, or options, money managers can purchase securities that are inherently attractive without concern for the currency denomination. A successful active strategy will place a limit on the downside impact of currency fluctuation while allowing the investor to participate in most of the upside.

Additionally, if a plan sponsor allows the currency manager to hedge exposures using currencies other than the U.S. dollar, more opportunities to increase total return arise. This strategy, known as cross hedging, would allow the manager to hedge, for example, a yen exposure into deutsche marks if it were more attractive than hedging the yen exposure into U.S. dollars.

COSTS

The four categories of costs associated with hedging are

- Cash-flow-related costs for contract settlement
- Contract trading costs
- Management fees
- Custodial costs

A currency hedging program may require cash to cover losses that may occur. Historically, contract settlement cash can amount to 20 percent of the international portfolio for a fully hedged program.[1] In a falling dollar period, security trading and transaction costs may increase. In contrast, a rising dollar period will generate cash. While optimal cash reserve for each plan is different, in general plans with large cash inflows will require smaller cash reserves than those plans with little or no cash inflows. The cash usually can be held in a reserve account at the custodian bank, which results in opportunity costs.

The opportunity cost of the reserve account can be measured by the difference between what the cash would have generated if it were invested like the rest of the portfolio and the return that the cash reserve generates. Estimates of the cost of maintaining the cash reserve have been set at approximately 10 basis points, while the level of opportunity cost is dictated by returns in the market at any given point in time.

Contract trading costs can be divided into two separate parts. The first part is the bid/ask spread on initial forward contract purchases. The second is the cost of rolling the monthly or quarterly forward contracts. Together these costs usually are not more than 10–15 basis points, but will be higher if contracts are rolled on a monthly, rather than a quarterly, basis.

Management costs of a hedging program typically range from 25 to 50 basis points. This margin is wide because fees vary depending on the style of hedging management chosen. In addition, the custodian bank charges two basis points for its services. The total hedging costs can be summarized as follows:

Category	Costs (Basis Points)
Cash-flow-related costs	10
Contract trading costs	10–15
Management fees	25–50
Custody Fees	2
Total	47–77

HEDGING VEHICLES

Currency managers may choose from three major hedging vehicles: forward contracts, futures, and options.

Forward Contracts

A forward contract is an agreement between two parties to exchange currencies at a specified price on a future date. The forward foreign exchange market is world's most liquid market; more than $600 billion a day in trades occur. Forward contracts as currency hedging vehicles allow investors to hedge almost any amount of any currency at a wide range of maturities. Investors, corporate plan sponsors, and multinational corporations find these contracts to be an effective way to eliminate exchange rate risk that is associated with international transactions. These contracts do, however, carry opportunity costs.

The size and liquidity of the forward foreign exchange market allow participants to create contracts in diverse sizes and terms. Contracts in any size may be issued for as short as a few days to as long as a year. In some cases, contracts are written for even longer periods. This flexibility enables investors to match currency hedging with the underlying asset.

No margin is required to establish a forward contract, nor is a daily position rebalancing necessary as would be the case with other derivative securities. Full settlement takes place when the contract expires, so risk of loss is limited. Profit-taking opportunity is limited as well, because despite where the market price for the currency is on the expiration date, the contract must be settled at the agreed-upon exchange rate. Actual delivery of currency takes place, requiring special accounts and administrative procedures. Some find this delivery to be a cumbersome and less efficient means of hedging.

Unlike the markets for other hedging vehicles, no central exchange for clearing forward contracts exists. Because of this, exchange rates can vary widely. Well-informed participants can take advantage of these disparities by using arbitrage techniques, especially between the futures and forward market. Less-informed participants are more likely to be quoted noncompetitive rates.

Contract prices quoted are also a function of the size and the term requested; contracts of $1 million or more for one-, three-, and six-month terms will be quoted most aggressively. Another pricing characteristic unique to the foreign exchange market is that most spot rates are quoted with a value date of two days forward. Transactions must be arranged at least two days in advance of delivery, leaving the participants open to short-term exchange rate risk.

Futures Contracts

A futures contract is an agreement to buy or sell a specific amount of a commodity at a particular price on a stipulated future date. Sold on the floor of a commodity exchange, these contracts have fixed sizes and maturity dates. Futures pricing and settlement are efficient; prices are quoted from the last executed trade, keeping the bid/ask spreads tight, and a central clearing system allows positions to be placed rather than offset. Delivery of the commodity, in this case currency, need not be taken.

While the futures market's fixed sizes and maturity dates contribute to more efficient contract pricing and settlement, they also can make it difficult to match hedging to underlying investments. Trading is ongoing, but contracts may mature on only four dates a year: one each in March, June, September, and December. These constrictions may not affect small international portfolios, but may make futures contracts less attractive to managers of large international portfolios.

Cash and credit requirements are different in the futures market than in the forward foreign exchange market. While the foreign exchange market requires full settlement, the futures market requires the ability to cover losses on a daily basis. Futures are marked-to-market daily and participants must be able to either raise cash, to maintain a cash pool to cover daily rebalancing needs, or be prepared to sell securities in the event of a shortfall. Maintaining a credit line and cash pool implies real and opportunity costs, while selling securities can disrupt an investment program. If the need to sell foreign securities arises, the higher transaction costs diminish total return.

Options

Options are the third type of derivative security that can be used as a hedge vehicle. The investor who decides to use options to hedge currencies has two choices. The first choice is to trade market options, which are essentially prefabricated securities that are traded through the various exchanges. The second, and more attractive, choice is the use of over-the-counter (OTC) options. When trading prefabricated securities, market options are created by the seller and then sold through normal security distribution channels. There is little flexibility with this type of option because the factors around the option are established before it is sold. With an OTC option, the security is structured to meet investors' needs. In fact, options can be created to the exact dollar amounts of the foreign assets that they are purchased to hedge against. The OTC options are virtually limitless in the style in which they can be manufactured.

The use of options also has some limitations and drawbacks. Some OTC options are sold only on a three- to five-year basis. The drawback to this type of option is its maturity. If the underlying assets are sold or reweighted within the portfolio during the time the option is in place, there can be a severe mismatch between the hedge and the underlying asset weightings. The option may undo a currency position on one hand and possibly overstate a position on the other. One of the features that makes OTC options attractive also is a detractor; if the option is created with specific factors, it may only be possible to resell the option at a sometimes deep discount to the brokerage firm that created it. Finally, market options are fairly liquid. However, they are not always consistent with investment strategies. In other words, the use of market options will provide the investor with a fairly liquid instrument, but at the same time it will not be tailored to meet the specific needs of the investor. An OTC option can provide flexibility to the investor, but at differing levels of liquidity.

HEDGING TACTICS

Sponsors may choose from several strategies to hedge international investments: passive hedging, cross hedging, and derivative strategies.

Passive Hedging

Description
Sell currency forward to hedge a predetermined percentage of the currency on a monthly or quarterly basis. This can be done for longer periods. However, it is recommended that it be done monthly or quarterly to ensure that the hedge is consistent with the underlying assets.

Advantages
- *Simplistic.* This is a straightforward strategy in which the plan can determine how much of a given currency they would like to hedge and use forward contracts to hedge the exposure. Forward contracts can be written in a wide range of expiration dates (monthly, quarterly, annually).
- *Low cost.* The absolute size of the forward contract market, coupled with the vast number of market participants, causes this to be an efficient market. Trading costs tend to be low because of the large number of participants. Market efficiency also lends itself to tighter bid/ask spreads on the contracts.
- *Performance measurement.* Measuring currency hedging's impact on performance is simple: The total return of the portfolio is equal to the local market return plus or minus the forward premium. This allows the plan to easily measure the effectiveness of the hedge versus trying to separate their managers' performance that is attributed to hedging as opposed to the performance that is the result of investment management.

Disadvantages

- *Sponsor capability.* A major drawback to this strategy is that the plan sponsor must make currency allocation decisions on a regular basis. In practice, the plan sponsors will have to obtain currency exposures from investment managers, assess which exposures should be hedged, and forward in the amount and the currency they desire to hedge.

Conclusion

It is more than likely that most plan sponsors have neither the desire nor the capability in-house to make effective currency decisions. Even though this is a very simplistic approach in theory, it could become impractical and costly in practice.

Derivative Strategy—Dynamic Hedging Using Options

Description

A derivative strategy is a method of managing currencies through over-the-counter put options on a basket of currencies. In this approach, the option's cost established the downside risk; the upside potential is the return less the cost of the option (see Figure 3.2). In practice, we have seen options with maturities as long as five years.

FIGURE 3.2   Dynamic Hedge Strategy

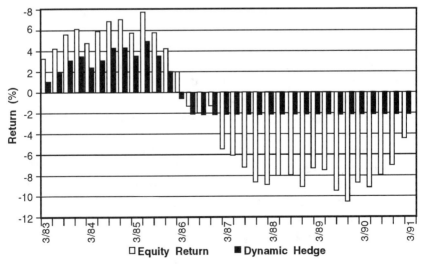

□ Equity Return   ■ Dynamic Hedge

Advantages

- *Predictability.* The cost and downside risk of this strategy are known at inception.

Disadvantages

- *Projectability.* This strategy is relatively new and untested. Little performance data is available. In many cases, the statistics available are client specific and not useful as a representative record of performance.
- *Liquidity.* The market for these options may be nonliquid. In many cases, the institution that issues the option is the only market so that if a plan sponsor chooses to unwind the option, he may pay a premium to do so.
- *Expensive.* Our survey of plan managers indicates that the transaction costs associated with these options can run as high as 275 basis points. This level of costs will significantly reduce the returns of the underlying international investment.
- *Exposure matching.* Options can be written for a variety of time periods of up to five years and even longer in some cases. During terms of this length, currency exposures will likely change, resulting in severe mismatches between the hedge and the underlying portfolio; this could leave the portfolio exposed to significantly more risk than it would have been if left unhedged.
- *Sponsor capability.* Plan sponsors will be responsible for determining the basket of currencies that will make up the option. The sponsor will have to get the currency exposures from the investment manager and then assess which exposure should be hedged.

Conclusion

Dynamic hedging through derivatives is a new strategy with a performance history that is specific to each participant and should not be used as a representative record of performance. The liquidity problems of these options coupled with their high transaction costs make them very expensive in both out-of-pocket and opportunity costs to plan sponsors. Lastly, the plan sponsor will have to determine the composition of currencies that will make up their basket and most sponsors have neither the desire nor the capability to undertake such an endeavor.

Derivative Strategy—Active

Description

An active derivative strategy uses a forward rate bracket on a basket of currencies to match the currency weighting of the underlying portfolio. A forward rate bracket uses put and call options to protect the portfolio from both a rising and falling U.S. dollar. By buying a put option and selling a call option on the currency basket, the portfolio is assured of a safety bracket. However, all returns must be forfeited when the basket price is above the level at which the call option was sold. Typically, the brackets are placed in equal amounts above and below the current spot rate (see Figure 3.3). In other words, loss protection can be placed at 2 percent, but the upside potential will also be limited to 2 percent. The brackets can be widened, but as the upside limit is increased, so is the downside limit. If the brackets are maintained at equal intervals above and below the spot rate, the strategy is essentially a zero cost strategy because the investor buys a put and sells a call to finance the strategy. It is only when an investor chooses to alter the symmetry of the brackets that he may incur a cost. An investor can choose to pay to increase upside potential while maintaining a

FIGURE 3.3   Forward Rate Bracket Strategy

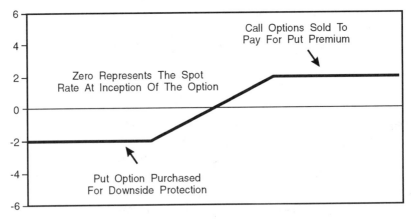

downside loss limit (see Figure 3.4). This strategy can be executed on a monthly or quarterly basis to allow for a careful match of the hedge and the underlying assets.

Advantages

- *Flexibility.* The active strategy allows plan managers to more carefully match their hedge to the underlying portfolio regularly because the structure of the forward bracket may be changed for rebalancing purposes. Generally, currency exposures do not vary significantly on a monthly basis, but can look quite different from quarter to quarter. This strategy will allow the plan sponsor to perform the rebalancing of the hedge and the underlying portfolio as often as desired.
- *Low cost.* The transaction costs of this strategy tend to be low, but only if the bracket is in equilibrium.

Disadvantages

- *Upside limit.* If a market begins to rise rapidly, the investor will lose any profits above the call sale price level; unwinding the option can be costly.
- *Sponsor capability.* The plan sponsor will be responsible for setting currency allocation. Recently, U.S. rates have been higher than foreign rates, leaving the sponsor with two unattractive choices. The first is to set a narrow bracket

FIGURE 3.4   Forward Rate Bracket Strategy

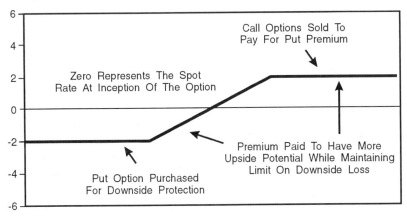

that will limit upside potential, the second is to pay a premium to widen the bracket to increase participation in rising markets.

Conclusion

An active derivative strategy with its flexible time periods is essentially cost free if the brackets are set at equal intervals above and below the spot rate. However, the upside will be limited to the amount the investor is willing to lose unless he or she pays a premium to participate in the upside market movements. As with the other derivative strategies, the plan sponsor will be responsible for setting currency allocation, which is a task that requires much knowledge and experience.

CURRENCY MANAGERS

Once a plan sponsor has decided to hedge currencies, someone must be designated to derive and implement the hedging plan. Currency management may be done in-house by existing managers or be contracted out to professionals such as currency overlay managers.

Existing Managers

Description

Existing international managers hedge their currency exposures.

Advantages

- *Cost-effective.* Since the manager is already in place, additional management fees will not be incurred for hedging.
- *Familiarity.* Since existing managers are intimately familiar with the portfolio, they will be able to closely monitor and match the hedges to the underlying assets.

Disadvantages

- *Expertise and experience.* The success of most international managers recently has been based on their ability to select countries, industries, or individual issues with little or no regard to the exchange rate of the currency. The currency environment of the past eight years has rewarded non-U.S. portfolios of the U.S. investors. International managers have not been required to hedge currencies. Our knowledge of international managers makes it apparent that many of them do not have the facilities, research, or knowledge to effectively hedge currencies. Therefore, a mandate to hedge could encourage a manager to attempt something beyond his or her capability.

- *Style conflict.* Many international managers employ a bottom-up stock selection style in which macroeconomic variables are not a consideration. For the most part, equity managers employing this style will resist or reject the mandate to hedge. This puts the plan sponsor in the position of either having to withdraw the mandate or terminate the manager in favor of one who will hedge. Fixed-income managers tend to focus more than their equity counterparts, although they too are assessing economic implication on bond prices as a first priority.

- *Performance measurement.* Using existing managers to hedge makes separate measurement of returns by currency and stock selection more difficult. A manager that does not hedge provides returns to a client on an unhedged basis. This allows the client to isolate a manager's performance in stock and bond selection. If the existing manager hedges the currency exposures, it will be very difficult to separate the performance that came from foreign exchange gains and performance that was generated from the capital appreciation of the asset.

Conclusion

It is clearly unwise to direct a manager to hedge an investment if such direction is counter to his or her investment style and he or she has neither the resources nor the inclination to hedge. It is risky to permit managers to hedge unless there is some track record to suggest capability in that area. Terminating managers who do not hedge in favor of those who will could be expensive and unproductive.

CURRENCY OVERLAY MANAGERS

Description

Plan sponsors may hire specialized external managers to hedge forward currency exposures. Currency managers tend to use a single currency as a proxy for an entire block of currencies. An example of this would be the German deutsche mark as a proxy for other European currencies. The forward contract is a hedge vehicle and the liquidity that the forward contract provides will allow the overlay manager to change positions as rapidly as is necessary to maintain a match with the underlying portfolio. The adoption of this strategy prohibits the active money managers to hedge any part of their portfolios. This applies only to active hedging, which will distort the activities of the overlay managers; it does not apply to the implicit hedging of currencies through currency and stock selection.

Advantages

- *Externally managed.* The plan sponsor does not have to make any currency allocation decisions. The overlay manager will be fully responsible for knowing the underlying positions of the portfolio and placing the hedges accordingly.
- *Return enhancement.* Since this strategy requires an ongoing active monitoring of the currency market and movements, a successful manager can add to return during strong and weak dollar markets; the expected return of an overlay strategy is to add 3 percent to 4 percent per year over the return of the underlying portfolio.
- *Performance measurement.* Measuring returns from currency management is simplified, since the active managers will not be hedging and the total impact of the currency manager will be revealed in the performance of his or her portfolio.

Disadvantages

- *Loss potential.* In a worst-case scenario, if the hedges were completely wrong, it is possible that currency losses could exceed the underlying portfolio's returns. This is an existing possibility that investors should be aware of, though it is not likely to occur.
- *Limited historical data.* As of this writing, there were less than fifteen managers engaged in overlay management. In most cases, the strategy is new and untested, although several managers do have track records that are longer than four years.
- *High fees.* Fees for currency overlay managers range from 40 to 70 basis points per year. As competition increases

and managers become more efficient, we expect fees to be reduced.

Conclusion

While some fixed-income managers are capable of making currency assessments, in most cases investment managers lack the experience to manage currency risks. Hiring overlay managers allows plan sponsors to take advantage of the profits available from hedging currencies without having to make currency allocation or timing judgments. Even after factoring in the fees, the overlay managers average 2.5–3.5 percent earnings for their clients while protecting the returns of the underlying portfolio from erosion due to adverse currency movements.

Two critical issues involved in the use of active overlay managers are timing and implementation. If a plan sponsor wishes to hire a manager to protect against a strengthening dollar environment and terminate that manager when a weakening dollar environment is expected, the sponsor must be able to predict changes in the direction of currency fluctuations. Additionally, the timing and logistics of hiring a manager make it difficult to take advantage of trend changes. By the time the need for a manager is established and one is actually hired, trends could have reversed themselves. We recommend that currency overlay managers be hired on a conditionally permanent basis as are other managers, with the understanding that there will be periods of time when the manager will be paid to be unhedged, unless cross hedging is authorized.

OVERLAY MANAGER DIFFERENTIATION

There are two categories of overlay mangers: technical managers and fundamental managers. The technical managers use computer modeling systems to drive their currency management process. The fundamental/technical managers use the technical data in the management process, but fundamental research drives the currency management plan.

Technical Managers

The technical currency overlay managers use sophisticated computer models to identify trend and contratrend movements in foreign exchange and global interest rates. These models look at different variables in an attempt to make precise time and price forecasts in currencies and interest rates. Technicians use relative strength as an indicator to compare currency prices and interest rates. Other indicators include moving averages, standard deviation, and momentum. Moving averages are used to assess trading patterns of currencies. The technical managers use standard deviation to try to predict or indicate trend changes among the various currencies. Lastly, momentum is used to show the changes of price movements. For example, year-over-year momentum changes are used to show longer-term changes as an indication of the start of a new trend.

The technical models are not static because the managers are constantly updating them to includes other variables when necessary. Purely technical managers follow their models exactly. They are confident that their input keeps up with the factors that drive currency markets and therefore are confident about the model's output.

Fundamental/Technical Managers

The fundamental/technical currency overlay managers use the same type of quantitative analysis that the purely technical managers use, but augment it with traditional macroeconomic fundamental analysis. The fundamental research includes tracking basic indicators such as GNP, growth rate of GNP, money supply, trade balances, consumption patterns, and the current account for each country/currency. Fundamental managers say that this research helps them to understand the output of the technical models and enables them to override the model when they deem it to be too aggressive or not aggressive enough. While all agree that the technical analysis is essential in currency management, each relies more heavily on the fundamental analysis, albeit in different degrees.

Conclusion

Empirical evidence shows that the purely technical managers have outperformed the fundamental/technical managers to date, through both strong and weak dollar periods. There are several possible explanations for this.

TABLE 3.6 Currency Manager Performance

| | Annual Periods | | | | | | | | | Annualized Cumulative Periods Ending 12/31/90 | | | |
| | Strong Dollar | | | | Weak Dollar | | | | | | | | |
	1982	1983	1984	1985	1986	1987	1988	1989	1990	Nine Years	Seven Years	Five Years	Three Years
Trend Trading	6.5	2.9	0.5	17.9	16.2	24.0	-0.9	3.5	5.8	8.2	9.2	9.3	2.7
Fundamental/Trend Trading	4.1	0.4	-0.3	8.6	4.3	2.2	1.1	1.1	1.3	2.4	2.5	1.9	1.1
EAI Average Int'l Mgr	3.8	27.5	-2.4	55.9	60.0	12.7	16.9	23.1	-11.1	18.6	19.6	18.2	8.6
EAFE Currency Effect*	-10.0	-6.0	-11.3	22.0	19.0	27.6	-4.1	-9.0	9.5	3.2	6.7	7.7	-1.5

*The EAFE currency effect is calculated by dividing the EAFE $ return by the EAFE local return to establish the currency effect.

41

First, currency movements have displayed trends over various cycles. This cyclical nature can be tracked very closely by the technical managers' charts and when acted upon, has proven to be accurate. When we interviewed managers who rely more heavily on fundamental data, they said that there were certain changes in momentum, particularly in the early part of 1991, that did not seem feasible and therefore, they circumvented the technical data and deferred to their fundamental analysis. This did not prove to be as profitable.

A second problem with relying on fundamental data is that countries are not concerned with the equilibrium pricing of currencies; rather they are focused on their own domestic economic issues, such as trade balances and inflation. The technician will look at various momentums and moving averages to assess the relative currency strength and invest accordingly. The same data can be looked at and then considered with a qualitative view of a country's economic and political outlook and generate completely different answers.

CONCLUSION

With the increase in international investing and the volatility of currencies, all plan sponsors must consider currency hedging as a means to protect their portfolios and enhance total return. The decision to hedge currencies is multi-layered and complex. Sponsors must first determine a currency hedging policy, then select hedging vehicles and tactics, and finally determine who will carry out these decisions. After a careful review of the plan sponsor's possible choices and interviews with currency managers, we suggest that hiring technically oriented currency overlay managers to actively hedge currency exposure through a variety of specialized techniques may be the best choice for most plan sponsors.

First the sponsors must choose one of the three strategies: never hedge, always hedge, or actively hedge. To never hedge currency means both to leave the portfolio open to currency exposure and to miss the opportunity to realize incremental gains on total return. To always hedge protects the portfolio from the risk of loss due to currency volatility, but this choice also precludes the possibility of incremental gains. To actively hedge, however, allows a plan to take advantage of short-term market moves either by hedging currency in a strong dollar market or leaving currency unhedged in a weak dollar market.

Once choosing to hedge currencies, a sponsor must then select hedging vehicles (forwards, futures, or options) and determine who will plan and carry out the hedging strategy (existing managers or currency overlay managers). Choosing what hedging vehicles to use when is a specialized job that requires knowledge and experience. For this reason we suggest that professionals be hired to handle currency management. Currency overlay managers handle all currency decisions. This frees investment managers to concentrate on stock and bond selection. Additionally, separating the investment management and the currency management makes it easier to assess the performance in each category.

Finally, if a plan sponsor chooses to hire a professional currency manager, one must be selected. Statistics gathered on the performance of both the technical overlay manager and the fundamental/technical overlay manager illustrate that the technical managers have outperformed managers who emphasize fundamental analysis when making currency hedging decisions. For this reason, we recommend that managers consider hiring technical overlay managers to handle their currency hedging.

NOTE

1. Michael Rosenberg, "Hedging a Non Dollar Fixed Income Portfolio," in Managing Currency Risk, The Institute of Chartered Financial Analysts, 1989, pp. 35–37.

In the News

4

Europe Central Banks Said to Have Lost Up to $6 Billion Trying to Help Currencies

Michael R. Sesit
Staff Reporter, *The Wall Street Journal*
Reprinted from *The Wall Street Journal*, Sept. 30, 1992

Currency traders and analysts estimate that Europe's major central banks lost a total of $4 billion to $6 billion in their mostly futile attempt to prop up weak currencies in September of 1992.

That money—which one analyst calculates as equal to about 10 percent of the allies' cost of fighting the Persian Gulf War—poured into the pockets of big international banks and big-time speculators.

Nobody was talking on the record about their profit and losses from the foreign-exchange war that began in early September, when traders, investors and speculators in the $1 trillion global currency market ganged up on the weaker currencies in the European Exchange Rate Mechanism.

The ERM is a joint float of nine European currencies that trade within tight bands of one another. It used to be 11 before Britain and Italy, unable to take the heat, pulled the pound and lira out the week of September 17, 1992.

British, French, Italian, Spanish and Swedish central banks together spent the equivalent of roughly $100 billion trying to prop up the pound, franc, lira, peseta and krona, figures Avinash Persaud, a senior currency economist at Union Bank of Switzerland in London. Germany, he adds, shelled out another $50 billion in marks.

To what result? "They suffered an estimated bookkeeping loss of $6 billion," says Mr. Persaud. "That's about

10 percent of the cost of the Persian Gulf War, the bulk of which was consumed in a critical fortnight in September."

Bank analysts are predicting that the trading operations of big money center banks—such as Bankers Trust New York Corp. and Citicorp—should report superb results for the third quarter of 1992. One market rumor has Citicorp's traders alone making a cool $200 million in just one week of September, 1992 from Europe's currency turmoil.

A spokesman for Bankers Trust declined to comment. A Citicorp spokeswoman said she couldn't comment because the company is in registration for a stock offering.

As a matter of policy, central bankers don't comment on the details of their intervention activity. But one senior official said: "You're talking very, very large amounts of money; it was an absolutely incredible operation."

"It seems that everybody lost money in these operations," says Wiltse Bailey, an economist at Banque Nationale de Paris in Paris. But "probably the central banks of the devalued currencies lost more than the Bundesbank."

The German central bank concedes that it shelled out 24 billion marks ($17 billion) defending the lira. In addition, other data indicate it spent another 40 billion or so marks trying to prop up other weak currencies.

However, the German central bank's claims on other European central banks shot up by 23.5 billion marks on Sept. 15, 1992 and by an additional 37.4 billion marks by Sept.

23, 1992. These jumps indicate that Germany was lending marks to other central banks for them to use in supporting their currencies. This money eventually must be repaid to Germany.

The rules of intervention within Europe call for both the central bank with the strong currency and the central bank with the weak currency to both buy the weaker and sell the stronger. But central bankers admit that in practice the obligation falls mostly on the weak-currency country.

The banks' intervention exercise basically consisted of selling marks and purchasing the currencies under attack. Eventually, they gave up. On September 17, 1992 Italy devalued the lira an effective 7 percent against the mark but later pulled its currency out of the ERM. Britain bailed out, too. Spain devalued the peseta by 5 percent against the mark. Since early September 1992, the mark has risen 15 percent against the lira and 11 percent against the pound.

The largest losses were incurred attempting to bolster these three currencies along with a few others. However, traders figure that the central banks have made money so far defending the French franc, but not nearly enough to make up for their other losses.

"The Bundesbank now has a lot of lire, pesetas and pounds and French francs in its reserves; it may not have wanted them, but it's got them," says Mr. Persaud of UBS.

In the end, the big losers could be European taxpayers. That's because most central banks turn over a large chunk of their profits—if any—to their national governments. Last year, for instance, the Bundesbank paid Bonn 14.46 billion marks. The Banque de France's profits are taxed like any other French corporation, says Philippe d'Arvisenet, deputy chief economist at BNP. "Sometimes there are years in which the Banque de France contributes more money [to the French treasury] than any other company," he adds.

In 1992, as usual, the German finance ministry budgeted a transfer of 7 billion marks from the Bundesbank. Analysts figure it may get that much, but probably not as much as 1991's 14 billion marks. They believe that high German interest rates will give the Bundesbank a plump return on its securities portfolio. And when the dollar eventually rises, the central bank will make a nifty profit selling dollars it purchased earlier in the year, they say.

Maybe, maybe not. As a spokesman for the Bundesbank in Frankfurt points out: "The profits are determined by our actions, but our actions are determined by policy motives rather than by any [need to produce] profits."

5

Currency Risk Management

Ezra Zask
Ezra Zask Associates, Inc.

INTRODUCTION

The past decade has witnessed an explosive growth in the international investments of financial institutions, including pension funds, insurance companies, and money managers. Overseas investments by U.S. pension funds, for example, had grown to 5 percent of assets by 1991 and, according to Intersec Research, should reach 10 percent of assets by 1996. The growth has been even more dramatic in the case of British and Japanese pension funds, whose overseas investments represent 7 percent and 20 percent of assets, respectively. (See Figure 5.1.) Between 1985 and 1992 the overseas assets exposure of mutual funds increased from $64 million to over $30 billion.

The increase in international investments has meant that financial flows now completely dominate the global currency market. In 1989, according to the *Economist* magazine, cross-border flows resulting from financial transactions amounted to $50 trillion compared to only $2 trillion in annual trade flows. Similarly, according to the world's central banks, only 7 percent of the $1 trillion daily volume in the currency markets is related to commercial hedging activity. The remainder is a result of investment and speculative activity.

47

FIGURE 5.1   World's Pension Assets (1991/96)

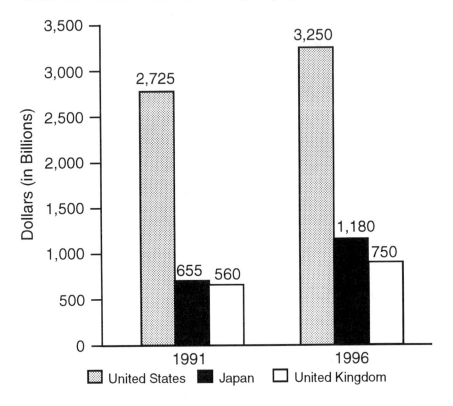

The initial reasons portfolio managers moved overseas were portfolio diversification and improved returns. The movement into international bonds and stocks was an extension of the familiar investment approach pension funds and institutional money managers were using domestically. The familiar tools of analysis of the investment community—portfolio optimization, mean-variance analysis, and efficient frontiers—were applied to overseas investments. Indeed, many of the large domestic money managers also became the leaders in managing international bond and stock portfolios.

Often overlooked in the process of international diversification was the key difference between international and domestic investment, especially the presence of country risk and currency exposure. As a by-product of their investment activities, institutional investors found themselves with substantial positions in the currency markets. Given the volatility of currencies and their impact on portfolios, pension funds and funds managers are beginning to agree that something needs to be done.

To some extent, international investors have enjoyed a respite from currency worries over the past five years. Currency exposure management has taken a back seat to risk management of equities and fixed income largely because the growth of international investments on the part of U.S. investors coincided with a period of dollar weakness. For the majority of the 1985–1992 period, international investors enjoyed a windfall profit from currency movements. However, to expect this to continue indefinitely is unrealistic. Investors could find themselves in the same situation as foreign investors who held U.S. investments when the dollar reached DM 3.47 in February 1985 and watched the "super" dollar decline by over 50 percent in the next five years.

In fact, the dollar has already appreciated by nearly 20 percent from its lows of 1992. While academic arguments regarding the true "nature" of currency trends may still rage on, few portfolio managers can afford losses of 20 percent a year due to a strong dollar. At that point, investors will need all the techniques of risk management to survive.

The major problem in formulating a strategy for managing currency risks is that the core questions regarding the role of currencies in global investment portfolios have not been resolved. Consultants, plan sponsors, money managers, bankers, and academics continue to debate such basic questions as:

- Are currencies an asset class? If yes, what is their risk and reward profile? The answer determines whether currencies are a nuisance to be eliminated or an asset to be managed for maximum return.
- Should currency exposures be hedged? If yes, what types of instruments should be used? What proportion of currency exposures should be hedged? For what length of time? Since currencies have different impact on equities and fixed-income portfolios, should different approaches be used to hedge them?
- Should currency exposures be managed separately from the underlying investments? How should currency risk management be organized? What's the best way to implement a currency hedge? Should hedging be done by an in-house or outside group?

- What approach is appropriate for hedging currency risk? What is an appropriate benchmark for currency management? How should forecasts be incorporated into the decision process?

PRESENT PRACTICES

A survey conducted by the Philadelphia Stock Exchange of 150 international portfolio managers in the U.S. and abroad found that over two-thirds of U.S.-based managers with responsibility for international fixed-income and equity portfolios say they *do not hedge* currency risk. By comparison, two-thirds of European managers say they do hedge currency risk. This disparity is partly caused by the relative levels of exposure. According to the study, "Almost half of all European managers have more than 50 percent of their holdings in assets other than those of their own country, while only 16 percent of the U.S. equities managers and 31 percent of the U.S. fixed-income managers have more than 50 percent of their portfolios in non-U.S. holdings." In the U.S. fixed-income managers were twice as likely to hedge currency risks as equity managers.

The survey also concludes that "there was a measurable lack of understanding of various currency products."

CURRENCY OVERLAY: DEFINITION AND CRITICISM

Currency exposure management of international investment portfolios is one of the most controversial in the investment arena. This is a result of the newness of the currency problem for funds managers and of the peculiar nature of currencies. While there is no common approach to currency management, a number of ad hoc approaches have been pieced together under the label of "currency overlay management."

The phrase "currency overlay management" has added confusion rather than help for managers. Currency overlay management means that currency exposure is treated separately from the equity and fixed-income investments that may have caused that exposure. In practice, this sometimes means assigning the responsibility for managing the currency positions in a portfolio to a separate manager (or group of managers) while decisions on the underlying equity and fixed investments remain in the hands of the original managers.

There are two major benefits to taking a currency overlay approach: First, it allows for the use of a specialized approach and set of skills, which may not necessarily be the same as those possessed by equity and fixed-income portfolio managers. Secondly, it allows investment managers to base their investment decisions on the merits of the equity and fixed-income investment without having to take currency into account.

Currency overlay management is not confined to one style or approach. In fact, it does not even state whether currency positions should be treated as an asset or as a risk. It does not imply anything about whether currency risk should be hedged nor suggest the means for hedging this risk. Almost any approach to currency management is consistent with a currency overlay program, including technical and fundamental approaches, passive hedging and active management, various options buying and selling strategies, and portfolio insurance approaches.

EFFECTS OF CURRENCIES ON INTERNATIONAL INVESTMENTS

The impact of currencies on volatility and return differs sharply for fixed-income and equity portfolios. Currencies have a much stronger impact on the results of fixed-income portfolios than on those of equity portfolios. (See Figures 5.2 and 5.3.) Currency movements account for a full 88 percent of the volatility of returns of fixed-income portfolios. This means that interest rate movements only account for 12 percent of the portfolio's volatility. Importantly, this relationship holds whether the investor is in the U.S. or Japan.

In contrast, returns on equity portfolios are primarily a result of foreign equity market movements. Currency movements only account for 33 percent of the volatility of international equity portfolios, with equity movements responsible for the remaining 67 percent of volatility. Again, the same holds for U.S. or Japanese investors.

The reason for the different effect of currencies on fixed-income and equity portfolios is relatively straightforward: the average annual volatility of currencies (12 percent) is substantially higher than that of fixed-income investments (7 percent), but

FIGURE 5.2   Composition of Risk: Foreign Bond Investments

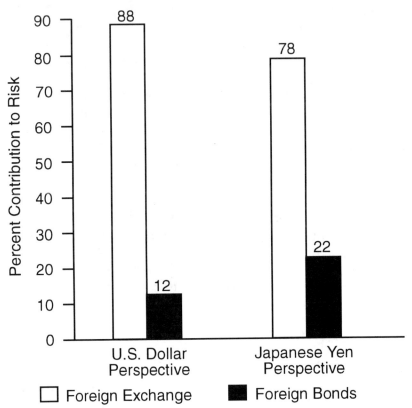

considerably lower than the volatility of equity investments (18 percent). If we add the emerging nations, the effect of currencies is further diminished since some emerging equity markets register volatility levels of 80 percent per annum compared to around 12 percent for currencies.

The implication of this difference between fixed-income and equity portfolios is that fixed-income managers need to pay considerably more attention to currencies than equity managers. In fact this largely turns out to be true. As one manager of a Global Fixed Income Group in an insurance company puts it: "Trading international bonds is really an excuse for trading currencies." A typical money management firm splits its Group into a Global Equity Management group and a Fixed Income and Currencies Group.

One caveat to this analysis is the steady rise in exchange rate volatility over the past 20 years. This has led to a greater impact of

FIGURE 5.3   Composition of Risk: Equity Investments

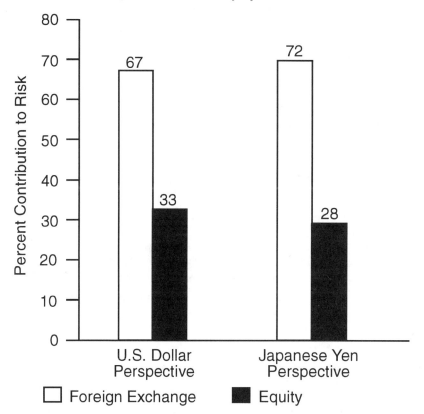

currency movements on both bond and equity portfolios, making currency management ever more important. The standard deviation of monthly currency returns over rolling five-year periods from 1977 through 1989 has risen by 50 percent over the past 17 years. Since 1973, the standard deviation of return for European and Pacific currencies has risen from 7 percent to over 12 percent (compared by around 8 percent for fixed income and 18 percent for stocks). If the recent high level of volatility of European currencies continues in the future, it is possible that currencies will play a greater role in portfolio management.

THE HEDGING DECISION

Because of the complexity of the issues involved and the lack of agreement among practitioners, it may take months or years to decide on a currency hedging strategy. Typically, the process includes extensive analysis and discussion with dozens of consultants, bankers, plan sponsors, and funds managers.

To Hedge or Not to Hedge

The first and fundamental decision that a funds manager needs to make is whether to hedge currency exposure. This will in turn depend on four factors:

1. The funds manager's view on currencies as an asset class
2. The sponsor's risk aversion
3. The size and composition of the international portfolio
4. The costs and benefits of hedging

If the decision is made to hedge the currency risk of the portfolio, the next decision is whether currencies should be hedged to minimize risk in the portfolio, or managed to add value to a portfolio? Clearly, the answer depends on the manager's feeling regarding currency as an asset class and expected return compared to the potential risk.

Risk and Return Considerations

When portfolio management theory first turned its attention to currency management, there was a popular school of thought that claimed that currency hedging was, in effect, a "free lunch." That is, the currency hedger would gain from a reduced volatility with little reduction in return. Over time, however, it has become clear that there is a real trade-off. Numerous studies have pointed out that while currency hedging reduces the risk of international portfolios, it also reduces their expected returns. Thus, the laws of finance still apply: lower risk comes at the expense of lower return.

A completely hedged international bond portfolio using currency forward contracts reduces the portfolio's volatility from 16 percent to 7 percent while reducing its expected return from 13 percent to 11 percent. (See Figure 5.4.) As expected, the impact of hedging on equity portfolios is less dramatic. A full hedge of an international stock portfolio reduces volatility from 19 percent to 14 percent while lowering expected returns from 23 percent to 21 percent.

FIGURE 5.4   Hedged and Unhedged Risk and Return: 1978–1987

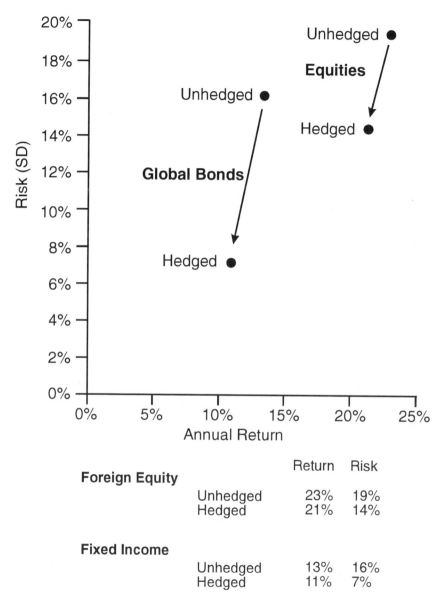

		Return	Risk
Foreign Equity			
	Unhedged	23%	19%
	Hedged	21%	14%
Fixed Income			
	Unhedged	13%	16%
	Hedged	11%	7%

Whether this risk/return trade-off makes hedging currency risk worthwhile is largely a question of the hedger's risk/return trade-off. In addition, there are efficiencies and costs to hedging that need to be taken into account.

Optimal Hedging Levels and the Cost of Hedging

Hedging is not an all or nothing proposition. The costs of hedging set a threshold level of overseas investments below which hedging may not be optimal. Virtually all hedging programs are based on a partial hedge using forward contracts, options, options replication, or some combination of these.

It turns out that there is a close relationship between the costs of hedging, the level of a fund's international asset allocation, and the optimal proportion of a portfolio that should be hedged (the hedge ratio). The greater the proportion of assets that are invested internationally, the greater the potential benefit of hedging. At low levels of international investment (i.e., 5–10 percent of assets), the cost of hedging quickly overwhelms any potential benefit of hedging. Assuming typical hedging costs of 30–60 basis points, it turns out that there is a cost rather than savings by hedging portfolios whose international exposure is less than 10 percent. On the other hand, portfolios with asset allocation above 15 percent should probably hedge at least a portion of their risk since the benefits of hedging are greater than the marginal costs.

The optimal hedge decision also depends on the relationship between the currency position and the other assets in the portfolio. For example, a currency position that is uncorrelated with the equity and fixed income positions in a portfolio may actually reduce the overall portfolio risk by adding an element of diversification. In this case, hedging the risk may increase the portfolio's overall volatility by removing a source of diversification. This is especially important since diversification is one of the primary reasons for investing abroad.

In other words, there is no clear-cut formula that yields a yes or no decision. Rather, we can point out the relative approaches and the cost/benefit analysis of each approach. The ultimate decision is a function of the hedger's own risk/return trade-off profile and opinion of currencies as an asset class.

CURRENCIES AS AN ASSET CLASS

Much of the controversy in the investment arena in recent years has revolved around the extent to which currencies can be said to be an asset class. The answer to this question is key. If currencies are an asset class, then they should be managed for maximum return, as are stocks or bonds. Otherwise, their effects should be eliminated from the portfolio in the most cost-effective manner possible.

The arguments for currencies as an asset class are often highly theoretical and mathematical. Unfortunately, the conclusions of the countless monographs and empirical studies are often contradictory. Their results are often not statistically significant or highly dependent on the time-frame or currencies used for their analysis.

One answer is provided by a senior investment manager who applies a three-part test for asset class status: Is there an investible, liquid marketplace for the asset? Are they securities? Do they produce returns? Currencies pass all three parts and should therefore be considered assets.

While there is no final answer, *a growing body of evidence points to the conclusion that currencies are an asset class* that is capable of yielding a return to the investor. If currencies are considered an asset class, the manner in which funds managers tackle currency exposures will need to change. Furthermore, portfolio managers will increasingly hire currency managers not only for currency overlay programs, but to gain income from currency investments.

The Arguments Pro and Con

The arguments for currencies as an asset class rely on the two ways of potentially making money in the currency markets: first, by earning the interest paid on currencies and, second, by correctly forecasting the direction of currency trends.

Currencies as Interest-bearing Instruments

Currencies are assets in one sense: the owner of a currency earns interest on that currency. This is a return as surely as dividends on stocks or coupon yields on bonds. This interest is earned by physically placing the currency on deposit with a bank or by buying a currency forward in the currency markets. Currencies can be invested with a bank in a currency's domestic market, in the Euromarkets, or in a multicurrency account in third-country markets.

An investor earns interest income by buying a currency forward because the investor needs to pay less for the currency in the future than he or she would pay today. The difference between today's rate (spot price) and the forward rate is merely the interest rate differential between the investor's local (home) currency and the foreign investment currency.

Figure 5.5 shows an international yield curve in which the real interest rates of various currencies are plotted, ranging from 1 percent for the U.S. dollar to 8 percent for the Danish krona. The total return to an investor is a combination of interest rates and the currency spot rate movement. While investors can earn interest by investing in currencies, the overall return is a function of the excess return above the risk they are assuming. The real question in deciding whether currencies are an asset class is the extent to

FIGURE 5.5   International Yield Curve: January, 1991

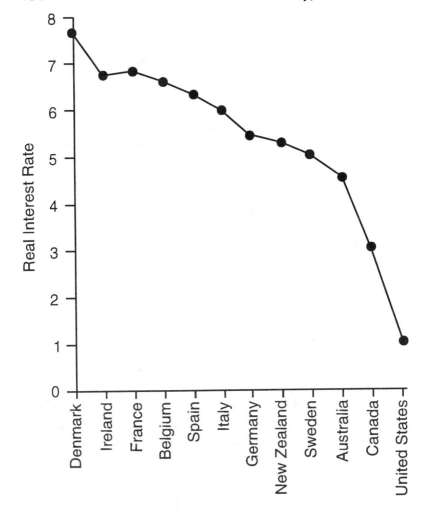

which the interest rates paid by the currency markets are more than sufficient to cover currency devaluation.

Total Return = Interest Rate + / – Currency Gain (Loss)

For example, an investor deriving 14 percent interest from an investment in Denmark, who loses 20 percent due to a devaluation of the Danish krona, shows a real return of 6 percent.

–6 percent = 14 percent – 20 percent

In this case, the interest rate was not sufficient to cover the risk of holding the currency.

A number of banks and institutions have attempted to take advantage of this "risk premium" through diversified investment baskets of currencies. A dozen or more mutual funds and money managers have attempted the same through variations of "global short-term income funds," which invest in higher-yielding currencies.

Currencies as Trending Assets

The other common approach to currencies as an asset class states that currencies trend or that their movements are "serially correlated." In other words, the argument states that it is possible to forecast (nonrandom) currency movements and thus gain a return from owning or selling short these instruments.

There is an important difference between this view of currencies as an asset class and the reasons for investing in stocks and bonds. While portfolio managers hope to "get the direction right" and earn a windfall profit from market moves in stocks and bonds, their investment strategy is often entirely based on picking up the yields (dividends and interest) on stocks and bonds. In the case of currencies as trend-following instruments, however, the premise is that a profit can be made even in the absence of any interest or dividend yield. In other words, currency markets are the only purely speculative markets in which the return depends entirely on getting the market moves right.

The argument against a currency asset class states that currency markets are efficient. Therefore, all the known information regarding currencies is embodied in the currency rate (price) and any future movement will be random. This implies that the direction of each day's currency movement is independent of the direction of the previous day's movement. In that case, it is impossible to correctly forecast a currency movement or to earn any profit from a trend in the market.

A large number of studies have shown, however, that currencies do trend. For example, PanAgora Asset Management has tabulated the serial correlation in the currency markets. They have regressed the results of one month's currency returns against those of the previous month to measure the extent to which currency movements are nonrandom. The results, shown in Figure 5.6, indicate that for every time period since 1971 the currency markets' movements are trending and nonrandom.

Indeed, a visual examination of currency markets shows the same. Critics of currencies as trend-following instruments point out that currencies have an expected return of zero since they often follow a long-term cyclical pattern. That is, today's currency rates may be the same as those of five years ago. However, advocates of currencies as trend-following systems point out that currencies have potentially large payoffs or big losses on a year-by-year basis and large point-to-point returns.

In fact, many argue that the current market alone of all the major markets exhibits a trend-following manner. The reasons presented for this are varied but revolve around the following:

1. The currency market is comprised of thousands of players in various countries of the world. Because none of these

FIGURE 5.6   Serial Correlation in the Foreign Exchange Markets

Regression Results of Monthly Currency Returns
versus Currency Returns One Month Prior

Period %	Sterling	Deutschemark	Yen
1/71–12/75	53	36	32
1/76–12/80	31	17	33
1/81–12/85	37	22	34
1/86–12/90	14	13	8
1/71–12/90	**31**	**26**	**24**

Small but positive correlations in all currencies in all periods.

dominate the playing field the way institutional players do in other markets, there is a ripple effect in the currency market. The movement starts in one center or location and spreads around the globe, creating trends.

2. Since currency values are ultimately the market's judgment of countries and country economic policy, their movements tend to reflect macro-economic factors and thus are longer moving.

3. The currency market has a unique actor—the central banks—whose motivation is not to make money but to stabilize markets. In this case, the central banks are willing to sustain and initiate a trend to meet policy objectives. The opportunity to make money with currencies *exists because central banks induce nonrandomness* in currency returns by intervening in foreign exchange markets to stabilize exchange rates. Nonrandom returns means that there is predictability in currency returns. That provides an investment opportunity.

In the world of investment managers, this has led to the most popular of approaches to both managing currency exposure and attempting to benefit from currency trends: The technical analysis approach.

APPROACHES TO HEDGING AND CURRENCY OVERLAY PROGRAMS

After analyzing the questions of hedging and currency as an asset class, a portfolio manager must decide which instrument or strategy to use in hedging a portfolio's currency exposure. Following the analysis described above, the funds manager should formulate an explicit policy statement that includes the following elements.

1. What is the objective of the portfolio manager regarding currencies?
2. Does the plan assume that currencies are an asset class and therefore managed for a return?
3. What are the costs of implementing various hedging strategies?

4. Are equity and fixed-income portfolios to be treated differently?
5. What benchmark will be used to measure performance?
6. Should hedging be performed in-house or should one use outside managers?
7. What approach and instruments should be used in hedging? (i.e., options, technical analysis, etc.)

In general, the currency overlay arena is divided into the following major groupings:

Type of Management	Unhedged	Forward Contract	Currency Options (and portfolio insurance)	Selective Hedging
Description	Unhedged investment	Sell a prespecified amount of foreign currency at a predetermined exchange rate for delivery on a specific date	1. Purchase a foreign currency put option 2. Purchase a put and sell a call to establish collar 3. Replicate an option via portfolio insurance	Use technical, momentum, or fundamental analysis to selectively hedge currency exposures
Advantages	1. No cash payment 2. Full participation in currency appreciation	1. No cash payment 2. No currency depreciation risk	Protection against downside risk with potential for upside appreciation	1. Potential for upside appreciation 2. No cost
Disadvantages	Full exposure to currency depreciation	No potential gain from foreign currency appreciation	Up-front cash payments (for some strategies)	1. Potential for loss from currency depreciation 2. Cost and complexity of program
View of Currencies as Asset Class	No	No	Yes	Yes
Implied Currency View	Foreign currency will appreciate (U.S. dollar will depreciate)	Foreign currency will depreciate (U.S. dollar will strengthen)	Foreign currency will appreciate (compared to forward rate) but with uncertainty	Currencies may appreciate or depreciate with time, but will trend

INVESTING IN A FOREIGN ASSET UNHEDGED

A U.S. investor purchases a U.K. stock share for 200 pence. Then, at purchase,

Price of U.K. Stock	200 pence
U.S./U.K. Exchange Rate	$2.00/pound sterling
Price of Stock in U.S. Dollars	$4.00

A year later, the investor sells the stock, which is still worth 200 pence, but the U.K. pound has changed in value. Depending on whether the pound has declined or strengthened versus the U.S. dollar, the investor will show a currency gain or loss. For example, let's assume that the U.K. pound either declines to $1.50 at the end of one year or rises to $2.50. The returns for the investor are as follows:

Scenario A: U.K. pound strengthens to $2.50
Price of Equity	200 pence
U.S./U.K. Exchange Rate	$2.50
Price of Stock in U.S. Dollars	$5.00

Thus, the investor has gained 25 percent from the movement of the currency.

Scenario B: U.K. pound weakens to $1.50
Price of Equity	200 pence
U.S./U.K. Exchange Rate	$1.50
Price of Stock in U.S. Dollars	$3.00

In this case, the investor has actually lost money on the investment although the stock did not decline in value.

HEDGING FOREIGN INVESTMENTS
WITH A FORWARD HEDGE

When purchasing a foreign asset, an investor actually purchases two assets at once: the stock or bond (which is denominated in the local currency) and the currency used to purchase the stock or bond. It works the same in disposing of foreign assets. The asset is first sold for local currency. The local currency is then sold for, say, U.S. dollars. Thus, the investor's return really depends on two markets: the local market for the asset and the currency market.

Often, however, investors may not wish to be exposed to currency movement. Far and away the most common form of hedge for funds managers is a forward contract. Costless, easy to understand, efficient, and liquid, they provide investors with a certainty of investment returns that no other instrument can provide. However, this comes at the cost of foregoing any currency appreciation gains and, depending on the currencies' relative interest rates, at the cost of a premium.

A forward contract entails an agreement between a funds manager and a financial institution (normally a commercial or investment bank) to sell a fixed amount of foreign currency (i.e., British pounds) and receive U.S. dollars on a future date at a rate of exchange agreed upon today. (A futures contract is the same except that the transaction is made through a futures exchange rather than a bank.) By entering into a forward contract, the funds manager has "locked in" the number of dollars he or she will receive for selling the British equity and converting the proceeds to U.S. dollars. In other words, the funds manager is fully "hedged" from any subsequent movement (positive or negative) in the forward market.

Example

An investor purchases the British stock at 200 pence with the pound spot rate at $1.50, and at the same time sells the British pound forward for three months at a rate of $1.5240/pound sterling. Thus,

At Purchase:

Price of British Share	200 pence
U.S. Dollar/Pound Sterling Exchange Rate	$1.50
Price of Share in U.S. Dollars	$3.00
200 Pence Sold Forward at Rate of	$1.4764

At Sale:

Price of U.K. Share	200 pence
U.S. Dollar and Forward Rate Fixed at Purchase	$1.4764
U.S. Dollar Proceeds of Sale	$2.9528

It is important to note that, unlike the unhedged example above, the U.S. dollar proceeds of the equity sale do not vary with the exchange rate at the time of sale. The investor will receive $2.9528/share whether the British pound has depreciated to $1.50 or appreciated to $2.50. Figure 5.7 shows the relative returns of an unhedged position compared to a position hedged using a forward contract.

A second point to note is that the forward price is not a forecast of future pound exchange rates. Rather, it is derived from the difference between the interest rates in the two countries (the U.S. and England) through a process known as covered interest rate arbitrage. The difference between the two rates (in this case 3.250 percent or 0.0236, or 236 "forward points") is known as the premium or discount of the forward rate from the spot rate of exchange.

FIGURE 5.7   Unhedged vs. Forward Hedge

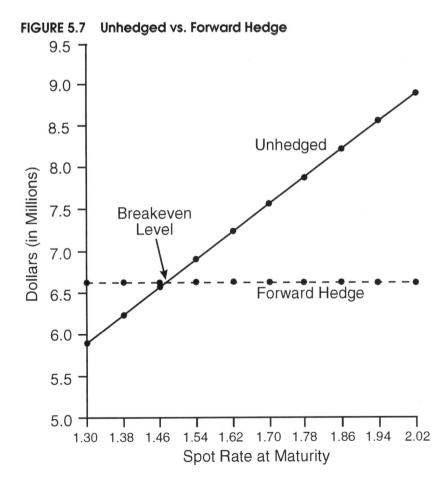

In our example, the pound is at a discount to the U.S. dollar because the forward rate for the pound ($1.4764) is weaker than the spot rate ($1.5000). By the same token, the U.S. dollar can be said to be at a premium to the pound since a British investor would need to pay more pounds to purchase dollars in the forward than in the spot market.

Forward rates are not a forecast of future market movements, but rather are rates calculated from the difference in the interest rates between the two currencies, which ensures that there is no risk-free arbitrate in the marketplace. Through a calculation known as covered interest arbitrage, the forward rate is determined so that a U.S. investor would see the same return through placing a given amount of U.S. dollars on deposit and converting the dollars to pounds, placing them on deposit in the U.K., and selling the proceeds forward back into U.S. dollars. The forward rate is that rate that makes the investor indifferent (excluding transaction costs) between holding U.S. dollars or converting the dollars to pounds and selling them forward. Arbitrage by dozens of major institutions and thousands of operators throughout the world ensures that the forward (or futures) rate is indeed in line with Covered Interest Arbitrage. (See Figure 5.8.)

FIGURE 5.8   Calculating Forward Rates: Covered Interest Arbitrage

Assume:

Spot Rate = $1.50/pound sterling
1 year Euro-Sterling = 9%
1 year Euro-Dollar = 4%

You have 1 million pounds to invest for one year
(At today's spot rate = $1,500,000)

Day One:	Deposit 1,000,000 pounds at 9% for 1 year	Equivalent Position	Deposit $1,500,000 at 4% for 1 year
	Earn 90,000 pounds interest		Earn $60,000 interest
In One Year	1,090,000 pounds		$1,560,000

The forward rate, in order to prevent arbitrage, must equate the two deposits so that the investor is indifferent between depositing his or her funds in U.S. dollars or pounds sterling:

$$\text{Forward Rate} = \frac{\$1,560,000}{1,060,000 \text{ pounds}} = \$1.4717/\text{pound}$$

Forward Premium and Discount

The forward premium or discount can be seen as the cost (or income) of hedging. In our example, it "cost" 3.250 percent per annum or 0.8125 percent per quarter in order to hedge the sale of the equity in one year's time. In other cases (where the local currency interest rate is lower than that of the U.S. for U.S. investors), the transaction would actually result in a gain through hedging. A British investor in the U.S., for example, would be able to sell the U.S. dollars forward for a premium of 3.250 percent and would realize a gain of 3.25 cents for each dollar sold forward. One of the key decisions confronting a funds manager is whether or not to hedge a transaction given the premium or discount.

This becomes especially challenging for high-yielding countries such as Spain or Portugal, where local interest rates of 15 percent mean that a forward contract entails a discount "cost" of 11 percent a year. How then does the funds manager decide if the cost of hedging is justified? The underlying key, of course, is his or her level of risk aversion. If this is high enough, then almost any cost would be worth bearing for currency protection.

However, if the funds manager has some leeway for protection, then the calculus of the decision must revolve around the anticipated movement in the currency market compared to the forward rate. For example, if the anticipated depreciation of the pound over a year is five percent, then the 3.25 percent discount of the forward contract seems reasonable. If, however, the funds manager feels that the pound will depreciate by only 1 percent over the year, he or she will not be anxious to sell pounds through the forward market. In other words, there is a *"break-even forward rate"* at which forward hedging makes sense.

Operational Aspects of Forward Contracts

Uncertainty of Proceeds

A number of technical issues confront funds managers who use forward contracts in their hedging practice. The first is the uncertainty of proceeds, which needs to be hedged. The amount of equity or fixed income (or real estate or equity) in local currency terms obviously changes over the life of a forward contract. The exact amount of this change cannot be known ahead of time. However, a forward contract is, by definition, based on a fixed amount of the currency to be sold forward. There are a number of ways of dealing with this problem:

1. Forward contracts can be maintained for three-month periods and "rolled over" or extended at expiration. This allows for adjustments of the amount of current that needs to be hedged.
2. A forecast of the growth of local currency amounts can be made at the beginning of the time period and hedged accordingly.

Cash Reserves

Typically, funds managers hedge their overseas exposure for a shorter maturity than their underlying investments, using 3-month or 6-month forward contracts. This is true for a number of reasons:

1. This allows for flexibility in changing the amount of hedge needed and in changing the hedge/no-hedge strategy.
2. The forward markets are extremely efficient until six months and even one year. Beyond one year, the bid-offer spreads begin to widen and some currencies become relatively illiquid. This makes hedging longer time periods an expensive proposition, which can only be solved by "asset swaps," long-term currency forwards that are based on the bond (as opposed to deposit) markets.

This maturity mismatch between the underlying investment and the forward hedge has important cash-flow implications in the need to provide cash to settle losses on forward currency contracts and to invest cash from forward contract gains. A declining dollar will mean that forward contracts will settle at a loss while a rising dollar will generate cash. The cash excesses and shortfalls can be met by liquidating overseas securities or, more efficiently, by having the sponsor establish a cash reserve to cover shortfalls.

Costs of Foreign Currency Hedging

There are a number of distinct costs in currency hedging. The first is the bid-offer spread on initial forward contract purchases. Because of the depth of the forward market, the spread on a three-month contract would not be more than around 0.01 percent. Secondly, management fees for currency programs might average between 5 and 15 basis points and custody costs another 2 basis points. The largest cost component to a hedging program may be the "hidden" points tacked on to currency transactions by custody banks, especially where the transactions are done on a noncompete basis. The total cost of hedging has been estimated at around 30 basis points.

USING CURRENCY OPTIONS

Currency options are ideally suited for currency overlay programs. When asked to express their objectives, most funds managers would state "protection of the portfolio's principal from downside risk and the opportunity of earning a return from favorable currency movements." Many of the problems found in the use of forward contracts—their inflexibility and the opportunity costs of giving up favorable currency movement and profits—are eliminated by the use of options. However, options also entail an up-front cost, which causes problems for many funds managers. Further, regulation in some (especially public) funds is either prohibitive or restrictive. Finally, accounting treatment may present a problem to some managers.

Despite these potential setbacks, a number of funds have used currency options to manage risk in their portfolios. The advantages of options over other forms of risk management include the following:

1. Options meet a pension plan's stated goal of absolutely protecting the downside risk while maintaining the potential for profit from favorable trends.
2. A number of analyses have found that options as a hedge strategy have significantly outperformed the hedge-all or hedge-nothing strategies.
3. The cash-flow problems associated with forwards are mitigated since the maximum potential negative cash flow is known at the beginning of the hedge.
4. Through a variety of strategies, strike prices, and combinations, it is possible to construct an almost infinite number of risk/reward profiles to meet almost any objectives.

Basics of Options

An understanding of currency options begins with the familiar risk/reward profile, which is familiar to all options users. Basically, there are four types of options strategies:

- Purchase a call
- Sell a call
- Purchase a put
- Sell a put

The profit-and-loss for each of these strategies is shown in Figures 5.9a–5.9d. The key points to observe are the "break-even" levels,

FIGURE 5.9a   Buy GBP Put Option: Profit and Loss Profile

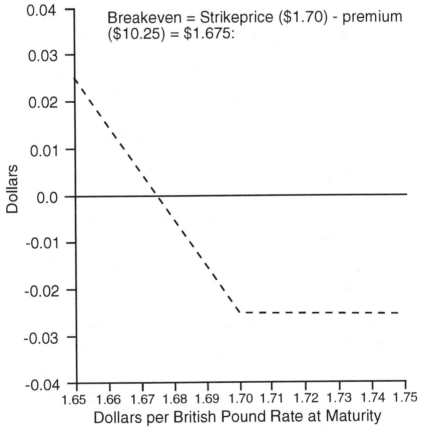

Breakeven = Strikeprice ($1.70) - premium ($10.25) = $1.675:

Dollars per British Pound Rate at Maturity

which are the levels at which an options strategy will outperform a do-nothing strategy, taking into account the premium paid for the option.

To see how options work in a foreign currency investment situation, we have presented a case study. In this case, a fund has invested in British sterling deposits to take advantage of the higher interest rates available in the U.K. The term of the deposit is 6 months (180 days), with the U.K. deposit yielding 11.00 percent per annum. (The issue of investing in stocks and bonds is more complicated in that the value of the underlying asset changes with time.) For simplicity, however, we begin with this example where the only variable that changes is currency.

FIGURE 5.9b   Buy GBP Call Option: Profit and Loss Profile

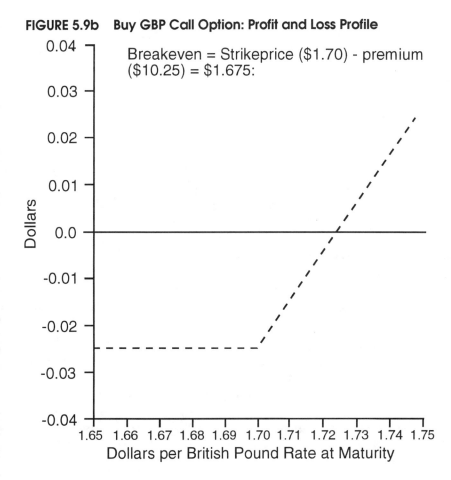

Breakeven = Strikeprice ($1.70) - premium ($10.25) = $1.675:

FIGURE 5.9c   Sell GBP Put Option: Profit and Loss Profile

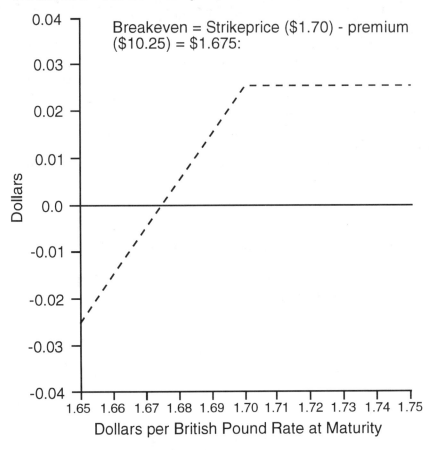

Open Position and Forward Cover

The first two alternatives, discussed above, open to the investor are to do nothing (maintain an open currency position) or to completely hedge his or her exposure with forward coverage. Maintaining an open position is the riskiest in that a downturn for the pound causes an unlimited loss for the investor. A fall of the pound from its present $1.50 to $1.30, for example, will cause a loss of capital of 13.33 percent.

Forward cover in this situation essentially turns a sterling investment into a U.S. investment because of interest rate arbitrage. Thus, investing in sterling and selling the proceeds forward in the forward market converts the return to 4.00 percent, which is exactly the U.S. dollar return on a six-month Euro-deposit. This is

FIGURE 5.9d   Sell GBP Call Option: Profit and Loss Profile

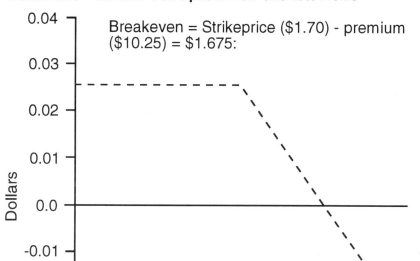

Breakeven = Strikeprice ($1.70) - premium ($10.25) = $1.675:

Dollars per British Pound Rate at Maturity

what we would expect from the covered interest arbitrage calculations described above.

Purchase of Protective Currency (Put) Options

The purchase of a put option is ultimately the simplest and most frequently used options strategy employed by investment managers. A sterling put option gives the buyer the right (but not the obligation) to sell his or her sterling proceeds at a guaranteed strike price in six months' time. The strike price can be determined by the buyer and will determine the premium that needs to be paid for this option.

As seen in Figure 5.10, the purchase of a put option gives the buyer complete downside protection from adverse currency

FIGURE 5.10   British Pound Put Option

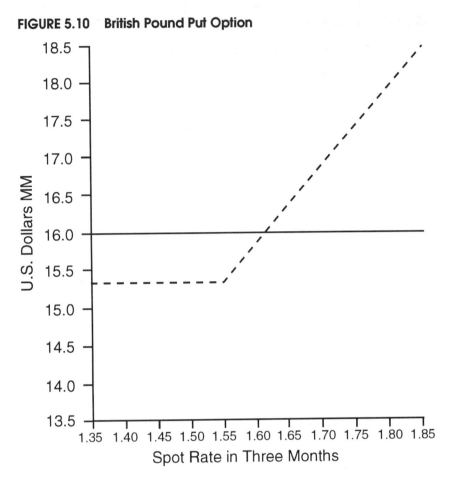

movements while allowing the benefit of participating in upside movement of the pound. The downside protection, in this case, is a function of the strike price of $1.7638 and the premium of 1.30 percent. If the pound falls below this level, the investor will experience a capital depreciation of 8.14 percent, of which 1.3 percent comes from the option premium cost and the rest from currency depreciation between today's spot rate ($1.9100) and the option strike price of $1.7638.

However, if at the expiration date the market is above $1.7638, the investor will sell his or her sterling in the market for the spot rate on that date. For example, a spot rate of $2.00 would result in an effective yield to the investor of 18.29 percent, of which 19.59 percent comes from the appreciation of the currency less the 1.3 percent premium cost.

Zero-Cost and Alternative Options Hedges

The idea of paying up-front for the cost of managing exchange and/or interest rate risk has not been a popular one in corporate circles. The cost of purchasing a put option has led to the development of alternative strategies and techniques for hedging currency risk. For a portfolio of $250 million in exposure, a put option that is 5 percent out of the money would cost $12,500,000 in premiums—a staggering number for any organization, especially investment firms who live in the regulatory, investor, and political limelights. The large number of options products that have appeared over the past five years are largely an effort to mitigate the up-front payment by hedgers for options products.

The first wave of such products was essentially "options portfolios"—that is, combinations of long and short positions of options and other derivative instruments to produce a portfolio with some option attributes. These portfolios were largely known as spreads by professional options traders who used them frequently in the markets. However, they were now rechristened with catchy names and sold on to the market as a new product. Examples include the cylinder option, participating forward, range forward option, zero-cost option, and so on. Thus, a cylinder option simply combined a long position in, say, a call option with a short position in a put option. The strike rates of the call and the put were chosen in such a way that the up-front cost of the portfolio would be very small or nothing, as in the case of a zero-cost option (i.e., cost of call equals cost of put).

A participating forward, on the other hand, combined a put and a call, possibly at different strike rates but also at different notional amounts. Again, the aim was to "minimize" the cost of the portfolio/product.

However, buying such portfolios required a thorough knowledge and understanding of the currency exposure confronting the funds manager. As we show below, the costs of misusing a collar or a put without the underlying cash flow and without adequate knowledge of the economics of these instruments could lead to severe losses. Indeed, a number of well-publicized cases involving corporate and financial institutions writing options either knowingly or unknowingly and consequently suffering substantial losses, served as timely reminders of an old proverb: there is no such thing as a free lunch.

The most popular zero-cost alternative to the purchase of a put is the range forward (or collar, fence, cylinder, etc.). This option strategy begins with the purchase of a put, as in the previous example. However, a call option is simultaneously sold whose strike price is such as to yield the same exact premium as that paid for the put option. In our example, the sale of a sterling call option with a strike of $1.9446 yields the investor a premium of $1.30, which exactly offsets the premium paid for the put option at $1.7638.

The profile of a collar strategy is presented in Figure 5.11. As indicated, the collar presents the same level of protection as the purchased put at the $1.7638 level. However, at this level the loss of principal is smaller since there is no option premium to be paid.

FIGURE 5.11   Put Option and Range Forward

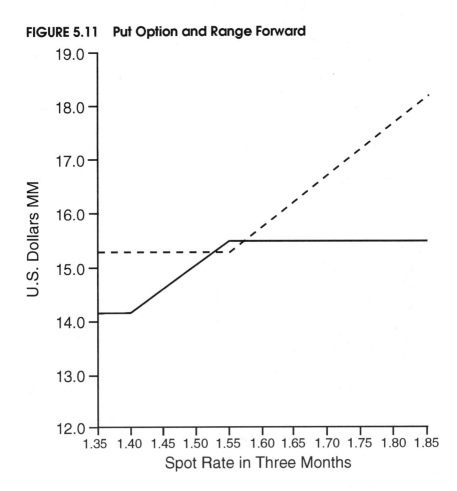

If the currency moves above $1.9446, however, the call that the investor sold will be exercised against him and he will be forced to sell his pounds at this rate of exchange. This will also cap his upside potential to a return of 14.87 percent, compared to the infinite return that a purchased option potentially delivers.

Clearly, the strategy that makes sense depends largely on a number of factors:

1. The extent to which an up-front payment for an option is viable
2. The extent to which an investor is willing to forsake unlimited upside potential in exchange for the elimination of an option premium
3. The currency view of the investor

In our example, if the investor is convinced that sterling will not rise above $1.9446, the collar option is clearly the best choice. However, a projection of currency movement to 2.00 makes either an open position or a purchased put the optimal choice. The composite graph, which draws the return profile of all the strategies, indicates how the investor's currency outlook is linked to the optimal strategy. For any forecasted value (i.e., $2.00 in six months), one or two strategies clearly dominate (i.e., open position or purchased put).

Like forwards, collar strategies have important implications for portfolio cash flows. A collar whose ending spot rate is above the strike price of the call that has been sold resembles a naked call option from a cash point of view. That is, the investor must make good the difference between the call option's strike price and the spot rate at expiration. This is, of course, offset by a comparable gain on the underlying investment portfolio. However, unless the funds manager wishes to liquidate this investment, there is an asymmetrical effect between the marked-to-market gain of the portfolio and the cash loss on the collar.

Participating Forward

A strategy that has received considerable publicity in the past several years, but that is a distant third in the risk management armory of investment managers, is the participating forward. This clever strategy entails the simultaneous purchase and sale of a put and call at the *same strike price*. Because the option sold is a call, it is in-the-money and provides more income than the cost of the option purchased. As a result, a smaller amount of the option needs to be sold than purchased.

In our example, the option sold is a pound call option at the strike of $1.55. This in-the-money option gives a premium of 6.634 percent, compared to the premium of the purchased put of 1.823 percent. Thus, only $2.363 million of the call option needs to be sold to provide the premium needed to offset the purchased put and provide a zero-cost strategy (i.e., $2,363 × 5.8 percent = $10mm × 1.3 percent).

The results of the participating strategy are as follows:

1. At any sterling rate below $1.55, the put option that has been purchased will provide complete downside protection to the investor, guaranteeing a worst-rate scenario of –5.36 percent return. Below this level, the call option that was sold expired worthless;
2. At any given spot price, 27.45 percent of the sterling amount to be sold will be sold at $1.55 (since the call option is profitable and is exercised in the market). The remaining 66.37 percent is sold by the investor in the spot market. The result is that the investor "participates" to the extent of 72.55 percent in any appreciation of sterling above the $1.55 level (see Figure 5.12).

Covered Write

A familiar strategy to Wall Street participants is the covered write option strategy. Similarly, investors can gain some protection from downside movement in the currency markets by selling a call option on their sterling investment. In this case, we show the sale of a sterling call at the strike price of $1.9446 in return for a premium of 1.30 percent.

The best way to show the economic relationship of a covered write is to compare its return profile to that of an open position. In our example, it will be noted that the depreciation of the sterling leads to losses in the cases of both an open position and a sell option strategy. However, the results of the covered write are always better by 1.3 percent because of the premium earned. On the other side, the maximum gain possible through a write strate-

FIGURE 5.12   Participating Forward and Put Option

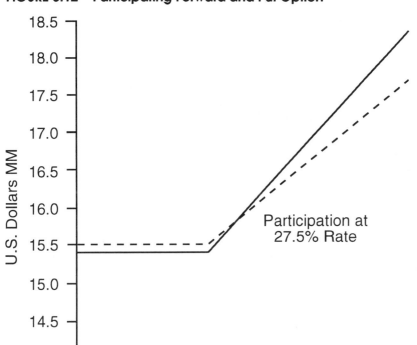

gy is equal to the strike price plus the 1.3 percent premium earned, since any sterling level above this strike price will lead to the options being exercised. Here, this caps the potential return of the investment at 17.65 percent.

Exotic Options Programs

The second wave of derivatives of the past three years comes from the increased sophistication of the financial institutions and the continuing demand from the corporate and funds management sector for derivative products. Again, the motivation, at least partly, was a possible reduction of the up-front premium. The "options portfolio" of the mid 1980s (i.e., collars) achieved this by simply buying and selling the right instruments in the "right" proportions. The second-generation options would achieve the reduction by offering insurance on a slightly different underlying asset or with certain exclusion clauses.

Examples of second-generation options are average rate options, down and out (barrier options), and options on options.

An *average rate option* would pay off at maturity the difference between the strike price and some average value of past spot exchange rates (for example, the arithmetic average of the last 20 daily closing prices before option maturity).

A *down and out option*, on the other hand, will pay off at maturity against the spot rate, but if, and only if, the daily spot rate during the life of the option never falls below a certain level.

An *cption on an option* is simply a call or a put on an underlying plain vanilla option. (It would be ideal "cheap" insurance for contingent financing or investment events that are hedged in advance.)

Unlike the option portfolio, however, second-generation options suffer from a major drawback: *liquidity*. Since these are normally structured by a financial institution for one customer on a customized basis, they can only be priced and marked-to-market with the same institution. This has obvious drawbacks in appeal for many potential users.

A DECISION-MAKING TOOL: THE RISK/REWARD MATRIX

While the ultimate decision regarding hedging strategies depends on the manager's risk/reward preferences, it is helpful to be able to evaluate the various approaches in one table. Table 5.1 presents the alternative strategies discussed above in one place. The numbers in the cells represent the dollar amount that the investor will realize from his or her investment in U.K. equities. This chart clearly demonstrates the relative advantages and disadvantages of each approach. One point is clearly demonstrated: no one strategy behaves best under all market conditions. An unhedged position is best suited to take advantage of favorable market movements, while a forward contract is ideal for adverse market moves. Options are never the best strategy, but they are never the worst.

TABLE 5.1 U.S. Dollar Receipt from Investing $20 Million in Sterling Under the Alternative Strategies at Varying Exchange Rates

	Exchange rate ate maturity (U.S./Stg)										
	11.35	1.40	1.45	1.50	1.55	1.60	1.65	1.70	1.75	1.80	1.85
Unhedged	20.250	21.000	21.750	22.500	23.250	24.000	24.750	25.500	26.250	27.000	27.750
Forward	22.148	22.148	22.148	22.148	22.148	22.148	22.148	22.148	22.148	22.148	22.148
Put Option	15.318	15.318	15.318	15.318	15.318	15.818	16.318	16.818	17.318	17.818	18.318
Range	14.103	14.103	14.500	15.000	15.500	15.500	15.500	15.500	15.500	15.500	15.500
Participating	15.500	15.500	15.500	15.500	15.500	15.863	16.225	16.588	16.950	17.313	17.676

PORTFOLIO INSURANCE: A COMEBACK

Portfolio insurance was proven to be a real problem in the equity markets in the 1980s. After becoming the most widely accepted form of managing equity risk, it showed its fundamental problem with the great crash of October 1987. As described below, portfolio insurance calls for an orderly market in which prices are available on a relatively continuous basis. Should this condition not hold, portfolio insurance can rack up open-ended losses for users.

Strangely, portfolio insurance is now making a comeback in the currency arena. It is offered by such institutions as Bankers Trust, Travellers Insurance, and Pareto-Mellon Bank. A number of highly publicized mandates have been given for currency overlay programs using portfolio insurance, including those from Calpers, Rockefeller Foundation, Hughes, and Illinois Teachers Fund.

What Is Portfolio Insurance?

Technically, portfolio insurance is a "path-dependent option." It is known by a number of other names, including dynamic hedging strategy, option replication, and dynamic asset allocation. While options are bought and sold on exchanges and over-the-counter, their true economic make-up is hedged by professionals using a technique known as delta hedging. In essence, the profile of an option is replicated by buying and selling the physical currency on the futures or interbank market.

As shown in Figure 5.13, portfolio insurance is meant to mimic the profile of a put option on the currency. It is assumed that the investor buys a put on the currency in which he has his investment.

Dynamic hedging entails a continuous readjustment (usually daily) of positions to adjust the portfolio for movements in the spot market. It is thus a transaction-intensive activity, which normally can be done only by a large staff with access to the marketplace. Most importantly, it is at risk from "discontinuous" pricing in the marketplace. The daily adjustment needs to be done at regular intervals. Any large gaps in the market would mean that the portfolio can incur a large loss. In October 1987 some portfolio insurance systems lost 20 percent or more as the market gapped before new "risk neutral" positions could be established.

FIGURE 5.13   Delta Hedge Payoff Objective

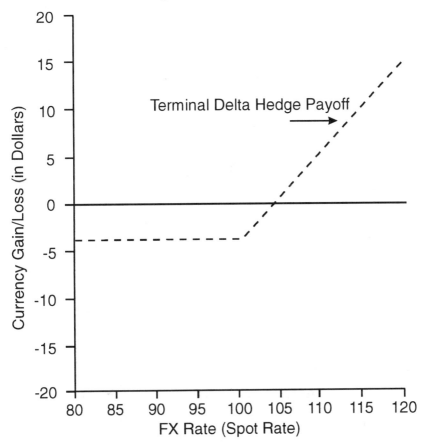

Protect dollar value of portfolio against declining FX rates,
and expose portfolio to dollar value gains from rising FX rates.

Source: Timco

Step-by-Step Portfolio Insurance

Figure 5.14: The hedge ratio that is used to simulate the option is
essentially derived from a calculation of delta—the hedge ratio
used to determine the "physical" position in the cash or futures
markets needed to exactly offset the risk of price movement in the
option position. All portfolios start at 50 hedge—that is, where
one half the amount to be hedged is sold or bought in the forward
market. As the spot rate moves, the delta also moves and the portfolio either accumulates the currency (if it is strengthening) or sells
the currency (if it is weakening).

FIGURE 5.14 Hedge Ratio Management

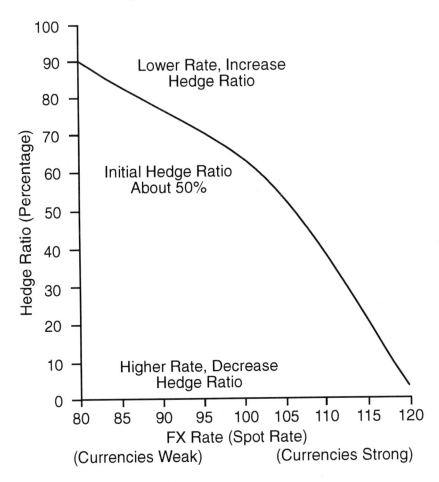

1. The hedge ratio of the portfolio is the percentage of the portfolio hedged with forward contracts.
2. As FX rate moves higher, decrease forward hedge ratio systematically.
3. As FX rate moves lower, increase forward hedge ratio systematically.

Source: Timco

FIGURE 5.15　Hedge Ratio Management

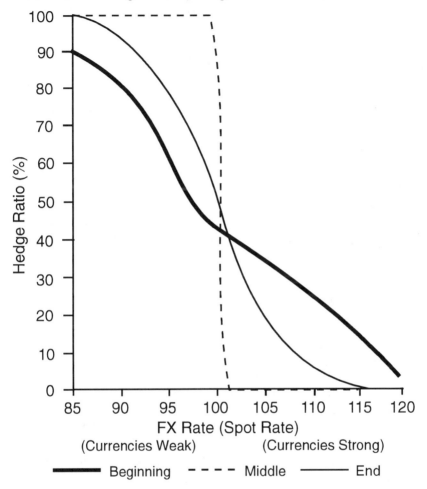

1. At every given FX rate the delta hedge target ratio changes slowly over time. The hedge ratio curve steepens as time passes.

2. At delta hedge expiration, the target hedge ratio will be 0% or 100% depending upon the level of the FX rate.

Source: Timco

Figure 5.15: More scientifically, the amount of currency bought or sold is determined by the hedge ratio (delta), which has a value of 0 percent to 100 percent. At expiration date, the hedge ratio will always be either zero (if the currency has strengthened) or 100 percent (if the currency has weakened). The currency owned by the program is a weighted average of all the daily currency purchased and sales made throughout the program.

Figure 5.15: Theoretically, hedging of simulated options portfolios needs to be done on an instantaneous basis. In reality, rehedging is normally done daily, so that the currency accumulation/disposition system looks like a step-function. As long as these steps are uniform and relatively small, the program proceeds safely.

Figure 5.16: Because the program starts with a 50 percent hedge, it will always entail a cost marked as differential A and B. This cost is identical to the cost of a purchased option if the implied volatility is the same as the historical. In either case, this cost is solely a function of the volatility in the marketplace. The higher the volatility, the more costly the hedging and the more the downside risk of a gap. Unfortunately, none of this is knowable ahead of time, but only after the fact.

Portfolio Insurance Versus Options

The reason firms use dynamic hedging over options (which has the same profile of limited loss and potential for gain) is twofold. First, there is the fact that no up-front payment is made using portfolio insurance. Second, when the traded options market is overvalued (i.e., when the implied volatility is higher than the actually volatility), replicated options do perform better than purchased options. One practitioner claims to be able to save between 50 and 100 basis points a year.

However, the key question is the risk involved in using dynamic hedging. As shown in Figures 5.13–5.17, the effectiveness of portfolio insurance depends on the ability of hedgers to approximate the hedge ratio since, in theory, the hedging should be done on a continuous basis. The more this rule is ignored, the more problematic is the hedge. Gross gaps in the market could lead to some serious losses.

One particularly terrifying worry is the *"five sigma" event.* Most models and market risk management strategies are effective in handling relatively small market shifts, but tend to break down when there are sharp, significant market shifts. It is similar to astrophysics: when you approach the speed of light, or get near a black hole, the old rule book stops working; you enter uncharted territory.

FIGURE 5.16 Delta Hedging Filter Rule

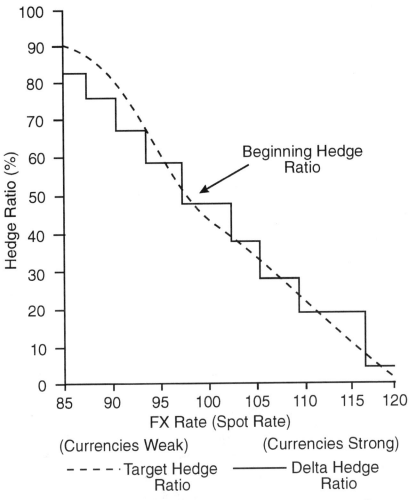

1. It is impractical and inefficient to attempt to replicate the hedge ratio on a continuous basis.
2. Forward contract cover is increased (as FX rates decrease) or decreased (as FX rates increase) in a stepped fashion.

Source: Timco

FIGURE 5.17   Delta Hedging Costs

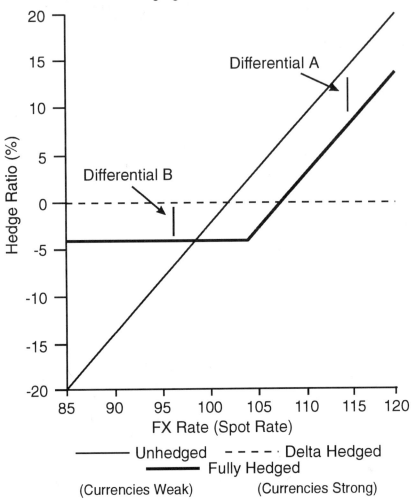

1. Because a delta hedged program will begin with a 50% hedge ratio, the portfolio will not be fully hedged as rates initially decline or fully unhedged as rates initially increase.

2. Delta hedge is not expected to capture the total profit potential of a rising FX market (differential A) and is expected to experience a limited loss in a declining FX market (differential B).

3. This projected performance differential to the two naive strategies represents the cost of the delta hedging program.

4. The more pronounced the market trend, the lower the cost of delta hedging.

Source: Timco

Two questions are often asked by those who use options as hedge instruments: First, do users of dynamic hedging realize that they are essentially speculating on volatility movements in the currency markets? For portfolio insurance to more effectively replicate an option profile, there must be a mispricing in the options marketplace. That is, implied volatilities must be higher than actual volatilities so that options cost more than they should. The question then is, should pension funds speculate in options volatility? Furthermore, with hundreds of professionals world-wide scouring the globe for arbitrage opportunities, is it likely that these pension funds have found a form of options volatility arbitrage that has escaped currency professionals? Finally, given the potential savings of portfolio insurance over purchased options, is it worth taking the gap risk entailed?

Part of the answer given by portfolio insurance providers is that currencies have never (and therefore by inference will never) "gap" to the extent of the stock market in October 1987. Of course, users of portfolio insurance for equity portfolios probably said the same thing up to that time. This argument is perhaps harder to make since the double-digit currency declines experienced by the Finnish markka, Italian lira, and the pound sterling in 1992. The point is that, as long as currency markets behave in a relatively orderly manner, portfolio insurance will have a prominent place in currency risk management.

MECHANICS OF A CURRENCY OVERLAY PROGRAM

Proxy Hedging Strategies

The typical portfolio of a funds manager may include anywhere from 10 to 25 currencies. This mix will vary, depending on the allocation between European and non-European currencies and between developed and emerging nations. It is usually expensive and inefficient to manage a normal portfolio on a currency-by-currency basis. In several emerging nations a forward currency market does not exist or is so illiquid that hedging currency risk is impossible.

Regardless of the hedging method used by a portfolio manager, the first step must be to reduce the original portfolio to a manageable number of currencies that can be hedged cheaply and efficiently.

The most common method of achieving this is known as basket hedge or proxy hedge. This hedge uses a surrogate portfolio of currencies to track the movement of the original investment portfolio. If properly designed, the proxy hedge basket contains fewer currencies and has a lower interest cost than hedging the original portfolio on a currency-by-currency basis. The risk in using this method was fully revealed during the upheaval in the European Monetary System in August and September of 1992. The premise of the method is that the investment and hedge portfolios move in tandem in response to currency fluctuations.

One time-honored method of creating a basket hedge is to segregate the investment currencies into blocks (i.e., deutsche mark, yen, and U.S. dollar) and hedge using these currencies as proxies for the actual investment portfolio. This is a rough approximation and has the advantage of ease of operation and an intuitive logic. However, it is at best a partial solution since it does not factor in the relationship between currencies. It also does not allow for the differences between the currencies within a currency block.

The latest technique for streamlining the hedge process is the use of portfolio optimization and portfolio volatility to create variance-covariance matrices, which can then be used to isolate a small number of currencies (normally 3–4) whose volatility closely mirrors that of the original portfolio. At times, it is possible to use this process to hedge currencies that are otherwise unhedgeable due to a lack of hedge instruments. In a typical portfolio, the proxy currencies will track the movement of the overall portfolio as much as 95 to 98 percent.

Finally, proxy hedging techniques can aid in finding low interest rate substitutes for higher interest rate currencies in the portfolio. For example, using Dutch guilders to hedge a portfolio consisting of Italian lira and Spanish pesetas represents an enormous cost savings in interest rates. In fact, it will often make the difference between being able to hedge a portfolio and the hedge being too expensive.

Once the proxy has been determined, it is possible to use these currencies as a surrogate for the portfolio as a whole. This step should be taken no matter which hedging technique is used by the managers: forward coverage, options, or portfolio insurance.

Proxy Hedging and the ERM

A substantial amount of proxy hedging assumed a high correlation among the currencies of the ERM. This correlation allowed managers to assume a "deutsche mark" block of currencies—high-yielding European currencies that could be hedged using the German mark as a proxy hedge.

The dramatic events that began with the defeat of the Maastricht accord by Danish voters in August of 1992 seriously upset this simple strategy. As shown below, the correlations between the German mark and other European currencies effectively disappeared.

Monthly Correlations with the Deutsche Mark

	British Pound	Italian Lira	Swedish Krona
August 1992	0.95	0.98	0.98
September	0.66	0.83	0.93
October	0.18	0.2	0.93

Benchmarks and Performance Evaluation

The selection of benchmarks is important for a variety of reasons. First, it establishes compensation levels for managers. More importantly, it should be used to strike a delicate balance between the desire of the pension fund to hedge its risk and to provide enhanced return through the selection of managers. Unless a fund has a policy of 100 hedge (which is rarely the case), the question becomes: Should currency overlay managers be judged on the actual positions of the fund or on a benchmark?

At Bechtel, for example, its $1.5 billion defined-contribution plan uses a subsidiary, Fremont Investment Advisors, to manage its pension fund. About 30 percent of the fund is internationally invested. Managers receive a performance benchmark to beat, which is 50 percent hedged for foreign equity and 80 percent hedged for overseas bonds. According to the firm, this works well in terms of letting managers know their responsibility for managing currency risk.

A benchmark that is too specific can act to stifle profitable asset selections of portfolio managers. For example, assume that a firm has general policy guidelines of investing 60 percent yen and 40 percent DM. At the same time, one of its managers makes a profitable decision to invest in 40 percent yen and 60 percent DM. If the currency overlay manager received a mandate to hedge the policy portfolio along 60 percent yen and 40 percent DM, the profitable trade would still go through. However, if the overlay manager hedged the revised trade, he or she would in effect reverse the manager's profitable decision.

The normal portfolio identifies the composition of the currency basket to be hedged. Examples might be the MSCI EAFE index or a fixed regional allocation. Some sponsors choose to hedge actual currency risk, rather than the risk assumed in the normal portfolio. For example, active managers may underweight Japan relative to the normal portfolio, reducing the yen exposure and increasing other currency exposures relative to the normal portfolio. The sponsor may want the overlay manager to know this and to hedge only actual currency exposures rather than normal exposures. In hedging actual exposures, however, an overlay manager may neutralize an active decision by an international manager, eliminating possible added return. This approach is also likely to result in a higher level of turnover, as the overlay manager must adapt to changing underlying portfolios. Hedging against the normal portfolio helps to preserve the integrity of other manager decisions and reduces transaction costs.

Longer-Term Trends in Currency Volatility

Anthony Foley
Pareto Partners

INTRODUCTION

In recent years there has been a good deal of work done on the nature of risk in financial markets. Several areas will be familiar to most people with an interest in finance. In the currency arena, a distinction can be drawn between essentially two sorts of approach. The open interest parity condition says that in the absence of a risk premium the interest rate differential between two separate currency areas should be just sufficient to offset the markets' expectation of the percentage change in the value of the currency concerned. The failure of this relation to hold even on average has been pointed out many times. The best-known response to this has been to baptize the difference between what should obtain under open interest parity and reality the "risk premium" and attempt to model this residual and its determinants as a separate process driven in some part by fundamental economic data. It seems fair to say that as yet nobody has put together a convincing model of this process and there are no particular grounds for optimism on this front.

In part the failure of risk premium modeling can be related to a more general problem for exchange rate economics and indirectly to the second of the two strands of risk modeling that have received most attention over the past few years. This problem is that the best efforts of economists to arrive at a general theory of exchange rate determination that will usefully explain all or even a large part of the behavior of currencies, let alone generate useful predictions of future exchange rate movements, have not really borne fruit. Relating the return on holding currencies to economic fundamentals has proved an intractable problem. See De Grauwe (1989) for a useful description of all the standard analyses and some empirical analysis on when each has worked and when it has nose-dived, and how this has affected subsequent theorizing. If it is impossible to provide a satisfactory account of the fundamental determinants of currency return, it is unsurprising that attempts to model the risk premium have met with little success.

The intractable nature of the currency return forecasting problem can be seen as part of the motivation behind the second sort of approach of interest in the currency area. This is the varied body of work that has been done on the risk characteristics of currencies. Most of this work has focused on trying to find structure in currency returns that is useful for forecasting the volatility of currencies even if there is no information there that would consistently help forecast the level of currency returns.

In this chapter, we will review some of this work. A contention is that the widely used GARCH framework may be supplemented in the affections of researchers working in the area of risk modeling by stochastic volatility modeling, which seems to have significant advantages, particularly when estimating the joint distribution of several currencies. For ease of comparison, a sketch of the workings of each technique is provided. Since empirical results for the stochastic volatility model are still relatively thin on the ground, a sample analysis is presented using this technique.

A second aim is to look in some detail at a more descriptive analysis of the behavior of volatility over the entire floating exchange rate period. This descriptive analysis will hopefully prove useful on a couple of grounds. Firstly, to give an intuitive perspective on the longer-run evolution of volatility. Secondly, to contrast the differing risk characteristics of the major currency blocs.

The main objective of the descriptive analysis, however, is to try and determine how unusual the events of 1992 were in a broader historical context. Clearly, the second half of 1992 was a very volatile time in currency markets generally. How volatile it was relative to previous episodes of high volatility, correctly measured, is a useful landmark to put in place.

To this end a simple regression model is used to see if there is any apparent structure in the longer run evolution of currency volatility over time. Some evidence showing mean reversion around a long-run upward trend is derived.

Finally, an economic rationale for some of the results presented is suggested.

INCREASE IN VOLATILITY VERSUS INCREASE IN ONE-OFF MOVES

The Distribution of Volatility

The data used in the analysis is weekly data from Datastream for the Australian dollar, Swiss franc, deutsche mark, French franc, Italian lira, Japanese yen, sterling, and the Dutch guilder. The Smithsonian Agreement in 1971 saw the dollar devalued against all major currencies, but it was not until 1973 (when major governments stopped guaranteeing the dollar price of their currencies) that the fixed-rate system really ceased to function. The data sample starts in June 1973, ensuring that the entire recent history of floating exchange rates is included, and finishes at the end of 1992.

To compare currency volatility across time and across currencies, the empirical distribution of exchange rate volatility was calculated. Nonoverlapping six-month volatilities were calculated based on the weekly data, giving a sample of 40 volatility points for each currency. A histogram of volatility for each currency was then constructed.

In order to place the events of 1992 in perspective, the volatility for the first half of 1992 and the second half of 1992 are highlighted. Figure 6.1 shows the distribution of six-month volatilities for an equally weighted basket of currencies against the U.S. dollar. In the first half of 1992 the volatility was in the 10 percent region, only mildly high relative to the historic average, but in the second half of 1992 volatilities reached levels very rarely exceeded since 1973. In fact, volatility was only significantly higher once, around the peak in the value of the U.S. dollar in February 1985.

This result can be dissected in several ways to further context the events of 1992 and the behavior of currency volatility more generally. Firstly, the increase in volatility was not uniform across currencies. Figures 6.2 and 6.3 show the distribution of currency volatility for the deutsche mark and Japanese yen, respectively.

These charts are typical of the contrast between the behavior of the European currencies and the yen and Australian dollar. The overall rise in volatility in 1992 would appear to be very much a European phenomenon. Secondly, the extreme level of volatility in the second half of 1992 should also be seen in the context of a gen-

FIGURE 6.1 Currency Basket vs. U.S. Dollar Annualized Six-Month Volatility Distribution

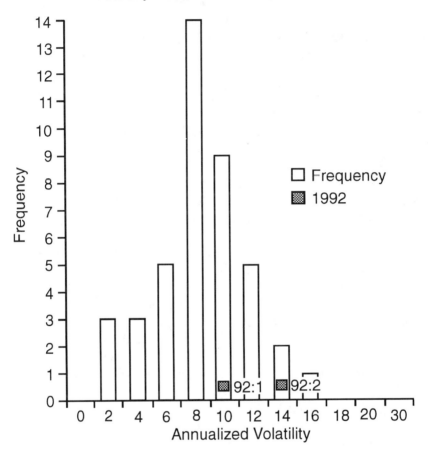

eral rise in the average level of volatility in the 1980s. This is illustrated in Figure 6.4, which breaks the overall data sample into two halves, pre- and post-December 1980.

Robust Estimation and Volatility

The increase in volatility in the second half of 1992 is very striking. Volatility as measured by standard methods can increase for two reasons: Firstly, as a result of an increase in the average absolute size of move, and secondly, as a result of as few as one very large

FIGURE 6.2   Deutsche mark vs. U.S. Dollar Annualized Six-Month Volatility Distribution

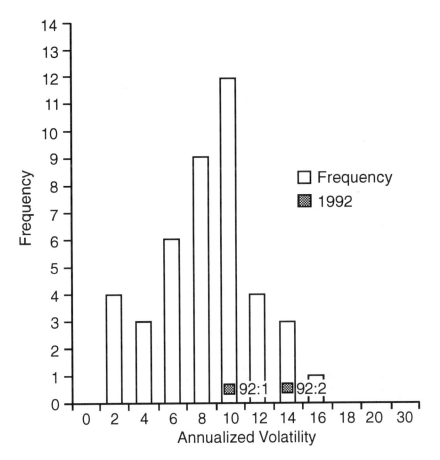

move. In such a case the observed "rise" in volatility could really be reflecting the events of as little as one minute in the entire six-month sample period.

Technically, the sample standard deviation is a nonrobust statistic. Robust statistics (see Huber [1981] for a good introduction to robust statistical techniques) are designed to limit the effect of extreme observations on estimated parameters in order to obtain a truer picture of what is actually occurring in the data. In this case an estimate of currency volatility that is not overly influenced by a few large moves is preferable.

FIGURE 6.3   Japanese Yen vs. U.S. Dollar Annualised Six-Month Volatility Distribution

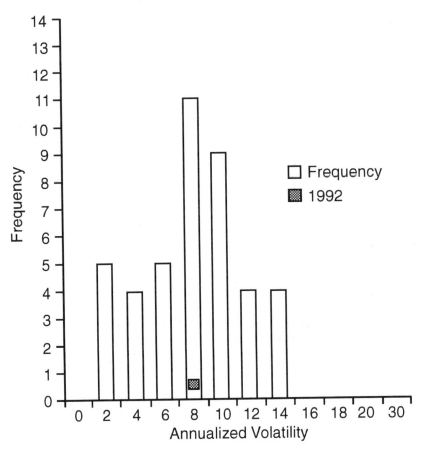

There are various ways of achieving this goal. The method used in this instance to get a robust estimate of volatility was to truncate each six-month sample of the absolute largest 20 percent of observations and then estimate volatility on the remaining 80 percent, the behavior of this volatility estimator over time should show whether the increase in volatility was a real event. Such an estimator is known as a trimmed distribution estimator.

Figure 6.5 is a "robustified" version of Figure 6.1 and is broadly similar to it (as are the robust versions of the other charts). This

FIGURE 6.4   Currency Basket vs. U.S. Dollar: Annualized Six-Month Volatility Distribution

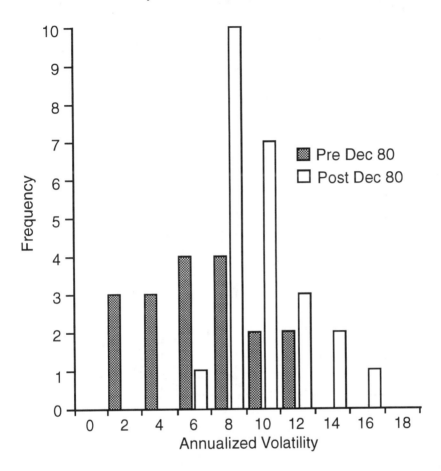

is good evidence for the rise in volatility being a genuine rise in the average size of exchange rate move.

STATISTICAL MODELLING OF EXCHANGE RATE DISTRIBUTIONS

Summary of Recent Research

A lot of work in recent years has been done on the evolution of short-term financial asset volatility over time. One approach in

FIGURE 6.5   Currency Basket vs. U.S. Dollar Annualized Six-Month Robust Volatility Distribution

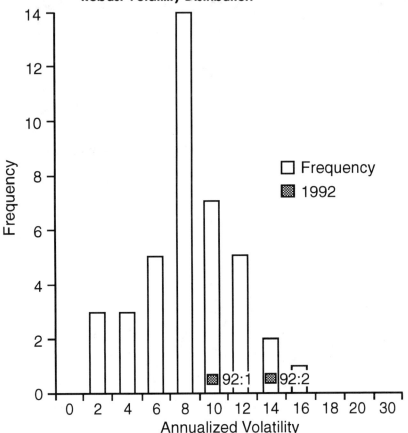

particular has received a lot of attention: Generalized Autoregressive Conditional Heteroscedasticity (GARCH) modeling and its variants. Bollerslev, Chou, and Kroner (1992) provide a comprehensive survey of the literature. The central theme in GARCH models is that volatility can often be modeled successfully purely as a function of squared past asset returns and past volatility values. This approach has gained widespread acceptance in the academic community as the appropriate tool for modelling the risk distribution of, in particular, financial time series such as exchange rate data.

The original ARCH model, as set out in Engle (1982), has subsequently been extended in many directions. For example, a more parsimonious representation can usually be obtained by including lagged values of the volatility estimates themselves, such models being described as Generalized ARCH, or GARCH, models, as described in Bollerslev (1986). Augmented ARCH models include the effect of cross-product terms on volatility, so that if two adjacent residual values are large, for example, this can have a bigger impact on the volatility estimate than would just be obtainable from a standard ARCH approach, and these are AARCH models. Engle (1990) suggests an Asymmetric ARCH model which includes the residuals themselves, rather than just their squared values, A-ARCH. A recent development is the quadratic ARCH model, which allows the sign as well as the size of past residuals to affect the future estimate of risk, this model being known as the QARCH model (see Sentana [1991]). Since the GQARCH model ("Generalized QARCH") model nests the others, the whole family of models can be obtained by placing restrictions on the parameters in the GQARCH(q,p) formulation:

$$\sigma_t^2 - \theta = \sum_{i=1}^{q} \psi_i X_{t-i} + \sum_{i=1}^{q} a_{ii} X_{t-i}^2 + \sum_{i \neq j} a_{ij} X_{t-i} X_{t-j} + \sum_{j=1}^{p} \delta_j \sigma_{t-j}^2$$

so that the original ARCH model includes only the second set of terms on the right-hand side, the AARCH the second and third, and the QARCH model the first three. The A-ARCH model includes the first two terms. In each case the generalized version of the approach also includes the fourth term. In the description GARCH(q,p), q is the number of lagged values of the variable included, and p the number of lagged values of the volatility estimator.

Empirical Results of ARCH Models of Currency Returns

The ability of models based on the ARCH formulation to improve the accuracy of risk estimation for exchange rate time series has been well-documented. Bollerslev (1990), McCurdy and Morgan (1988), and many others apply variants of ARCH models to foreign exchange rate data. The conclusions could be summarized as saying that at a minimum, whether daily or weekly data is considered, over a wide range of currencies, a GARCH(1,1) model is a clear statistical improvement over the assumption of unconditional normality.

Such a framework can capture some important characteristics of currency markets. See Hsieh (1988) for a typical study. GARCH models will also give some guide to the extent of any mean-reversionary tendencies in the behavior of volatility over time. However, GARCH models are not well suited to accommodating the existence of skew in a distribution, which can be shown to be an important feature of currency behavior. Liesching and Foley (1992) addresses this issue in more detail. This is in part because in the GARCH framework, the conditional distribution is always symmetric. Furthermore, to extend a GARCH framework to a multivariate context where several currencies are being considered jointly, for example, requires the estimation of a very large number of parameters. This has serious implications for the degrees of freedom in the estimation process. Typically, to reduce the problem to manageable levels, a number of simplifying assumptions need to be introduced. These simplifications often result in dubious assumptions about the degree and type of correlation between volatility processes among different currencies.

Stochastic Volatility Modeling

A lot of recent econometric research work in this area is concentrated on a newer technique, stochastic volatility modeling. Good introductions to this technique are provided in Harvey, Ruiz, and Shephard (1992) and Taylor (1993). This approach models the behavior of volatility as an unobserved stochastic process. In other words, the dependence on past price movements is less direct than is the case with GARCH models. Although both models are estimated on the basis of a past price history, there is a distinct difference between the approaches. In the GARCH framework, these movements directly bring about changes in the estimate of volatility. In the stochastic volatility model, past price movements provide information as to how the separate random process driving volatility is evolving. This can be an important distinction.

Taylor, for example, concludes that in the context of an information counting model in which volatility is a function of the amount of information available, the stochastic volatility model can be interpreted as being driven by this process while past price movements remain the primary source of volatility in the GARCH framework.

To illustrate the way in which this technique may be applied in practice, a set of univariate models were estimated using the data set already described. The idea was to generate results for weekly exchange rate movements, which could be compared to the daily results obtained by Harvey et al.

A typical model might look like:

$$x_t = \varepsilon_t * \exp(h_t/2)$$
$$h_t = \gamma + \varphi h_{t-1} + \eta_t \qquad \eta_t \sim \text{NID}(0,\sigma_\mu^2)$$

where h_t represents the stochastic process driving volatility. In the above example the process is assumed to be AR(1), although a more general specification could easily be accommodated. The theoretical properties of this model are examined in some detail in Harvey et al. and Taylor. One very important point is that the properties of (in this case) the exchange rate process follow directly from the properties of the process governing h_t. This makes such models easy to work with because the properties of ARMA models are so well-known. It is also easy to generalize such models to the multivariate case without having to impose a large number of restrictions on the form of the co-persistence in volatility. A disadvantage is that the model is not conditionally Gaussian, which does make estimation and interpretation of the parameters more complicated than in the GARCH framework.

There are several ways of going about estimating the above model. The technique employed here is Kalman filtering with quasi-maximum likelihood estimation of the hyperparameters. See Harvey (1989) for an introduction to Kalman filter modelling. The following table reports estimates of the AR(1) model over the entire sample period:

	$\hat{\gamma}$	$\hat{\varphi}$	$\hat{\sigma}_\eta^2$	Log L
Deutsche mark	−0.87	0.90	0.10	−932.7
Swiss franc	−0.075	0.99	0.01	−970.0
French franc	−0.125	0.99	0.02	−928.2
Italian lira	−0.33	0.96	0.04	−993.7
Japanese yen	−0.054	0.99	0.004	−1000.2
Sterling	−0.37	0.96	0.05	−979.7
Dutch guilder	−0.18	0.98	0.02	−975.0
Australian dollar	0	1.00	0.001	−975.12

In general, the results are quite similar to those reported by Harvey et al. The typical result would seem to indicate that the volatility process can be well characterized as following a random walk, but that the degree of divergence from this is much higher for the European currencies than for the Japanese yen and Australian dollar.

These results are very similar to those that would have been obtained using a GARCH-type approach. This is shown to hold theoretically by Harvey et al. for processes that have the sort of parameter values that we have found. At the univariate level more work needs to be done to assess the relative merits of the two approaches. Results obtained by Taylor over a different data set again indicate that the stochastic volatility model will give similar results to the most appropriate ARCH model in the univariate case.

In the multivariate case, the simplicity of the stochastic volatility model structure results in a substantial fall in the number of parameters needed to characterize the process compared to GARCH formulations.

To estimate a GARCH(1,1) model for just two variables conjointly requires the estimation of no fewer than 21 parameters. For a five-variable model, the equivalent number would be 465. This means that to estimate a multivariate GARCH model realistically requires the use of some fairly ruthless pruning assumptions. This is, generally speaking, a poor position to be forced into. The issue is well described in Harvey et al.:

> "The multivariate GARCH specification contains a large number of parameters and some restrictions have to be imposed for the model to be manageable. These restricted models do not necessarily have a natural interpretation, and even with the restrictions there are often still large numbers of parameters and estimation is not easy."

The stochastic volatility framework generalizes to a multivariate case in a much smoother fashion. Essentially, what is required is the estimation of a straightforward VAR model. This means that, for example, in the two-currency case with the first order autoregressive scheme used in our empirical analysis, only nine parameters would need to be estimated, a significant gain on the GARCH requirement. In the five-variable case this number would be 45, an order of magnitude smaller than the GARCH model requirement. The requirement to impose arbitrary limitations on the structure of the model is consequently more or less eliminated.

Because of this gain in degrees of freedom, it may well be that in the multivariate case, which will very often be the reality in an investment context, stochastic volatility modelling will be the more appropriate technique. Current research being undertaken at Pareto Partners into the structure of bond and currency returns is employing this technique, and preliminary results are encouraging.

It should, of course, be noted that the stochastic volatility approach, like the GARCH model, does not take account of the existence of skew in currency returns, which is, as mentioned, a significant drawback for any currency model.

Longer-Run Modelling

To look at the longer-run evolution of volatility, a different approach is called for. Neither GARCH nor the stochastic volatility approach is really suitable for the small sample size at our disposal. There is simply not enough data and stationarity assumptions are violated. It is also not clear that one would expect the same sort of model to describe longer-run swings in volatility as well as the short-term change in volatility patterns found in currency movements.

In fact, the questions addressed here fall more naturally into a simple error-correction model framework very closely related to that employed in co-integration analysis. See Engle and Granger (1987) for the theory and Perman (1991) for a good explanation of the technique and the merits of alternative estimation techniques. Here the focus is on detecting longer-run relationships in the data, rather than the explicit modelling of short-term trends.

The analysis here is limited in scope: how much evidence is there for mean-reversion in longer run volatility in our sample? To answer this question, a two-stage estimation procedure was employed. In the first stage a linear regression of volatility on a constant and time trend was performed. The hypothesis that volatility fluctuates around an upward long-term trend could not be rejected using the Augmented Dickey-Fuller test. Given this result, the residuals from this equation can be interpreted as deviations of volatility from this long-run upward trend. These residuals were then used as the independent variable in a regression of changes in volatility, the idea being to try and see the extent to which the deviation from the longer-run trend affects subsequent moves in volatility.

The estimated coefficient from this second regression can be interpreted as the proportion of the divergence of volatility from its changing equilibrium level rate eliminated in a given time period.

The results are consistent with longer-run volatility having a noticeable upward trend over time, amounting to some 20 basis points a year. More importantly, the results characterize the process as tending to revert quite rapidly from deviations around this trend, which are both large and frequent.

Regression Results

Dependent Variable: Average Volatility—Estimation by Least Squares

Semi-Annual Data From 72:02 to 92:02
Degrees of Freedom   39   R Bar **2   0.18
Standard Error of Estimate   2.6
Durbin-Watson Statistic   1.26

Variable	Coeff	Std Error	T-Stat
1. Constant	7.22	0.828	8.72
2. Trend	0.11	0.034	3.08

The augmented Dickey-Fuller test statistic from this regression using two additional lags was 3.65.

Dependent Variable: Change in Volatility—Estimation by Least Squares

Semi-Annual Data From 73:01 to 92:02
Degrees of Freedom   39   R Bar **2   0.33
Standard Error of Estimate   2.40
Durbin-Watson Statistic   1.53

Variable	Coeff	Std Error	T-Stat
1. Lagged Error	−0.66	0.15	−4.41

ECONOMIC INTERPRETABILITY

Two important conclusions have been suggested by this analysis of longer-run currency volatility: firstly, that currency volatility has rarely been as high as it was in the second half of 1992, and secondly, that longer-run volatility has shown a trend rate of increase over the course of the floating exchange rate period.

In addition, the data supports a conclusion found at higher data frequencies: the risk distribution of European currencies and those of the Pacific Rim can be very different.

Economic modeling of time-varying conditional variances is still in its infancy. Nevertheless, a few thoughts occur. Firstly, the fact that the level of volatility in the second half of 1992 was only exceeded around the last major turning point in the value of the U.S. dollar is interesting. It does seem, at the least, plausible that volatility should be high when market views about the prospects for the asset in question are undergoing substantial revision. This was clearly the case in early 1985. In 1992 there appeared to be a widespread agreement that the dollar was substantially undervalued against European currencies but that until some combination of a substantial recovery in the U.S. and a significant easing of monetary policy occurring in Germany, prospects for the dollar were muted.

Therefore, it can be argued that the sharp rise in volatility could be associated with the possibility at any rate of a sharp change in the value of the U.S dollar in terms of the European currencies. This is of course highly tentative given the data at our disposal, but seems worthy of consideration.

Note that such a notion would be different from the causality implied in ARCH-M models. Here the idea is that higher volatility should be associated with higher expected return. The theoretical rationale for this process is normally the CAPM model, but we believe there are serious problems with applying this model to currency holdings. The majority of research completed on this basis has in any case come up with negative results.

The partial fracturing of the ERM was also likely an important source of the increase in volatility in the second half of 1992. The Bundesbank was reluctant in the extreme to pursue a monetary policy more accommodative to the real shock of unification than already dictated by internal considerations. Other European central banks with economies mired in recession (or in the case of the U.K., slump) found the deflationary impact of this reluctance difficult or impossible to bear.

It is important, however, not to overstate the impact of the ERM crisis on the findings. The turbulence of the early years of the ERM was very pronounced, with several instances of large-scale speculative attacks on currencies thought to be in line for devaluation, just as occurred in 1992. The influence of the very large one-day moves in, for example, sterling when the U.K. suspended membership of the ERM will have been greatly reduced by the robust procedure, which was shown to have very similar characteristics in terms of the scale of the increase in volatility.

The other empirical finding concerns the upward drift in volatility over time. Two common explanations are, firstly, during the 1980s, an explosion in the size of this market occurred, with many new entrants whose motives were primarily rent-seeking. This could well induce an upward trend in volatility. Secondly, the growth in world trade volume over time could have had some influence. It should be noted though that foreign exchange transactions directly related to trade form a minute portion of daily transaction volume.

An additional longer-term source of an uptrend in volatility could be the coalescing of the currency market into essentially three blocs, the yen bloc, the dollar bloc, and the European bloc. Such a tripartite regime could be considerably less stable than one with a single dominant currency and many satellite currencies, as was the case at the start of the floating exchange rate regime.

CONCLUSION

A longer-run analysis of currency volatility has shown that for European currencies relative to the U.S. dollar the events of the second half of 1992 were close to previous highs in volatility. This was a robust conclusion.

It was suggested that of the standard approaches to estimating volatility, the newer stochastic volatility technique deserves to be taken very seriously as an alternative to GARCH-type models.

Although standard approaches to the estimation of currency volatility were not suitable for the task at hand, a simple model of the evolution of volatility over the floating period was estimated, and some evidence of mean reversion in volatility was found and of an upward trend in volatility over time.

We have put forward several thoughts as to what economic processes might be behind the longer-run evolution of volatility and believe this to be an interesting area for future research.

REFERENCES

Bollerslev, T., "Generalised Autoregressive Conditional Hetero-scedasticity," *Journal of Econometrics*, 31, 307–327, 1986.

Bollerslev, T., "Modelling the Coherence in Short-Run Nominal Exchange Rates: A Multivariate Generalized ARCH Model," *Review of Economics and Statistics*, 72, 1990, 498–505.

Bollerslev, Chou, and Kroner, "ARCH Modelling in Finance: A Selective Review of the Theory and Empirical Evidence with Suggestions for Future Research," *Journal of Econometrics*, 52, 5–59, 1992.

De Grauwe, "International Money, Post-War Trends and Theories," Clarendon Press, Oxford, 1989.

Engle, R. F., "Autoregressive Conditional Heteroscedasticity with Estimates of the Variance of United Kingdom Inflation," *Econometrica*, 50, 987–1007, 1982.

Engle, R. F., "Discussion: Stock Market Volatility and the Crash of '87," *Review of Financial Studies*, 3, 103–106, 1990.

Engle and Granger, "Co-Integration and Error Correction: Representation, Estimation and Testing," *Econometrica*, 55, 251–276, 1987.

Harvey, A. C., "Forecasting, Structrual Time Series Models and the Kalman Filter," Cambridge University Press, 1989.

Harvey, Ruiz, and Shephard, "Multivariate Stochastic Variance Models," *L.S.E. Financial Markets Group Working Paper*, 132, 1992.

Hsieh, D. A., "The Statistical Properties of Daily Foreign Exchange Rates: 1974–1983," *Journal of International Economics*, 24, 129–145, 1988.

Huber, P. S., "Robust Statistics," Wiley, New York, 1981.

Liesching and Foley, "The Estimation and Management of Currency Risk," *Pareto Partners Research*, 1992.

McCurdy, T. H., and Morgan, I. G.,"Testing the Martingale Hypothesis in Deutschemark Futures With Models Specifying the Form of Heteroscedasticity," *Journal of Applied Econometrics*, Vol. 3, 187–202, 1987.

Perman R., "Cointegration: An Introduction to the Literature," *Journal of Economic Studies*, Vol. 18, No. 3, pp. 3–30, 1991.

Sentana, E., "Quadratic ARCH Models: A Potential Re-Interpretation of ARCH Models," Discussion Paper No. 122, 1991, *L.S.E. Financial Markets Group*.

Taylor, S. S. "Modelling Stochastic Volatility," working paper, Lancaster University, 1993.

7

Going Global in Chaotic Times

Martha Eden
Hanseatic Group, Inc.

INTRODUCTION

Despite the fact that individual American investors are still years away from viewing a dollar-denominated portfolio as depicting the result of a currency decision, most U.S. fund managers have at this time at least seriously contemplated the opportunities presented by offshore markets. Of course, incorporating foreign market instruments in a domestic portfolio forces participation in the currency markets and confrontation of the risk control peril that that implies. Characterized by a free-wheeling, anyone-can-play attitude, it is estimated that the currency markets encompass some $1 trillion in transactions daily from all corners of the earth. Add to that the fact that there are no daily limits to price moves, no collars, no clearing houses of last resort, no institutional oversight or regulatory agencies, and no opening or closing hours, and it would be difficult to devise a more humbling environment.

There is a strong case to be made that present conditions in the currency markets, conditions marked by extreme daily volatility as well as the absence of enduring multimonth trends in the U.S. dollar, will be more the norm than the exception for the rest of the decade. Because of stagnant economic performance in the United States and the likelihood of unsatisfactory annual returns from conventional American markets for possibly as long as the next three to five years, a hunker-down mentality that restricts investments to U.S.-dollar-denominated markets is not a viable path for fund managers whose performance is publicly compared monthly with global competitors.

If looking to offshore markets becomes the only way to produce acceptable performance, some innovative ways to address currency risk amid chaotic conditions must be incorporated. While there is no hard and fast answer to this dilemma, some of the more advanced quantitative analytical methods and statistical tools can point the way to logical alternatives that are available to managers who are willing to expand their horizons.

WHY THE CHAOS WILL NOT GO AWAY

The economist Robert Heilbroner has theorized that throughout history global prosperity has closely coincided with the presence of a dominant and recognized world leader with a dependably supported hard currency. Prosperous times seem to flow naturally when businessmen and financiers can rely on certain fixed assumptions about inflation, taxes, and currency values. Likewise, successful experiments in fixed currency values tend to usher in or certainly walk in tandem with periods of global prosperity. The era of the British Empire and the American-dominated 1940–1970 era both spring to mind as excellent examples supporting this theory. However, since the abandonment of most currency controls and fixed rates in the early 1970s, no nation or group of nations has successfully assumed the leadership mantle in its entirety. The United States has military power to spare, which bestows upon it a form of global domination, as it readily demonstrated during the Persian Gulf War, but the exercise in financial inadequacy that followed that war as the U.S. was forced to pass the plate to help pay for its services precluded its acceptance as any sort of global financial leader. The Japanese have advanced to nearly the richest nation in the world by virtue of a trade surplus that will exceed $100 billion this year, yet they are unable and unwilling to assume all the accoutrements of a recognized world financial leader, refusing as they do to take the necessary steps to boost the yen to official reserve currency status. Germany, from its position as leader of the European Monetary System (EMS), and recognized globally as the only issuer of a hard currency in the world that is both proud of that status and appreciative of what it takes to maintain that status, has been hamstrung in its ascension to global financial leadership. For one thing, like Japan, Germany is still considered tainted by its actions during World War II. Additionally, for two years now, Germany has been single-mindedly preoccupied with the unexpectedly disruptive reunification of its East and West pieces, and this preoccupation played a significant role in the recent breakdown of the Exchange Rate Mechanism (ERM) of the EMS. As events unfolded, the failure of the United States economy to recover with anywhere near the vigor expected of it served to turn the slowdown of European economies into a full-blown recession. Thus, when the pressure on the ERM structure intensified in the fall of 1992, Germany lacked both the economic energy and the financial wherewithal to hold it together.

There is another intriguing body of economic research that supports the conclusion that economic stagnation and general disorder in the currency markets will not subside much before the end of this century. As it happens, the decline of American hegemony and the end of the most recent period of tightly controlled capital access and allocation occurred virtually simultaneously with the peak of the ascending economic cycle, according to Long Wave theory as developed by Professor John Sterman of the Sloan School of Management, Massachusetts Institute of Technology. By this theory, the "waves" typically cover between 45 and 60 years. During the ascension part of the cycles, peaks of business cycle expansions are successively higher and valleys of recessions or slowdowns are also successively higher. The ascension phase is typically characterized by progressive social mores, and the peaking phase by an evolution to more cosmopolitan values. As the descending phase takes over, societies grow more politically conservative. Business cycle upturns tend to reach lower successive peaks and recessions lower lows. At the trough, which can last several years, cycles tend to be relatively flat, with little differentiation in overall economic pain between upturns and downturns. Societies turn defensive, parochial, and paranoid. The Western world is presently considered to be slogging its way through the trough of its Long Wave cycle after the peak was reached in the early 1970s. It is surely not considered a coincidence by developers of this theory that several measurements of the American real standard of living peaked in 1973 and have been declining ever since. In the Long Wave trough, such indicators as serial single-term politicians, economic stagnation, declining manufacturing capacity utilization, insufficient money supply growth, and extremes of social parochialism all work to hold economic performance hostage to the forces of time and history. Whether or not one buys into this type of analysis, it is difficult not to notice how aptly long-wave theory premises apply to the 1990s in the so-called First World economies.

Very much in tune with this line of reasoning is the recent upheaval that has occurred in the ERM of the EMS. After the abandonment by the United States of the gold standard in the early 1970s and the subsequent collapse of fixed currency values, Europe launched the European Monetary System in an attempt to create an orderly European currency market consisting of worthy partner currencies tied to the much-respected German mark. Efforts to peg currency values to each other and to control their volatility are of variable success in the best of times. Such programs are doomed to fail miserably in a difficult economic environment.

The Exchange Rate Mechanism of the European Monetary System was set up with certain European currencies pegged to the deutsche mark, allowing only 2.25 percent fluctuation on either side of a peg rate for the harder currencies and a 6 percent fluctuation on either side of a peg rate for softer currencies or those currencies that had been only recently allowed to enter the mechanism. Whenever a currency approached its floor or ceiling, the central banks were obligated to enter the market and intervene as massively as was necessary to rebalance prices. While there are twelve currencies in the EMS, all of which were considered potential candidates for the ERM, there were never more than ten included in the ERM, and two of those were included within the last two and a half years. Great Britain and Portugal were the most recent entrants to the mechanism, and the entry date of each was hailed as marking a new era of European togetherness and prosperity. In each of these cases, the ERM was attempting to embrace currencies that had literally been ravaged by inflation for years. According to figures published by the Bundesbank recently, the weaker EMS currencies experienced inflation on average of 35 percent between 1987 and 1992, while the worst of the stronger currencies had allowed only 15 percent inflation in that period. To appease the rather prickly British instinct that the U.K. probably did not belong in the ERM or the EMS or the EC at all, the pound was allowed to enter the ERM at a peg rate to the D-mark that was probably higher than the facts warranted. The hope was that better economic times would quickly make everything right.

The EC summit at Maastricht put the icing on the unity cake with a treaty that set a timetable for monetary union and strict rules of economic performance set for eventual entry of each country into the monetary system. The U.K. had its ambiguity essentially institutionalized by a few special rules governing it, and referenda to ratify the treaty were scheduled. In the first popular test of a United States of Europe, the Danes shocked the world by voting "no."

Unfortunately the timing for Maastricht could hardly have been worse. It did not help that when outside pressure was brought to bear on the ERM, West Germany was far more concerned with its reunification problems than with its position as Europe's financial leader. Germany's expensive return to nationalistic concerns and its need to keep monetary policy tight to shore up the D-mark not only created difficult economic times for its ERM partners, it also served to alienate some of the softer-core members of the European experiment in unity. At about the time of the German reunification, the Anglo-Saxon economies were hit by an extremely stubborn recession, made the more so by politicians who largely ignored it at first due to the First World fixation with the Persian Gulf War. The Thatcher/Reagan political legacy had been passed on to Major and Bush, compatriots with their mentors philosophically, but neither capable of filling his predecessor's shoes when it came to rhetoric and moving the masses to consensus on a policy of uncertain popular appeal. Once the pound hit the floor of its allowed band against the deutsche mark, it was just a matter of time until the German and English central banks realized they were up against more pressure than they could allay with intervention. Chancellor of the Exchequer Norman Lamont and Prime Minister John Major staunchly insisted the pound would remain at its level in the ERM and would not devalue. Financial pressure from without and political pressure from within finally caused Lamont and Major to abandon ship and take the pound out of the ERM. The by-product of the whole mess was that credibility on both sides suffered, the sharks smelled blood, and every member of the ERM, with the exception of the D-mark itself and its sister currency the Dutch guilder, were considered vulnerable to being torn out of the ERM cocoon.

The extreme pressure that was put on the ERM last fall, which caused both the lira and the British pound to drop out of the mechanism indefinitely, was the by-product of an increase in parochialism among ERM members coupled with severe economic contractions, which were made more painful by the very tight hold the German central bank kept on its interest rates. Member countries were left with only painful choices. They could lower interest rates to stimulate their economies, which would mean their currencies could remain tied to the deutsche mark but only at greatly devalued levels. Alternatively, they could leave the mechanism and lower interest rates but at the expense of global financial respectability and possible future exclusion from any successful European union. The Spanish peseta and Portuguese escudo both devalued sharply within the ERM. At this writing, further ERM turmoil is considered very much on the front burner with the Danish krone, French franc, and Belgian franc as well as peseta and escudo again all viewed as potential candidates for high-pressure speculative selling.

The net effect of the failure of the ERM to stand under pressure has wide-ranging consequences for American investors. The function performed by the ERM provided businessmen, borrowers, and investors with predetermined inter-currency volatility that they could rely on not to be exceeded. The extent to which even outsiders relied on the durability of the ERM is amply demonstrated by a look at a debt issue floated by America's own Federal National Mortgage Association in August of 1992. The issue was of seven-year maturity, with the interest rate set initially at 12.35 percent and adjustable based on a formula tied inversely to moves in the cross-rate of the Swiss franc to the Italian lira, with a ceiling of 24 percent and a floor of zero. While the Swiss franc was not an ERM member, it was considered a close deutsche mark sister in terms of its value and volatility. A table showing monthly rates of the SF/IL cross from 1987 to 1992 was presented in the prospectus to show how stably it traded within an 820–920 range. As long as the ERM kept the mark/lira cross in its designated band, the Swiss/lira cross could be counted on to stay in its range, and the implied interest rate payable on the FNMA notes in dollars would be extremely attractive. At a price of 1011 or higher, the bond became a zero coupon bond with no interest due until maturity. The rest, as they say, is history. The very next month the lira was forced out of the ERM and reached a price well outside its multiyear band against the D-mark. As would be expected, the Swiss/lira cross rose to nearly 1100 at its highest level. The FNMA bond is now effectively a zero coupon issue and can only be liquidated at a large loss. Unfortunately, this rather interesting idea will have the effect of driving away a multitude of investors from any product even remotely related to currency markets.

Despite poor experiences in investing such as the hapless investors in the FNMA issue are facing, avoidance behavior on the part of U.S. investors at this juncture simply is not an option. Like it or not, U.S. investors must come to grips with the chaos of the currency markets. The view of the United States based on the dollar as the hub of the international investing wheel, with every other market merely a spoke responding passively to the motion of the hub, must be relinquished.

WHY THE CHAOS MUST BE CONFRONTED

The 1940–1990 era was notable for the enormous wealth creation that took place in the United States, to the point where few investment managers needed or wanted to look elsewhere for profit-making opportunities. However, the evidence abounds that these managers must accept and deal with the possibility that the somnolent character of the early 1990s might plague the United States' economy for several more years. As long as debt is growing two and a half times faster than GDP, there is a strong case to be made that the trough of the Long Wave (or whatever label one wishes to apply to these stagnant times) will continue to extract economic pain in the United States, and that it could be as many as three to five years before really excellent profit-making opportunities recur in this country. It is not logical to expect U.S. stocks and bonds to be able to maintain levels of appreciation of the last few years. The total return index of U.S. long government debt has reached new high ground after appreciating 18.5 percent in calendar 1991 and another 15.5 percent from the end of calendar 1991 to the present. Unless one wholeheartedly accepts the premise that the government deficit in the U.S. will be substantially cut—not just slowed but cut—such gains in bonds will likely not continue. American stocks are considered overvalued from virtually any method of measurement. The dollar is in a long-term bear market, which may be temporarily interrupted by the overanticipated rally of 1993, but is unlikely to be reversed into a bull trend. Both the stock and bond markets are technically at places where ugly accidents can happen. Treacherous as currency risk can be, the case for diversifying investments offshore has never been more compelling. Where and how to diversify, then, becomes an interesting analytical exercise.

For better or worse, the world seems intent on dividing itself into three main regions—Asia, Europe, and the Americas. At the present time, Asia is dominated by Japan, Europe by Germany (with occasional stabs at leadership by the U.K.), and the Americas by the United States. Each of these regions has several corollary markets in addition to the dominant ones. Within each of the regions, there are what is known as "emerging markets." In Asia—Thailand, South Korea, and Malaysia could all be considered emerging markets, trying as they are to develop liquid, freely trading stock, bond, currency, and short-term money markets. In the Americas, most Latin American countries, including Mexico, are literally clawing their way up from third-world status to market-driven economies. In Europe—Turkey, Greece, and many of the former Soviet Union's republics and satellites are striving for market-oriented economies with viable capital conduits. In the absence of strictly observed fixed currency rates and a clear leader in capital formation and allocation, the world has become quite literally an investment kaleidoscope. There are no limits and few boundaries to the choices confronting the growth-oriented investment manager. It is essential that logical ways to measure and compare the choices be developed. Which markets to enter, how long to stay, and how to control the currency risk are the questions that must be addressed.

REARRANGING THE CHAOS

Since fixed rates for currencies were abandoned in the early 1970s, the search for profitable ways to approach currency risk has perhaps waylaid as many American investment managers as it has propelled to success. It is true that some of the time, currencies are the most trended trading instruments in the world. In the past, the dollar has had periods of appreciation or depreciation not just for two or three percentage points, but for five, six, or ten percent before it corrected sharply. If, however, the premises of a Long Wave trough are sound predictors of the character of markets for most of the rest of this decade, currency volatility will be much more the norm than the exception. While economies are more or less expanding, experiments such as the ERM have a chance to succeed. However, when tougher economic times coupled with increased social parochialism take hold, it implies that the likelihood of the foreign exchange markets' seeing enduring unidirectional trends in any of the non-Asian currencies for the rest of this decade is extremely small. If this proves true, it astronomically complicates the task of managing the currency risk assumed by the U.S. investor looking for profitable global investments; non-trended markets do not lend themselves to a "hold and pray" approach. Grappling with this risk, then, forces one to select some kind of quantitative analytical strategy.

The debate over fundamental versus technical analysis has been raging literally for years, and there is little point in rehashing the relative merits of the two approaches to investing. However, there is absolutely no contesting the point that the decline in discernible long-term trends in many of the currency markets—plus the plethora not only of new types of trading instruments, but also of new markets on which to trade them and new countries in which markets are just now opening—reduces the approach to investments to a game of sheer numbers. As a result of the capital flow free-for-all now taking place, the massive amount and kind of information that can logically be brought to bear on any given investment simply limits the usefulness of conventional fundamental analysis, and most successful traders today will admit to using one or more technical tools, usually in computer model form, to aid their decision making.

Whether or not one views technical trading as a useful tool, even the most ardent critic must admit that to approach offshore investing without some sort of computerized analytical tools is folly. It is enough to have to cope with the arcane pronouncements of the American Financial Accounting Standards Board and how they affect financial statement presentation in the United States without having to add the variables of a foreign language, foreign accounting quirks, and foreign financial idioms. Without doubt, the highest and best use of technical analysis occurs when it is applied to streams of price data from foreign assets, reducing masses of significant data to a quantifiable and comprehensible picture, which then can easily be compared to other quantifiable and comprehensible pictures generated by other streams of data.

In addition to reducing price data to easily comparable graphic form, most working technical models add the perspective of differing time dimensions, so that longer-term views can be generated as easily as shorter-term ones. A comparison of three graphs prepared by one technical system eloquently demonstrates this concept. The top graph in Figure 7.1 shows the price of Hamburg schillings per British pound for the period 1776 to 1827, constructed with one data point per year. The middle graph shows the British pound expressed in "New York dollars" from 1923 to 1992, again using one data point per year. The bottom graph depicts a daily model of the dollar/yen rates built with two price points every 24 hours and covering several weeks, spanning the period January 22, 1993, to March 11, 1993.

To make sense of these graphs, it is necessary to know that the solid line represents a mathematically smoothed price. The line of small circles is a more sensitive oscillator, which measures momentum and acceleration, and the line of pluses is a less sensitive oscillator. A "2b" designates a buy of a certain type, just as a "3s" designates a sell of a certain type. The main point to be made is that a good technical system will allow any stream of price data gathered on any regular basis to be reduced to a picture that is interpretable using essentially the same principles no matter when or where or over what period the data is generated. (The author thanks Brian Turner of Henderson's in London who, provided the eighteenth- and nineteenth-century data.)

Taking this unique ability of a good technical model to reduce different types of data to pictures that can readily be compared, it is a fairly small progression to the point where it is possible to take any one market in the world and compare it as an asset allocation function to any other market in the world. For instance, to lend support to the premise that investments limited to domestic markets will provide few high-growth years during the remainder of this decade, it is possible to reduce the regional stock markets to index numbers and compare them, using the Financial Times Actuaries Indexes. Figures 7.2 and 7.3 show the symbol NAMER (for North American stock markets) compared to PACIFIC and to EUROPE. The graphs show both a monthly and weekly time frame, with monthly depicting the period July 31, 1987, through March 31, 1993, and weekly showing December 20, 1991, through April 16, 1993. As in the previous graphs, the solid line is a

FIGURE 7.1

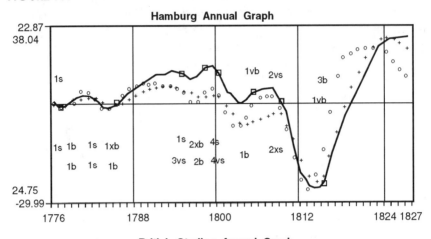

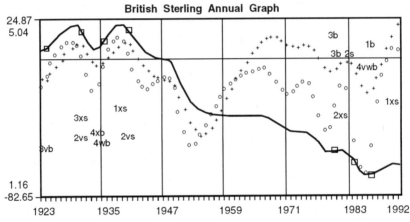

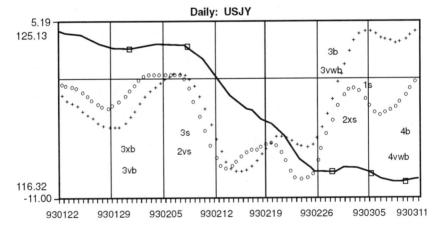

FIGURE 7.2

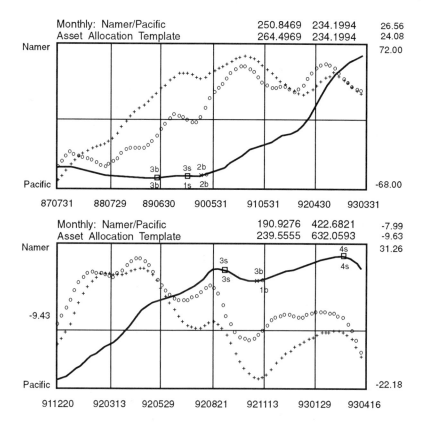

smoothed price line, and the line of pluses and line of small circles each represents an oscillator measuring momentum and strength of the price direction. In an asset allocation, when the solid line is moving up, price direction favors the first item of the pair being compared; when the solid line is moving down, price direction favors the second-named item of the pair. These two graphs both clearly have favored North American stock markets (of which the United States is by far the dominant factor) for the last three years.

Figures 7.4 and 7.5 show equivalent measures of credit markets in these regions by viewing asset allocations among the three key short-term interest rates. Figure 7.4 is JAPINT/USINT, showing monthly and weekly series of short-term deposit rates for Japan and the United States. Figure 7.5 shows a similar series for

FIGURE 7.3

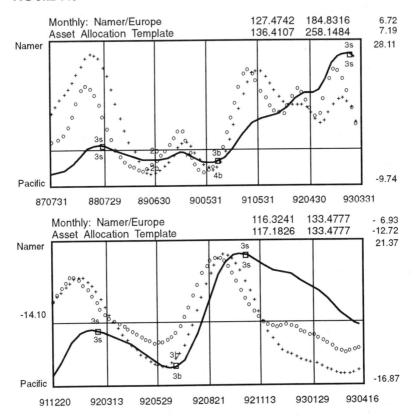

German and U.S. short-term rates. In both cases, short-term rates in both Germany and Japan rose faster than those (or fell slower than those) in the United States for a number of years.

Top-picking is more art than science, but each of these monthly/weekly pictures shows a trend that is mature and reaching a point technically where a change in trend would not be at all out of line. These illustrations are used partly to support the theory expounded in the previous section that the United States stock and bond markets are unlikely to provide exceptional returns relative to other regional investment opportunities for the intermediate to long term, and also to illustrate what a powerful analytical tool a technical system can provide in choosing one market over another.

FIGURE 7.4

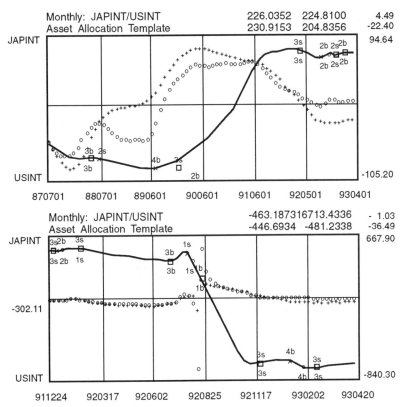

CREATING POCKETS OF ORDER
AMID THE CHAOS

The next logical step in this analysis is in fact to abandon the
notion that the United States is the hub of an international wheel
and that all global investments must somehow be tied to the U.S.,
particularly to the U.S. dollar. Instead, the world must be viewed
as a menu of investment opportunities that often have nothing to
do with the United States other than to provide an opportunity for
the investor who happens to be dollar-based. One such opportunity is the notion of cross-rate trading, or trading one nondollar currency against another. At least in theory, and often in fact, this
type of trading provides investors with a way to profit from currency movements without necessarily taking a view on dollar
direction. If a positive interest rate differential can be gained from

FIGURE 7.5

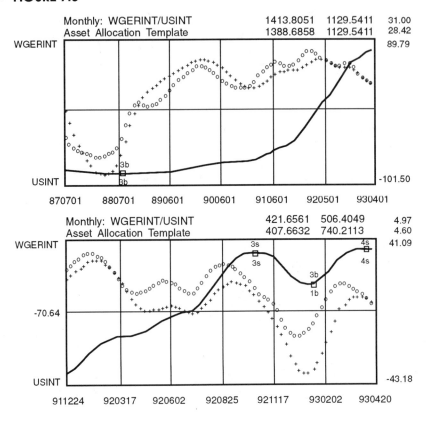

the chosen spread, that is all the better. It is intriguing to note that nondollar currency trading within blocs can provide a fairly tame experience, even after the near-destruction of the ERM. For instance, annual volatility as measured by Standard Deviation has been very low for the U.S. dollar to Canadian dollar historically and is even quite low for the U.S. dollar to Mexican peso in recent years. The crosses Australian dollar to Malaysian ringgit, yen to Malaysian, and Mexican to Canadian are all three less volatile than the dollar itself to either the yen or the deutsche mark. These kinds of relationships may seem beyond the pale to the American investment manager who is just learning to grapple with the problems caused by the sterling and mark moves against the dollar, or who has ventured into some European crosses based on continuation of the European Exchange Rate Mechanism and found more countries leaving that safe haven than entering it. However, some

FIGURE 7.6

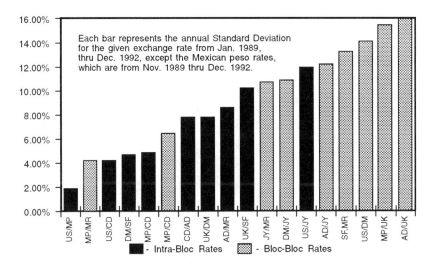

Each bar represents the annual Standard Deviation for the given exchange rate from Jan. 1989, thru Dec. 1992, except the Mexican peso rates, which are from Nov. 1989 thru Dec. 1992.

■ - Intra-Bloc Rates   ▨ - Bloc-Bloc Rates

of these more exotic markets are growing by leaps and bounds, are nowhere near levels customarily associated with overvaluation, and are increasing in accessibility and liquidity every day. Figure 7.6 is a bar graph of some inter-bloc and intra-bloc crosses, showing their annual volatility over a recent three-year period.

One area of trading opportunities that is suggested by Figure 7.6 and that probably deserves a book all of its own is the use of one nondollar currency to hedge exposure in another nondollar currency otherwise known as cross-hedging. As the three global regions solidify, their currencies will tend to correlate even more closely in their direction than they do now. One can neutralize dollar direction, reap the benefit of a hedge with a positive interest rate spread built in, or take advantage of pairs of currencies that correlate in direction versus the dollar but vary in the magnitude of their moves against the dollar. All of these strategies bear far less risk and offer far less volatility of returns and drawdowns than traditional outright dollar/currency trading. The bottom line is that currencies are not just a corollary market that must be addressed on the way to achieving other investment goals. They can legitimately claim the right to be considered an asset class on their own. Not only can currency/dollar crosses be an asset class, but the enormous universe of nondollar currency pairs should eventually also earn its right to be viewed as an asset class.

FIGURE 7.7

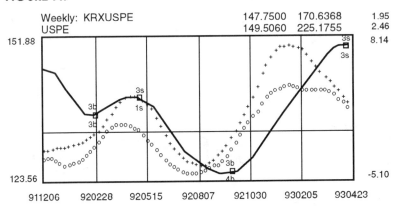

The possibilities from both an investment and a hedging standpoint are virtually endless. For instance, Figure 7.7 shows a weekly picture of the moves the Portuguese escudo made against the U.S. dollar between December of 1991 and April of 1993. For approximately half of the period, price moves favored the escudo, and for the other half, the moves favored the dollar. During the whole period, the escudo paid a much higher interest rate than the dollar. However, this positive interest rate spread would have been eaten up quickly once the dollar began appreciating against the escudo.

Now take a look at Figure 7.8, which shows an asset allocation between the escudo and its sister currency the Spanish peseta. The line clearly favors the escudo for the entire period, regardless of the dollar direction. In fact it is difficult to pinpoint where the dollar bottom occurred. Astonishingly, it is impossible to tell where the escudo and peseta were both forced to undergo heavy devaluation within the ERM. Again the interest rate for most of this period favored the escudo over the peseta, but the forex move clearly would have compensated during those periods the interest rate spread was negative.

One more example, very much in the spirit of the bar graph shown in Figure 7.6, is the Malay ringgit to the U.S. dollar (see Figure 7.9) and the Malay ringgit to the Australian dollar (see Figure 7.10). A Malay/U.S. exposure would have made money from December of 1991 to August of 1992, but then would have given up half of the profits by April of 1993. Had the investor bought Malay and hedged it with the Australian dollar, however,

FIGURE 7.8

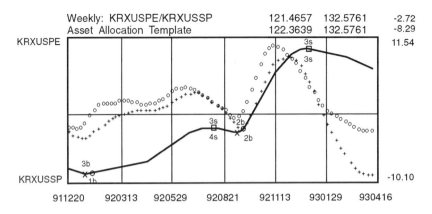

the cross would have remained profitable from December of 1991 through January of 1993, and on the correction would have given up very little.

However markets evolve over the next few years, the investment manager who incorporates consideration of some of these less conventional markets and trading techniques into his or her repertoire will be richly rewarded, particularly if, as seems highly possible, the United States and Europe both find emergence from

FIGURE 7.9

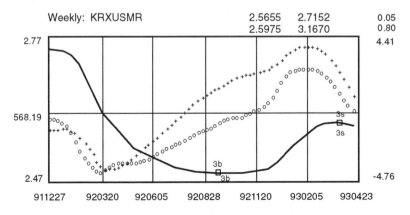

FIGURE 7.10

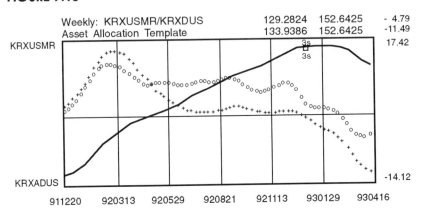

their present stagnation a much tougher assignment than it has been in fifty years.

CONCLUSION

Twenty years ago, the question "What will life be like in the twenty-first century?" would encourage exercises in sheer mind-expanding fantasy. Now the question can be addressed more rationally. If Long Wave theory has any validity at all, the century will begin with some exceptionally stimulating economic times and will improve from there for at least a few decades. The emerging markets will provide the best leverage for investment results, and investment managers will see their list of viable candidates for controlled-risk investment increase geometrically. When the next Long-Wave expansion does begin, it will be launched from a broader base than ever before in history and will enhance the wealth and living standards of more people in more countries than ever before. The amount of new wealth that could be created is staggering. For instance, at the present rate of growth of both population and GDP in China, the amount of new wealth that country could reasonably be expected to generate is half a trillion dollars between now and the end of the decade. Considering the economic reforms that are being instituted there, that figure may vastly underestimate the potential new wealth to be generated from that source. The number of investment-grade stock markets that could double or triple in total value will itself be higher than ever before in history.

Considering that the Mexican stock market literally quintupled in value from the beginning of 1990 to the present, that statement may also prove to be too pessimistic a forecast. The number of currencies that will offer liquid alternatives to the dollar and the deutsche mark will be the highest in the history of the world. The number of futures contracts, option choices, and individual exchange-listed stocks will dwarf those available at any other time in history. There can be no more serious message to be delivered to fund managers in the U.S. today than that one more day is too long to wait to learn how to handle the mind-numbing growth in the number and kind of markets. They must grow comfortable with quantitative measuring tools and imaginative methods of currency risk control.

As cycles evolve, there will no doubt be a time in the twenty-first century when a successful program of currency rate pegging will develop, probably along with the emergence of some form of borderless common market in Europe. The Asian countries have been discussing an ACU or Asian Currency Unit, analogous to Europe's ECU, which would be pegged to the yen and could eventually supplement or even replace many of the present Asian currencies. Regardless of how it occurs, who leads it, or how it is defined, the next period of general global prosperity will very likely be accompanied by some form of reduced currency volatility through dominance of one currency or through the evolution of baskets of currencies pegged to the strongest one within a bloc, such as the ERM nearly achieved. The dominance is most likely to be regional. That is to say, the deutsche mark or an ECU clone of the deutsche mark will dominate Europe and western Russia, the yen or yuan will lead the Asian and eastern Russia bloc, and the dollar will dominate the American bloc.

For better or worse, the development of this more stable environment could still be many years away. In the meantime, the best that can be said is that eras of mature economy stagnation and a dearth of financial leadership do provide unlimited opportunity in less mature markets to the willing investor. The potentially heady character of the 1990s should at least be mind-expanding; rules and limitations to where and how investments will prosper for the rest of this decade are few. It will be a time when above-average investment growth will accrue generously to those willing to be stimulated by emerging markets, to be educated in the use of new types of tools to analyze those markets, and to brave the growing multitude of hard choices.

8

Currency in International Investing

Adrian F. Lee
J. P. Morgan Investment Management, Inc.

INTRODUCTION

When an investor wishes to purchase a foreign asset, he or she is required to purchase the currency of that country in order to settle the transaction. This second decision, or hidden purchase of currency in international investment, has associated with it a significant risk. Irrespective of the asset return, currency values can fluctuate to impact the market value of the investment in base currency terms.

Historically, 30 percent of the volatility (as measured by standard deviation) of an international equity portfolio has been associated with its inherent currency exposure. The equivalent statistic for international fixed income is 60 percent. This risk has been persistent and fairly stable since the beginning of the most recent period of floating exchange rates, i.e., 1973. See Figures 8.1 and 8.2.

This risk, due to inherent currency exposure associated with international investments, does not appear to be rewarded with an associated expected return. Currency exposure, unlike asset exposure, is not expected theoretically to generate a long-run return in order to compensate for its risk. Empirical data since 1973 on the return to currency is very time period and base currency specific, but is not inconsistent with this long-run zero return hypothesis. It should be pointed out that compared to

FIGURE 8.1   Sterling Currency Return vs. the Dollar %

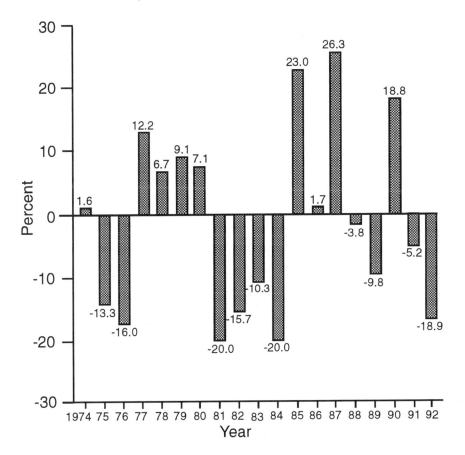

other areas such as equity and bonds, historical data on currency
is rather short and for all practical purposes dates back to only 20
years ago.

Currency rates and the associated investment returns are driven by a different set of economic fundamentals than those that
drive local market asset returns. Conceptually, currency is a medium of exchange between two different national money supplies
and the demand for currency itself derives from the demand for
cross-border purchases of real goods and assets. Net demand for a
given currency is a function of net foreign demand for that country's goods and assets. These demands themselves being a func-

FIGURE 8.2   U.S. and Non-U.S. Asset Class Returns and Risks

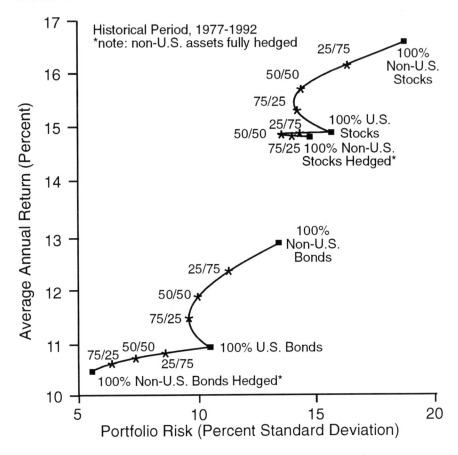

tion of cross-border differences in price levels, quality of traded goods, and expected risk-adjusted return on assets. From the foregoing, it is clear that the fundamentals that drive currency are different from those that drive local market returns. This implies a lack of systematic relationship between asset market return (particularly equities) and currency return. Empirically, there is no evidence of any relationship between equity market returns and currency, as evidenced by the low and unstable correlation of equity markets and their own or foreign currency. See Figures 8.3 and 8.4.

Finally and importantly, despite the fact that most evidence points to the long-run return of currency being zero, significant

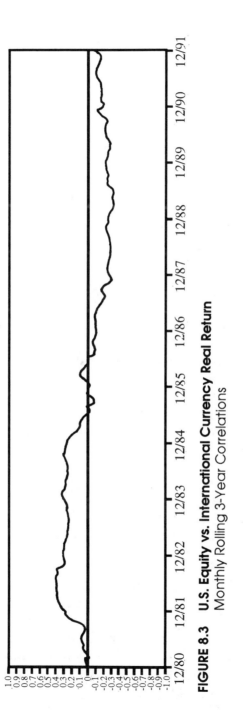

FIGURE 8.3   U.S. Equity vs. International Currency Real Return
Monthly Rolling 3-Year Correlations

FIGURE 8.4

CORRELATION		91–85	84–78	77–73
Yen Return vs. Dollar	Japanese Equity Local Return	0.10	0.25	0.14
DM Return vs. Dollar	German Equity Local Return	–0.11	0.11	0.06
Sterling Return vs. Dollar	UK Equity Local Return	–0.10	–0.01	0.25

evidence exists that active management of currency can add value over time, e.g., through a market cycle. The inefficiencies of currency with respect to tactical fundamental analysis and technical analysis are discussed below.

A FRAMEWORK FOR ADDRESSING CURRENCY

The implication of the foregoing is that the currency exposure inherent in international investment ought to be managed and not simply assumed as a hidden investment. Because of the separate nature of currency from assets one should and can prudently unbundle currency from assets and explicitly resolve for currency the main policy issues that need to be addressed for any separate asset class.[1] These are:

1. What is the appropriate strategic or long-run exposure to currency?
2. Should currency be managed actively around this strategic position?
3. Who should manage currency exposure and how?

It is important to emphasize that these currency policy issues, while they may appear new and alien, are in fact issues that most pension plans have in fact addressed already and have made decisions about implicitly. For example, a typical plan not having looked at currency explicitly, would probably have adopted a strategic currency exposure equal to their strategic international exposure, engaged in active currency management through the country allocation decision of international managers, and allowed these currency decisions to be made by their international equity managers. We present below a methodology for addressing these issues more analytically and allowing overt policies rather than covert ones to be identified. We discuss each area in turn, emphasizing that the solution to one issue has little or no implication for the solutions to the others. In other words, these issues are separable and independent. In the final section, we discuss some interactions and implementation issues that modify this statement somewhat, but for now the assumption of independence is a reasonably valid one.

The Strategic Currency Allocation Decision

This decision is similar to many other strategic decisions made by long-term investors, such as the stock/bond allocation decision or, for example, the decision to allocate a specific percentage of a portfolio strategically to international equity.

The long-run allocation to currency should be thought of as quite separate and different from the allocation to international assets. One should think of international investments as made up of two unrelated investments—hedged assets and currency. These, after all, are the component economic exposures.

In this improved structure the portfolio choice directly focuses on essentially five separate components: domestic stocks and bonds, hedged foreign stocks and bonds and foreign currency.[2] The appropriate allocation to each is theoretically determined in an overall portfolio context on the basis of risk and return expectation for each asset and investor risk preference for the overall portfolio, as well as transaction cost for hedging currency exposure.

Standard mean variance analysis in this expanded opportunity set then indicates the level of foreign currency expense consistent with investors' expectations and risk preference. Comparison of optimal currency exposure with optimal allocations to hedged assets reveals the implied optimal hedge ratio.

Clearly in this framework optimal hedge ratios become unique to each investor's expectation, risk preference, and overall asset mix. Therefore, no optimal currency hedge ratio exists for all international investors. Each investor should undertake such analysis to identify the hedge ratio that is consistent with its overall plan characteristics.

Nevertheless, several tentative generalizations are possible. On the basis of largely historical risk and correlation results, an assumption of zero long-run return to currency and a 15 basis points annual cost of hedging currency, the following observations can be made:

1. Partial hedging of currency exposures may appear optimal for investors who have greater than five international assets and a typical 60/40 stock/bond mix.
2. Obviously, the greater the allocation to international assets the larger the hedge ratio, by simple arithmetic, e.g., an investor with 10 percent international assets might hedge 50 percent; the same investor with 20 percent international assets correspondingly should hedge 75 percent, to maintain the same optimal 5 percent allocation to currency.
3. The more aggressive the investor the lower the optimal hedge ratio—a 70/30 stock/bond investor may hedge zero percent, whereas a 50/50 investor may hedge 100 percent, for a given level of international assets.

Overall, such analysis tends to be considerably more sensitive to input assumptions than is normally the case with mean variance analysis. This is because currency is a "noncompeting" asset class—in other words, currency can be invested in without displacing other assets, and any slight return to currency will make it desirable as it offers a purely additional return. Of particular importance in the strategic currency hedging equation is the overall portfolio exposure to fixed income. Historical data and economic theory weakly support a positive relationship between foreign currency return and domestic bond return, through the link of interest rates, particularly short rates. This implies that the greater the domestic bond allocation, the less desirable is foreign currency exposure strategically because of its nondiversifying characteristic.

The role of a dynamic hedge or an option-based hedging strategy for currency is also appropriately viewed in the overall strategic/long-run portfolio context. However, because of the asymmetric payoff pattern associated with options, quadratic optimization of mean variance analysis masks the short-run distributional characteristics of this strategy. Monte Carlo simulation under equilibrium assumptions indicates that such a policy in the long run is equivalent to some level of fixed partial hedging (about 50 percent, depending on the structure of the dynamic hedge) with higher transaction costs. The short-run asymmetry of return—say on a one-year basis—begins to dissipate after about 5–10 years. While dynamic hedging has often been viewed as a style of active currency management, research suggests that it is essentially equivalent to a passive 50 percent hedge with special short-run risk management characteristics. It does, however, have a built-in technical characteristic that may provide excess return, to the extent that currency markets exhibit persistent trends in the shorter run. Historical results associated with trend-following strategies are discussed below.

Active Versus Passive Currency Management

While currency may offer a zero long-run return to an investor, it is clear that currency returns can be quite significantly positive or negative in the short run (3–5 years). Therefore, to the extent that active management of currency can capitalize upon this volatility and add return, then actively managed currency will have a positive return despite the strategic long-run zero return of a passive exposure. This excess return can be thought of as purely additive over the international portfolio, and incremental to any excess return for active asset management.

Before we discuss the evidence relating to active currency management it is important to point out that international investors who make active country allocation decisions are indeed engaging in the active management of currency with respect to their benchmark. For example, if a manager underweights Japan in favor of Europe, a hidden currency decision is implemented shorting yen in favor of European currency. Active currency management is not generally a new activity for investors. The issue is one of overt versus covert currency management.

Equilibrium currency rates are determined on the basis of the relative economic fundamentals of the countries involved. These fundamentals are essentially the relative demands for goods and assets and expectations thereof. Overtime spot rates tend toward this equilibrium, which itself is dynamic and changing in accordance with the relative fundamentals.

Significant evidence exists in the public and private domain that active currency management undertaken in a structured way, based on the relevant network fundamentals, adds value over time. An example of such evidence in the public domain is work done in 1985 by John Bilson indicating nominal short-term interest rate differentials provided insight and excess risk-adjusted return to currency management. More recently Jack Glen at the University of Pennsylvania provided evidence that relative inflation differences or PPP has provided insight into currency return over longer periods of time. This evidence is in sharp contrast to the popular perception of the usefulness of this factor.

Proprietary currency research undertaken by various firms over the last five years and actual experience confirm that significant opportunity exists to add return to international portfolios by actively managing the currency inherent to the portfolio.

Interestingly also, but more complex to explain conceptually, is the significant body of literature in the public domain confirming statistically that technical analysis or trend following has been a profitable trading strategy (in spite of the high turnover associated with such techniques). This research has also been confirmed by Morgan in-house research.

In summary, it is fair to say that unlike other asset classes, it appears that the burden of proof is not with the case for active management but with the case for passive management of currency.

Who Should Manage Currency Exposure—Individual Asset Managers or Specialist Managers?

The key conceptual issue here is to recognize that currency management inevitably will take place in some form or other—even passive—and that because of the unique characteristics of currency, particularly compared to equity markets, there are significant benefits to using a specialist. These benefits, some quite obvious and some less so, are listed below:

1. Higher long-run return to the portfolio through a specialist approach adding value.
2. Lack of disruption to individual asset managers, who can continue to focus on allocation and asset selection with or without implied currency bets.
3. Improved cash flow and transaction cost management associated with currency hedging. International asset managers sell international assets to fund currency hedging activities. Specialist currency managers integrate their cash flow management with the overall cash of the fund.

4. Specialist currency managers trade foreign exchange on a competitive basis with a diversified range of counterparties. International asset managers normally trade foreign exchange spot and forward with the custodian only.

5. Specialist managers generally use dedicated and specialized in-house traders to execute client orders, provide separate performance measurement and a range of other specialized reports relating to currency separate from the underlying assets that originally generated such exposures.

PRACTICAL/IMPLEMENTATION ISSUES AND OTHER MATTERS ASSOCIATED WITH SPECIALIST CURRENCY MANAGEMENT

Within the area of specialist currency management, there is a range of multiple-manager, benchmark/performance measurement and operational issues that arise.

Multiple-Manager Issues

1. Should currency management be handled differently for international equity portfolios versus international bond portfolios? Is the case for overlay less valid for international fixed-income portfolios? Do local bond market allocations imply a hidden currency strategy that should be left intact?

2. While strategic exposure and active management are conceptually separate, are there any interactions that might argue for a different benchmarks? For example, asymmetric benchmarks distort ability to add value and symmetric ones maximize a manager's excess return, but increase total risk.

3. If one overlays an international manager should that manager be dissuaded from currency management? Should all equity portfolios be included in an overlay program? Should active and passive equity portfolios be treated differently?

4. Is it necessary, and if so, what alternative currency management styles should I use to give diversification across currency managers?

Benchmark Issues

1. If the underlying asset managers hold U.S. dollars, is that hidden currency bet to be included in the program or ignored?
2. For performance measurement purposes in partially hedged policies, what is the appropriate normal position for non-U.S. currency exposure—EAFE, G.D.P. weights, the underlying asset exposures, or some other normal position?

Operational/Performance Measurement

1. How much cash is required, if any, to undertake a currency overlay program and what are the associated opportunity costs? How can they be minimized? How should this cash be managed and when should it be reinvested?
2. How often should the overlay manager get updates on asset positions? How should underlying manager hedges, if any, be taken into account? Who is responsible for the consolidation of various international portfolios at different custodians?
3. Should performance be rebased when new asset exposures are given as frequently as weekly?

NOTES

1. While there are significant methodological and investment benefits to encourage the separation of assets and currency, this does not imply that currency is a "separate asset class." The latter notion, which is often associated with advocating a strategic investment in that class, is difficult to justify in face of the long-run zero return hypothesis.
2. In this format, total investment adds up to 100 percent in assets *plus* currency. In other words, it need not add up to 100 percent.

9

Internationally Diversified Bond Portfolios: The Merits of Active Currency Risk Management

Richard M. Levich, New York University, Stern School of
  Business, and National Bureau of Economic Research
Lee R. Thomas, Investcorp Bank E.C., Bahrain

INTRODUCTION

Some international investors believe they should always hedge the currency risks in their nondollar securities; others never hedge.[1] In this chapter we consider a third approach—active currency management.

The active currency manager turns his or her currency problem into an opportunity. Why not treat foreign exchange as an incremental source of return? To do so, of course, implies an ability to beat the foreign exchange market. Surprisingly, this may not be as difficult as it sounds. Various studies have shown that active trading strategies based upon simple technical trading rules often produce foreign exchange profits.[2]

This chapter draws together two strands of research. In the next section, we update past studies of technical trading rules in the foreign exchange market using a new data base and a new, nonparametric statistical test. Then, we examine the performance of a global bond portfolio that uses technical trading rules as the basis of an active currency hedging strategy. Unlike previous research, which has focused on only two hedging strategies—"always hedge" and "never hedge"—we examine strategies that sometimes hedge, sometimes partially hedge, and even sometimes overhedge. A summary of the main results and conclusions appears at the end of this chapter.

In brief, our results reveal that profits could have been earned in the currency futures market over the 1976–1990 period by applying simple technical trading rules. These results apply to currency speculators—investors who begin trading with a null balance sheet and who are free to take both long and short currency futures positions as guided by the technical rules. As for hedgers—investors who initially hold a portfolio of foreign securities, our results show that selectively hedging can lead to superior results when compared to never hedging or to always hedging. And when an active currency overlay that can take long or short foreign currency positions is adopted, our results show that hedgers can realize even greater improvements in the Sharpe performance ratio.

EXCHANGE RATE TRENDS AND THE PROFITABILITY OF TECHNICAL TRADING RULES

Our argument that an active currency risk management strategy may be beneficial rests on the assertion that foreign exchange futures markets can be "beaten" by simple trend-following trading rules. This suggests that the foreign exchange markets are inefficient.[3] We do not undertake lightly the task of demonstrating such an improbable assertion. Consequently, we have (1) examined a long-time series of exchange rate futures prices; (2) explicitly measured risk and transactions costs; and (3) developed a procedure to test the statistical significance of the profits we observed. To avoid selection bias we report the results for every trading rule we have examined to date.

We collected closing futures prices for five currencies (the German mark, British pound, Swiss franc, Japanese yen, and Canadian dollar) for the period January 1, 1976, through December 31, 1990, yielding approximately 3,800 daily observations per series. Concatenated series of returns were constructed for each currency by splicing together observations from successive near-term contracts.[4]

We have chosen to use futures prices rather than spot prices because the former reflect contemporaneous short-term interest rate differentials, or the "carry" earned by a foreign exchange position. Consequently, changes in futures prices represent the total excess return—interest income, less the interest expense of funding a foreign currency position, plus capital gain or loss—accruing to the holder of a foreign currency. Futures prices also capture the total incremental gain or loss resulting from hedging away the foreign currency exposure embedded in a foreign security investment.

Weak-form efficiency of the foreign exchange market is commonly tested by calculating the profitability of mechanical trading rules. We use two kinds of trading rules to generate buy and sell signals, filter rules and moving average crossover rules. We chose filter rules because they have been widely used in academic studies of market efficiency.[5] Moving average crossover rules are more commonly used by foreign exchange market practitioners.

A filter rule is defined by a single parameter (f), the filter size. If we express exchange rates in American terms (the dollar price per one unit of foreign currency), then the filter rule can be defined as follows: "Buy the currency whenever it rises by f percent above its most recent trough; sell the currency whenever it falls f percent below its most recent peak." We examined seven filter rules with f valued at 0.5%, 1.0%, 2.0%, 3.0%, 4.0%, 5.0%, and 10%.

Specifying a moving average crossover rule requires two parameters: the length (L, in trading days) of the longer moving average (MA_L) and the length (S) of the shorter moving average (MA_S). A L/S moving average rule can be defined as follows: "If $MA_S > MA_L$, then buy the foreign currency. If $MA_S < MA_L$, then sell the foreign currency. If $MA_S = MA_L$, take no position." We examined three moving average crossover rules: 5/1; 20/5; 200/1.

Statistical Significance of Trend-Following Profits

It is relatively easy to measure the returns that mechanical filter rules earn when they are applied to foreign currency futures. But the observed profits (if any) may have resulted from chance alone. So we need to test to verify that any profits we measure are statistically significant. We could use a conventional t-test if exchange rate volatility has been constant throughout our sample period. Unfortunately, exchange rate volatility has varied substantially.[6] This empirical finding invalidates classical statistical tests that depend on repeated draws from a stationary distribution. Consequently, we have developed a nonparametric test, motivated by the bootstrapping methodology developed by Efron (1979). Put simply, the test compares (a) the profits earned by applying a technical trading rule to a historical exchange rate series, to (b) the profits earned by applying the same trading rule to many simulated exchange rate series. By construction, the simulated exchange rate series have the same empirical distribution as the actual series.[7]

We examined seven filter rules and three moving average crossover rules for each of five currencies, yielding fifty profit values, as reported in Table 9.1. All fifty values were positive. The trading profits were highly statistically significant (at the 1% level as measured by our simulation approach) in thirty-five of fifty cases, significant (at the 5% level) in an additional nine cases, and not statistically significant (but positive) in the remaining cases.[8]

These results demonstrate that simple trend-following trading rules have earned statistically significant profits in the foreign exchange futures markets. They do not prove that the profits are economically significant. To do so, we must consider the size of the profits, risk, and transaction costs and compare active currency strategies with a passive "buy-and-hold" strategy.

Regarding transaction costs, in Table 9.1 we also report the number of transactions entailed by following each trading rule. As expected, small filter sizes and trading rules based on short-term moving averages result in considerably more trading signals than larger filters and rules based on long-term moving averages. We calculate that the likely cost of transacting in the currency futures market is about 2.5 basis points (0.025%) per transaction for a large institution, but we have used instead a more conservative estimate of 4.0 basis points.[9] Transaction costs of this magnitude would substantially eliminate the 3.3% annual profit for the 1/5 moving average rule for the Canadian dollar that generated 65 trades per year at an annual cost of 2.60%, and reduce the profits of the 1/5 rule for other currencies. For the other trading rules we consider, the volume of trading is considerably smaller, so transaction costs do not significantly reduce profits.

The returns from buying and holding each foreign currency, and buying and holding an equally weighted currency portfolio, are reported in Table 9.2. The rate of return and risk figures in Table 9.2 do not account for transaction costs. However, the returns are in excess of the risk-free rate.[10]

The performance of the buy-and-hold strategy was generally disappointing. The annual (excess) rates of return ranged from 1.9% on the British pound to –0.2% on the Swiss franc. These modest returns were associated with substantial risks: Canadian dollar volatility was 4.8% but the other currencies' volatility ranged from 12.1% (German mark) to 13.8% (Swiss franc). These results sup-

TABLE 9.1 Profits of Technical Trading Rules in Currency Futures Markets, 1976–1990

Strategy	Currency SF	DM	CD	BP	JY
Filter	8.1[a]	2.2	3.3[a]	9.9[a]	7.5[a]
0.5	901	825	305	791	784
1.0	6.8[b]	9.3[a]	3.4[a]	7.5[a]	8.3[a]
	533	409	121	424	410
2.0	3.7	5.5[b]	1.7[b]	7.4[a]	7.0[a]
	253	195	51	188	174
3.0	7.2[b]	7.9[a]	0.9	8.4[a]	7.1[a]
	127	97	28	106	98
4.0	10.1[a]	8.1[a]	1.6[b]	8.0[a]	10.1[a]
	78	62	15	65	60
5.0	6.7[b]	8.2[a]	1.1	4.3[c]	8.4[a]
	62	41	11	55	44
10.0	6.0[a]	3.5[b]	1.8[a]	4.5[a]	4.8[a]
	15	15	2	14	15
MA 5/1	5.2[b]	6.4[a]	3.3[a]	7.4[a]	7.3[a]
	980	964	987	943	929
20/5	8.9[c]	11.2[a]	2.7[a]	10.5[a]	10.6[a]
	211	215	196	187	191
200/1	6.9[a]	8.1[a]	2.3[b]	8.7[a]	9.2[a]
	81	75	81	60	85

Notes: Profits in percent per annum, U.S. dollar returns

Second line is number of trades in full sample

[a]Significant at the 1% level in a bootstrap test

[b]Significant at the 5% level in a bootstrap test

[c]Significant at the 10% level in a bootstrap test

Japanese yen data are for 1977–1990.

port the view that foreign currencies are not an attractive buy-and-hold investment.[11]

In applying the technical trading rules to hedging currency risk in a global bond investment, it will be convenient to collapse the information in our ten technical rules. To do this we construct a composite trading rule for each currency. The composite rule gives an equal weight to each of the ten technical rules. Each day for each currency, our currency position is $P = (N_L - N_S) \times 10\%$, where N_L is the number of rules recommending a long currency position

TABLE 9.2   Profits Using a Buy-and-Hold Trading Rule in Currency Futures Markets, 1977–1990

	SF	DM	CD	BP	JY	Portfolio
Mean Excess Return	–0.17%	0.31%	0.48%	1.48%	1.82%	0.86%
Volatility	13.75%	12.07%	4.78%	12.28%	13.06%	9.04%
Sharpe Ratio	–0.01	0.03	0.10	0.12	0.14	0.10

Note: Profits in percent per annum, U.S. dollar returns

and N_S is the number of rules recommending a short currency position, and $-1 \leq P \leq +1$. So, for example, if five rules recommend a long position and five rules recommend a short position, we take no currency position at all. If seven rules recommend being long and three recommend being short, our composite position is long 40% of our capital. Similarly, if eight trading rules are short and two are long, our net position is short the foreign currency, in an amount equal to 60% of our capital. Notice that the composite trend-following rule is usually only partially invested.

The performance of the composite technical trading rules is summarized in Table 9.3.[12] For each currency, the composite trading rule earned a substantially higher return than the buy-and-hold strategy, even though the trading rule was usually only partially invested. The annual (excess) rate of return in Canadian dollars was 2.1%; the other returns ranged from 8.2% on the Japanese yen to 6.8% on the German mark. Moreover, in all but one case the composite trading rule was less risky than the buy-and-hold strategy. The Sharpe ratios for the trading rules ranged from 0.84 to 1.08.

TABLE 9.3   Profits Using a Composite Trading Rule in Currency Futures Markets, 1977–1990

	SF	DM	CD	BP	JY	Portfolio
Mean Excess Return	7.00%	6.84%	2.06%	7.60%	8.18%	6.26%
Volatility	8.38%	7.47%	2.76%	7.02%	8.05%	4.69%
Sharpe Ratio	0.84	0.92	0.75	1.08	1.02	1.33

Note: Profits in percent per annum, U.S. dollar returns

The results in Table 9.3 also show the value of diversification across currency positions. The volatility of the equally weighted currency portfolio (4.7%) was lower than the volatility of all but one of the single currency positions. Lowering the volatility of currency investing by diversifying resulted in a much improved Sharpe ratio. The diversified currency portfolio's Sharpe ratio, 1.33, is superior to that available in U.S. common stocks during the same sample period.[13] Moreover, the currency portfolio's return was uncorrelated with the return on equities (sample correlation = –0.08). As a result, foreign currency investment governed by technical trading rules was an attractive diversification instrument for a U.S. equity investor.[14]

GLOBAL BOND PORTFOLIOS AND HEDGING STRATEGIES

We now apply our trading rules to hedging global bond portfolios. An investor who buys foreign bonds has two sources of return: (1) the own-currency return, equaling interest income plus capital gain or loss—reflecting an exposure to interest rate risk, and (2) exchange rate gains or losses—reflecting an exposure to currency risk. The availability of inexpensive, effective currency risk hedging instruments (forwards and futures) means that an international portfolio manager can be exposed to foreign interest rate risks only (currency-hedged foreign bonds), currency risks only (pure positions in forwards or futures) or to both (unhedged foreign bonds).[15] That is, the decision to hold foreign bonds can be made independently of the decision to bear currency risk. In this chapter, we investigate currency hedges applied to foreign bonds and executed in the currency futures markets.[16]

Description of the Hedging Strategies

Passive Currency Hedging Strategies

Several arguments can be made for passive currency hedging. These strategies are relatively easy to implement and they have low administrative costs. They are easily understood and performance evaluation is simplified. Passive strategies offer a good alternative if active currency hedging strategies are costly to implement, risky, or often unsuccessful.

In this chapter we consider two passive currency hedging strategies: "Always Hedge" and "Never Hedge."[17] The always-hedge strategy presumes that currency insurance is inexpensive, so that the costs of always being covered are low. This would be the case if the forward rate used for hedging ($F_{t,1}$) and the expected future spot rate ($E[S_{t+1}]$) were on average equal and if transaction costs are low. The case for always hedging would be enhanced further if the period-to-period discrepancies between $F_{t,1}$ and S_{t+1} were often large. Always hedging would then smooth out period-to-period results without reducing long-run returns.

An argument for a passive strategy based on never hedging can also be made. Clearly this case presumes that currency insurance is expensive, so that the cost of hedging is high. Hedging costs could be high because transaction costs are high or because the forward price of foreign currency systematically underpredicts the future spot price. If the discrepancies between $F_{t,1}$ and S_{t+1} are small, or if period-to-period variability in returns is not penalized, then always hedging offers few benefits. Managers could claim that return variability is a normal part of an international portfolio and that some of this volatility is naturally dampened in the context of the larger portfolios that investors hold.

Active Currency Hedging Strategies

The case for active (or selective) currency hedging strategies also relies upon several arguments. First, it presumes the existence of a trading rule that can beat the currency futures market. By this we mean that, on average, the trading rule earns a profit after accounting for transaction costs. And second, since no trading rule will earn a profit in every period, an active strategy presumes that these returns are large relative to the risks.

As was the case with passive strategies, a large number of active strategies could be investigated. This is especially so when a large number of forecasting rules exist, and various composite forecasts could be generated based on these individual forecasts. In this chapter we examine only two active strategies similar in spirit to the composite trading rules previously proposed.

A *tactical hedging strategy* is one where the percentage of currency futures to sell for currency i ($P_{T,i}$), based on our ten technical rules, is determined by the formula:

$$P_{T,i} = [10 - (N_{L,i} - N_{S,i})] \times 10\%, \quad \text{for } N_{L,i} \geq 5$$
$$= 100\% \quad\quad\quad\quad\quad\quad\quad \text{for } N_{L,i} \leq 4$$

where $N_{L,i}$ and $N_{S,i}$ are the number of technical rules advocating long and short currency positions. When all technical rules expect the value of FC to rise ($N_{L,i} = 10$), no hedging is recommended ($P_{T,i} = 0$). But when the trading rules are evenly split ($N_{L,i} = N_{S,i} = 5$), the tactical strategy results in a 100% hedge of the currency risk in a foreign bond portfolio. When most trading rules recommend a short foreign currency position, the tactical strategy also hedges fully. The return on the tactically hedged portfolio (R_T) is simply

$$(1) \qquad R_T = R_U (1 - P_T) + R_H (P_T)$$

where R_U is the return on the unhedged bond and R_H is the return on the currency-hedged bond.[18]

The *currency overlay strategy* is actually a combination of two separate investments: (1) a foreign currency bond position that is always hedged against currency risk, and (2) a currency position governed by the composite currency trading rule [$P = (N_L - N_S) \times 10\%$] as described previously. At one extreme, if all trading rules recommend a long position, the currency overlay strategy will be 100% unhedged, just like the tactical hedge. But at the other extreme, if all trading rules recommend a short position, the currency overlay strategy will "overhedge" to become net 100% *short* in the foreign currency. Recall that in this case, the tactical hedge resulted in a full hedge, yielding no net currency exposure. As the range of currency positions is wider with the currency overlay strategy, it is more aggressive than the tactical hedge strategy. The return on the currency overlay strategy (R_{CO}) is given by

$$(2) \qquad R_{CO} = R_H + R_A$$

where R_A is the return on the active composite trading rule, or $R_A = \Sigma_t P_t * \ln(F_{t+1}/F_t)$, and P_t, the percentage of futures contracts to *buy*, satisfies $-1.0 \leq P_t \leq +1.0$.[19]

Empirical Results

Our bond data reflect the monthly returns (interest income plus capital gain or loss in local currency) on foreign government bonds with approximately 10-year maturities.[20] Most of the data are available for the 1975–1990 period, but because of limitations on Japanese yen currency futures data, the effective sample period is 1977–1990. The returns are converted into U.S. dollars by using end-of-period spot rates (for unhedged returns) and the one-month Eurocurrency rate differential (for hedged returns).[21]

For calculating the returns associated with the "always hedge" strategy, the currency hedge is repeated (or rolled over) each month. Since the maturity of the foreign currency bonds far exceeds the maturity of the currency hedge, the bond portfolio continues to reflect essentially all of its initial foreign currency interest rate risk.

The results for the two passive strategies are reported in Tables 9.4 and 9.5. As a benchmark, we also computed the returns for a U.S. dollar government bond portfolio with similar maturity. The mean return for the dollar portfolio over the entire 14-year period was 9.00% with standard deviation 8.91%. The mean excess return, over and above the risk-free rate, was 1.06%, producing a Sharpe ratio of 0.12.[22] For the unhedged portfolios (Table 9.4), we see that mean returns were higher for three of the four currencies (BP, DM, and JY) and for an equally weighted portfolio than for the U.S. dollar portfolio. However, volatility measures for these foreign currency bonds were all considerably higher than the U.S. dollar portfolio. Nevertheless, the Sharpe ratios for the BP, DM, and JY portfolios and the global portfolio all equal or exceed the U.S. dollar bond benchmark.[23]

The unhedged global portfolio, however, is imperfectly correlated with the U.S. dollar portfolio, so opportunities exist for diversification gains. In Figure 9.1, we see that a mixture of roughly 40% global portfolio and 60% U.S. dollar bonds would have improved the total returns-to-risk measure. The Sharpe ratio, however, is maximized with a full investment in the global unhedged portfolio.

The results for the portfolios with 100% currency hedging are shown in Table 9.5. The effect on mean return is mixed, with two

TABLE 9.4   U.S. Dollar Returns from Unhedged Ten-Year Bonds, 1977–1990

	DM	CD	BP	JY	Global Portfolio	US $
Mean Return	9.75%	8.59%	14.07%	12.90%	11.33%	9.00%
Mean Excess Return (a)	1.81%	0.65%	6.13%	4.96%	3.39%	1.06%
Volatility	15.53%	11.17%	17.42%	16.89%	11.68%	8.91%
Sharpe Ratio	0.12	0.06	0.35	0.29	0.29	0.12

Note: Calculations based on N = 168 monthly observations. (a) The risk-free return for the period was 7.94% per annum.

The global portfolio is an equally weighted portfolio of the four nondollar bonds.

TABLE 9.5   U.S. Dollar Returns from Fully Hedged Ten-Year Bonds, 1977–1990

	DM	CD	BP	JY	Global Portfolio	US $
Mean Return	10.05%	8.31%	10.95%	11.07%	10.10%	9.00%
Mean Excess Return (a)	2.11%	0.37%	3.00%	3.14%	2.16%	1.06%
Volatility	6.06%	9.03%	10.10%	6.38%	5.68%	8.91%
Sharpe Ratio	0.35	0.04	0.30	0.49	0.38	0.12

Note: Calculations based on N = 168 monthly observations. (a) The risk-free return for the period was 7.94% per annum.
The global portfolio is an equally weighted portfolio of the four nondollar bonds.

currencies (BP and JY) showing 2–3% lower returns, and two currencies (DM and CD) showing little change.[24] The effect on the reduction of volatility in each foreign currency bond portfolio is unambiguous. The trade-off between risk and return is reflected in the Sharpe ratios, which are little changed (compared to Table 9.4) for two currencies (BP and CD) but much improved for two others (DM and JY). The Sharpe ratio is 0.41 for the equally weighted global portfolio, higher than for the unhedged portfolio and higher than for the U.S. dollar benchmark. The opportunities for diversification with the fully hedged global portfolio are shown in Figure 9.2. Here it is clear that the fully hedged global portfolio completely dominates the U.S. dollar portfolio. Ex-post, a 100% weight on the fully hedged global bond portfolio would have maximized either a Sharpe ratio or the total return/risk trade-off.[25]

The results for the two active currency hedging strategies are summarized in Tables 9.6 and 9.7.[26] The more conservative, tactical hedging strategy bests the two passive approaches. In Table 9.6, all mean returns are higher than either of the two passive foreign currency strategies. And all volatilities are bounded within the two measures reported in Tables 9.4 and 9.5. The tactical currency hedging strategy improves the realized Sharpe ratios for every currency compared to either passive strategy. The Sharpe ratio for the tactically managed global portfolio is 0.75, nearly twice that of the fully hedged global portfolio and more than six times that of the U.S. dollar portfolio.

FIGURE 9.1   International Portfolios: Unhedged
US$ Investor, 1977–1992

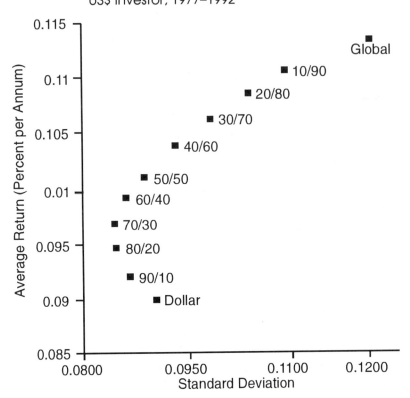

The results for the currency overlay strategy (Table 9.7) are still more encouraging. Without exception, mean returns are higher than for the tactical hedging program, and volatility measures are about the same. The effect on the Sharpe ratio is unambiguous. For three currencies (DM, BP, JY) the return/risk ratios are substantially higher than for the pure U.S. dollar bond portfolio. For the global portfolio, the Sharpe ratio is 1.23, more than ten times that for the U.S. dollar bond portfolio. These two active strategies are illustrated in Figure 9.3.

The results presented above are evidence that active hedging strategies would have been very beneficial to international bond portfolio managers. However, in light of the wide swings in currencies over the sample period, it is possible that our results might have been largely determined by events in a single year or two. To investigate this possibility, we examined the robustness of our results by breaking the sample into three sub-periods and into five

FIGURE 9.2 International Portfolios: Frontiers
US$ Investor, 1977–1992

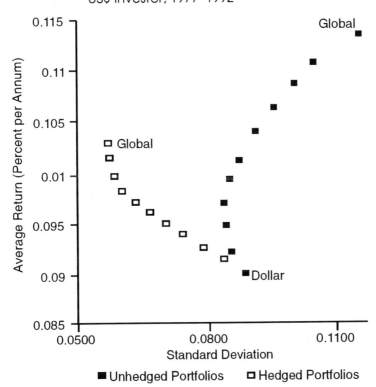

■ Unhedged Portfolios   □ Hedged Portfolios

TABLE 9.6 U.S. Dollar Returns from Tactically Hedged Ten-Year Bonds, 1977–1990

	DM	CD	BP	JY	Global Portfolio	US $
Mean Return	12.63%	9.04%	16.80%	15.57%	13.51%	9.00%
Mean Excess Return (a)	4.69%	1.10%	8.86%	7.63%	5.57%	1.06%
Volatility	9.29%	9.50%	13.24%	11.10%	7.47%	8.91%
Sharpe Ratio	0.50	0.12	0.67	0.69	0.75	0.12

Note: Calculations based on N = 168 monthly observations. (a) The risk-free return for the period was 7.94% per annum.

The global portfolio is an equally weighted portfolio of the four nondollar bonds.

TABLE 9.7   U.S. Dollar Returns from Hedged Ten-Year Bonds Combined with Active Currency Overlay, 1977–1990

	DM	CD	BP	JY	Global Portfolio	US $
Mean Return	17.68%	10.52%	19.38%	19.58%	16.79%	9.00%
Mean Excess Return (a)	9.75%	2.58%	11.44%	11.65%	8.85%	1.06%
Volatility	9.15%	9.18%	13.68%	10.43%	7.30%	8.91%
Sharpe Ratio	1.07	0.28	0.84	1.12	1.21	0.12

Note: Calculations based on N = 168 monthly observations. (a) The risk-free return for the period was 7.94% per annum.

The global portfolio is an equally weighted portfolio of the four nondollar bonds.

FIGURE 9.3   International Portfolios: Active and Passive Hedges

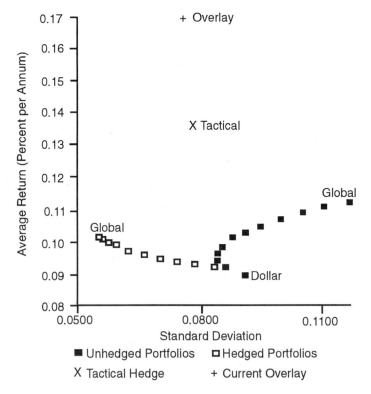

sub-periods. The results for the five sub-periods are summarized in Figures 9.4 and 9.5. The active overlay strategy had the highest total return and the highest Sharpe ratio in four of the five sub-periods. Moreover, in every sub-period, the currency overlay strategy produced a positive Sharpe ratio and a Sharpe ratio greater than the U.S. dollar portfolio. That is, a foreign bond portfolio that includes an active currency risk management strategy based on a currency overlay approach dominated the performance of a passively held U.S. dollar bond portfolio.

SUMMARY AND CONCLUSIONS

In this chapter we described a new test for weak-form market efficiency, applied it to foreign currencies, and decisively rejected the hypothesis that exchange rates have evolved randomly. While foreign exchange has not been attractive as a buy-and-hold investment, we found that simple trend-following trading rules historically earned economically and statistically significant profits.

Should international investors, then, routinely currency hedge all of their foreign investments? To date, most contributors to the currency hedging debate have either implicitly or explicitly assumed that foreign currency positions do not promise abnormal, risk-adjusted returns. But if foreign exchange markets offer unusual profit opportunities, the arguments for always hedging are weakened. Our results suggest that selective hedging may produce superior investment performance. However, it appears that the greatest

TABLE 9.8   Sharpe Ratios for International Portfolios with Alternative Currency Hedging Strategies, 1977–1990

Strategy	DM	CD	BP	JY	Global Portfolio
No Hedge	0.12	0.06	0.35	0.29	0.29
Always Hedge	0.35	0.04	0.30	0.49	0.38
Tactical Hedge	0.50	0.12	0.67	0.69	0.75
Currency Overlay	1.07	0.28	0.84	1.12	1.21

Note: Sharpe Ratio for U.S. dollar portfolio is 0.12.

FIGURE 9.4   Total Returns and Five Strategies
1977–1990 and Five Sub-Periods

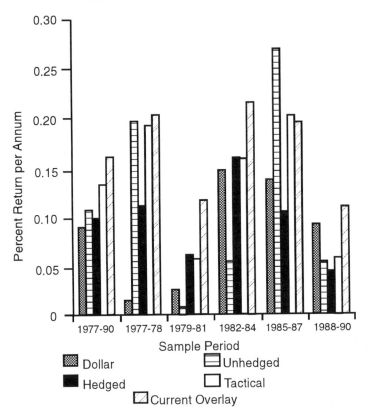

opportunities are present if investors are not restricted in their ability to overhedge in currencies where they hold long positions in bonds. This finding was supported by an examination of performance over shorter time periods, where the currency overlay strategy consistently produced a positive Sharpe ratio, and one exceeding that for a U.S. bond portfolio. Our results suggest further that foreign exchange may be an attractive asset class for return-seeking investors, even if they do not own foreign securities.

In light of these findings, international investors may wish to reconsider the advice to always hedge all, or always hedge a set percentage of, their portfolio's currency exposures. Using simple tactical hedge/no hedge rules based on signals from technical currency trading models would have increased the risks of foreign

FIGURE 9.5 Sharpe Ratios and Five Strategies
1977–1990 and Five Sub-Periods

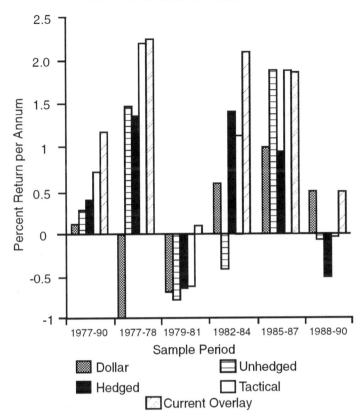

investing compared to a strategy of always currency hedging. But tactical hedging rules would have increased returns too. A more aggressive strategy using an active currency overlay earned the highest returns (both gross returns and excess returns relative to volatility) of any strategy we examined, yet was less risky than not hedging at all.

REFERENCES

Adler, Michael, and David Simon. "Exchange Risk Surprises in International Portfolios," *Journal of Portfolio Management*, (Winter 1986): 44–53.

Alexander, Sydney S. "Price Movements in Speculative Markets: Trends or Random Walks," *Industrial Management Review*, 2 (May 1961): 7–26.

Aliber, Robert Z. *Exchange Risk and Corporate International Finance* (London: Macmillan), 1978.

Bilson, John F.O. " 'Technical' Currency Trading," in Lee Thomas (ed.) *The Currency Hedging Debate* (London: IFR Publishing), 1990.

Black, Fischer. "Equilibrium Exchange Rate Hedging," *Journal of Finance*, 45, No. 3 (July 1990): 899–907.

Dooley, Michael, and Jeffrey Shafer. "Analysis of Short-Run Exchange Rate Behavior: March 1973–November 1981," in D. Bigman and T. Taya (eds.), *Exchange Rate and Trade Instability* (Cambridge, Mass.: Ballinger Publishing), 1983.

Efron, B. "Bootstrap Methods: Another Look at the Jackknife," *The Annals of Statistics*, Vol. 7, No. 1 (1979): 1–26.

Fama, Eugene F., and Marshall Blume. "Filter Rules and Stock Market Trading Profits," *Journal of Business*, 39 (1966): 226–41.

Froot, Kenneth A., and Richard H. Thaler. "Anomalies: Foreign Exchange," *Journal of Economic Perspectives*, 4, No. 3 (Summer 1990): 179–92.

Gadkari, Vilas, and Salvador Demafeliz. *The Role of Currency Hedged Bonds in Fixed Income Diversification*, Salomon Brothers, Inc., June 1987.

Hsieh, David A. "The Statistical Properties of Daily Foreign Exchange Rates: 1974–1983," *Journal of International Economics* 24 (1988): 129–45.

Jorion, Philippe. "The Exchange-Rate Exposure of U.S. Multinationals," *Journal of Business* (July 1990): 331–45.

Koh, Annie, and Richard M. Levich. "Synthetic Eurocurrency Interest Rate Futures Contracts: Theory and Evidence," in R. Sato, R. Levich, and R. Ramachandran (eds.), *Japan and International Financial Markets: Analytical and Empirical Perspectives* (Cambridge: Cambridge University Press), 1993. (forthcoming)

Levich, Richard M. "Is the Foreign Exchange Market Efficient?" *Oxford Review of Economic Policy*, Vol. 5, No. 3 (Fall 1989): 40–60.

Levich, Richard M., and Lee R. Thomas. "The Significance of Technical Trading-Rule Profits in the Foreign Exchange Market: A Bootstrap Approach," *Journal of International Money and Finance*, 1993. (forthcoming)

Perold, Andre F., and Evan C. Schulman. "The Free Lunch in Currency Hedging: Implications for Investment Policy and Performance Standards," *Financial Analysts Journal*, May/June 1988.

Sweeney, Richard. "Beating the Foreign Exchange Market," *Journal of Finance*, (March 1986): 163–82.

Thomas, Lee R. "The Performance of Currency-Hedged Foreign Bonds," *Financial Analysts Journal* (May/June 1989): 25–31ff.

Thomas, Lee R. *The Performance of Currency-Hedged Foreign Equities*, Goldman Sachs & Co., July 1988.

NOTES

1. For example, studies by Perold and Schulman (1988) and Thomas (1989) showed that the risk/return trade-off offered by U.S. government securities could be improved by diversifying into a portfolio of government bonds. Moreover, they showed that a passive strategy of hedging the currency risk embedded in foreign bonds could further enhance the risk-return trade-off from this class of international investments compared to never hedging. See also Gadkari and Demafeliz (1987). For the case of currency-hedged equity investments, see Thomas (1988).

2. See for example, Dooley and Shafer (1983), Sweeney (1986), or Levich (1989). Unfortunately, all of these studies rely on severe statistical assumptions that make their inferences somewhat suspect. This chapter remedies this problem.

3. An alternative hypothesis—that there is a foreign currency risk premium that fluctuates in sympathy with the positions taken by trend-following models—is logically possible. The possible economic explanation for such a premium, which would necessarily frequently change its sign over a period of days or weeks, is obscure.

4. The data on currency futures are daily settlement prices on the Chicago Mercantile Exchange collected through the I.P. Sharpe Company. The Japanese yen data begin only in 1977. Returns are calculated as logarithmic first differences of successive prices.

5. See, for example, Alexander (1961) and Fama and Blume (1963).

6. See the evidence presented in Hsieh (1988).

7. The bootstrap test for statistical significance as applied to foreign exchange is described in detail in Levich and Thomas (1993).

8. The results were fairly robust across three five-year subperiods. For a more complete description of the test results, see Levich and Thomas (1993).

9. We consider two elements in the cost of transacting: first, the bid/ask spread, which we take as $0.0002 or $0.0001 per transaction, and second, the brokerage commission, estimated at $11.00 per round-trip. Since the sizes of currency futures contracts are fixed and futures prices are variable, the percentage cost transacting varies somewhat across currencies and over time. Our estimate reflects an average of these circumstances.

10. This is because margin on account can be held in U.S. Treasury bills that earn the risk-free rate for the speculator.

11. This is the basis of the argument that an international investor's base case should be to currency hedge. See for example, Perold and Schulman (1988), or Thomas (1989). Black (1990) argues that a portion of your foreign equity investments should be permanently

unhedged. This is equivalent to taking a buy-and-hold position in foreign exchange with a fraction of your capital.

12. Again, the returns do not account for transaction costs. In effect, each of the ten trading rules governs how 10% of the portfolio is invested. The transaction costs for the portfolio would then be a weighted average based on the number of transactions for each rule. From Table 9.1, we see that all DM trading rules resulted in 2,898 total transactions, or less that 20 transactions per rule per year. Thus, transaction costs would reduce profits by between 50 and 80 basis points per year (see note 9 also).

13. By comparison, the Sharpe ratio achieved by the Standard and Poor's 500 stock index was 0.5 for the same 1976–1990 period.

14. See Bilson (1990).

15. Foreign interest rate risk could be hedged as well using actual or synthetic interest rate futures contracts. (See Koh and Levich [1993].) We do not consider this case, as a foreign currency bond hedged against both exchange rate and interest rate risk effectively becomes a synthetic U.S. dollar bond.

16. Currency forward contracts differ from currency futures contracts in two important ways: forward trades involve bearing the credit risk of a bank counterparty, and forward positions are usually not marked-to-market daily. Neither of these differences has a material effect on forward and futures prices, which are ordinarily very close. As a practical matter, forward and futures market hedges produce the same result.

    We do not treat the question of how to measure currency exposures. See, for example, Adler and Simon (1986). Many corporations use the accounting value of their foreign investments as a proxy, but this practice is conceptually flawed. A measure of exposure analogous to beta is justifiable in some cases. See Jorion (1990).

17. Many other passive currency risk management rules could be proposed. For example, policies based on (1) maximizing nominal interest earnings, (2) persistent forward exchange prediction bias, or (3) a contrarian view based on hedging forward premia but not discounts could be followed in a passive manner. See Aliber (1978) for further discussion of these issues.

18. Note also that R_U and R_H are related by $R_H = R_U + R_{FH}$ where R_{FH} is the return on the futures hedge, i.e., the return from selling currency futures [$-\ln (F_{t+1}/F_t)$]. Equation (1) can then be rewritten as $R_T = R_U (1 - P_T) + (R_U + R_H) (P_T) = R_U + R_F P_T$; with $0 \leq P_T \leq 1$. We use this expression to compute R_T, taking R_U from the monthly series of bond prices and taking $R_F P_T$ from the daily series of trading signals and futures prices, accumulating these to a monthly series.

19. We use equation (2) to compute R_{CO}, taking R_H from the monthly series of bond prices and taking R_A from the daily series of trading signals and futures prices and accumulating these to a monthly series.

20. For the period 1975–1985, data are for individual bonds and are from Goldman Sachs. For the 1986–1990 period, data are for liquid bond indices and are from J.P. Morgan Securities.

21. Equating the interst differential to the cost of a forward hedge relies on the covered interest rate parity principle, which is robust in the Eurocurrency market. We use these data rather than futures to establish an exact one-month hedge.

22. The sequence of one-month U.S. Treasury bill yields from the Center for Research in Security Prices (University of Chicago) is used as a risk-free return. The Sharpe ratio is calculated as $(R_i - R_F)/\sigma(R_i)$.

23. Had we measured performance on the basis of mean return relative to volatility, the U.S. dollar portfolio would come out ahead of the other portfolios in Table 9.4. Even based on the $R_i/\sigma(R_i)$ measure, the foreign portfolios presented in Table 9.8 will be superior to the U.S. dollar portfolio. See Thomas (1989) for an analysis using the total returns to volatility measure.

24. The results in Table 9.5 do not include the incremental transaction costs associated with hedging. Always hedging our monthly returns implies 12 hedging transactions per year at a cost of 2.4–4.0 basis points each (see note 9) or 30–38 basis points per year.

25. These results correspond generally with those reported earlier in Thomas (1989).

26. Again, the returns are measured before transaction costs. With the most active hedging strategy producing an average of 20 transactions per currency per year (see note 9), the impact on returns would be 50–80 basis points per annum.

10

Approaches to Currency Management

Kevin Bailey
Record Treasury Management Ltd.

So many questions face a pension fund when investing overseas that it is something of a miracle that anyone ever gets around to it! If I am a plan sponsor, for example, I have to decide whether the foreign investments are intended mainly for diversification or whether I genuinely believe that the foreign market will outperform the domestic. And is there really an associated currency risk to worry about, or am I having the wool pulled over my eyes by rapacious currency managers?

It will probably not take too long for most plan sponsors to convince themselves that there is a currency problem to be faced, since in practice the returns from foreign investments will often be dominated by currency moves. However, is it really possible to quantify the currency risk? If the plan buys a stock in, say, a Japanese company exporting goods to Europe, that company may well be hedging currencies on its own behalf, and doesn't that turn what is ostensibly completely yen risk into, well, something else? Closer examination reveals that this effect is actually second-order and can be largely ignored, but it does illustrate the complexity of the issues. Even if the currency exposure can be accurately assessed, some plan sponsors may ask how a currency overlay program can possibly benefit them given that the foreign exchange market is a "zero-sum game" (i.e., what one player gains another loses) and surely over time gains and losses will even out. Perhaps this simply indicates that we must choose the strategy we use very carefully—a random approach may well not give a long-term benefit.

One major hurdle to be overcome by a plan sponsor before tackling currency issues is the question of a benchmark. When investing abroad, the sponsor can appoint managers and give them, say, the Morgan Stanley EAFE index as a benchmark to judge performance. This index is one of the industry standards, and performance against it will be recognized as such by virtually the entire pension fund world. In the currency field there is no equivalent widely recognized benchmark, and this is sometimes felt keenly by individual plans, since what seems to them good performance from their currency managers may not be recognized as such by their peers. It is possible that in time an "industry standard" benchmark may arise, although an individual plan's assets are very unlikely to be allocated exactly to any one index's weightings and so perhaps a tailor-made benchmark may be more appropriate. Until this situation has been resolved, individual plans will have to continue to decide what performance means to them—and after all, who can better judge this than the plan sponsors themselves?

The plan sponsor, being satisfied that the problem is real, quantifiable, and "solvable" must then look for a solution. One common approach is to use forecasting techniques to decide when to put a hedge in place. If, for example, the plan has sterling-denominated assets and the sponsor thinks that sterling will weaken against the dollar, it makes sense to sell sterling for dollars in the forward foreign exchange market for some horizon in the future. Or does it? The trouble with this approach is of course that if the forecast is wrong, the decision based on it will be equally wrong, and may prove expensive. The plan sponsor is entitled to ask how accurate such currency forecasts have been in the past. (See Figure 10.1.)

Figure 10.1 is compiled from data published by Euromoney Treasury Manager, which annually prints forecasts from 30 or 40 eminent organizations. The figure shows the range of one-year forecasts of the dollar/sterling exchange rate, and compares these to the actual spot rate during the subsequent year. A policy based on these forecasts wouldn't have had much success, and must be of very limited use in managing currency exposures. Having said

FIGURE 10.1   Is Forecasting Useful?

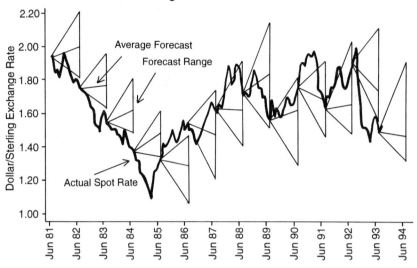

Source: Euromoney

that, it is of course possible for an individual forecaster to "score a home run" and the much publicized successes of, for example, George Soros are tempting. The plan sponsor might, however, feel that such triumphs belong more properly to a "currency as an asset class" category, and look for other methods to reduce risk and manage the plan's strategic currency exposure.

Having discarded discretionary policies, the plan sponsor will have to turn to systematic strategies for currency management. The main question to be asked here is whether cover based on simple forward contracts executed in the foreign exchange market can give the risk reduction and added value that our plan sponsor will naturally desire. It has been argued elsewhere at length that a 100 percent forward hedge is not desirable in that this completely neutralizes the currency risk, and therefore removes one of the main benefits of foreign currency investments—asset diversification. Some analysts argue that while the foreign investments remain a relatively small percentage of the total 5 to 10 percent), a forward hedge is unnecessary, the size of the recommended forward hedge rising as the percentage of the total plan invested abroad rises. This analysis is detailed and well reasoned, and certainly forms the basis of a practical and systematic policy. We might question, however, whether the relatively simple forward cover generally used gives the most desirable result. It is of course cheap to put into place, since there is no up-front cost involved in executing a forward contract, but the main disadvantage of simple forward cover is that it can cause large cash outflows at times when perhaps the plan would prefer not to have to pay out cash. This situation occurs when paradoxically the relevant currency moves in the plan's favor, creating windfall gains in the dollar valuations of the foreign assets, since the forward hedge will neutralize the currency effect by incurring equal and opposite losses.

The plan sponsor may by now be asking whether a simple forward hedge would have benefited the plan in the past. As we all know, past performance is no guarantee of future results, but it is certainly interesting to note that in general over any significant period of time such a policy would not have added value. It would have smoothed the dollar valuation of the foreign assets, reducing risk in that sense, but would almost certainly have had substantial cash implications for the plan over the years. As we have seen in actual cases in the past, periods in which the dollar is very weak will cause large accounting gains on the foreign assets and require correspondingly large cash payments to be made; this can be the source of great excitement to any outside commentator who doesn't understand the strategy being followed.

At this point the plan sponsor may well feel like giving up entirely; after a great deal of agonizing he or she may feel that the available solutions to the currency problem, namely leaving the exposure uncovered or using a simple forward hedge, don't seem that attractive. Fortunately there are other possibilities, and we can now move on to look at management using other instruments such as currency options. The advantage of an option over forward cover is obvious, in that if the dollar strengthens the benefit is enjoyed from both instruments, but if the dollar weakens, the forward cover incurs losses, whereas the option can simply not be exercised. If currency options cost nothing, one would naturally use them in preference to forward cover; the "catch" is of course that they do have an up-front premium associated with them. Managing currency exposures in this way might cost 4 or 5 per cent per annum, and the question has to be whether this is good value. Again we can look at past history to give an indication of this, and the broad answer is that over the past decade cover using currency options would have not only protected a portfolio but would have added value as well.

Currency management using options is sometimes likened to taking out currency insurance, and some purchasers of options rationalize the premiums paid as being their "currency insurance premium." The insurance analogy can't be taken too far, since currency risk is two-way (there can be both favorable and unfavorable moves), whereas a conventional insurance risk is one-way in that a factory can burn down but not up (!), but it is still an interesting way to look at this type of cover.

If the plan sponsor has now become interested in options, he or she probably feels close to a decision about currency management. Now would seem the time, therefore, to introduce the concept of "dynamic hedging" in order to shake the new-found confidence. Dynamic hedges are essentially constructed to give an option-like (or currency insurance) result—that is, the user will benefit from the dynamic hedge if the currency moves unfavorably and will just pay the cost of the hedge should the currency move favorably. Typically, this will be achieved by the user, taking strategic positions in the spot or forward foreign exchange markets and managing these on a continuing basis to achieve the desired end result. A dynamic hedge is often seen as a development of the option hedge in that the techniques used are similar in concept to those used by the seller of a conventional option to hedge his own risk. In some cases (including ours) the techniques used are radically different from the normal ones used, but the end effect will be somewhat similar, the main difference being that the total cost of the hedge should be less over time. This cost saving, again for dollar/sterling, is illustrated by Figure 10.2.

Our informed plan sponsor might well ask at this point whether a dynamic hedge is more "risky" than a simple forward hedge or a hedge constructed using conventional options bought from a bank. Curiously enough, the answer is that probably it is not, and we should examine the reasons. As already discussed, a forward hedge taken out to protect a foreign asset portfolio will be loss-making if the dollar weakens, and depending upon the size of the move, this can lead to very substantial cash demands. Given that these losses would not have occurred had the cover been in the form of options (which could have been allowed to lapse), the losses could be regarded as the option premiums that had to be paid in order to obtain currency insurance. On this basis, a simple forward hedge turns out to be expensive, and the currency insurance premiums paid very variable. One might, however, be forgiven for thinking that a hedge constructed of conventional options would involve less risk than a dynamic hedge. Again, this is less clear-cut than one might think, since the factors that make a dynamic hedge expensive, of which the main one is volatility in the foreign exchange market, also make conventional options expensive. It is true that when one purchases a currency option from a bank one is buying certainty, as opposed to a dynamic hedger who almost by definition has to react to market movements, but our experience has been that the risk is very manageable. Certainly the cost savings available in terms of the overall currency insurance premiums paid are substantial enough to make this a viable approach and enable value to be added. An idea of the value that can be gained is given by Figure 10.3, which shows the effect of overlay programs using various hedging techniques on an EAFE portfolio in terms of the gain or loss to the index value.

FIGURE 10.2   Cost Comparison of Conventional Option and Dynamic Hedges

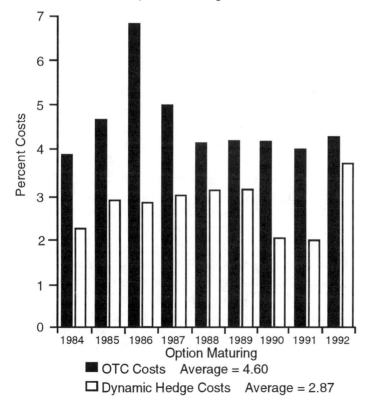

FIGURE 10.3   Performance of an EAFE Hedge

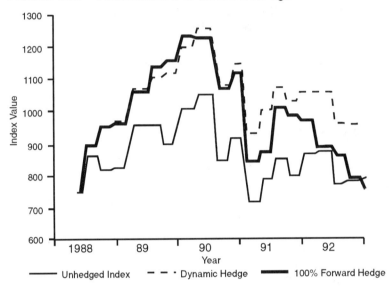

The plan sponsor may now ask if it is worth looking at even more exotic instruments that could be used to manage currency. For example, what about the so-called zero-cost options widely available from banks? In this context, however, many of these instruments may be judged inappropriate, as they sometimes increase risk rather than reduce it. The zero-cost option, to take a case in point, involves simultaneously buying one conventional option and selling another (so that the premium received on one equals the premium paid for the other), and selling (or writing) an option can of course lead to large cash losses.

Finally, if the plan sponsor believes that managing currency exposures through a currency overlay program can add value as well as give protection, isn't there a strong argument for having currency as a separate asset class? Some plans may not be particularly interested in the risk reduction aspect of overlay, in that their foreign portfolios may be small, but may well be interested in adding value. How then does currency as an asset class differ from currency overlay, and are the risks involved different? The techniques involved are often, as one might suspect, very similar—a manager involved in both activities who claims to add value through forecasting in overlay will probably use the same approach for a currency fund. Certainly we have found that the positive performance of our currency funds lends weight to our

FIGURE 10.4   The Profitability of Dynamic Hedges

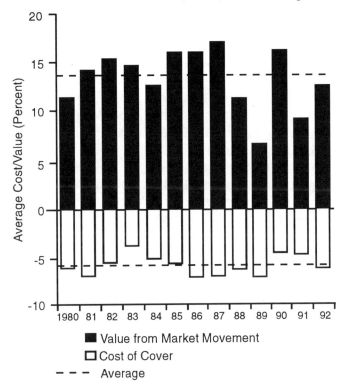

statements concerning the added value that can be generated through dynamic hedging. However, the two applications differ in concept in that, in the great majority of cases, an overlay program is trying to protect purely against a weakening in the currency in which a foreign investment is denominated, whereas a currency fund will attempt to benefit whichever direction the currency moves in. The fact that value can be captured on a consistent basis is shown by Figure 10.4, which shows the average costs and values at maturity for one-year dollar/sterling dynamically created options. It is based on setting options at monthly intervals to capture currency movements in either direction.

Another difference is that when treating currency as an asset class—running a currency fund—the manager will commonly be able to take positions in a greater number of currencies. The extent to which he or she will do this is of course dependent on the type of techniques used, and a manager using discretionary or forecasting methods may perhaps feel more inclined to take large positions in any one currency.

More importantly, most currency fund managers will take a more aggressive approach than used in currency overlay, using varying degrees of leveraging. This will alter the risk profile of the activity, but the manager should be able to describe that profile—if there is a significant chance that the investor will lose 80 percent of his or her investment for example, this should obviously be stated in advance. In general, a more structured approach will allow the potential risk to be more fully analyzed.

The same argument that has been made for the potential costs of a currency fund can also be applied to the expected returns from that fund. Again, the greater the degree of structuring involved, the greater the chance of estimating and putting "confi-

FIGURE 10.5   Currency Fund—Actual vs. Expected Outcome

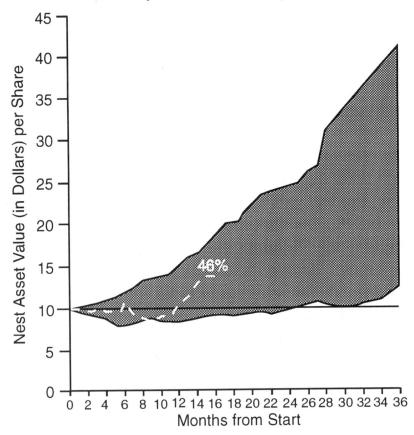

dence limits" on what the return will be. Performance from the most successful currency funds has been excellent, although as we all know, this is not always the case and it's important that a potential investor should search carefully to find a manager who can offer the right risk profile—if this can be determined in advance. That this is possible can be seen from Figure 10.5, which shows the performance of one of our public currency funds against an expected "envelope of results" produced before the fund was launched.

We would argue strongly from our own experience that currency overlay can both reduce risk and add value, and that this is best achieved by using a dynamic approach to hedging. In our particular case the same techniques used in overlay are applied to our currency fund activities, lending weight to the suggestion that the two applications are closely related. They should not however be confused, and the plan sponsor's objectives will of course be crucial in deciding whether currency overlay or currency as an asset class is the most suitable application.

11

The Case for Active Currency Management

John R. Taylor, Jr.
FX Concepts, Inc.

INTRODUCTION

There has always been a foreign exchange market. Even in the most primitive societies, the movement of goods from one family or settlement to another requires a medium of exchange that is less bulky than the goods themselves and that can be readily valued. Metallic bits and small shiny stones were obvious candidates, and even today some of these objects have retained their value. The first traders had to be foreign exchange specialists as well as merchants who knew the products being traded. One could make an entertaining, and half-true, argument that the world's oldest profession was actually foreign exchange trading. And, as a profession, it has often been held in equally low regard.

In fact, the reason foreign exchange traders were disliked in ancient cultures is that they were very successful and very rich. Trading gold and other money successfully was often the difference between great success and great failure. These traders were the famous asset and liability managers of their time. There was no stock market or bond market, and foreign exchange—moving from one convertible asset to another—was the best way to invest your way to wealth. Knowing the valuation, safety, and liquidity of many different specie and metals was very difficult. It took a cold-hearted and critical mind to evaluate the strength and weakness of these different mediums of exchange. Modern investment analysis should trace its roots to the minds of these men trading in the Middle Eastern marketplaces. Both fundamental and technical analysis, as well as market expertise, had their place in a studied analysis of the value of a specific bag of coins or weight of gold.

Foreign exchange is still attached to every trade transaction, whether export or import, but in the last few centuries it has grown beyond trade. International investing must involve foreign exchange, but the element of time plays a much more important role. Moving goods and accepting payment for them is quickly done when compared to the time required to take an equity position in a company or project, to nurture its growth, and finally to liquidate the position and repatriate the profits. A savvy example of foreign exchange positioning is the story of the Rothschilds. In the second half of the eighteenth century, the Rothschild family dispersed its five children to five different national capitals in Europe to pursue the banking and investment business that the family had developed in Germany. They did what every modern global asset and liability manager dreams about. The Rothschilds took deposits, borrowed, and otherwise collected funds in weak currency countries of the time, like France and the Kingdom of Naples, and diversified their assets, investing it primarily in strong currency countries like England, Germany, and the Netherlands. The Rothschild family symbol became five arrows bound together, but some of those arrows were borrowers and some were investors. The story of the homing pigeon that flew from the battlefield at Waterloo, bringing the news of Napoleon's defeat, is not only a famous story about equity timing, but also part of a decades-long, and spectacularly successful, foreign exchange strategy.

The overwhelming economic position of the United States after World War II temporarily eliminated the fluctuations in currency values. Twenty-five years later, as the economic dominance of the United States waned, the imposed relationships among the currencies of the free world collapsed. Then, foreign exchange was rediscovered by the international marketplace. The Bretton Woods agreement, between the victors of World War II, relegated foreign exchange to a minor role in international trade and investment. The elimination of foreign exchange as a critical variable brought a boom in international transactions. In effect, the money changer of previous times was eliminated from the calculations, with an increase in profits to all the other participants. Returns on individual equities and bonds, as well as on entire asset classes, and on the export and import process itself, became far more important to the trader and the investor than the returns on the underlying currency. All assets were effectively dominated in dollars, and the fluctuating value of one country's currency against its neighbors' no longer was a factor.

During this period, international money managers lost sight of the important contribution that currency movement had historically made to international return. After twenty-five years of almost no movement, from 1946 to 1971, when the world operated on a dollar standard, this could be excused. The number of people who practiced currency management dwindled and those that remained were marginal members of the investment community. In 1971, the Bretton Woods system broke down; for the most part, bankers, money managers, and other investment professionals simply yawned. Very few remembered the world before the war and could see this as an important event in the world financial scene. Foreign exchange fluctuations began immediately and defied all the current economic theories. The volume of currency trading grew rapidly at the commercial banks in the 1970s, as all trade and commercial transactions were impacted by volatile exchange rates. Over the next twenty years, the analysis of currency movements expanded from a perfunctory paragraph or two in an annual country study to a science practiced with statistics, mathematical theory, and computers by highly paid "quants" educated with Ph.D.'s in mathematics or physics, who devoted their lives to the analysis of a few major currency relationships. By 1993, twenty-two years after the breakdown, the historical results—both from the risk side and the reward side—are compelling: foreign exchange is once again the critical factor that makes the difference between a good and a bad international transaction.

Foreign exchange is now an integral part of most international investment decisions, but very seldom is it being used as effectively as it might. Much of today's emphasis is negative: foreign exchange is seen as an added risk to international investing, a risk that must be controlled. At best, this wild and uncertain variable is seen as lowering the correlations between domestic equity and fixed-income returns and international returns. Because lower correlations among asset classes is seen as positive, foreign exchange might be viewed as a positive factor in the total portfolio. In response to this perceived need of plan sponsors, the most prominent products offered by foreign exchange managers attempt to mitigate the risk of foreign exchange first, and only then to add return. Sometimes the adding of return is a far distant second.

Although these early risk reduction strategies all look at foreign exchange as an added component—of risk and not of return—that must be handled by the manager, foreign exchange can stand on its own as an investment vehicle. Even though many academic studies show, and empirical experience seems to confirm, that foreign exchange does not have an underlying intrinsic rate of return, currency rates tend to move up and down in long waves lasting months or even years. As Figure 11.1 makes clear, in almost half of the quarterly periods during the past twelve years the dollar has moved by 5 percent or more against the EAFE weighted currency basket.

Also, half of the quarterly moves have been up and half down. As might be expected after a reading of the academic studies, at the end of 1992, the dollar had moved only marginally from where it began twelve years before in 1980, but adding the absolute quarterly movements over this period gives a number several times the original value of the dollar. For many years, a few strategies have existed to capture this volatility and profit from it, but the development of computers and active forward markets has meant an explosion of possibilities.

The nature of the foreign exchange market combined with continuous movement, volatility, and advanced computer analysis

FIGURE 11.1   Currency Impact on EAFE Portfolio
Quarterly 1980–1992

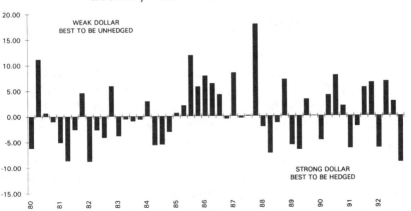

has bred an entirely new class of investments that offer high returns and relatively low risk. Many of these products were developed internally at the very largest commercial and investment banks, where they were used primarily to manage these institutions' asset and liability strategies and other principal accounts. Earnings from this area often contribute over 50 percent of the total earnings of these major institutions.

The futures market also explored these profitable avenues, but often buried their successes under extremely high management fees, which masked the returns. Despite these high carrying costs, the management of currency funds has grown exponentially over the past decade. Only recently has currency analysis become more widely available to the institutional manager—this book is a good example of that trend. Although the tremendous analytical and management advances in foreign exchange are finally becoming apparent, the possibilities offered by these changes are still unknown to the majority of managers.

Before describing some of the techniques that have been developed to turn foreign exchange fluctuations into investment products, it would be valuable to understand the characteristics, including the participants and the major factors, of the foreign exchange market since 1971. Like all the other markets, it is continuously changing. This change has been primarily a function of the change within the world system, and far less a function of the fate of an individual economy or nation-state. The nature of the foreign exchange market itself dictates the techniques used to analyze the market and defines the limits in the development of profitable decision-making strategies.

THE GIANT THAT NEVER SLEEPS

The foreign exchange market is the largest in the world, dwarfing all the others. According to statistics collected by the Bank for International Settlement during the spring of 1992, the average daily volume is $880 billion. The second largest market, that for U.S. government obligations, is estimated at about $150 billion per day, and the New York Stock Exchange is less than a tenth the size of the U.S. government market.

The foreign exchange market has grown dramatically over the past ten years, quadrupling in size, and the market in the early 1980s was probably five times the market ten years before.

Although some of this growth is tied to the expansion of international trade, not all is trade-related; and capital flows have come to dominate the market's expansion. The Eurodollar market and the international banks expanded rapidly in the early years of the post-Bretton Woods period, making it far easier to arrange cross-border financings and commercial investments. The accelerated growth of the "swap" market, which was born around 1980, has allowed almost any creditworthy institution to efficiently tap any pool of financial liquidity in the world. Swaps allow long-term assets and liabilities to be recharacterized: for instance, one could switch a long-term loan from floating rates to fixed rates or redenominate a Swiss franc asset into a Japanese yen asset. Swap volume now outdistances loan volume at many banks. The final boost to the currency market's phenomenal growth is the accelerating trend toward cross-border investment. Global diversification of asset pools has coincided with the growth in multinational companies, the globalization of almost all the world's economies, mounting worldwide liquidity, and the increasing reach of modern investment and portfolio theory.

All these factors have led foreign exchange volumes to higher and higher heights. However, this market is very different from an equity market. The participants approach an equity market with generally similar goals: they want a positive return on their investment. Often, foreign exchange transactions are done with very different purposes in mind; only a few of the major participants in this market are entering transactions with the hope of making a positive return. For instance, central banks transact business in this market, buying and selling their own currency and the currency reserves that they hold. They act with their countries' national interest in mind, not to make a profit. When the Bundesbank is selling dollars and buying marks, it might be doing so to reduce the money supply in Germany, to help the U.S. keep its currency lower within the G7 framework, or perhaps to adjust its currency holdings within the European Rate Mechanism (ERM). It is not making the trade because a profit will ensue.

Corporations execute a large number of currency transactions, but very few of these companies are trading for a profit. Their primary business is not currency, but something else, and they are acting to secure the profits on their primary activity. An effective example would be a Canadian firm that produces goods sold in the United States. Its sales are priced in U.S. dollars and its competition is American, but its costs are all Canadian. This firm must be very active in the currency market, but its goal is certainly not the profit gained from buying low and selling high. When the U.S. dollar is at a level that will ensure a good profit for the exported goods, the U.S. dollars will be sold forward and the Canadian profit will be ensured. The Canadian company has achieved its goal: profitable sales.

Another example concerns a European airline that purchased a large number of Boeing 747 jets in early 1985 for delivery several years in the future. Company analysts had done their work and analyzed traffic needs, ticket price levels, and operating costs, including the cost of the new planes. The numbers worked; it was a good investment. Because their forecasts saw a profitable transaction flying those planes around the world in the years ahead, the airline contracted to buy all the dollars needed to pay for the planes at their future delivery date. The dollar dropped to 50 percent of its original value before the planes were delivered, but the airline was not worried, as this variable cost was ensured at an acceptable level. Its goal was the purchase of a fixed asset at a known local currency cost.

Very few corporations will take chances in the currency market, attempting to minimize costs or maximize revenues. They are almost always acting to cut risk and ensure future cash-flow levels. Corporations consider themselves winners when their basic business is profitable, even when the transaction was executed at a level far worse than the optimal one. The tremendous volume of foreign exchange associated with international trade is not traded as an investor would, in a profit-seeking manner.

Commercial banks are the largest participants in the market, but in most cases, they are not investors. Their role is usually that of an intermediary, making a market between the buyers and the sellers of currency. There are no commissions or fees in the market, only the difference between bid and asked. Despite the fact that this spread is very narrow, usually around 0.05 percent (the value of the difference between a bid such as 1.6110 for marks and an offer of 1.6120), this is a very profitable business for the banks. Most banks make all of their money acting as an intermediary and not as an investor of their own capital. Although the figures are guarded very closely, several years ago, a major U.S. bank's internal figures showed that more than 100 percent of the profit was generated by the customer traders, those who dealt with nonbank outsiders, while the positioning of the bank, taking long or short positions against different currencies for inventory reasons or speculation, lost money two years in a row. The profitability of the intermediary function does not rely on a directional view of the market. Banks do not usually profit by investing in currencies at low prices and selling them at high prices—there are too many more-promising avenues they can follow.

Although all international portfolio investors must participate in the foreign exchange market when they buy and sell securities, almost all regard it as a hindrance to be overcome. Over the past ten years, while international investment has grown rapidly, managing currency for a profit has lagged badly. Prior to 1987, when FX Concepts entered the market, only one outside manager held itself out as a currency manager to this marketplace, and it had less than a handful of clients. Despite this, commercial banks were seeing more and more foreign exchange transactions from pension funds. Groups of bank traders were formed that focused entirely on pension plans and their managers. Although plan sponsors were moving tremendous amounts of foreign currency out of and back into U.S. dollars, there was no plan, rational or irrational, behind this movement.

These four major participants in the foreign exchange market, the central banks, multinational corporations, commercial banks, and international investors, now combine to trade almost 100 percent of the total volume in this market. However, not one of these trades currency with the goal of buying it low and selling it high—the common profit-making motive in most markets. The only participants trading to make a profit have been the commodity managers, among whom are John Henry, Campbell and Company, and Millburn, and those few commercial and investment banks that have emphasized principal dealings rather than customer trading. Bankers Trust, Solomon Brothers, and Goldman Sachs stand out in this group. Our company, FX Concepts, is the largest of the new firms that specialize in foreign exchange that have grown up over the past ten years. There are still very few of these. Although the last year or two has seen tremendous growth in trading foreign exchange as an investment, it is unlikely that this contributes as much as 5 percent of the total volume in the market.

The fact that foreign exchange is not always traded with the profit motive foremost in mind makes this market easier to analyze and trade for those who are driven by this motive.

Government policies pursued by the central banks can maintain certain arbitrage situations, perhaps not perpetually, but certainly for as long as it is in the interest of the government to continue the specific internal or external policy that is causing the arbitrage. The most blatant example of this over the past decade has been the series of arrangements between the countries of the European Economic Community (EEC), most recently known as the European Rate Mechanism (ERM). The ERM has linked the European currencies together in a tight grid, allowing a range of fluctuation with each other of only 2.25 percent in most cases, at the same time as the individual governments have applied domestic economic policy aimed at different goals. The result has been a persistent interest rate differential while the foreign exchange rates have remained bound together. By borrowing the currency with the lower interest rate and investing in the one with the higher, or by making the same transaction through the swap market, as long as EEC policy remained unchanged, generally risk-free profits were recognized. The profits have been gigantic: the application of this arbitrage has resulted in earnings of many billions of dollars for financial institutions operating in Italy during the last ten to fifteen years alone. For many of them, profits using this technique dwarfed all other operations combined. This is the most extreme example, but the interplay between government policy exercised through the central banks creates many other opportunities every month.

Corporate transactions also tend to create a consistent bias in the market. For instance, trade activities always lead to a flow of foreign exchange from the purchasing country back to the seller. This will result in a persistent long-term decline in the currency of the country with the surplus of imports. Eventually this might reverse itself as the importer's currency declines continuously, but other factors such as inflation and interest rate levels are likely to intervene, causing the trade deficit to persist. This downward pressure becomes locked within fairly tight calendar time frames as liquidity and accounting considerations at the exporting firm demand that foreign sales be converted back to domestic use to pay suppliers and workers. The Japanese yen has rallied throughout the last ten years on the back of exports, and self-correcting global interest rate and inflation levels make this trend look as persistent today as it did ten years ago.

ANALYZING THIS MARKET

The many interlocking factors that influence this market, plus the difficulty in analyzing the relative strengths of the two sides of a currency pair, have made it extremely difficult to succeed with a fundamental economic approach to foreign exchange movement. Political decisions also play a critical role in currency movements, but the most effective course of analysis has proven to be quantitative. Through close analysis of currency movements and price changes, the supply and demand for each currency can be monitored and the future trend can be ascertained. Political understanding, economic fundamentals, and quantitative relationships can all play a part in understanding the market's movements, but the quantitative anticipates the future better, while the political and the economic make the whole process seem rational after the fact.

Political considerations can shape the terrain of the foreign exchange market, substantially altering it from the positions it would have naturally assumed. Certainly the ERM example is illustrative; and any analysis of the Italian lira that ignored the Italian government's desire to be part of Europe during the recent past would have missed the point—and the direction of the lira. Another clear example concerns the dollar. Throughout the decade of the eighties, the movement of the dollar can be divided into two political phases. The "cowboy" dollar ruled through the first half of the decade. This dollar was strong because Ronald Reagan and his policy makers wanted to strengthen the U.S. internationally, and dominate the Soviet Union, reversing the decline in U.S. prestige growing out of the loss in Vietnam. Historically, a strong country had a strong currency. All of Reagan's words on this subject display this linkage, and the dollar obeyed, rising almost continuously for five years. The second half of the decade was dominated by fears of job losses, and the "rust belt" dollar was born. Although the signs were obvious before the Plaza Accord in September 1985, this event rang the bell and informed the world that the "cowboy" dollar period had ended. The U.S. was worried about declining international competitiveness in general and the loss of jobs in the industrial heartland in particular. World leadership was no longer tops on Reagan's list and the global economic strategy of the U.S. had shifted. From this time, the Americans began to debase their currency both verbally and through policy actions, pursuing a weak dollar strategy during the rest of

Reagan's presidency and throughout Bush's as well. The result of this was a dramatic decline in the dollar from a position of extreme economic overvaluation to equally extreme economic undervaluation in less than three years. Politics is important; and dismissing the power of the politicians can often destroy the analysis.

If any economic approach makes the most sense as a starting point in analyzing foreign exchange, it should be monetarism. Money supply is what we are trying to value, and foreign exchange rates are nothing but the price applied to different money supplies. To understand the value of a given currency, however, we must not only know what its money supply is and its relative position with regard to that of the currency we wish to value it against, but we must also know the demand for both of the currencies. The relationship between the size of the two money supplies and the demand for each is the exchange rate at the moment. Analyzing the supply of money and the demand for it in order to come up with a price makes common sense. If a government undersupplies its economy with the money that it needs to operate, interest rates should rise, and foreign investors would convert their currencies to take advantage of the abnormally high interest rates. This would cause the first currency to climb until the tight monetary conditions eventually bring on a recession and force the central bank to reverse its policy and oversupply the local currency, or until the trade picture deteriorates dramatically. In retrospect, this seems to explain the dollar's movement under Reagan, as well as many other situations.

The problem comes in measuring the demand for a currency. Demand is not only a function of economic growth and inflation, but also of the public's willingness to hold balances in that currency. How willing are governments, exporters, corporations, and individuals to hold it? This critical input is impossible to measure and does not stay steady. If no one wants to hold a currency, it can decline for a long time, even though it is becoming less plentiful; the opposite is true as well. For example, throughout the last three years of the 1970s, the U.S. undersupplied its economy with dollars; that is, the money supply grew less than nominal economic growth (growth unadjusted for inflation) and dramatically so. However, the dollar continued lower; no one wanted to hold dollars. Dollar holdings had increased throughout the Bretton Woods period and corporate, national, and individual balance sheets were too crowded with this newly uncertain asset. At the same time, Switzerland had negative interest rates and the Swiss allowed their money supply to grow far faster than economic growth and inflation levels would dictate—yet this currency continued to strengthen. The Swiss mystique was at its height, while the U.S. dollar was a pariah, and no one seemed aware that the situation had changed. Eventually the world ran out of dollars, American interest rates took off, and the dollar followed along; but this analysis would have been wrong for several years before it was right.

Economic and monetary fundamentals are wonderful tools for explaining why currencies moved in the past but unfortunately, adequate information is only available after the fact, and sometimes, only long after the fact. Usually many alternative analytical scenarios exist while the market is moving, and a decision must be made. Government data about the strength of the economy, inflation, and the growth of the money supply are always incomplete and come several months after the fact. Far worse, they are very often wrong, and are restated several years later. Furthermore, data are not comparable across national boundaries. Finally, among the thousands of different important data series, the market seems to choose one or two factors on which to focus. Some analysts can find their way through this thicket of data to project currency movements and make management decisions on their outlook, but the growth of inexpensive computer power has enabled many firms, including our own, to find a much easier and—if investment records are taken as the proof—a more successful way.

Our analysis depends upon the computer, plus mathematics and statistics, to pinpoint the direction of currency movement. Because we cannot analyze fundamental data in real time due to their unavailability, we analyze the market's reaction to the participants' perception of the economic fundamentals and the supply-demand balance of the market. This reaction is seen in the price that market participants will pay for dollars, other currencies, interest rates, oil, gold, and other commodities. This is the best information available to analyze this marketplace.

Our technique combines both a trend-following and a cyclical analysis. Actually these two conceptual ways of approaching the market are at odds with each other. Trend-following depends on the fact that the trend will tend to continue as new ideas and conceptions spread through the market. Simplistically, one would argue that what went up for the last week will go up tomorrow. Cyclicality, by definition, says that trends will end. If cycles exist, then trends must be interrupted by cyclical reversals.

We have found that both processes exist simultaneously. Trend-following has been tested by thousands and has a ritual following among commodity traders. Many empirical studies have shown it to be very successful in currency trading. Trends do tend to persist. Looking back at the market in the past, some trends have had phenomenal staying power—certainly the dollar decline from early 1985 to the end of 1987 had it—but there have also been periods when it was hard to know what was going on.

Cycles are far less known among market followers, but the empirical analysis of at least some cycles is far more advanced. Economic and business cycles have been widely studied. There is also related literature on cycles in nature, especially concerning the symbiotic relationship among different species of animals. Whether the analysis concerns the economy or animal survival, cycles have been shown to be multivariate, with timing lags between the variables creating a complex cyclical picture. In economic cycles, the reactions of the political and business decision makers take place concurrently, adding to the variability of each cycle. Although history never repeats itself, there are enough similarities that business cycles recur over and over again.

Our analytical method uses cycles as its base, and trend-following techniques between the reversals. The critical cycle is one that is slightly less than four years in length. We have found this cycle length in the dollar's relationship to the German mark, the U.S. stock market, the U.S Treasury market, American trade statistics, producer prices, gold, and many fundamental variables. Although we have no guarantee, we believe that this concurrence of cycles must mean that this is the business cycle. This cycle has been generally stable for over 100 years, at least according to our analytical method. Although they have the same mean length, the many different cycles tend to lead or lag each other, peaking at different times. Of course, considering the multitude of exogenous events, these cycles do not run precisely, but have a standard deviation from trough to trough between 9 percent and 12 percent of their length. After the repetition of several cycles, the timing can become quite complex, but the cycles do tend to persist—which means that the standard deviations of multiple cycles are not additive, and a string of cycles will tend toward their mean length.

We follow six or seven cycles for each currency, some as short as three days, and we attempt to capture the movements of those cycles that have the largest amplitude. Our system generally works with two cycles—one slightly over a month in length and the other slightly under a year. We have created one model based on each cycle. Because of the wide standard deviations, our knowledge of the moment at which a year-long cycle will reverse is not too precise. With that cycle, we can only pin the reversal down to an eighteen-week range. To improve our precision, we use the shorter cycles to identify whether the longer cycles are still moving in their previous direction or whether they seem to have turned. A series of very short cycles should have higher highs and higher lows if the major cycle is no longer declining. Short cycles moving higher should mean that the major bottom has been passed. To prevent the system from abandoning the position too easily, we take advantage of trend-following to confirm the change in direction.

The improvement of computer speed and the incredible expansion of available memory, plus the ability to feed data directly from the marketplace into memory has increased our ability to measure cyclical changes, helping further pinpoint the reversals in major trends. Nevertheless a critical component of our management process is the manager himself. In the foreign exchange market, there is a great deal of random noise that affects the market. This is a function of news reports, political pronouncements, and new economic data, all of which continually bombard the market. These impulses can cause sharp movements that quite often are quickly reversed. An experienced manager can better withstand these erratic fluctuations, knowing when to avoid them and when they are a sign of a new emerging trend. The combination of an excellent analytical system with experienced and intelligent managers, who have worked together in harmony, is the optimal condition.

INVESTING WITH CURRENCY

Knowing which way the foreign exchange market is going to go, or at least having a consistently good idea about the direction of its next movement, is a giant step forward, but the clincher is figuring out how to use this knowledge to create an investment that adds value with an acceptable level of risk, year after year.

In evaluating an investment opportunity, the two premier criteria to weigh are risk and return. Can a reasonable return be produced at a tolerable level of risk? Another critical variable is the reproducibility of the results; are the risk and return characteristics stable over a long time period? As analysts of foreign exchange since 1980 and managers since 1987, our firm believes that the answers to these questions are an emphatic yes.

There are four investment products that we would like to describe. Each of these fits the criteria above, but in a slightly different way. The first, we call Selective Hedging. It is a currency overlay product and focuses both on risk reduction and on added investment return within a portfolio of international equities or bonds. Writing Covered Calls is also an overlay product. Its goal is the consistent recognition of profit from currency positions already held within an international equity or bond portfolio. With the writing of covered calls, especially at the correct cyclical junctures, this strategy gains by selling volatility.

The two other products do not depend on a pre-existing portfolio, but stand alone as pure foreign exchange investments. They focus primarily on investment return with an acceptable level of risk. The first is the most straightforward. Currency as an Asset Class takes short and long foreign currency positions against the dollar with the goal of profiting from their movement. Gains and losses are made from currency movements. Preferred Risk is similar to Currency as an Asset Class, but adds interest rate positioning to the foreign exchange portfolio, further enhancing return. Gains and losses are made from currency movements abetted by interest rate movements. Each of these investment ideas has risk and return characteristics that make them suitable candidates for an ERISA portfolio as well as for a stand-alone investment.

Currency overlay is the most widely used currency management strategy. As practiced by many managers, this overlay is often used more to reduce risk than to add investment returns to the underlying portfolio of equities or fixed income instruments. There is no doubt of the fact that volatility is a nuisance in a portfolio, adding nothing on its own but lessening predictability of future value, thereby increasing risk and cost. Currency does add volatility to an international portfolio, and it is true that volatility can be greatly reduced by hedging the currency out of the portfolio. This strategy has its followers, especially in the academic world, but plan sponsors have been unwilling to adopt fully hedged positions because of two negatives. First, a fully hedged portfolio would lose the entire currency appreciation imbedded in the portfolio when the dollar declined, and second, the cash cost of the hedges while the foreign currencies were moving higher would forcibly re-allocate assets. The results of the period from February 1985 to December 1987, while the dollar collapsed (losing over 50 percent of its value against an EAFE weighted index of currencies), showed that the cash cost could be astronomical. Currency overlay programs answered these problems by eliminating much of the volatility while allowing some of the currency gains to flow through while lessening the cash cost. The questions to ask of overlay systems are: how much volatility, how much gain, and what is the cash cost?

Some currency overlay programs are better than others. A perfect one would allow the profits generated while currencies are rising to flow through to the bottom line while protecting against any currency declines if the dollar were to rise. This process would also be accompanied by a reduction in currency volatility equal to the reduction achieved if currency were eliminated completely, while suffering no negative cash flow periods. This is the ideal—all the gains, no loss, no volatility, and only positive cash flows. Ideals cannot be reached, but we should try. Evaluating a currency overlay program involves measuring the currency gains and the reduction in volatility, versus the increase in cash-flow volatility compared to an unhedged position. All of this should be done over a time period of several years.

An analysis of our currency overlay strategy, which we have named Selective Hedge, shows very positive results. Looking at the past four years, during which our position under management grew from about $150 million to over $1.5 billion, we have compared our results against the two passive alternatives, unhedged and fully hedged. The three bars in the graph in Figure 11.2 represent, from left to right:

- The foreign currency exposure is left unhedged and the prevailing spot price is used to evaluate the U.S. dollar value of the investment at each month end, and the results are totalled for each year.
- The foreign currency is managed by FX Concepts by selectively selling forward the currency exposure for U.S. dollars in the forward market for up to 100 percent of the value of the investment. These hedges are taken whenever market analysis indicates that a currency decline and a dollar ap-

preciation is expected. When the analysis changes, and the currencies are expected to appreciate, the hedge is eliminated by offsetting it with another equal foreign exchange contract. The profit or loss from this hedging contract is added to the return of the investment at the end of the month. These are the annual composite results of this strategy.

- A rolling hedge is constructed to hedge the foreign currency exposure. One-month forward contracts are used to sell forward the foreign currency. The amount sold forward in each currency is the amount of the original investment. By using one-month forwards, distortions are limited. The monthly results are totalled for each year.

The results over the four-year period are clear. Either of the two passive strategies resulted in a loss. The unhedged strategy caused a negative return from currency exposure of 456 basis points, which would have to be subtracted from local market return. The fully hedged strategy was also unsuccessful as local market returns were adversely affected by being hedged to dollars by 687 basis points. Over the same period, our Selective Hedge strategy added 1038 basis points to the local market returns, out-

FIGURE 11.2   Results of Selective Hedge Management 1989–1992

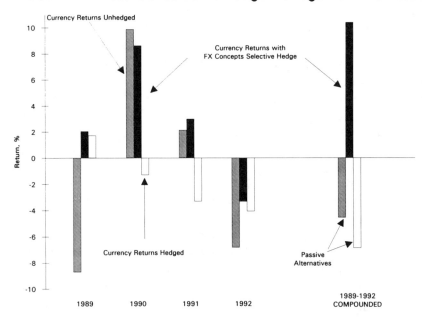

FIGURE 11.3   EAFE Returns 1989–1992

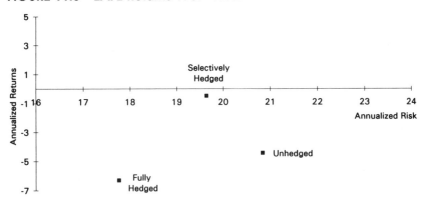

performing unhedged results by 1494 basis points and outper-
forming hedged results by 1725 basis points. These results mean
that a gain in overall performance of roughly 4 percent per annum
has been added to the returns of our composite portfolio during
this four-year period—nothing less than a tremendous shot in the
arm for any international equity portfolio.

Looking at these results from a risk/return point of view, the
improvement offered by Selective Hedge is once again apparent
(see Figure 11.3). In the 1989 to 1992 period, the fully hedged strategy reduced the portfolio's return, but lessened volatility only
marginally more than the Selective Hedge strategy.

A monthly analysis of the cash flows attendant on the two
hedging strategies, fully hedged and Selective Hedge, makes it
abundantly clear that volatility of cash balances should be an
important factor to consider before adopting a fully hedged strategy. Cash flows are not very significant in our Selective Hedge
strategy, never causing a drawdown of more than three percent in
a quarter. Over the four-year period, they are strongly positive,
adding over 13 percent to cash balances. And these results were
generated in a four-year period of overall dollar weakness when
hedging programs tend to lose cash and penalize the overall
unhedged return (see Figure 11.4).

It should be clear from the above analysis that the Selective
Hedge process adds a great deal to an international equity portfolio. The same thing is true regarding international fixed-income
portfolios. The major difference between the management of these
two asset classes is the difference between the managers of the

FIGURE 11.4   Quarterly Cash Flows on a $100M Account

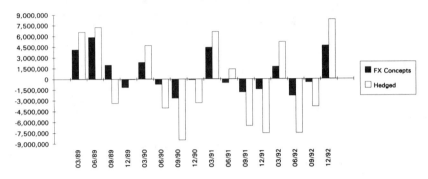

underlying assets. International equity managers generally admit that they have minimal foreign exchange knowledge and concede the management of foreign exchange to expert managers. International bond managers almost never do. In all other ways, the impact of foreign exchange fluctuations are identical.

The Selective Hedge process adds significant return to an international fixed income portfolio while lowering the standard deviation of returns. It is significant that the fully hedged strategy is a very successful one for bonds. A fully hedged international portfolio of bonds offers a more impressive decline in volatility than an equivalent equity portfolio while surrendering less of the total return in the portfolio. The figures in Figures 11.5 and 11.6 use the Salomon Brothers Non-US$ World Government Bond Index, with the investment revalued at the end of each month; interest gains and losses are re-invested. The foreign exchange management is handled in exactly the same way as it is for equities.

The results show that foreign exchange management is a critical component of portfolio return. Using the period from January 1, 1980, to the end of 1988, unhedged and hedged strategies returned 319.5 percent and 294.5 percent respectively, while a Selective Hedge strategy had a total return of 514.1 percent. The risk-return analysis displayed in Figure 11.5 clearly reinforces these numbers. The volatility of the average unhedged returns is more than twice as high as the volatility of the fully hedged returns—a standard deviation of 14.1 percent for the unhedged portfolio, compared with 6.0 percent for the fully hedged portfolio. The Selective Hedge strategy cut volatility to 10.9 percent from 14.1 percent, and at the same time increased return to 19.8 percent from 14.6 percent for the unhedged portfolio.

FIGURE 11.5   International Fixed Income Portfolios

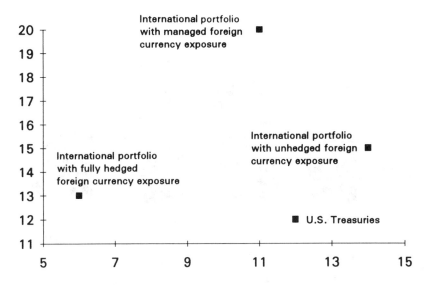

Annualized
average monthly
return in %

An analysis of return per unit of risk clearly illustrates the fact that a fully hedged portfolio outperforms the hedged and the Selective Hedge strategy in this category (see Figure 11.6). The conservative strategy, which invests in hedged international bonds, certainly seems to be a wise one, but the aggressive strategy, which invests in international bonds and uses a Selective Hedge approach, also looks very wise. For slightly more risk per unit of return, it performs much better—19.8 percent compared to 12.8 percent. However, the most interesting point in this graph might be that a fully hedged portfolio of the Salomon World Index bonds tremendously outperforms the U.S. Treasury index on a risk-reward basis. The implication is that no one should invest in U.S. Treasuries if international bonds are available.

The conclusion is inescapable. The benefits of international fixed income diversification can be expanded using a Selective Hedge strategy to manage currency risk. Actually, the investor has two logical alternatives depending on his risk preference. If his goals are a higher level of return he should actively manage foreign exchange with our Selective Hedge. If her goal is an asset with a very predictable rate of return, she should fully hedge her interna-

FIGURE 11.6   International Fixed Income Portfolios

**Average
annualized monthly
returns per unit**

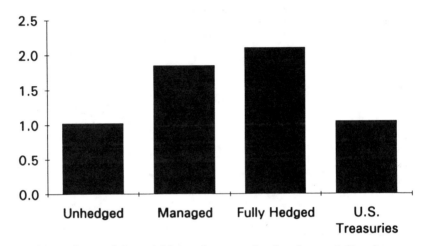

tional bond portfolio. Although an unhedged portfolio does not seem to be a logical choice, very few bond portfolios are hedged, either by our firm's Selective Hedge process or by any other.

Many foreign exchange management firms, including our own, have created another set of strategies to limit volatility and improve return on international equity and bond portfolios using the foreign exchange market. These strategies use options rather than forward contracts. If one envisages an international equity position as being both an equity and a currency exposure at the same time, it is a short step to separating the two pieces and looking for ways to profit from each of them. That currency piece could be sold outright or an option could be sold on it; or the currency could be sold outright and an option could be bought back.

The Selective Hedge strategy is simple. It just sells the currency piece and depends on analytical knowledge to know whether that sale is smart or not. When it hedges the currency exposure, it is actually selling that currency to a third party for dollars, and when it chooses not to hedge, it is holding the currency as an asset. An option strategy would not sell or buy the currency, but only sell or buy an option on that currency. Many different option strategies have been devised to add some return and eliminate some risk on currency portfolios, but they can never be as effective as a correct policy of hedging and unhedging. Because these strategies often are not dependent on directional analysis, return is often very dependent on the nature of options and the strategies applied, and much less dependent upon any timing or directional analysis.

Our firm takes a different view of options. As we feel that timing and directional analysis of foreign exchange is possible, we combine this knowledge with options to add further value. For example, we have a strategy that we call Writing Covered Calls. The volatility imbedded in the currency is sold, and over time, if this strategy is applied consistently, it will yield a positive return and a lower volatility for the entire portfolio. This is a parallel strategy to that of writing covered calls on equity positions. Although this strategy will prevail over time, leading to positive returns and diminished volatility, with currency analysis added, it will perform consistently. Combining this strategy with cyclical timing increases the probabilities of writing calls that will expire worthless, which makes it possible to consistently add between 3 percent to 5 percent a year to an unhedged return, depending on the underlying portfolio, while greatly lessening the probability of a negative year.

There are many ways to structure a strategy with options, but most of those being used are primarily defensive, striving to improve the risk-return qualities of underlying portfolios. Our Writing Covered Calls technique above is of this type. However, options can also stand on their own. One technique that our firm has tested buys currency volatility, especially when it is low, and then follows the trends that develop. This strategy often yields high returns. Although it is erratic on a quarter to quarter basis and does not perform at a continuously high level, it has only very small drawdowns and over several years should give far above average returns.

These new option strategies have been developed to provide return to the investor—and not as an addition or alteration to another asset. They are part of the trend toward treating currency as a separate asset class. This trend started about ten years ago in the commodity arena and has only recently spread to institutional investors. Our firm, FX Concepts, has been managing currency in this manner since the middle of 1988. We call our most popular product Currency as an Asset Class. Presently, we have about $1.5 billion under management for this strategy.

The concept behind Currency as an Asset Class is very easy. We asked a simple question: if we can successfully protect an overseas portfolio of foreign currencies from depreciating against the dollar when the dollar is strong, why can't we take advantage of our knowledge to also buy foreign currencies when the dollar is weak? The answer seemed obvious, and we began trading Currency as an Asset Class. When the dollar is weak, we own foreign currencies; when the dollar is strong, we go short the foreign currencies.

This strategy needs more than cash balances, or equity positions, to carry it out, it also needs to borrow. If the foreign currencies are strong, cash can be denominated in those foreign currencies, but if the dollar is strong, then the cash can only be placed in the dollar, but this does not create a short foreign currency position. This short position can be created only by borrowing the foreign currencies. Currency as an Asset Class demands the ability to go short foreign currencies.

The simplest way to use this strategy is to open a short-term Eurodollar deposit and a foreign currency trading line. When the analysis says the dollar should strengthen, the currencies are sold forward and the gains or losses are credited to the deposit. If the analysis says the dollar should weaken, then the currencies are bought forward. Once again, the gains and losses are credited to the deposit. The total results are calculated by adding the interest earned on the deposit to the foreign currency gains from either being short or long the foreign currencies. Table 11.1 shows the actual quarterly and annual results of this simple strategy in column 3, Total Return-No Leverage. This column is the sum of the first two columns, Currency Return and Eurodollar Return. Using foreign exchange this way is effectively a cash strategy. It is extremely liquid, as it can be withdrawn or turned into another asset in a day; it has no credit risk; and it also has a low volatility. In fact, for an institutional investor with access to bank credit, the Currency as an Asset Class strategy does not need a cash Eurodollar deposit as the underlying asset. An equity or a fixed-income portfolio would be fine. The only difference in the results are the numbers that would be placed in column 1.

The returns in column 3 with No Leverage do not have the kind of return that would make plan sponsors or other corporate asset managers alter their asset allocation. On the other hand, they do not have the risk of an equity or a bond portfolio either. If we were to roughly even the risk between Currency as an Asset Class and an equity portfolio, the amount of currency being traded would have to expand by a factor of five. If the currency portfolio

TABLE 11.1   Currency as an Asset Class Composite

	Currency Return	Eurodollar Return	Total Return No Leverage	Total Return 5:1 Leverage	Total Return 7:1 Leverage
1Q89	2.05	2.44	4.52	13.09	17.52
2Q89	2.83	2.41	5.29	15.64	20.10
3Q89	2.55	2.22	4.81	14.29	18.41
4Q89	−0.44	2.15	1.71	−0.07	−0.97
1Q90	−0.56	2.08	1.51	−0.89	−2.16
2Q90	0.61	2.08	2.70	4.80	5.62
3Q90	0.18	2.01	2.19	2.65	2.71
4Q90	2.00	1.99	4.02	11.84	15.58
1Q91	2.36	1.67	4.06	13.01	17.11
2Q91	−2.75	1.50	−1.27	−12.32	−17.79
3Q91	0.54	1.42	1.96	4.02	4.98
4Q91	3.19	1.21	4.42	17.65	24.50
1Q92	−0.29	1.02	0.73	−0.66	−1.48
2Q92	3.31	1.01	4.35	17.92	24.83
3Q92	2.11	0.88	3.00	11.78	16.35
4Q92	1.67	0.87	2.55	9.14	12.35
1989	7.15	9.55	17.32	49.36	65.52
1990	2.23	8.41	10.81	19.24	22.68
1991	3.27	5.93	9.38	21.27	25.83
1992	6.94	3.84	11.03	42.91	60.75
Annualized Return	4.87	6.91	12.09	32.55	42.36
Annualized St.Deviation	4.68	0.62	4.69	23.37	32.72
Sharpe's Ratio	—	1.01	1.24	1.12	1.10
Worst Quarter	−2.75	0.87	−1.27	−12.32	−17.79

is leveraged five times, a $1 million Eurodollar deposit would support a $5 million currency position. These results—the Eurodollar Return in column 1 plus five times the Currency Return in column 2—are shown in column 4. Currency as an Asset Class managed this way substantially outperforms an equity portfolio over the four year period, returning 32.55 percent annually over the period. It would even be possible to leverage this strategy further, trading seven times the underlying equity. The returns for this more aggressive strategy appear in column 5 of Table 11.1.

An interesting way to look at these results would be to place them on a risk-return graph. Figure 11.7 shows the Currency as an

Asset Class strategy with no leverage (point number 1) all the way up to the same strategy with seven times leverage (point number 7). For reference, the S&P return and the EAFE return over this same time frame have been added to the graph. Even these brief comparative results should make it clear that this currency strategy would be a powerful addition to any well-managed asset portfolio.

There is one more asset strategy that FX Concepts has developed over the last few years. It is what we call a Managed Swap Portfolio. This strategy combines the currency outlook with the interest rate outlook to create a portfolio of multicurrency borrowings and deposits through the Swap market, which are continuously managed using the same techniques as in Selective Hedge strategy. This more complex strategy has the advantage of using the interest rate market as well as the foreign exchange market, profiting from currency movements as well as from interest rate differentials and movements. There are three ways to profit rather than one: currency movement, interest rate differentials, and interest rate movement.

The starting point of this portfolio is similar to that in Currency as an Asset class. A cash deposit is established. However, Managed Swaps start not with a Eurodollar deposit but with deposits in a currency or currencies, selected because of their high interest rates or because of projected rallies in their fixed-income markets. An offsetting short position is also established. This one is selected because the currency has low interest rates or a fixed-

FIGURE 11.7   Currency as an Asset Class Returns with Various Leverage 1989–1992

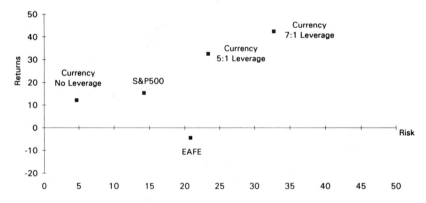

income market that is about to decline. The resulting foreign exchange position is managed and the profits or losses are credited to the deposit accounts.

Managed Swap Portfolios can be conservative, with no leverage added beyond the original deposits, or aggressive, with leverage added up to seven times the original deposit. The results of this strategy show a slightly lower return, but with less volatility than the Currency as an Asset Class strategy. The Sharpe ratio, a common measure of risk-return, is 2.00 times. The reduction in volatility is a function of the continuous positive income stream created by the offsetting deposits and borrowings.

Our historical results are not strictly comparable, as the portfolios we have managed have almost always been a function of a commercial financing proposal rather than a dispassionate portfolio strategy, and in all cases have been carried out for individual corporate users. Even with the restrictive conditions, this has been a very successful concept. As Figure 11.8 illustrates, with leverage

FIGURE 11.8   Managed SWAP Portfolio

7:1 Leverage
Average Annual Return 38.14%
Annualized Standard Deviation 15.78%
Sharpe Ratio 2.42

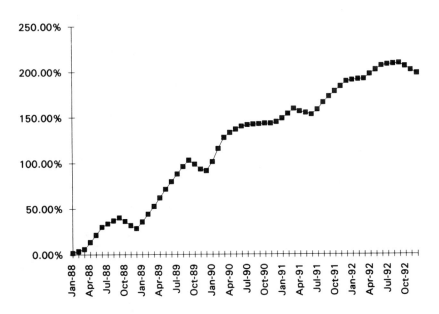

adjusted to seven times the underlying deposit base, swap strategies have returned 38.14 percent over the period from 1988 to 1992.

This foreign exchange strategy will become the basis for an
offshore mutual fund later this year. We expect the public unveil-
ing of this technique will lead to the construction of many portfolios of this type in the next few years.

This brief review of foreign exchange products, developed
both as an addition to other underlying assets and as the basis of a
new asset class, allows only a glimpse at the possible alternatives
still ahead. We expect that the rewrite of this chapter in a few
years' time will be much more enticing even if it is much longer.

12

An Option-Based Approach to Currency Risk Management

David F. DeRosa
Swiss Bank Corporation

Here is a simple yet effective way to manage a multicurrency exposure to exchange rate risk:

Step 1: Measure the exposure of your portfolio to each separate currency. As an example, the currency exposure embedded in the MSCI EAFE index, as of December 31, 1992, is shown in Table 12.1.

Step 2: If you are exposed to more than four currencies, use a quadratic optimizer to isolate the basket consisting of three or four major currencies that has the minimum tracking error with respect to the index. In practice, you will at least want to use the British pound, the German mark, and the Japanese yen for portfolios with a large number of currency exposures, like EAFE. You can experiment by adding more currencies (the French franc, Swiss franc, and Australian dollar are good candidates). Any reduction in predicted tracking error from the addition of a new currency must be balanced against the reality that although the currency option market is the largest option market in the world, options on currencies other than the majors tend to be less liquid and have wider bid-ask spreads. Output from a commercially available software

TABLE 12.1   Currency Exposure of MSCI EAFE Index as of 12/31/92

Japan	43.16%
United Kingdom	19.72%
Germany	6.60%
France	6.73%
Switzerland	4.44%
Netherlands	3.33%
Hong Kong	3.01%
Australia	2.84%
Spain	1.96%
Italy	1.93%
Sweden	1.41%
Singapore	1.47%
Belgium	1.27%
Denmark	0.69%
Austria	0.49%
Norway	0.36%
New Zealand	0.33%
Finland	0.26%
Total	100.00%

program that is capable of making currency baskets is shown in Table 12.2.[1]

Step 3: Buy put options on the individual currencies in the optimized basket. You must choose how much protection you want, but in practice, most investors want a floor of 100 percent or 95 percent—meaning that the maximum annual loss to exchange rate risk cannot exceed zero percent or 5 percent, respectively. Naturally, the higher the

TABLE 12.2   An Optimized Currency Basket*

Japan	46.13%
United Kingdom	21.73%
Germany	17.42%
France	9.15%
Unhedged (USD)	5.57%
Total	100.00%

*Expected Annual Tracking Error of 0.83%.

TABLE 12.3   One Year At-The-Money Option Basket Hedge

Currency	Weight	Implied Volatility	Foreign Interest Rate	U.S. Dollar Interest Rate	Strike As a % Of Spot	Cost As a % Of Spot
Japan	46.13%	9.10%	3.31%		100.00%	3.33%
United Kingdom	21.73%	13.80%	5.62%		100.00%	6.24%
Germany	17.42%	12.80%	7.45%		100.00%	6.86%
France	9.15%	12.80%	9.57%		100.00%	8.14%
Unhedged (USD)	5.57%			3.68%	100.00%	
Total/Average	100.00%	11.22%	4.92%		100.00%	4.83%

floor, the more expensive will be the basket of puts. A basket that protects to a 100 percent floor for one year on an EAFE portfolio is shown in Table 12.3. The overall cost of this basket of put options is 4.83 percent of the underlying portfolio.

At this point, your portfolio will be protected against currency fluctuations to the level of the floor up to the option expiration date. Moreover, you will not be encumbered in any way from capturing any upside profits, were your index of currencies to appreciate. In other words, you would be in possession of "currency insurance;" the cost of the option basket would represent the insurance premium and the difference between 100 percent and the floor that you choose would be the "deductible loss."

Going forward, you might have to rescale the size of your hedge for changes in portfolio size. For example, it would be necessary to buy more puts if the local market values in which you have invested rise considerably. If local market values fall, you would have the option of selling off part of your currency option hedge to recover some of your initial cost—that amount would represent your having been overhedged.

Now it is possible that one or more of the minor currencies in your index might suffer a catastrophic decline. In other words, some tracking error might occur. Usually, this is not a major concern because most portfolios are exposed primarily to the same currencies that are in the basket. For EAFE, 69.5 percent is taken up by the pound, mark, and yen, as of December 31, 1992. If you count the French franc, the Swiss franc, and the Netherlands guilder as close substitutes for the mark, then the number becomes 84 percent.[2] Also, tracking error can be positive, meaning that one of the nonbasket currencies might appreciate against the dollar by more than the basket.

The only other concern that you should address is the possibility that your option counterparty might not be able to perform. If you buy exchange-listed currency options, the credit risk is associated with the exchange's clearing house (the Options Clearing Corporation for the Philadelphia Stock Exchange's currency options and the Clearing House of the Chicago Mercantile Exchange for the IMM currency futures options). These entities are considered to have the same bullet-proof balance sheet strength of a triple-A institution. Plus, there are a whole host of banks and other institutions in the over-the-counter currency option business. You will have to decide for yourself what it takes to satisfy your peace of mind, triple-A, double-A, single-A, or lower, as they are all available.

Otherwise, it is hard to see what else could go wrong as long as you are planning to hold the options until expiration.

But this is not the end of the story because it is possible for you to recover some portion of your initial cost if you monitor the cross rates. This is what is known as exploiting the dispersion option:

Step 4: Monitor the basket, watching for movements in the cross exchange rates. By definition, a cross exchange rate is any exchange rate that does not involve the U.S. dollar. The pertinent rates in question probably will be pound/mark, pound/yen and mark/yen. Whenever there is a large movement in a cross rate, it may be possible to create a cheaper hedge! In other words, under some circumstances, it may be possible for you to swap your basket of put options for another, cheaper basket, with no loss of floor protection.

This means that you may be able to recover portions of the purchase price of the original basket, without ever losing the protection of your initial currency insurance program. Furthermore, you will never be under pressure to have to do this trade. In a well-managed program, it may be possible for you to do a profitable basket trade once every 30 to 60 days, depending on how much cross rate movement occurs, and the size of the bid-ask spread that must be paid to transact.

Why not just buy an over-the-counter put on the EAFE currency exposure? The answer is that although there are option dealers who specialize in writing custom-made calls and puts, multicurrency options on broad indexes tend to be expensive and bid-ask spreads can be wide. Moreover, the dealer may not fully price the value of the dispersion option.

To understand how the dispersion option phenomenon works, consider an at-the-money put on the German mark with the following characteristics (as prevailed in February 1993):[3]

Option Type:	German mark put (U.S. dollar call)
Spot Exchange Rate:	$0.6046 per mark
Strike:	$0.6046 per mark
Time to Expiration:	1 year
Assumed Volatility:	12.8%
U.S. Dollar Interest Rate:	3.68%
German Mark Interest Rate:	7.45%
Exercise Convention:	European

Garman and Kohlhagen's adaptation of the famous Black-Scholes option pricing model to work on currency options values this put as being worth $0.0415 per mark of underlying deliverable currency. The model also tells us that the delta of this option is –0.549. Now consider two cases. One is what happens when the spot exchange rate rises by 10 percent and the other is what happens when it falls by 10 percent. The new deltas would be –0.283 (spot level having risen) and –0.792 (spot level having fallen). The important thing to realize is that the absolute values of the changes in the deltas are not equal to one another, which is not surprising because options are convex instruments. The option on the rising spot gained 0.266 delta points, whereas the option on the falling spot lost only 0.243 delta points. The implication is that when one basket currency rises relative to another, meaning that the cross rate has moved, there exists a cheaper basket that can provide the same hedge on the index.

Frequently, investors take the attitude of "why bother to do anything about currency risk." Some argue that "currency risk is a zero-sum game" or "in the long run, gains and losses on foreign exchange should average out flat" or "currency risk has a zero risk premium." The answer to why you should bother to worry about currency risk is that even if all of the above points are correct, you might not want to experience the variation in returns that currencies can inflict on a portfolio. Table 12.4 shows annual spot levels for the British pound, the German mark, and the Japanese yen, as well as calculated annual rates of return on these currencies from the perspective of a U.S. dollar investor for the period 1973–1992.

TABLE 12.4 Annual Spot Exchange Rates on the British Pound, German Mark, and Japanese Yen; Rates of Return to a Dollar-Based Investor

Date	British Pound Spot	British Pound Rate of Return	German Mark Spot	German Mark Rate of Return	Japanese Yen Spot	Japanese Yen Rate of Return
31-Dec-73	2.32		2.70		280.11	
31-Dec-74	2.35	1.13%	2.41	12.27%	301.20	–7.00%
31-Dec-75	2.02	–13.90%	2.62	–8.09%	304.88	–1.20%
31-Dec-76	1.70	–15.86%	2.36	11.02%	293.26	3.96%
31-Dec-77	1.91	12.10%	2.11	11.92%	240.38	21.99%
31-Dec-78	2.04	6.80%	1.82	15.60%	194.55	23.56%
31-Dec-79	2.23	9.25%	1.73	5.71%	239.81	–18.87%
31-Dec-80	2.38	7.10%	1.96	–11.94%	202.43	18.47%
31-Dec-81	1.91	–19.90%	2.25	–12.73%	219.78	–7.89%
31-Dec-82	1.62	–15.24%	2.38	–5.65%	234.74	–6.37%
31-Dec-83	1.45	–10.35%	2.72	–12.56%	231.48	1.41%
31-Dec-84	1.16	–20.17%	3.15	–13.69%	251.26	–7.87%
31-Dec-85	1.45	24.74%	2.45	28.94%	200.40	25.38%
31-Dec-86	1.48	2.46%	1.95	25.50%	158.48	26.45%
31-Dec-87	1.88	26.94%	1.57	24.14%	121.07	30.90%
31-Dec-88	1.81	–3.75%	1.78	–11.56%	125.00	–3.15%
31-Dec-89	1.61	–10.86%	1.69	4.98%	143.68	–13.00%
31-Dec-90	1.93	19.62%	1.50	12.96%	135.69	5.89%
31-Dec-91	1.87	–3.24%	1.52	–1.59%	124.69	8.82%
31-Dec-92	1.52	–18.85%	1.62	–5.98%	124.84	–0.12%
Average Return		–1.16%		3.64%		5.33%
Standard Deviation		14.72%		13.80%		14.54%
Average Absolute Value		12.75%		12.47%		12.23%

Although exchange rates do go through some quiet periods, there are many years when the absolute value of the rate of return exceeds 20 percent. This is in agreement with the hypothesis that the distribution of rates of return on currencies is leptokurtic. More to the point, exchange rates can move in one direction against the dollar for several consecutive years without a reversal. Even more compelling is the fact that relative to the U.S. dollar, foreign currencies do not materially diversify one another. This can be seen in Figure 12.1, which shows a time series plot of the FINEX USDX index[4] of the U.S. dollar relative to ten currencies.

But how expensive are currency options? The conventional sentiment is that they are very expensive. The one-year at-the-money put on German marks that was used as an example earlier

FIGURE 12.1   FINEX® U.S. Dollar Index®

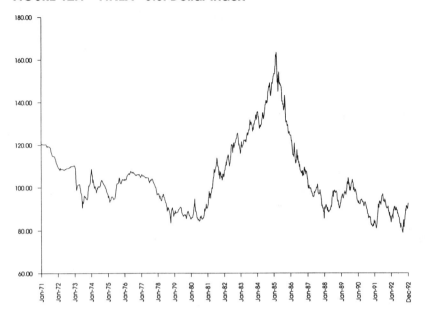

is a case in point. It was quoted at $0.0415 per mark; at the spot exchange rate of $0.6046, the put costs 6.86 percent of the value that it would protect. But one has to remember that in February 1993, the dollar was at steep premium to the mark (i.e., dollar interest rates for one-year paper were trading a full 377 basis points below German rates) and that this is built into the price of the option. You can think of a put as a conditional forward exchange contract: It gives you the right but not the obligation to sell foreign exchange at the fixed strike price on expiration day. Since we know from interest parity that the forward price of currency always encapsulates the interest spread, we can say that the forward points make up more than half of the put's price (3.77 percent out of 6.86 percent), in the case at hand of the German mark. The remainder of the option's price, 3.09 percent, is a function of the length of its life and the assumed volatility. An assumption of 12.8 percent is high by historical standards. Mark volatility of 11 percent is more normal (the 12.8 percent level in February 1993 was an artifact of the ERM crisis of autumn 1992 and winter 1993). At an 11 percent volatility, the total price of the at-the-money put would be 6.22 percent, or 2.45 percent net of the interest rate spread.

As an alternative to making an outright purchase of put options, you might decide to create the option synthetically. Option

replication programs function by buying and selling forward foreign exchange in amounts that correspond to the delta of the target
option. Because the delta of the target changes over time—primarily with movements in the underlying spot exchange rate but also
in response to changes in interest rates, volatility, and the passage
of time—it is necessary for you to be prepared to adjust the position on a regular basis. When properly implemented, the profit and
loss from the replication strategy should duplicate the payoff pattern to owning the actual target option. The biggest risk with
dynamic option replication is that you will not be able to adjust the
forward position fast enough to keep up with the target option's
delta in a rapidly moving or discontinuous market (see Jorion for a
discussion of the importance of jump process movements in
exchange rates). This would certainly have been a problem during
the autumn 1992 EMS crisis, especially with respect to movements
in the British pound upon its withdrawal from the ERM. Also, you
will have the problem of path dependency. When you buy actual
options, your maximum cost is locked in until the option expiration. But with dynamic replication, your full cost of a risk management program is not bounded. Ideally, spot rates will move on
monotone increasing or monotone decreasing paths—this is the
best environment. But when exchange rates move in up-down
whipsaws, the cost of dynamic replication will be high because you
will be caught buying at high levels and selling at low levels.

Alternatively, the cost of the program might be mitigated by
using cross hedging (also known as proxy hedging), especially for
the EMS currencies. The idea of a cross hedge is you can substitute
a low interest rate currency for a high interest rate currency in the
basket, and therefore save on the forward interest rate points that
are embedded in option and forward prices. The problem is that
you will then be long a cross rate of exchange that is not included
in your index. But as long as the cross exchange rate is stable, you
may get some savings. Unfortunately, this was not the case in
autumn 1992 and winter 1993, when the exchange rate mechanism, upon which the success of this strategy largely depends, all
but failed. Two currencies (the British pound and the Italian lira)
were forced out of the system and several others were devalued,
all giving an object lesson in the danger of this strategy.

Whatever the actual form of implementation of this strategy
that you elect to use, you must face the practical matter of how to
judge the success of your program. An option-based strategy

should be judged on the basis of two criteria. First, if foreign currencies decline, does the downside protection work? Second, if currencies rise, how much upside capture can be achieved? But the obvious benchmarks are problematic. An unhedged currency benchmark is clearly not appropriate because there is no recognition of the potentially significant downside protection that an option program is designed to provide. Nor is a fully hedged benchmark correct, for the symmetrically opposite reason that it ignores the potential upside capture with options. But at least it recognizes the role of the interest rate spread that is present in any hedging program.

NOTES

1. Note that 5.57 percent of the index is left unhedged. This is an intentional rescaling of the hedge to account for the fact that some currencies in the index, like those of Hong Kong and Singapore, trade closely to the U.S. dollar.
2. Where there is one currency that does have a large weight in the portfolio but is not included in the optimized basket, you may wish to execute a hybrid basket hedge. In this technique, you create a separate, one-off option hedge for the specific currency in question and then hedge the remainder of the exposure using the optimized basket approach. See DeRosa (1991).
3. Here we are using the convention of the IMM listed futures and futures options contracts that spot rates should be quoted in U.S. dollars
4. The USDX index seems to have a reasonable level of correlation with the currency component of EAFE. (See FINEX report in References.)

REFERENCES

DeRosa, David F., *Managing Foreign Exchange Risk: Strategies for Global Portfolios.* Chicago, IL: Probus Publishing, 1991.

DeRosa, David F., *Options on Foreign Exchange.* Chicago, IL: Probus Publishing, 1992.

FINEX, "Re-Examining Foreign Exchange Risk in the ERM Interregnum," 1993.

Jorion, Phillipe, "On Jump Processes in the Foreign Exchange and Stock Markets," *Review of Financial Studies* 1 (1988) 427–45.

13

A Dual Protection Approach to Foreign Currency Overlay Management

James T. Kneafsey
Cambridge Financial Management, Inc.

INTRODUCTION

With the state of the art in currency overlay management having advanced dramatically since 1987, the chief question facing any investor in international equity and fixed-income markets should not be whether to hedge but rather how best to hedge. Additional questions, then, are how much to hedge and who should do the hedging.

In this chapter, we offer some answers to these questions, based on our experience as a specialized currency overlay manager protecting more than $800 million in foreign investments for several pension plan sponsors and public funds.

Our approach is a dynamic hedge, which uses a combination of interbank forwards, OTC options, futures, and listed options. We have developed a unique dual-directional protection for our clients—irrespective of whether the U.S. dollar rises or falls.

THE ATTRACTIVENESS
OF INTERNATIONAL INVESTMENTS

The international markets have provided excellent opportunities for foreign equity and fixed-income managers over the last several decades, and especially since February 1985, when the U.S. dollar last peaked. With the eventual European Community alignment and new opportunities in a more unified Eastern Europe, the potential for international investing to continue to provide competitive returns remains strong. The added "kicker" for foreign investments between 1985 and September 1992 (when the dollar may have bottomed) has been the "currency" gain associated with the 50 percent decline in the value of the dollar.

However, the complexity of the business cycle in the United States as well as in many other countries, coupled with the fact that the dollar could rise sharply in the future against foreign currencies, may mean that these steady increases in the value of international holdings could become less attainable. The recent declines in the Japanese stock market and the ERM currency crisis may be harbingers of difficulties that may lie ahead in these and in other countries. On the other hand, the extremely resilient performance of the U.S. equity market along with many other major bourses during this same time period could augur well for the future and could produce super bull markets in local currency market terms over the next few years.

THE IMPORTANCE OF THE U.S. DOLLAR

How does the dollar fit in? Let's look at the possibilities. There are three alternative scenarios for international stock markets: rising, falling, or unchanged stock prices. Within each scenario there also exists the potential for a rising, falling, or unchanged dollar (with or without cross trends). In Table 13.1 is a synopsis of the three dollar scenarios and their impacts on an international portfolio using a format of a 100 percent hedge, a 50 percent hedge, no hedge, and the dynamic hedge (as used by Cambridge). The first two hedge types are generally labeled as "classic" hedges and are of the passive variety. The chief advantage of the dynamic hedge is that it is active (and therefore responsive to dollar volatility).

As shown in Table 13.1, in the case of a rising dollar the value of any dollar hedge is realized (in greater or lesser percentage terms). In the case of a falling dollar, the dynamic hedge adds value, whereas the classic hedges result in losses. The falling dollar scenario is the only one where it would pay to be unhedged (if it could be accurately predicted ahead of time). With an unchanged dollar, there is still an attractive outcome provided by the dynamic hedge. While this case is unlikely to persist for lengthy periods, it is the only case where some price erosion

TABLE 13.1 Potential Currency Environments

DOLLAR SCENARIO	100% HEDGE	50% HEDGE	UNHEDGED	DYNAMIC HEDGE
RISING DOLLAR	RETURN BOOSTED BY DOLLAR GAIN	RETURN BOOSTED BY 50% DOLLAR GAIN	RETURN HURT BY DOLLAR GAIN	RETURN BOOSTED BY DOLLAR GAIN
FALLING DOLLAR	RETURN HURT BY DOLLAR GAIN	RETURN HURT BY 50% DOLLAR LOSS	RETURN BOOSTED BY DOLLAR LOSS	RETURN ENHANCED BY DYNAMIC HEDGE
UNCHANGED DOLLAR STABLE CROSSES	NO IMPACT	NO IMPACT	NO IMPACT	RETURN ENHANCED BY HEDGE OR NO IMPACT
UNCHANGED DOLLAR TRENDING CROSSED	MIXED IMPACT	MIXED IMPACT	MIXED IMPACT	RETURN ENHANCED BY DYNAMIC HEDGE

would occur. In the sub-case of stable cross-rates, the dynamic hedge should not behave significantly differently from any other hedge program, except that some minor value addition should occur. Finally, in the sub-case of trending cross-rates with dollar neutrality, the dynamic approach should shine, as value additions would be experienced on both sides of the trending crosses.

THE NEED FOR UNLEVERAGED ALLOCATIONS FOR PLAN SPONSORS

Pension fund currency hedges should be based on an unleveraged, dollar-for-dollar allocation of foreign currency forwards, futures, and options contracts. The advantage of using options in a totally unleveraged format is that the maximum risk incurred is limited to the total amount paid for the options. The analogy of a premium for insurance coverage fits—the art is in the selection.

Options premiums do take into account the full value of the option contract. The full dollar value of the option should be used to calculate both risk levels and rate of return, so that the integrity of this investment as a hedge (rather than as a high risk speculative investment) is maintained.

The outstanding benefit of an unleveraged strategy to plan sponsors and other conservative investors is that it allows for a 100 percent hedge against a dollar rise, while maintaining a prudent level of risk (which essentially is the "insurance cost" of the options premiums) in periods during which the dollar declines. With options being used to trade against the long dollar anchor position, the unique feature of this approach is that gains will be experienced if the dollar moves sharply overnight in either direction—all the while maintaining a limited risk level. This is why our recommendation is for a 100 percent hedged benchmark depending, of course, on minimal transaction costs or the sponsor's risk level, and on the amount of international exposure relative to the total portfolio.[1]

THE APPROPRIATENESS OF A PERFORMANCE BENCHMARK

As with any form of investment, it is of utmost importance to establish a means of easily assessing performance. The first use of a performance benchmark is to act as a means of measurement in assessing ongoing investment strategy and its applicability to stated goals. The second use for a benchmark is as a means of monitoring investment results. It is imperative that the benchmark be easily available, widely known and comprehensive in scope.

The Federal Reserve Board's U.S. Dollar Index and the Morgan Stanley Capital International (MSCI) EAFE Currency Index meet these criteria. They are reported worldwide and quoted by every foreign and U.S. exchange, and since they are based on leading currencies, they are comprehensive. Another positive characteristic of the U.S. Dollar Index is that the closing value on any given trading day can be used as a commencement date value and/or for addition or withdrawal values. The Dollar Index can be used as a proxy for EAFE accounts because of the high correlation between it and the (MSCI) EAFE Index for currencies (97.6 percent).

Recognizing that no benchmark is perfect for all accounts, we monitor an EAFE Index of currencies and, in fact manage one specialized EAFE account, (where we normally trade four currencies—pound sterling, mark, yen, and Australian dollar—and use the U.S. Dollar Index for the rest of the exposure). In trying to balance the residual risk of additional currencies in the forward markets and the associated incremental transactions costs, we have calculated that this combination yields optimal coverage, both in terms of the long-dollar anchor and any enhancements.

PERFORMANCE EVALUATION POLICIES

The evaluation of the overlay manager's performance should be directed toward the fulfillment of each of three main goals: (1) effectiveness in guarding against a sustained dollar increase, (2) flexibility and ability to "add value" in the event of a sudden dollar decrease, and (3) minimization of overnight risk. Considering the ongoing nature of the risk (as long as investments are made in foreign countries, risk will exist), the hedge should not be designed to meet precise quantitative objectives over any specific time period—to that extent, its success or "performance" is dependent upon the path of the U.S. dollar.

Since this is an innovative form of risk containment, it is important that all related parties are kept informed as to the progress of its performance. A monthly performance evaluation would serve to communicate planned strategy adjustments or refinements and to give a general review of major foreign currency markets. This close co-ordination is essential to matching the allocation requirements (country by country) to foreign currency hedge positions.

THE VALUE OF THE DYNAMIC APPROACH

As suggested earlier, our dynamic approach is distinctive in the area of risk control. The bi-directional coverage relies on trading experience, accurate exchange rate projections, and money management strategies specific to foreign currency markets. The ability to price the total hedge portfolio, calculate daily portfolio exposure, and place adequate coverage is essential. Through the application of these diverse abilities, we respond to the sponsor's needs with minimal risk, volatility, and cost. The consistent application of the dynamic hedge relies upon an infrastructure of computer models, sophisticated pricing data, and key hedging personnel.

While monthly foreign currency price projections are created and updated by our computer models, the actual day-to-day application of hedging strategies depends upon daily comparisons of foreign currency futures contracts, options prices, and our forecast values. Money management and timing techniques are developed to determine the percentage of the total international exposure that should be protected, the general direction of the hedge (geared toward a higher or lower dollar) and the overall volatility in the market. As long as a 100 percent protection against a rising dollar is the stated policy, a full anchor position is always in place (i.e., long puts, short currency futures, or short interbank forwards).

We use specific guidelines in providing this risk coverage:

1. The aggregate value of the currency hedging program will never exceed the value of the underlying equities.
2. The program will use the primary currencies for the most part (i.e., the deutsche mark, pound sterling, Swiss franc, and Japanese yen). Secondary markets used will include the Australian dollar, Canadian dollar, Irish pound, Dutch guilder, Italian lira, French franc, etc.
3. All foreign currency transactions for the program will be executed in the United States.
4. The program will never "write" futures options, due to the unlimited risk of these vehicles (although we do sell some options as synthetics, we are never "naked" short).

The argument that currency gains and losses are a "wash" in the long run is bogus, especially as modern computer technology and improved software capabilities provide the currency overlay manager with tools that were not available even four years ago. The only way that the "wash" argument can be put forward today would be if the plan sponsor or investor was indifferent to the possibility that the value of its foreign holdings could decline by 20 percent to 30 percent in dollar terms during periods of dollar strength—hardly reassuring by today's aggressive and competitive yardsticks.

THE EMERGENCE OF THE CURRENCY OVERLAY MANAGER—A FINAL THOUGHT

Sponsors have two choices regarding who should undertake foreign currency hedging. They can allow the individual managers to hedge their own currency exposure or they can hire a currency specialist. Most international equity managers, by their own admission, are not strong currency experts. International fixed-income managers are usually better equipped to hedge currency exposure (because currency variations can be a large portion of the total returns from various international bonds) — but even here, the lack of currency management expertise can be costly during periods of dollar weakness.

In the early 1980s, most hedging was conducted on an ad hoc basis, but the dollar's rise from 1980 through early 1985 led to currency losses exceeding 50 percent. This phenomenon led to the evolution of currency specialists (primarily at commercial banks) and to the trendy belief that money managers could do their own hedging. But the sharp drop in the dollar from 1985 to 1988 led to substantial interbank trading losses even though the foreign equity and bond markets were appreciating—and to the false confidence that hedging was unnecessary.

In 1988 and 1989, the dollar again spurted sharply, leaving most foreign investors, who were then unhedged, in the lurch. It became clear that programs were required to protect against a dollar rise while avoiding losses during a dollar decline. This is when a more sophisticated group of currency overlay managers surfaced. With all the intricacies associated with contemporary currency trading, the appeal of a new breed of specialist currency manager should be obvious. If nothing else, this specialist manager can take the onus of currency volatility away from the foreign equity and fixed-income managers, whose tasks are already formidable.

SUMMARY

The currency overlay approach used by Cambridge Financial Management is an active one, but with the unique features of providing enhancements and simultaneously reducing overnight risk. The primary focus of our approach is to furnish an improved way to manage foreign equity and fixed-income investment currency risk. Specifically, the approach is designed to provide institutional plan sponsors with a reliable means of reducing currency exposure. Traditionally, this risk has been managed by adjustments in the portfolio in any given country or by ad hoc decisions made by the individual managers to hedge or not. However, these remedies often prove costly and can be inconsistent with the sponsor's desired investment strategies.

The dynamic hedge is a structured investment approach, which uses foreign currency futures, options, and forwards in a consistent manner to offset the devaluation of foreign holdings due to the impact of any rise in the value of the dollar. Therefore, the primary goal is to match dollar gains using a 100 percent dollar benchmark. As such, this goal reflects a perpetual "long-dollar" anchor position using the forward markets.

A secondary goal is to contribute additional value to the international sector of the sponsor's portfolio. This goal is implemented through short-term positions in foreign currency futures and options in order to profit from periods in which a dollar retracement may take place. This secondary goal is regarded as a "value-added" enhancement.

A third goal is the minimization of risk. With our combined strategy format, the risk is always limited to the transaction costs paid for the protection (in the case of a rising dollar) and to the cost of the premiums paid for the enhancement (in the event of a precipitous fall in the dollar). The total risk is limited to the combined costs of the premiums, unlike most traditional overlay programs, where the risk can be substantial—this is a distinctive feature of our dynamic hedge approach.

If the expansion of international investing continues as evidenced by articles appearing recently in *Pensions & Investments, Institutional Investor,* and other financial publications, dynamic currency protection will be essential. The main question, then, becomes "How should it be done?" This chapter offers one contemporary solution.

NOTE

1. See Stephen L. Nesbitt, "Currency Hedging Rules for Plan Sponsors," *Financial Analysts Journal* (March–April 1991), pp. 73–81, for a discussion of the trade-offs. However, Nesbitt recommends optimal hedge ratios of less than 100 percent for his types of hedges.

14

Profiting from Diversified Managed Currency Strategies: An Investor's Perspective

Virginia R. Parker
Ferrell Capital Management

INTRODUCTION

The objective of this chapter is to explore the significant investment opportunities afforded traditional investors through managed currencies. We begin with an overview of the foreign exchange markets and the leadership that some of the major banks and investment banks have provided in their proprietary trading operations. Our discussion on benchmarks for managed currencies begins by highlighting the dynamics of trading strategies, including positioning, the role of leverage, and earning of interest on the capital investment. Next, we examine the risk and return characteristics of managed currencies using the Ferrell FX Manager Universe™. We analyze the performance of the composite, the median, and individual managers. We compare the investment results of managed currencies to traditional asset classes. We conclude by showing the benefits of adding diversified strategic currencies to traditional investments.

Foreign exchange is the world's largest, most liquid market, and it is unregulated. Over the past decade, the size of the interbank and derivative markets has grown dramatically. While interbank volume is difficult to measure accurately, estimates show that during 1992 volume at banks reached as high as $1 trillion a day and general activity is thought to be about five times the daily volume of the U.S. Treasury market, or around $600 billion a day. The total number of futures and exchange-traded options grew from 729 million contracts in 1991 to 886 million in 1992. Over 70 percent of the derivative growth occurred in non-U.S. markets. The trend is expected to continue to the point where exchanges outside the U.S. will take the lead in trading volume, perhaps as early as 1993 or 1994.

For decades, foreign exchange market making has been a major source of revenue for commercial banks. Providing liquidity and inventory to support international trade and the ever increasing volume of financial asset transfers between currencies was a source of relatively low risk profit margins. Today, customers are well informed about prices and market direction. Many dealers are willing to sliver spreads to gain market share. The niche players and the major market makers are squeezing the other participants. This fierce competition, coupled with information flow, has made the traditional business of market making considerably less profitable. More important, the risks associated with positioning for customer business are often not compensated by these narrow margins.

As a result, the most successful dealers are now focusing on three important areas for generating profits—*financial engineering* of complex customer transactions, *swaps,* and *proprietary trading.* It is the latter, generating consistently impressive earnings for a few major players, that we believe has important implications for traditional investors. The development of successful methodologies to take advantage of directional market moves and complex arbitrage opportunities can be constantly guided and controlled with sophisticated risk management techniques. The resulting consistency allows these firms to allocate a growing percentage of their equity capital to trading for their own account.[1] What is important for traditional investors is that the explosive expansion in the global markets and related derivatives provide opportunities for traders *outside* the banks and investment banks as well. In fact, over the past several years, there has been an enormous growth in the number of firms trading foreign currencies as an investment strategy. In addition to the banks and investment banks, there are three major sources for managing currencies for outside investors:

- foreign exchange advisory firms
- registered investment advisors
- commodity trading advisors

Skeptics frequently question how traders profit in a market where there are no underwriting fees for new issues, and all trading is conducted in the *zero-sum* secondary market. The answer is pure and simple. Foreign exchange markets are inundated with activity designed to facilitate asset transfers, international trade, financial transactions, hedging, and speculation. Thus, the opposite sides of a transaction are not necessarily made up of a winning trade and a losing trade. Central banks, multinational corporations, large investors, even small businesses need to exchange currencies. Many are willing to pay premiums to hedge against future exchange rate exposures. The interbank and futures markets supply the vehicles for hedging, while the speculators supply liquidity. Traders may be hedging, capturing a spread, or initiating or closing out a position. Due to different entry points and different time horizons, two traders on opposite sides of a transaction may both be profitable or unprofitable. Through the lackluster performance of some of the market makers, trading is not a *zero-sum* venture.

Information flows freely and quickly throughout the marketplace. Nevertheless, opportunities are ripe for nimble traders. Anomalies are created in a number of ways, including the inefficiencies of market-making activities in many locations (both over-the-counter and exchange-traded) and pricing that includes not only the currency value of the spot market, but also the interest rate component of the forward markets, future expectations for inflation, and the influence of correlations between markets. Although the market is complex and generally in flux, currencies tend to trend better than most other markets due to the interrelationships among the major global economies. Market efficiency cannot preclude a good trader from finding opportunities to make profits from directional or arbitrage strategies. Moreover, the efficiency is an important ally, allowing traders to commit large sums to positions.

Ferrell Capital has conducted research to explore the efficacy of currency trading as a prudent investment strategy. In our efforts to analyze the usefulness of currencies for traditional investors, we have created a performance index to provide objective analysis of the firms that trade currencies for outside clients. The index cannot provide a comprehensive overview of *all* proprietary currency trading. Among the largest players are the commercial and investment banks who trade for their own account. These institutions publish only gross trading figures that also include components of customer hedging, swapping, and market-making activities. Nonetheless, we can read published financial reports and quickly learn that a number of large money center banks and investment banks generate over $500 million annually in trading profits from currency markets alone. Moreover, as speculative trading and arbitrage have become a more important activity for these institutions, the position of speculators themselves has become a major force in the marketplace. Such was the case in the much publicized trading activity of George Soros' Quantum Fund in September 1992. For a handful of large, legendary proprietary trading operations, performance data is not made available.

Rather than be concerned about the returns produced by the dealers and large private trading operations, our study is limited to a universe of practical importance to investors. Without bias to any qualitatively selected group, we include those firms offering their trading strategies and expertise to outside clients. Our Index measures their composite performance, net of fees, as a group and the Universe shows the median performance, net of fees, of the trading firms. The results are two performance-driven indexes demonstrating that conservative investors may lower volatility and enhance total, as well as risk-adjusted, returns with currency trading added to their overall investment strategy.

Currency investing is often considered a speculative endeavor. But it is no more speculative than investing internationally. Over the past several years there has been an enormous thrust among U.S. pensions to invest internationally to gain the diversification benefits of exposure to overseas markets. Managed currencies as an investment strategy is simply the *currency* component of international investing. Strategic currency investing has several important advantages over international equity and fixed-income investments:

- Executing currency transactions is considerably more efficient and less expensive than equities and fixed income.
- There are no custody requirements, since the investor is dealing in contracts rather than deliverable securities.
- All transactions may be effected through domestic exchanges or banks, allowing the investor's assets to remain in his or her own country.
- Currency strategies may be implemented with a minimal use of capital.

TABLE 14.1   Sources of Total Return by Asset Class

FOR INTERNATIONAL EQUITY PORTFOLIOS
   Profit/loss in value of securities + dividends + change in local exchange rate
   versus investor's base currency

FOR INTERNATIONAL BOND PORTFOLIOS
   Profit/loss in value of securities + interest + change in local exchange rate
   versus investor's base currency

As shown in Table 14.1, traditional international investing has three components that make up *Total Return:* profit or loss in the value of the security, dividends or interest, and change in foreign currency translation.

Managed currencies have two of the three sources of returns of international investing:

$$\text{Interest}^2 + \text{change in the local exchange rate}$$
$$\text{versus investor's base currency}$$

In a given year, it is not unusual for half or more of the total return on an international equity or bond portfolio to be the result of the movement in the foreign exchange rate, as may be seen in Table 14.2. It is a mistake to ignore foreign currency fluctuations for traditional international portfolios. From January 1986 until January 1993, 69.6 percent of the return of the Morgan Stanley Capital International EAFE Index was due to the currency component. Studies may demonstrate that over a ten-year period the international investor was no better off for hedging. But few, if any, investment portfolios are subject to review just once every ten years. Investors must confront the currency issue. For this reason, many institutional investors have adopted overlay programs that dynamically hedge—*hedge when it seems necessary*—their foreign currency exposures. Where dynamic hedging is a *defensive* strategy, managed currencies is an *offensive* strategy, attempting to exploit the same foreign exchange movements that may help or hinder the total return of a traditional international investment portfolio.

BENCHMARKS FOR CURRENCY MANAGERS

Determining appropriate benchmarks for the trading of foreign currencies as an investment strategy is challenging, at best. Passive benchmarks have long been pension consultants' preferred perfor-

TABLE 14.2   Annual Change in Foreign Exchange Rates U.S. Dollar Versus Major Currencies[a] 1984 Through December 1992

Year	deutschemark Price	Change Percent	Japanese yen Price	Change Percent	British pound Price	Change Percent	Swiss franc Price	Change Percent	EAFE[b] Change Percent	Int'l Bonds[c] Change Percent
1984	2.2772		233.95		0.7040		2.2250			
1985	3.1835	39.8	252.20	7.8	0.8651	229	2.6310	18.2	22.0	21.6
1986	2.4570	-22.8	199.80	-20.8	0.6835	-21.0	2.0640	-21.6	19.0	18.1
1987	1.9265	-21.6	158.65	-20.6	0.6684	-2.2	1.6180	-21.6	27.5	25.6
1988	1.5905	-17.4	123.35	-22.2	0.5283	-21.0	1.2905	-20.2	-4.1	-4.4
1989	1.7725	11.4	124.95	1.3	0.5463	3.4	1.5025	16.4	-9.0	-5.8
1990	1.7170	-3.1	146.80	17.5	0.6150	12.6	1.5850	5.5	9.1	10.2
1991	1.4995	-12.7	136.20	-7.2	0.5140	-16.4	1.2785	-19.3	3.2	1.8
1992	1.5288	2.0	124.47	-8.6	0.5353	4.1	1.3632	6.6	-6.4	-7.3
1993	1.6393	7.2	125.35	0.7	0.6662	24.5	1.4800	8.6		
Change from 1984 to 1/1/93	-28.0%		-46.4%		-5.4%		-33.5%		69.6%	

[a] In this table, spot prices are quoted as of January 1 for each year in foreign currency unit per U.S. dollar. British pounds are usually quoted in U.S. dollars per British pound but are inverted here for ease of comparison.

[b] Foreign exchange component of the Morgan Stanley Capital International EAFE index, including dividends.

[c] Salomon Non–US$ World Bond Index

mance measurement for managers of traditional asset classes. For trading strategies, the construction of a *meaningful* passive index or benchmark portfolio is impossible. In fact, developing benchmarks for any type of *trading strategy* is enormously complex. The very dynamics of trading strategies require that performance be measured on the basis of *absolute returns, absolute risk,* and the *ratios* thereon. In applying benchmarks to the performance of currency managers, we must work with the information available to us and be respectful of the differences between trading strategies and management of traditional *long* investment portfolios.

The Dynamics of Trading Strategies

The dynamics of trading strategies that affect performance are the result of several important distinctions between trading strategies and traditional long investment strategies:

- ability to take long, short, and arbitrage positions
- use of leverage as both a common and important element of a trading strategy
- earning of interest on the capital base being traded—to the extent the capital base is funded

Ability to Establish Long, Short, and Arbitrage Positions

Unlike the traditional manager, who has the choice of establishing a long security position or remaining in cash, a currency manager has the flexibility to take long as well as *short* and *arbitrage* positions in the market. This flexibility in positioning means that the currency manager's performance should be independent of the traditional long market *beta,* or risk. The currency manager may position himself for a directional move—*up or down*—in one or more exchange rate relationships, or the manager may capture an anomaly between two or more price relationships and *arbitrage* the profit. Using a long, passive index as a benchmark—*a routine practice for measuring the performance of traditional managers*—is inappropriate for trading strategies. The long market performance has no direct relationship to the currency manager's performance. Applying a passive index like the Finex US Dollar Index is meaningless, since the US Dollar Index is always long the dollar against the currencies of which it is composed. An appropriate passive benchmark must have a mechanism for going short. Additionally, an index may begin and end the year near the same price while experiencing a strong trend up and back down, or vice versa, over the 12 months. Skilled traders should make easy profits given this scenario. It is naive to believe there could be meaning in measuring the performance of traders based on the beginning and ending points of a passive index. Consideration must be made for the factors that foster market opportunity or wreak havoc—*volatility, congestion, sharp, sudden reversals, and strength of trends*. A passive index based on the performance of an underlying market or composite performance of markets tends to breed mediocrity. Many traders would be forced to focus on trying to beat, or at least meet, the underlying market performance rather than relentlessly scrutinizing the markets for profitable trading opportunities. Strong benchmarks must measure trading *skill*.

The construction of a benchmark portfolio has two inherent flaws. Most currency managers are trading a diversified portfolio of currency positions, usually long or short the deutschemark, the Japanese yen, and British pound against the U.S. dollar. Some managers also include several European currencies, Canadian dollars, and Australian dollars against the U.S. dollar. Many are now trading nondollar cross rates as well. A passive benchmark portfolio would need three components:

- a selection process to determine which currencies should be included
- an allocation process among each of the currencies selected
- a mechanism for going neutral or reversing a position

A benchmark portfolio for currency trading including the three key components listed above is essentially a trading model. The first flaw is that developing a benchmark portfolio is similar to building a trading model against which currency managers would be measured. This is creating a trading *standard*. A strong benchmark portfolio would require the development of a superior trading model. The second flaw is that a benchmark portfolio, by definition, is static. Static trading systems eventually collapse as markets evolve. A benchmark portfolio should stand the test of time. Even the strongest trading models eventually experience an excessive—*30 percent or considerably more*—losing period. An appropriate benchmark portfolio should be immune to such large losses. This is the essence of the futility in developing a passive index and a benchmark portfolio for currency management. In the final analysis, it is *absolute returns* and *absolute risk* with which investors must be concerned.

Use of Leverage

Another complication for structuring a passive benchmark for foreign currency managers is that the use of leverage is both a common and important element of a trading strategy. Whether a trader is using the futures market or the interbank forward market, only a small portion of the position size represented by the contract is required as a *good faith deposit* with the clearing broker or the bank through which the transaction is effected. The requirement of a partial deposit is what creates leverage in trading accounts. Most currency investment portfolios are fully funded. The good faith deposit represents only a small portion of the actual capital allocated to the strategy. The currency manager and the investor determine the size of the *capital investment* against which positions will be traded. The typical ratio of good faith deposits to capital invested ranges from 10 percent to 20 percent (although the amount of good faith deposits is actually dictated by gross position size). Given $50 million in capital, good faith deposits would normally range from $5 million to $10 million.

Gross position size, as measured by gross foreign currency positions, may be five or more times larger than the capital base. On a given day, a portfolio with a capital base of $50 million may have gross positions of $250 million. Gross position size is constantly changing, as the relationship between the foreign currency spot, forward, and futures rates change against the base currency or cross currency rates. But what the trader and the investor are monitoring is the performance of the portfolio as measured by the profit and loss of the *capital invested.* The currency managers engineer their strategies' expected returns, expected standard deviations, and expected maximum losses to conform to the capital base against which they are trading. With most trading methodologies, the higher the ratio of good faith deposits to capital base, the more aggressive the strategy.

Leverage may be measured by the ratio of good faith deposits to account equity or the ratio of good faith deposits to gross position size. Most often in trading portfolios, leverage is referred to as the former—*ratio of good faith deposits to account equity.* Leverage is probably the most feared and misunderstood concept of trading strategies. Leverage has different meaning with different trading methodologies, instruments, and markets. In fact, it is not leverage, per se, that exposes the investor to risk.[3] *Risk is a function of the price volatility of positions held and the correlation in price movement between positions held.*[4] As with traditional investments, the best way to protect a portfolio against the price volatility of individual positions is through diversification. In structuring currency portfolios, managers must carefully monitor and respond to both *price volatility* of individual currency positions and the *correlation* between markets being traded. The best currency managers adjust gross position sizes for each market to reflect the market's current price volatility and the correlation between the markets being traded.

Tracking the daily leverage used over a broad range of currency traders becomes quite difficult unless one has actually hired the trader and is monitoring the portfolio positions on a daily basis. Most often, as one is conducting a search for one or more currency traders, the investor is dependent upon the currency trader to release information of the trader's degree of leverage. The most adroit traders increase leverage when market volatility, and therefore risk, is low and decrease leverage when market volatility, and therefore risk, is high. Two benchmarks that are good measures of a trader's skill in navigating the markets are the *maximum peak-to-trough loss*[5] in the performance record and the *compounded annual return divided by the maximum peak-to-trough loss.*

Earning Interest on the Capital Base

In currency trading portfolios, like in all trading portfolios, 100 percent of portfolio assets are kept in cash instruments. In purchasing a position, whether in the futures or interbank market, good faith deposits are typically held in Treasury bills with the clearing firm. That portion of the portfolio in excess of good faith deposits is also earning interest, either through investments in Treasury bills, money market, or other short-term instruments. Firms reporting trading performance will often include profits from these cash balances. An appropriate risk-adjusted benchmark for currency managers' performance is the *Sharpe ratio,*[6] because this measure considers the risk-free alternative. The trader always has the choice of going to a cash position. The Sharpe ratio is an excellent combination of a cash and volatility benchmark measurement.

THE FERRELL FX MANAGER UNIVERSE

The above distinctions between trading strategies and traditional *long only* investment strategies make the construction of relevant passive benchmarks and benchmark portfolios for trading strategies meaningless. We believe that the most effective method for judging an individual firm's success in trading foreign currencies is to measure the firm's performance over a wide range of variables and to compare the results with a representative universe of firms trading foreign currencies for outside investors. Our analysis of benchmarks and performance for foreign currency traders will rely on information we have compiled for the Ferrell FX Manager Universe[TM].

The Ferrell FX Manager Universe[TM] is a universe of 30 managed currency programs available to outside investors. The Universe includes foreign exchange advisory firms, registered investment advisors, and commodity trading advisors located in the United States, the United Kingdom, Switzerland, and Ireland. The Universe includes firms that are technical, fundamental, and quantitative in their approach to currency trading.[7] Our purpose in constructing the Universe was to examine the performance characteristics of managed currencies from January 1987 through December 1992. The Universe tracks the actual real-time monthly performance of each of the 30 programs, net of all fees and expenses. Each program's monthly performance is added to the Universe upon commencement of trading client assets.[8] Figure 14.1 shows the number of firms participating in the Universe from January 1987 through December 1992. Collectively, the firms manage over $6.16 billion in currency assets. We measure assets under management using the *equity base* against which the firms are trading for their clients.[9] Figure 14.2 shows the growth in currency assets under management for the Ferrell FX Manager Universe[TM] over the same time period. Currency assets under management represented in the Universe have grown an impressive 63 percent from December 1991 until December 1992 as investors have committed more funds to strategic currency investing.

The Ferrell FX Indexes

From the Universe, we have developed two indexes to serve as a source of benchmarks for tracking the performance of managed currencies:

FIGURE 14.1   Ferrell FX Manager Universe Historical Participation 1987–1992

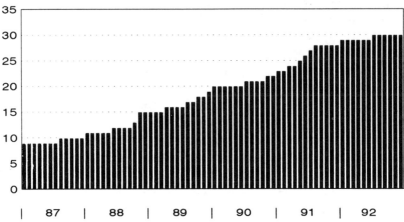

Chart I illustrates the growth in participation in the Ferrell FX Manager Universe from January 1987 through December 1992. The Universe originated with 9 currency programs and at year end, 1992, had grown to a total of 30 participating programs.

- The Ferrell FX Manager Universe™ median performance is an index that serves as a benchmark source for individual currency managers.
- The Ferrell FX Index™ is a benchmark source for multi-advisor currency portfolios.

Universe Analysis

The Ferrell FX Manager Universe™ results include the monthly performance of a representative currency portfolio or composite of currency portfolios, net of fees and expenses, and including interest, for each currency advisor. In applying universe analysis we have ranked each of the 30 currency programs from highest to lowest performance and removed the top and bottom 5 percent to preclude outlier bias. The remaining programs in the Universe are divided into first through fourth quartiles. These quartiles represent the top, second, third, and bottom 25 percent of performance. The 50th percentile, also representing the top of the third quartile, is the *median* performance of the currency programs. The median represents the middle performance, with half the programs performing above and half below. The median performer will change

**FIGURE 14.2   Ferrell FX Manager Universe Annual Growth
in Currency Assets Under Management, 1987–1992**

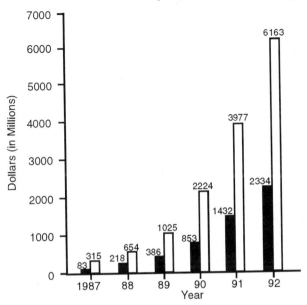

■ Assets specifically tracked by Ferrell FX Indexes.

□ Includes pure currency programs, currency componenet of
   more diversified programs, and currency overlay programs.

Chart II illustrates the annual growth in dollars in currency asstes under management in the Ferrell FX Index and the more broadly defined currency programs. Over the six year period, currency assets grew by 27 times in the Ferrell Index and by 186 times in the more expansive currency programs.

when a particular variable is measured over different time horizons. One should also note that it is impossible to always invest in the median performance, because one cannot predict at the beginning of the time period which firm will have been the median performer by the end of the time period.

Nevertheless, the median performance of the Ferrell FX Manager Universe™ provides a useful benchmark for individual currency managers. By examining a number of performance variables over different time horizons, we may analyze an individual firm's ranking against a universe of firms trading the same markets and improve our understanding of the risk and return characteristics of currency managers individually and as a group. We apply universe analysis over monthly, quarterly, and annual periods.[10]

The Ferrell FX Index

The Ferrell FX Index™ is equally weighted and represents the *average* performance of the 30 currency programs comprising the Ferrell FX Manager Universe™. We track the Ferrell FX Index™ performance from January 1987 through December 1992. Because the Index represents the composite performance of the 30 Universe programs, it is an appropriate benchmark for *multimanager* currency portfolios. The Ferrell FX Index's consistent outperformance of the Ferrell FX Manager Universe™ median supports our conviction that a managed currency investment strategy should be *diversified* among several currency managers. The rolling 12-month performance for the Ferrell FX Index™ ranges from a high of 82.8 percent to a low of 0.8 percent. This compares favorably to the S&P 500, with a high and low rolling 12-month return of 34 percent and –9 percent, and to the Morgan Stanley Capital International EAFE Index with a high rolling of return of 22 percent and a low of –22. A summary of the rolling 12-month and 3-month returns is found in Figures 14.3 and 14.4. The Ferrell FX Index™ results[11] outperform those of the Median each year

FIGURE 14.3   Ferrell FX Index Rolling 12 Month Compound Returns January 1987–December 1992

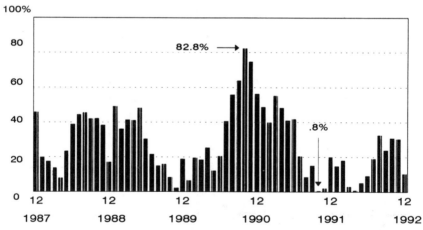

Chart III shows the rolling twelve month returns for the Ferrell FX Index from January 1987 through December 1992. The lowest 12 month return is .8% comparing very favorably to the S&P 500 and EAFE at –18% and –29%, respectively. The "high" rolling return of 82.8% for the Index is also substantially above other asset classes, 39% for the S&P 500 and 30% for EAFE.

**FIGURE 14.4 Ferrell FX Index Rolling Annual and Quarterly Return
Comparison by Asset Class
January 1987–December 1992**

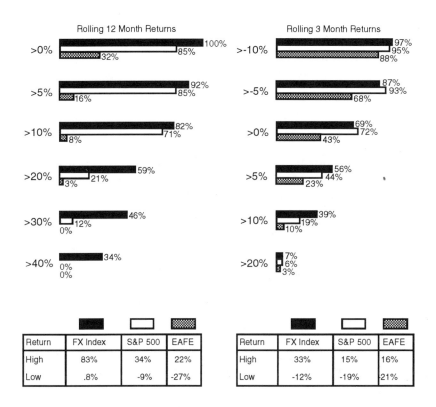

Chart IV illustrates what percent of time both rolling annual and quarterly returns of the FX Index, the S%P 500, and EAFE exceed the specified percentage barriers over the period January 1987 through December 1992. It is interesting to note that in all but two cases, the FX Index returns exceed those of both the S&P 500 and EAFE by a minimum of 5 percentage points and a maximum of 35 percentage points. In analyzing rolling 12 month returns, both the high and low for the FX Index performed above the 0% level, with the high standing 44 percentage points above the high of the S&P 500. While the FX Index's low for the rolling 3 month returns was –11%, it still remained substantially above the low returns for both the S&P 500 and EAFE.

from 1987 through 1992, except 1988. The reason for the outperformance of the Index is the diversification effect of the composite. Over the six-year period from January 1987 through December 1992, the compounded annual return of the FX Index is 27.4 percent, compared to 17.7 percent of the Universe median.

APPLYING MODERN PORTFOLIO THEORY TO MANAGED CURRENCIES

Asset allocation is the single most important determinant of performance for any investment portfolio. Through the asset allocation process, one carefully structures portfolios to maximize expected returns and minimize volatility, selecting the risk/reward point most appropriate for the investor's rate of return objective and risk profile.[12] The same principles that apply to modern portfolio theory for traditional investments apply to managed currencies. Currency investing diversified across managers, markets, and trading styles increases returns and lowers volatility. Unlike traditional long investment portfolios, currency portfolios may be profitable regardless of market direction and volatility, throughout various stages of economic, political, and market cycles.

Similar to traditional investment strategies, three levels of diversification benefit the investor. First, individual managers diversify across currencies, reducing the risk of the individual portfolio of currency positions. Next, the investor may diversify across managers and styles with low correlation, providing another layer of diversification for the overall currency strategy. Finally, the diversified currency program's lack of correlation to traditional asset classes increases the expected return and reduces expected risk of an overall investment portfolio. Currency managers have an enormous advantage over portfolio managers who apply traditional long investment strategies. Through establishing long *or* short positions, currency managers may profit in declining as well as rising markets. The flexibility to profit from either market direction severs the portfolio's link to traditional benchmark performance. Thus, managed currencies allow both internal and external diversification for the investor:

- The correlation between trading methodologies is usually quite low, creating opportunity for significant diversification within a multimanager currency portfolio.[13]
- The correlation between the performance of managed currencies and traditional equity and fixed-income securities is also quite low, creating powerful diversification opportunities for existing domestic and international portfolios.

To be consistently profitable, managed currencies must include a diversified combination of strategies. Figure 14.5

FIGURE 14.5   Ferrell FX Manager Universe 1987–1992

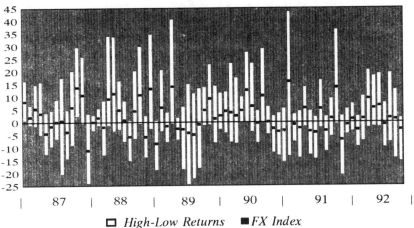

☐ *High-Low Returns*   ■*FX Index*

Chart V represents the performance range, highest to lowest, reported by the Ferrell FX
Manager Universe participants, and the performance of the Ferrell FX Index marked by the
point on the range. Results are illustrated on a monthly basis from January 1987 through
December 1992.

demonstrates the diversification benefits from using multiple
managers for strategic currency investing. The chart shows the
range of highest to lowest performance for the Universe on a
monthly return basis. The portion of the range above the zero line
represents positive performance; the portion of the range below
the zero line represents negative monthly performance. The point
marked with a box on each range represents the composite performance of the Ferrell FX Index™. Although the worst performer in
the Universe has negative returns in all but 2 of 72 months, or 97
percent of the monthly observations, the composite is positive for
24 months, or 61 percent of the monthly observations.

Investors in managed currencies are seeking attractive *absolute*
returns that have little or no correlation to their current investments.
As an investor considers whether managed currencies would be an
appropriate diversification tool for his or her portfolio, the absolute
return benchmarks of the currency manager should also be compared to those of the traditional asset classes. In comparing the
results of the FX Index to the S&P 500 from January 1987 through
December 1992 in Table 14.3, the Index outperformed the S&P 500
four out of six years. The Index's compounded annual return of 27.4
percent far surpassed that of the S&P 500's 13.6 percent.

TABLE 14.3   Ferrell FX Manager Index™ Versus
S&P 500 Comparison of Annual Returns
January 1987 Through December 1992

Year	FX Index (Percent)	S&P 500 (Percent)	Outperformance
1987	42.2	5.3	FX Index
1988	17.4	16.6	FX Index
1989	19.2	31.6	S&P 500
1990	56.7	-3.1	FX Index
1991	20.3	30.7	S&P 500
1992	10.8	7.6	FX Index
Compounded Return 1987- December 1992	27.4%	13.6%	FX Index

For this study, we will also compare the Ferrell FX Manager Universe™ and Ferrell FX Index™ results with those of the S&P 500, EAFE, the Shearson Lehman Corporate Bond Index, and the Salomon Non-US$ World Bond Index, and the U.S. Dollar Index, as summarized in Table 14.4. Because the Index consistently outperforms the Universe median, our discussion focuses on comparing the Index results with those of traditional asset classes:

- *Compounded Annual Return.* Examining the compounded annual returns from January 1987 through December 1992, the FX Index significantly outperforms the traditional asset classes, delivering a 27.4 percent return. This compares quite favorably to 13.6 percent for the S&P 500, 5.2 percent for EAFE, 9.9 percent for the Lehman Corporate Bond Index, 12.9 percent for the Salomon Non-US$ World Bond Index, and –1.2 percent for the Finex U.S. Dollar Index.
- *Standard Deviation.* The volatility of the FX Index is 21.1 percent. This is higher than the S&P 500 at 17.5 percent, but as seen above, the returns of the FX Index are considerably higher to compensate for the additional volatility risk. The FX Index is slightly higher than the 20.7 percent standard deviation of EAFE. The domestic and international bond indexes have lower volatilities at 5.0 percent and 12.1 percent, respectively.
- *Sharpe Ratio.* The Sharpe ratio of the FX Index, 0.9, is the highest of all asset classes examined over the six-year peri-

od. The next highest ratios are from the bond indexes—the
Lehman Corporate Bond Index at 0.7 and the Salomon
Non-US$ World Bond Index at 0.6. The equity indexes and
the U.S. Dollar Index are the low performers at 0.5 for the
S&P 500, 0.1 for EAFE, and –0.4 for the Dollar Index.

- *Maximum Monthly Loss*. The lowest maximum monthly
  loss over the period was the domestic bond index at 3.3
  percent, followed by the U.S. Dollar Index at 5.9 percent,
  international bonds at 6 percent, and the FX Index at 11.1
  percent. The largest monthly losses were in the S&P 500
  and EAFE, at 21.5 percent and 14.0 percent, respectively.
- *Maximum Peak-to-Trough Loss*. The FX Index's maximum
  peak-to-trough was 14.7 percent, comparing very favorably to EAFE and the S&P 500 at 30.6 percent and 29.6 percent, respectively. The Lehman Corporate Bond Index had
  the lowest peak-to-trough loss at 6.3 percent.

**FIGURE 14.6   Growth of $1,000 by Asset Class
January 1987 through December 1992**

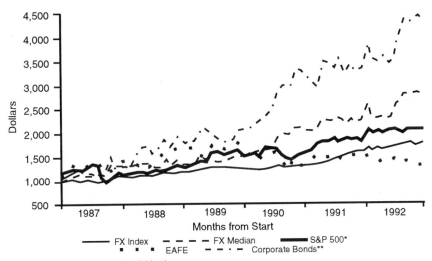

* Adjusted to include dividends
** Merrill Lynch Corporate Master Bond Index

Chart VI represents the growth of a hypothetical $1000 investment by asset class. The out-
performance of the Index over the median performance of the Ferrell FX Manager Universe
supports the conviction that over time, multi-advisor managed currency portfolios are
superior to those dependent on one strategy.

TABLE 14.4 The Ferrell FX Manager Universe™ Median and Index Performance January 1987 Through December 1992

	1-yr Return	Compounded Annual Return	Standard Deviation	Sharpe Ratio	Max. Monthly Loss	Max. Peak-to-Trough Loss	Percentage Profitable Periods
1987							
FX Index	46.2	46.2	19.5	1.5	-4.4	8.8	75.0
FX Median	31.9	36.3	43.3	1.3	-10.1	16.2	66.7
S&P 500	5.3	5.3	30.6	0.1	-21.5	29.6	66.7
EAFE	24.9	24.9	23.9	0.7	-14.0	15.3	66.7
Bonds	2.6	2.6	6.8	-0.5	-3.3	6.3	50.0
Int'l Bonds	35.2	35.2	15.1	1.5	-3.6	7.5	66.7
U.S.$ Index	-17.7	-17.7	10.3	-1.0	-5.9	17.7	33.3
1988							
FX Index	17.4	31.0	24.3	0.5	-11.1	11.1	66.7
FX Median	18.1	25.0	51.2	0.5	-12.6	20.4	56.4
S&P 500	16.6	10.8	10.2	0.9	-3.6	3.8	66.7
EAFE	28.6	26.8	15.8	1.1	-6.5	9.0	75.0
Bonds	9.2	5.8	5.4	0.4	-1.0	2.1	58.3
Int'l Bonds	2.4	17.6	12.5	-0.3	-5.5	9.5	41.7
U.S.$ Index	6.9	-6.2	10.5	0.0	-3.9	8.1	58.3
1989							
FX Index	19.2	26.9	26.2	0.5	-8.7	14.7	41.7
FX Median	13.2	10.3	61.5	.4	-10.3	16.8	58.3
S&P 500	31.6	17.3	12.6	1.5	-2.6	2.6	66.7
EAFE	10.8	21.2	17.6	0.2	-5.4	7.9	58.3
Bonds	14.1	8.5	4.6	1.2	-1.1	1.1	83.3

TABLE 14.4 (continued)

	1-yr Return	Compounded Annual Return	Standard Deviation	Sharpe Ratio	Max. Monthly Loss	Max. Peak-to-Trough Loss	Percentage Profitable Periods
Int'l Bonds	-3.4	10.1	12.7	-0.9	-6.0	10.7	58.3
U.S.$ Index	3.2	-3.2	12.1	-0.3	-4.0	7.6	41.7
1990							
FX Index	56.7	33.8	15.6	2.1	-2.5	2.6	75.0
FX Median	50.0	35.5	40.9	1.3	-7.7	8.6	75.0
S&P 500	-3.1	11.9	18.2	-0.5	-9.2	14.5	41.7
EAFE	-23.2	8.1	30.1	-1.0	-13.9	30.6	33.3
Bonds	7.1	8.1	5.0	-0.1	-1.6	1.9	75.0
Int'l Bonds	15.3	11.4	10.2	0.7	-3.1	6.2	66.7
U.S.$ Index	-12.2	-5.5	7.1	-1.0	-3.6	12.7	25.0
1991							
FX Index	20.3	31.0	25.3	0.6	-4.5	7.9	41.7
FX Median	19.3	20.4	40.6	.5	-8.6	14.8	50.0
S&P 500	30.7	15.4	15.8	1.3	-4.6	4.6	75.0
EAFE	12.5	9.0	18.5	0.4	-7.3	11.0	66.7
Bonds	18.5	10.2	2.9	3.8	-0.0	0.0	91.7
Int'l Bonds	18.9	12.9	8.6	1.3	-3.1	3.4	66.7
U.S.$ Index	8.2	-2.9	10.3	0.3	-3.2	7.5	41.7
1992							
FX Index	10.8	27.4	15.9	0.5	-7.6	9.8	58.3
FX Median	9.7	18.6	23.2	0.3	-8.2	11.9	58.3
S&P 500	7.6	14.1	17.2	0.6	-21.5	30.6	63.9
EAFE	-11.9	5.2	14.6	-1.0	-6.6	13.2	41.7

TABLE 14.4 *(continued)*

	1-yr Return	Compounded Annual Return	Standard Deviation	Sharpe Ratio	Max. Monthly Loss	Max. Peak-to-Trough Loss	Percentage Profitable Periods
Bonds	8.7	9.9	4.8	1.0	−2.1	2.1	75.0
Int'l Bonds	4.6	11.5	9.8	0.1	−3.6	6.3	50.0
U.S.$ Index	7.7	−1.2	11.6	0.4	−4.0	12.4	58.3
1987–1992							
FX Index	27.4	27.4	21.1	0.9	−11.1	14.7	59.7
FX Median	18.6	17.7	14.6	0.9	−7.5	9.9	66.7
S&P 500	13.6	13.6	17.5	0.5	−21.5	29.6	62.3
EAFE	5.2	5.2	20.7	0.1	−14.0	30.6	56.9
Bonds	9.9	9.9	5.0	0.7	−3.3	6.3	71.6
Int'l Bonds	12.9	12.9	12.1	0.6	−6.0	12.6	60.0
U.S.$ Index	−1.2	−1.2	10.6	−0.4	−5.9	21.8	43.1

THE PERFORMANCE RESULTS OF INDIVIDUAL CURRENCY MANAGERS

Firms specializing in managed currencies as an investment strategy have had mixed success in their ability to deliver consistently attractive results to their clients. Nevertheless, there are a few firms who consistently outperform the Ferrell FX Universe™ median performance. We examine the performance of the 30 firms comprising the Universe over a broad range of performance measurements, including:

Absolute Returns
- Compounded annual return
- High-rolling quarterly return
- Low-rolling quarterly return
- High-rolling 12-month return
- Low-rolling 12-month return

Absolute Risk
- Maximum peak-to-trough loss
- Standard deviation of monthly returns
- Probability of 35 percent peak-to-trough loss

Risk-Adjusted Returns
- Sharpe ratio
- Annualized return/maximum peak-to-trough loss

We have included a summary of the Ferrell FX Manager Universe by trading firm in Table 14.5 on the following three pages.

CONCLUSION

We believe there is objective evidence that investing in managed currencies is a profitable venture. Strategic currency investing provides important diversification benefits to the investor. The volatile trading performance of individual managers, as seen in the median performance of the Ferrell FX Universe™, may be mitigated by careful diversification and disciplined risk management.

TABLE 14.5   FERRELL FX Manager Universe Benchmark Comparisons

Advisor	Pct Perform > 1st Qrtl	Rank 1st	2nd Quartile	Pct Perform > Median	Rank 2nd	Total Quarters	Quarters Losses > -10	Pct. Qtrs. Losses > -10	Largest Quarterly Loss	Rank Largest Qtr. Loss
J	41.7%	23	12	50.0%	14	24	7	29.2%	30.7	26
R	29.2%	17	11	45.8%	9	24	5	20.8%	50.6	30
L	36.8%	21	12	63.2%	25	19	5	26.3%	28.4	25
E	33.3%	20	3	33.3%	6	9	1	11.1%	15.1	20
Y	47.1%	26	10	58.8%	22	17	3	17.6%	43.2	29
D	na	1	na	na	1	na	0	na	na	1
G	20.8%	12	11	45.8%	10	24	3	12.5%	11.4	13
Z	45.8%	25	14	58.3%	21	24	6	25.0%	39.1	27
I	33.3%	19	13	54.2%	18	24	6	25.0%	21.6	23
C	31.8%	18	12	54.5%	19	22	4	18.2%	27.5	24
A	28.6%	15	2	28.6%	5	7	0	0.0%	12.9	18
F	45.8%	24	18	75.0%	29	24	4	16.7%	42	28
O	8.3%	6	3	12.5%	2	24	6	25.0%	5.7	8
X	0.0%	4	1	16.7%	4	6	0	0.0%	9.5	12
V	17.6%	9	8	47.1%	12	17	1	5.9%	14.2	19
U	0.0%	3	4	16.7%	3	24	0	0.0%	0.0	2
B	23.1%	14	6	46.2%	11	13	1	7.7%	11.9	16
Q	41.7%	22	6	50.0%	13	12	2	16.7%	21.1	22
W	29.2%	16	13	54.2%	17	24	1	4.2%	12.8	17
CC	8.3%	5	12	50.0%	16	24	0	0.0%	6.3	9
N	13.3%	7	6	40.0%	8	15	0	0.0%	4.1	7
DD	0.0%	2	9	37.5%	7	24	0	0.0%	1.0	4
M	17.6%	10	10	58.8%	23	17	0	0.0%	7.7	10
H	20.0%	11	5	50.0%	15	10	0	0.0%	3.5	6
T	23.1%	13	9	69.2%	26	13	0	0.0%	9.1	11
K	50.0%	28	10	71.4%	27	14	1	7.1%	18.1	21
BB	14.3%	8	4	57.1%	20	7	0	0.0%	2.5	5

TABLE 14.5 *(continued)*

Advisor	Pct Perform > 1st Qrtl	Rank 1st	2nd Quartile	Pct Perform > Median	Rank High	Rank 2nd	Total Quarters	Rank Low	Quarters Losses > -10	Pct. Qtrs. Losses > -10	Largest Quarterly Loss	Rank Largest Qtr. Loss
S	50.0%	29	5	62.5%	29	24	8	24	1	na	11.8	15
AA	100.0%	30	3	100.0%	24	30	3	30	0	0.0%	0.3	3
P	50.0%	27	6	75.0%	27	28	8	23	1	12.5%	11.5	14

Advisor	Probability of 35% Loss	Rank Prob.	High-Rolling 3-Month (%)	Rank High	Low-Rolling 3-Month (%)	Rank Low	High-Rolling 12-Month (%)	Rank High	Low-Rolling 12-Month (%)	Rank Low	Number of Months of Record	Quarterly 1st Quartile Perform
J	26.13	28	99.40	29	-37.20	24	416.90	30	-52.70	28	72	10
R	14.22	24	70.20	24	-50.60	30	133.30	25	-48.50	27	72	7
L	24.12	27	74.90	27	-32.30	23	195.00	27	-33.60	26	56	7
E	18.74	25	63.90	22	-39.20	26	49.40	12	-7.60	15	26	3
Y	22.88	26	64.30	23	-43.40	29	195.70	28	-32.60	25	50	8
D	100.00	30	0.10	1	-6.40	5	na	2	na	30	6	na
G	10.26	21	35.00	16	-18.80	19	72.20	16	-31.50	24	72	5
Z	13.67	23	79.30	28	-39.00	25	144.80	26	-25.80	22	72	11
I	8.88	20	46.80	19	-24.50	22	127.80	24	-16.90	18	72	8
C	11.96	22	142.50	30	-40.60	27	311.40	29	-30.90	23	65	7
A	30.38	29	31.20	14	-16.60	16	45.80	11	-13.10	16	19	2
F	6.72	18	70.90	25	-42.10	28	122.80	23	-17.10	20	72	11
O	0.24	12	10.40	5	-9.40	11	4.50	3	1.80	5	17	2
X	0.60	13	7.50	3	-9.50	12	5.90	4	-3.50	9	18	0
V	6.29	17	37.90	17	-16.80	17	71.10	15	-18.90	21	39	3
U	0.14	11	15.90	8	-9.30	10	26.60	7	-6.90	13	72	0
B	0.08	10	16.60	9	-12.00	15	42.00	10	-13.40	17	37	3
Q	7.26	19	62.70	21	-22.00	21	106.90	22	-2.20	8	36	5
W	1.58	15	71.00	26	-21.60	20	106.50	21	-17.00	19	72	7
CC	0.00	3	18.70	11	-7.40	6	40.70	9	-3.60	10	72	2

TABLE 14.5 *(continued)*

Advisor	Probability of 35% Loss	Rank Prob.	High-Rolling 3-Month (%)	Rank High	Low-Rolling 3-Month (%)	Rank Low	High-Rolling 12-Month (%)	Rank High	Low-Rolling 12-Month (%)	Rank Low	Number of Months of Record	Quarterly 1st Quartile Perform
N	0.04	9	33.10	15	-7.60	7	76.00	17	-7.10	14	45	2
DD	0.00	5	9.00	4	-1.30	2	17.80	5	1.10	7	72	0
M	0.00	1	17.20	10	-7.70	8	53.10	13	-6.50	12	50	3
H	0.00	4	6.60	2	-6.20	4	20.80	6	3.30	4	30	2
T	0.02	8	31.10	13	-9.10	9	91.40	19	-4.70	11	39	3
K	1.67	16	40.80	18	-18.10	18	99.20	20	1.20	6	40	7
BB	0.00	2	12.30	6	-3.20	3	31.80	8	12.30	2	20	1
S	0.01	7	28.70	12	-11.80	14	57.80	14	8.90	3	24	4
AA	0.00	6	14.30	7	-0.30	1	na	1	na	29	8	3
P	0.80	14	54.80	20	-11.50	13	90.60	18	12.90	1	22	4

Advisor	Comp. Return (%)	Strength	Max DD (%)	Std. Dev. (%)	Rank SD	Return/ Std. Div.	Rank CR/SD	Return/ Max DD	Rank Ret/MD	% of Periods with Gain
J	13.10	100.0%	58.86	44.82	24	0.29	27	0.22	28	54.17
R	17.71	100.0%	55.25	39.05	21	0.45	23	0.32	26	58.33
L	19.20	77.8%	47.17	49.93	27	0.38	25	0.41	23	51.79
E	6.38	36.1%	40.44	53.31	29	0.12	29	0.16	29	53.85
Y	24.75	69.4%	47.31	53.20	28	0.47	22	0.52	20	54.00
D	-12.15	8.3%	6.41	7.29	3	-1.67	30	-1.90	30	16.67
G	12.21	100.0%	32.70	27.51	14	0.44	24	0.37	24	50.00
Z	34.31	100.0%	40.28	47.52	26	0.72	17	0.85	18	59.72
I	25.20	100.0%	39.29	40.09	22	0.63	19	0.64	19	61.11
C	45.09	90.3%	47.94	58.56	30	0.77	15	0.94	15	50.77
A	8.39	26.4%	24.26	34.98	19	0.24	28	0.35	25	42.11
F	40.53	100.0%	43.65	40.61	23	1.00	12	0.93	16	58.33
O	5.15	23.6%	11.06	9.86	6	0.52	21	0.47	22	64.71

TABLE 14.5 *(continued)*

Advisor	Comp. Return (%)	Strength	Max DD (%)	Std. Dev. (%)	Rank SD	Return / Std. Div.	Rank CR/SD	Return / Max DD	Rank Ret/MD	% of Periods with Gain
X	3.54	25.0%	11.31	9.68	5	0.37	26	0.31	27	72.22
V	26.01	54.2%	20.05	36.36	20	0.72	18	1.30	13	52.94
U	5.70	100.0%	11.82	9.60	4	0.59	20	0.48	21	52.78
B	15.49	51.4%	17.69	14.82	11	1.05	11	0.88	17	67.57
Q	34.19	50.0%	27.88	45.32	25	0.75	16	1.23	14	52.78
W	29.65	100.0%	21.56	31.43	17	0.94	13	1.38	11	56.94
CC	12.96	100.0%	9.49	10.51	7	1.23	10	1.37	12	61.11
N	21.71	62.5%	9.22	27.68	15	0.78	14	2.35	7	55.56
DD	7.78	100.0%	2.33	3.22	1	2.42	2	3.34	4	84.72
M	18.34	69.4%	8.16	10.80	8	1.70	4	2.25	8	62.00
H	12.96	41.7%	6.23	5.37	2	2.41	3	2.08	9	83.33
T	28.19	54.2%	11.86	21.27	12	1.33	8	2.38	6	69.23
K	41.51	55.6%	23.67	32.22	18	1.29	9	1.75	10	63.41
BB	17.14	27.8%	3.18	10.98	9	1.56	5	5.39	2	65.00
S	35.08	33.3%	13.55	23.35	13	1.50	6	2.59	5	70.83
AA	31.09	11.1%	1.59	11.58	10	2.68	1	19.55	1	75.00
P	45.70	30.6%	13.44	30.97	16	1.48	7	3.40	3	54.55

**TABLE 14.6   Portfolio Comparison January 1987
Through December 1992**

Investment	Balanced Portfolio	Including Managed Currencies[a]
S&P 500	60%	50%
Bonds	40	40
Ferrell FX IndexTM	0	10
Rate of Return (%)	12.5	14.3
Standard Deviation (%)	11.8	10.1
Maximum Peak-to-Trough Loss (%)	19.6	15.1

[a]As represented by the Ferrell FX Index[TM]
[b]Shearson Lehman Corporate Bond Index

The compounded returns of the Ferrell FX Index[TM], representing a diversified portfolio of currency managers, are higher than those of the traditional asset classes. Diversified managed currency strategies allow investors to improve the returns of a traditional investment portfolio while reducing volatility (see Table 14.6).

Since currency trading generally includes long and short dollar exposures and cross-rate positioning and arbitrage, the results from this activity do not correlate with traditional equity and fixed-income investments. By adding managed currencies to a traditional balanced account, the portfolio's total return would have increased by 1.8 percent while its standard deviation would have decreased by 1.7 percent, and its maximum peak-to-trough loss would have decreased by 4.5 percent. Unlike many nontraditional investment strategies, currency trading is very liquid. Investment capital may be expanded or contracted without disruption to the market or trading performance.

NOTES

1. P. Bernstein, *Capital Ideas* (New York: Free Press, 1992) provides an excellent history of proprietary trading on Wall Street.
2. The investor will earn interest on his or her capital invested to the extent the capital base is funded. For trading accounts, portfolio assets always remain in cash.
3. Other sources of risk include liquidity, counterparty, and sovereign.
4. For example, a convergence strategy capturing interest rage differentials between currencies can support much higher leverage, under most market conditions, than an technical trend-following strategy.

5. *Maximum peak-to-trough* loss refers to the maximum percentage loss in the value of an investor's NAV. In analyzing the performance of an individual trading firm or a multi-advisor trading portfolio, one must examine the "winning" versus "losing" periods. One must examine not only the size of losses but also the frequency and duration to recovery.

6. The Sharpe ratio is calculated as follows: (investment return – risk-free rate)/standard deviation of investment.

7. *Technical strategies* use hindsight to forecast behavior. These strategies track internal market dynamics, including pattern recognition, price momentum, volume, moving averages, stochastics, and oscillators. The most common technical strategies are technical trend-following. *Fundamental strategies* are anticipatory. They evaluate external market influences, including supply and demand, interest rates, economic data, and market psychology. *Quantitative strategies* are contrarian and usually apply econometric models to determine when markets are over- or undervalued.

8. The Universe does not include extracted records where currency trades have been separated from a more diverse portfolio to create a "currency only" track record for the period preceding the firm's managing of a "currency only" program.

9. *Gross position* size would approximate $30 billion for the Universe of trading firms.

10. See Appendix I at the end of this chapter for the Universe Bar Charts summarizing Universe returns over the annual, quarterly, and monthly periods from January 1987 through December 1993.

11. Including return, standard deviation, Sharpe ratio, maximum monthly loss, and maximum peak-to-trough loss.

12. Markowitz, Harry, "Portfolio Selection," *The Journal of Finance, 7* (March 1952), pp. 77–91.

13. See Appendix II at the end of this chapter for the Correlation Matrix of managers composing the Ferrell FX Manager Universe™. The highest correlations are between those firms applying a technical trend-following approach.

14. Although quantitative analysis is quite important in judging the strength of an individual firm, appropriate analysis must also include a thorough investigation of the qualitative strengths and weaknesses of an organization and its performance history.

APPENDIX I: FERRELL FX MANAGER UNIVERSE™ STATISTICAL INFORMATION

FIGURE 14.7 Ferrell FX Manager Universe Annualized Total Return

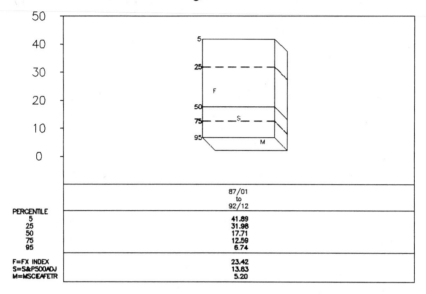

PERCENTILE	87/01 to 92/12
5	41.89
25	31.98
50	17.71
75	12.59
95	6.74
F=FX INDEX	23.42
S=S&P500ADJ	13.63
M=MSCIEAFETR	5.20

FIGURE 14.8 Ferrell FX Manager Universe Annualized Sharpe Ratio

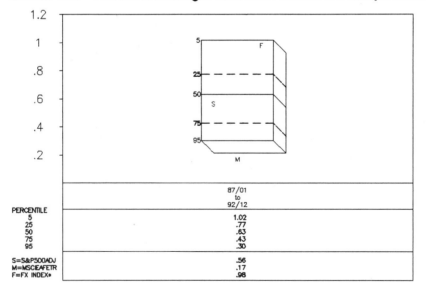

PERCENTILE	87/01 to 92/12
5	1.02
25	.77
50	.63
75	.43
95	.30
S=S&P500ADJ	.56
M=MSCIEAFETR	.17
F=FX INDEX*	.98

**FIGURE 14.9   Ferrell FX Manager Universe
Maximum One Period Loss**

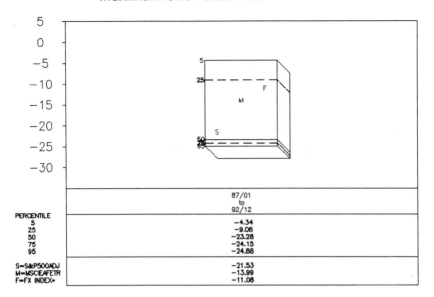

PERCENTILE	87/01 to 92/12
5	−4.34
25	−9.06
50	−23.28
75	−24.15
95	−24.88
S=S&P500ADJ	−21.53
M=MSCIEAFETR	−13.99
F=FX INDEX•	−11.08

**FIGURE 14.10   Ferrell FX Manager Universe
Maximum Capital Drawdown**

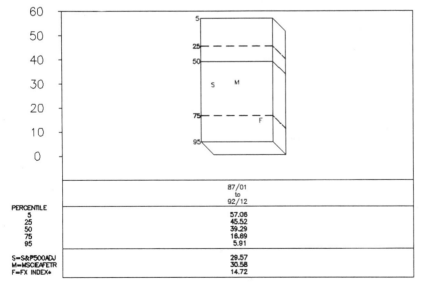

PERCENTILE	87/01 to 92/12
5	57.06
25	45.52
50	39.29
75	18.69
95	5.91
S=S&P500ADJ	29.57
M=MSCIEAFETR	30.58
F=FX INDEX•	14.72

FIGURE 14.11 **Ferrell FX Manager Universe**
Percent of Periods with Positive Gain

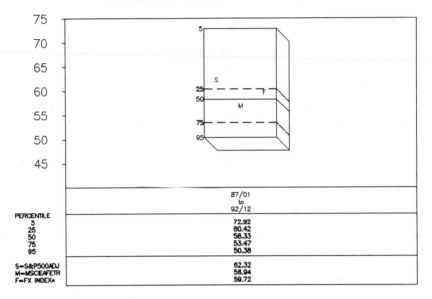

PERCENTILE	87/01 to 92/12
5	72.92
25	60.42
50	58.33
75	53.47
95	50.38
S=S&P500ADJ	62.32
M=MSCIEAFETR	56.94
F=FX INDEX*	59.72

FIGURE 14.12 **Ferrell FX Manager Universe**
Annualized Total Return

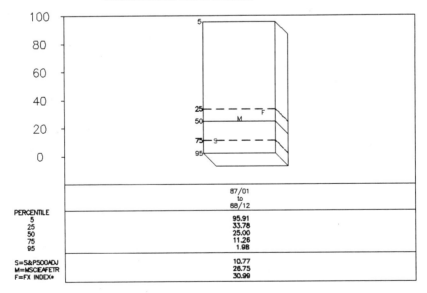

PERCENTILE	87/01 to 88/12
5	95.91
25	33.78
50	25.00
75	11.26
95	1.98
S=S&P500ADJ	10.77
M=MSCIEAFETR	26.75
F=FX INDEX*	30.99

**FIGURE 14.13   Ferrell FX Manager Universe
Annualized Total Return**

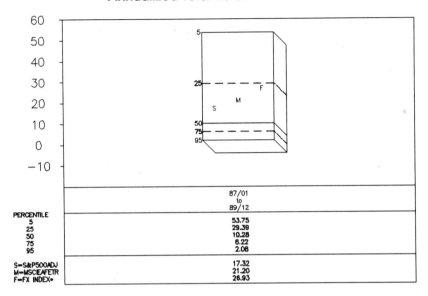

**FIGURE 14.14   Ferrell FX Manager Universe
Annualized Total Return**

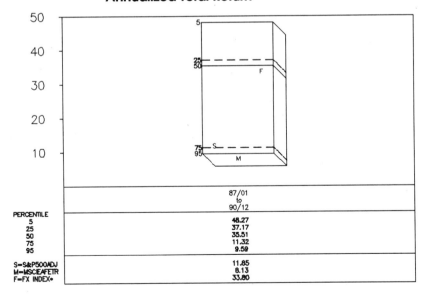

FIGURE 14.15 Ferrell FX Manager Universe Annualized Total Return

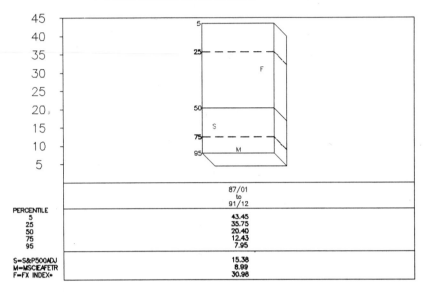

	87/01 to 91/12
PERCENTILE	
5	43.45
25	35.75
50	20.40
75	12.43
95	7.95
S=S&P500ADJ	15.38
M=MSCIEAFETR	8.99
F=FX INDEX•	30.98

FIGURE 14.16 Ferrell FX Manager Universe Annualized Total Return

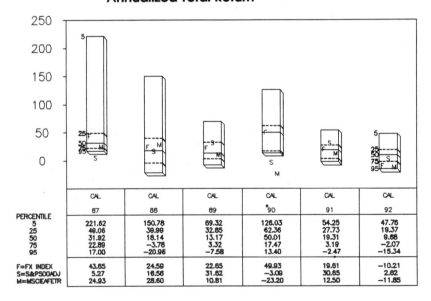

	CAL	CAL	CAL	CAL	CAL	CAL
	87	88	89	•90	91	92
PERCENTILE						
5	221.62	150.78	69.32	126.03	54.25	47.76
25	49.06	39.99	32.85	62.36	27.73	19.37
50	31.92	18.14	13.17	50.01	19.31	9.68
75	22.89	−3.78	3.32	17.47	3.19	−2.07
95	17.00	−20.96	−7.58	13.40	−2.47	−15.34
F=FX INDEX	43.65	24.59	22.65	49.93	19.61	−10.21
S=S&P500ADJ	5.27	16.56	31.62	−3.09	30.65	2.62
M=MSCIEAFETR	24.93	28.60	10.81	−23.20	12.50	−11.85

FIGURE 14.17   Ferrell FX Manager Universe
Annualized Standard Deviation

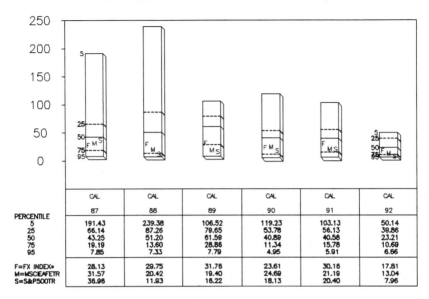

	CAL	CAL	CAL	CAL	CAL	CAL
	87	88	89	90	91	92
PERCENTILE						
5	191.43	239.38	106.52	119.23	103.13	50.14
25	66.14	87.26	79.65	53.78	56.13	39.86
50	43.25	51.20	61.59	40.89	40.58	23.21
75	19.19	13.60	28.86	11.34	15.78	10.69
95	7.85	7.33	7.79	4.95	5.91	6.66
F=FX INDEX∗	28.13	29.75	31.78	23.61	30.18	17.81
M=MSCIEAFETR	31.57	20.42	19.40	24.69	21.19	13.04
S=S&P500TR	36.96	11.93	18.22	18.13	20.40	7.96

FIGURE 14.18   Ferrell FX Manager Universe
Maximum One Period Loss

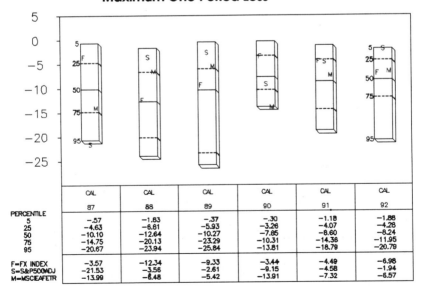

	CAL	CAL	CAL	CAL	CAL	CAL
	87	88	89	90	91	92
PERCENTILE						
5	−.57	−1.63	−.37	−.30	−1.18	−1.86
25	−4.63	−6.61	−5.93	−3.28	−4.07	−4.28
50	−10.10	−12.64	−10.27	−7.65	−8.60	−8.24
75	−14.75	−20.13	−23.29	−10.31	−14.38	−11.95
95	−20.67	−23.94	−25.84	−13.81	−18.79	−20.79
F=FX INDEX	−3.57	−12.34	−9.33	−3.44	−4.49	−6.98
S=S&P500ADJ	−21.53	−3.56	−2.61	−9.15	−4.58	−1.94
M=MSCIEAFETR	−13.99	−8.48	−5.42	−13.91	−7.32	−6.57

**FIGURE 14.19   Ferrell FX Manager Universe
Annualized Sharpe Ratio**

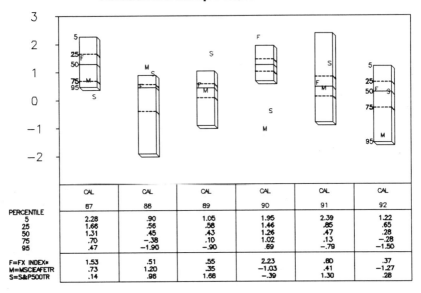

	CAL	CAL	CAL	CAL	CAL	CAL
	87	88	89	90	91	92
PERCENTILE						
5	2.28	.90	1.05	1.95	2.39	1.22
25	1.66	.56	.58	1.46	.85	.65
50	1.31	.45	.43	1.26	.47	.28
75	.70	−.38	.10	1.02	.13	−.28
95	.47	−1.90	−.90	.69	−.79	−1.50
F=FX INDEX*	1.53	.51	.55	2.23	.80	.37
M=MSCIEAFETR	.73	1.20	.35	−1.03	.41	−1.27
S=S&P500TR	.14	.96	1.66	−.39	1.30	.28

**FIGURE 14.20   Ferrell FX Manager Universe
Maximum Capital Drawdown**

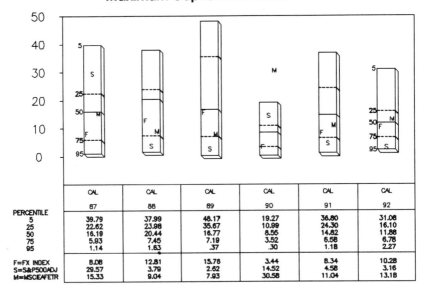

	CAL	CAL	CAL	CAL	CAL	CAL
	87	88	89	90	91	92
PERCENTILE						
5	39.79	37.99	48.17	19.27	36.80	31.06
25	22.62	23.98	35.67	10.99	24.30	16.10
50	16.19	20.44	16.77	8.55	14.82	11.88
75	5.93	7.45	7.19	3.52	6.58	6.78
95	1.14	1.83	.37	.30	1.18	2.27
F=FX INDEX	8.08	12.81	15.78	3.44	8.34	10.28
S=S&P500ADJ	29.57	3.79	2.62	14.52	4.58	3.16
M=MSCIEAFETR	15.33	9.04	7.93	30.58	11.04	13.18

**FIGURE 14.21   Ferrell FX Manager Universe
Percent of Periods with Positive Gain**

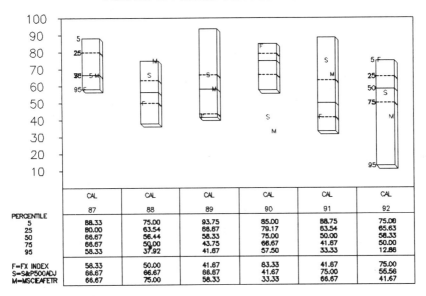

PERCENTILE	CAL 87	CAL 88	CAL 89	CAL 90	CAL 91	CAL 92
5	88.33	75.00	93.75	85.00	88.75	75.00
25	80.00	63.54	66.67	79.17	63.54	65.63
50	66.67	56.44	58.33	75.00	50.00	58.33
75	66.67	50.00	43.75	66.67	41.67	50.00
95	58.33	37.92	41.67	57.50	33.33	12.86
F=FX INDEX	58.33	50.00	41.67	83.33	41.67	75.00
S=S&P500ADJ	66.67	66.67	66.67	41.67	75.00	55.56
M=MSCIEAFETR	66.67	75.00	58.33	33.33	66.67	41.67

**FIGURE 14.22   Ferrell FX Manager Universe
Compound Capital Gains for Interval**

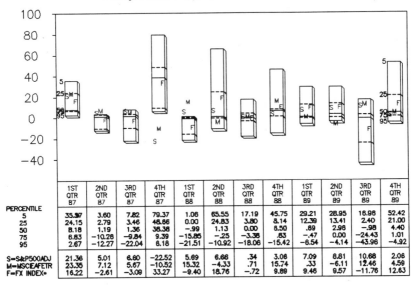

PERCENTILE	1ST QTR 87	2ND QTR 87	3RD QTR 87	4TH QTR 87	1ST QTR 88	2ND QTR 88	3RD QTR 88	4TH QTR 88	1ST QTR 89	2ND QTR 89	3RD QTR 89	4TH QTR 89
5	35.97	3.60	7.82	79.37	1.06	65.55	17.19	45.75	29.21	28.95	16.98	52.42
25	24.15	2.79	3.46	48.66	0.00	24.83	3.80	8.14	12.39	13.41	2.40	21.00
50	8.18	1.19	1.36	38.38	-.99	1.13	0.00	6.50	.69	2.96	-.98	4.40
75	6.83	-10.26	-9.84	9.39	-15.85	-.25	-3.38	.83	-.47	0.00	-24.43	1.01
95	2.67	-12.27	-22.04	8.18	-21.51	-10.92	-18.06	-15.42	-6.54	-4.14	-43.96	-4.92
S=S&P500ADJ	21.36	5.01	6.60	-22.52	5.69	6.66	.34	3.06	7.09	8.81	10.68	2.08
M=MSCIEAFETR	23.35	7.12	5.67	-10.52	15.32	-4.33	.71	15.74	.33	-6.11	12.46	4.58
F=FX INDEX*	16.22	-2.61	-3.09	33.27	-9.40	18.76	-.72	9.89	9.46	9.57	-11.76	12.63

**FIGURE 14.23 Ferrell FX Manager Universe
Compound Capital Gains for Interval**

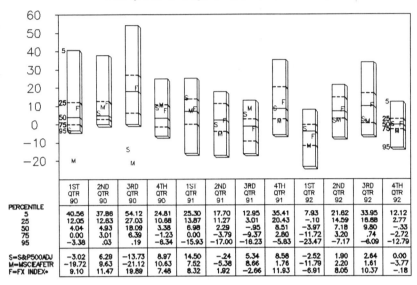

	1ST QTR 90	2ND QTR 90	3RD QTR 90	4TH QTR 90	1ST QTR 91	2ND QTR 91	3RD QTR 91	4TH QTR 91	1ST QTR 92	2ND QTR 92	3RD QTR 92	4TH QTR 92
PERCENTILE												
5	40.56	37.86	54.12	24.81	25.30	17.70	12.95	35.41	7.93	21.62	33.95	12.12
25	12.05	12.63	27.03	10.68	13.87	11.27	3.01	20.43	-.10	14.59	16.88	2.77
50	4.04	4.93	18.09	3.38	6.98	2.29	-.95	8.51	-3.97	7.18	9.80	-.33
75	0.00	3.01	6.39	-1.23	0.00	-3.79	-9.37	2.80	-11.72	3.20	.74	-2.72
95	-3.38	.03	.19	-6.34	-15.93	-17.00	-16.23	-5.63	-23.47	-7.17	-6.09	-12.79
S=S&P500ADJ	-3.02	6.29	-13.73	8.97	14.50	-.24	5.34	8.58	-2.52	1.90	2.64	0.00
M=MSCIEAFETR	-19.72	9.63	-21.12	10.63	7.52	-5.38	8.66	1.76	-11.79	2.20	1.61	-3.77
F=FX INDEX=	9.10	11.47	19.89	7.48	8.32	1.92	-2.66	11.93	-6.91	8.05	10.37	-.18

**FIGURE 14.24 Ferrell FX Manager Universe
Compound Capital Gains for Interval**

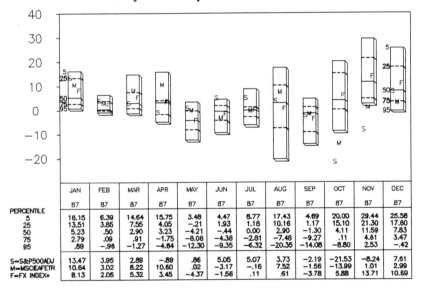

	JAN 87	FEB 87	MAR 87	APR 87	MAY 87	JUN 87	JUL 87	AUG 87	SEP 87	OCT 87	NOV 87	DEC 87
PERCENTILE												
5	16.15	6.39	14.64	15.75	3.48	4.47	8.77	17.43	4.69	20.00	29.44	25.58
25	13.51	3.85	7.55	4.05	-.21	1.93	1.18	10.16	1.17	15.10	21.30	17.80
50	5.23	.50	2.90	3.23	-4.21	-.44	0.00	2.90	-1.30	4.11	11.59	7.83
75	2.79	.09	.91	-1.75	-8.06	-4.38	-2.81	-7.48	-9.27	.11	4.81	3.47
95	.89	-.96	-1.27	-4.84	-12.30	-9.35	-6.32	-20.35	-14.08	-8.80	2.53	-.42
S=S&P500ADJ	13.47	3.95	2.89	-.89	.86	5.05	5.07	3.73	-2.19	-21.53	-8.24	7.61
M=MSCIEAFETR	10.64	3.02	8.22	10.60	.02	-3.17	-.16	7.52	-1.56	-13.99	1.01	2.99
F=FX INDEX=	8.13	2.05	5.32	3.45	-4.37	-1.56	.11	.61	-3.78	5.88	13.71	10.69

**FIGURE 14.25   Ferrell FX Manager Universe
Compound Capital Gains for Interval**

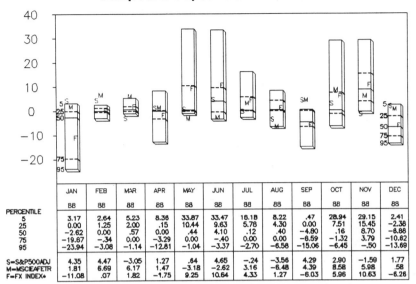

	JAN	FEB	MAR	APR	MAY	JUN	JUL	AUG	SEP	OCT	NOV	DEC
	88	88	88	88	88	88	88	88	88	88	88	88
PERCENTILE												
5	3.17	2.64	5.23	8.36	33.87	33.47	18.18	8.22	.47	28.94	29.15	2.41
25	0.00	1.25	2.00	.15	10.44	9.63	5.78	4.30	0.00	7.51	15.45	−2.38
50	−2.62	0.00	.57	0.00	.44	4.10	.12	.40	−4.80	.16	8.70	−8.88
75	−19.87	−.34	0.00	−3.29	0.00	−.40	0.00	0.00	−8.59	−1.32	3.79	−10.82
95	−23.94	−3.08	−1.14	−12.81	−1.04	−3.37	−2.70	−6.58	−15.06	−6.45	−.50	−13.69
S=S&P500ADJ	4.35	4.47	−3.05	1.27	.64	4.65	−.24	−3.56	4.29	2.90	−1.59	1.77
M=MSCIEAFETR	1.81	6.69	6.17	1.47	−3.18	−2.62	3.16	−6.48	4.39	8.58	5.98	.58
F=FX INDEX*	−11.08	.07	1.82	−1.75	9.25	10.64	4.33	1.27	−6.03	5.96	10.63	−6.26

**FIGURE 14.26   Ferrell FX Manager Universe
Compound Capital Gains for Interval**

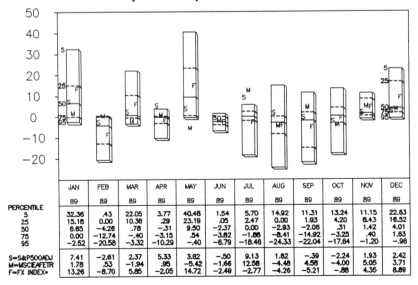

	JAN	FEB	MAR	APR	MAY	JUN	JUL	AUG	SEP	OCT	NOV	DEC
	89	89	89	89	89	89	89	89	89	89	89	89
PERCENTILE												
5	32.36	.43	22.05	3.77	40.48	1.54	5.70	14.92	11.31	13.24	11.15	22.63
25	15.18	0.00	10.36	.29	23.19	.05	2.47	0.00	1.93	4.20	8.43	16.52
50	8.65	−4.26	.78	−.31	9.50	−2.37	0.00	−2.93	−2.06	.31	1.42	4.01
75	0.00	−12.74	−.40	−3.15	.54	−3.82	−1.88	−8.41	−14.92	−3.25	.40	1.63
95	−2.52	−20.58	−3.32	−10.29	−.40	−6.79	−18.46	−24.33	−22.04	−17.84	−1.20	−.98
S=S&P500ADJ	7.41	−2.61	2.37	5.33	3.82	−.50	9.13	1.82	−.39	−2.24	1.93	2.42
M=MSCIEAFETR	1.78	.53	−1.94	.95	−5.42	−1.66	12.58	−4.48	4.58	−4.00	5.05	3.71
F=FX INDEX*	13.26	−8.70	5.85	−2.05	14.72	−2.49	−2.77	−4.26	−5.21	−.88	4.35	8.89

FIGURE 14.27 Ferrell FX Manager Universe Compound Capital Gains for Interval

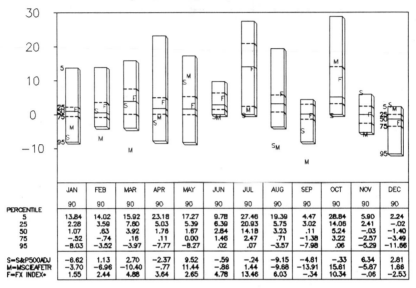

	JAN	FEB	MAR	APR	MAY	JUN	JUL	AUG	SEP	OCT	NOV	DEC
	90	90	90	90	90	90	90	90	90	90	90	90
PERCENTILE												
5	13.84	14.02	15.92	23.18	17.27	9.78	27.46	19.39	4.47	28.84	5.90	2.24
25	2.28	3.59	7.60	5.03	5.39	6.39	20.93	5.75	3.02	14.06	2.41	-.02
50	1.07	.63	3.92	1.76	1.67	2.84	14.18	3.23	.11	5.24	-.03	-1.40
75	-.52	-.74	.16	.11	0.00	1.46	2.47	.71	-1.38	3.22	-2.57	-3.49
95	-8.03	-3.52	-3.97	-7.77	-8.27	.02	.07	-3.57	-7.98	.06	-5.29	-11.66
S=S&P500ADJ	-6.62	1.13	2.70	-2.37	9.52	-.59	-.24	-9.15	-4.81	-.33	6.34	2.81
M=MSCIEAFETR	-3.70	-6.96	-10.40	-.77	11.44	-.88	1.44	-9.68	-13.91	15.81	-5.87	1.68
F=FX INDEX•	1.55	2.44	4.88	3.64	2.65	4.78	13.46	6.03	-.34	10.34	-.06	-2.53

FIGURE 14.28 Ferrell FX Manager Universe Compound Capital Gains for Interval

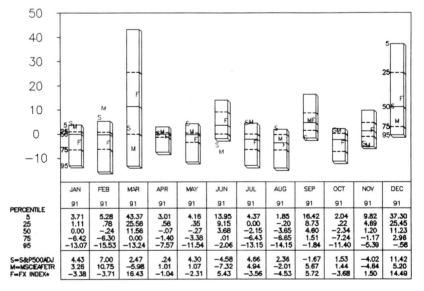

	JAN	FEB	MAR	APR	MAY	JUN	JUL	AUG	SEP	OCT	NOV	DEC
	91	91	91	91	91	91	91	91	91	91	91	91
PERCENTILE												
5	3.71	5.28	43.37	3.01	4.16	13.95	4.37	1.85	16.42	2.04	9.82	37.30
25	1.11	.78	25.58	.56	.35	9.15	0.00	-.20	8.73	.22	4.89	25.45
50	0.00	-.24	11.56	-.07	-.27	3.68	-2.15	-3.65	4.60	-2.34	1.20	11.23
75	-6.42	-6.30	0.00	-1.40	-3.38	.01	-6.43	-6.65	1.51	-7.24	-1.17	2.96
95	-13.07	-15.53	-13.24	-7.57	-11.54	-2.06	-13.15	-14.15	-1.84	-11.40	-5.39	-.58
S=S&P500ADJ	4.43	7.00	2.47	.24	4.30	-4.58	4.66	2.36	-1.67	1.53	-4.02	11.42
M=MSCIEAFETR	3.26	10.75	-5.98	1.01	1.07	-7.32	4.94	-2.01	5.67	1.44	-4.84	5.20
F=FX INDEX•	-3.38	-3.71	16.43	-1.04	-2.31	5.43	-3.56	-4.53	5.72	-3.68	1.50	14.49

**FIGURE 14.29   Ferrell FX Manager Universe
Compound Capital Gains for Interval**

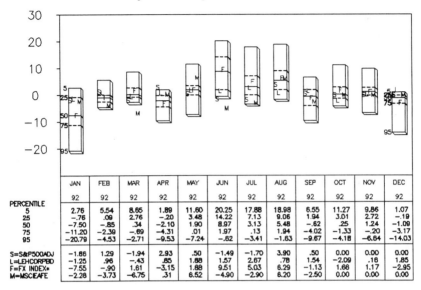

	JAN	FEB	MAR	APR	MAY	JUN	JUL	AUG	SEP	OCT	NOV	DEC
	92	92	92	92	92	92	92	92	92	92	92	92
PERCENTILE												
5	2.76	5.54	8.65	1.89	11.60	20.25	17.88	18.98	6.55	11.27	9.86	1.07
25	-.76	.09	2.76	-.20	3.48	14.22	7.13	9.06	1.94	3.01	2.72	-.19
50	-7.50	-.85	.34	-2.10	1.90	8.97	3.13	5.48	-.62	.25	1.24	-1.09
75	-11.20	-2.39	-.69	-4.31	.01	1.97	.13	1.94	-4.02	-1.33	-.20	-3.17
95	-20.79	-4.53	-2.71	-9.53	-7.24	-.62	-3.41	-1.63	-9.67	-4.18	-6.64	-14.03
S=S&P500ADJ	-1.86	1.29	-1.94	2.93	.50	-1.49	-1.70	3.90	.50	0.00	0.00	0.00
L=LEHCORPBD	-1.25	.96	-.43	.85	1.88	1.57	2.67	.78	1.54	-2.09	.16	1.85
F=FX INDEX*	-7.55	-.90	1.61	-3.15	1.88	9.51	5.03	6.29	-1.13	1.66	1.17	-2.95
M=MSCIEAFE	-2.28	-3.73	-6.75	.31	6.52	-4.90	-2.90	6.20	-2.50	0.00	0.00	0.00

APPENDIX II: CORRELATION MATRIX

FX Manager Universe Correlation Coefficients

	A	B	C	D	E	F	G	H	I	J	K	L	M	N	O	P	Q	R	S	T	U	V	W	X	Y	Z	AA	BB	CC	DD
A	100																													
B	64	100																												
C	5	-18	100																											
D	52	66	-54	100																										
E	51	73	-38	54	100																									
F	31	52	3	40	30	100																								
G	45	51	-41	65	62	46	100																							
H	-9	9	-28	-12	-23	3	-1	100																						
I	43	39	-9	51	35	52	48	-5	100																					
J	26	46	14	24	26	15	6	-21	9	100																				
K	25	64	-6	29	25	62	47	-15	59	5	100																			
L	45	59	-78	44	29	30	-4	49	59	32	22	100																		
M	10	-4	17	20	11	26	12	27	23	-9	34	7	100																	
N	16	-20	89	-17	-36	-14	-31	3	36	-22	-25	-39	8	100																
O	51	55	-14	32	16	28	58	-5	40	22	23	-35	27	-31	100															
P	39	71	-46	81	93	63	51	-8	42	22	67	8	-4	-38	66	100														
Q	16	-7	-14	-8	2	-4	-14	-5	7	44	71	27	-15	-4	19	82	100													
R	52	-25	-30	64	71	32	68	-6	33	22	27	-35	24	21	87	87	-18	100												
S	52	70	-53	88	87	55	61	-8	56	44	65	19	-13	-49	59	86	-11	91	100											
T	46	76	-14	74	65	34	40	1	46	35	31	24	-11	-21	-11	76	-11	76	81	100										
U	-11	24	-2	4	15	-1	21	-7	62	13	16	9	13	-15	13	35	9	7	12	19	100									
V	30	49	-15	53	41	36	42	-7	60	33	37	-2	16	-2	39	57	-8	53	63	46	18	100								
W	46	54	-41	42	47	48	70	-6	22	66	39	-32	37	17	71	69	8	50	78	58	10	60	100							
X	-15	38	-43	47	59	34	32	-18	34	64	65	-48	-13	17	38	64	-20	68	76	66	54	62	64	100						
Y	51	76	-27	77	77	42	57	-9	55	39	39	16	-30	17	23	82	-6	80	76	68	19	67	60	67	100					
Z	48	65	-38	78	78	40	64	-4	48	36	33	17	-14	55	32	87	0	84	87	71	7	54	56	59	78	100				
AA	28	56	-8	75	58	31	8	36	-9	23	74	21	-2	-8	59	68	-3	74	53	74	66	76	69	57	72	76	100			
BB	36	33	11	76	31	8	36	-23	11	28	12	18	-34	-6	31	-4	53	74	28	35	54	35	62	48	71	93	50	100		
CC	-13	25	-11	4	11	7	8	4	11	12	18	-6	35	18	15	32	28	21	-7	59	28	21	-7	59	9	10	66	50	100	
DD	51	64	-32	37	47	23	39	36	36	17	36	-50	14	72	47	56	66	16	26	27	16	26	27	62	55	43	51	54	49	100

Of the 30 programs comprising the FX Index™, 26 apply a technical trend-following system. The 4 above that are bold face indicate those that are not trend followers.

APPENDIX III: CURRENCIES TRADED BY PARTICIPANTS

Japanese yen
British pound
Swiss franc
deutschemark
Canadian dollar
Australian dollar
French franc
Belgian franc
Italian lira
Spanish peseta
Austrian schilling
Dutch guilder
European Currency Unit
Swedish krona
Danish krone
Norwegian krone
New Zealand dollar
Hong Kong dollar
Malaysian ringget
Singapore dollar
Saudi riyal
Indian rupee
Philippines peso
Finnish markka
Kuwaiti dinar
Mexican peso
Portuguese escudo
Venezuelan bolivar
South African rand
Various Cross Rates

15

Exploiting the Interest Rate Differential in Currency Trading

William Fung, Falcon Investment
    Management Corporation
David Hsieh, Fuqua School at Duke University
James Leitner, Falcon Investment
    Management Corporation

RISK-RETURN FROM CURRENCY POSITIONS

In order to establish the risk and return characteristics of holding a currency position, we present a more formal economic interpretation of a foreign exchange transaction. Drawing from the analogy of familiar fixed-income (or bond) investments, we can think of the purchase of a unit of the British pound in much the same way as purchasing a U.S. Treasury bond. In the case of the bond transaction, we are in fact exchanging *cash* (or U.S. dollars) for *a series of future cash-flow obligations of the U.S. Treasury* (or for British pounds). The currency analog of the bond transaction is shown in parentheses. The key point is that the notion of a transaction to exchange one financial asset for another was always present. Extending this argument, we can generalize all financial transactions into an *exchange* setting, thus making a foreign exchange transaction no different from everyday stock/bond purchases (sales can be compared to a short pound, long dollar position). This somewhat abstract interpretation allows us to uncover the common ground between foreign exchange transactions and standard financial transactions. With this in mind, we can import the traditional risk return analyses of standard financial assets to the arena of foreign exchange.

The total return from bond investments has two components, income and capital appreciation—income in the form of interest receipts and capital appreciation in the form of higher bond prices reflecting improved interest rate outlook. In much the same way, the total return from investing in a currency position also has two components—the interest rate differential component in the form of forward points, and the capital appreciation component reflecting improved outlook on the *external value* of the British pound relative to the U.S. currency unit.

The following example illustrates our points and introduces some common terminology:

On August 7, 1992, we observed the following foreign exchange quotations:[1]

	Spot	*30 Days Forward*	*Forward Points*
USD/GBP	1.9279	1.9170	–109

	U.S. Dollar	*British Pound*
1-month interest rates	3.34%	10.18%

The spot exchange rate tells us that it costs 1.9279 dollars to purchase one British pound for spot delivery. The forward exchange rate, on the other hand, shows that it costs 1.9170 dollars to purchase one British pound for 30 days' delivery. The difference between the forward exchange rate and the spot exchange rate is 1.9170 – 1.9279 = –0.0109 and is often referred to as the forward points, which are commonly quoted in 10,000 times the actual rate for convenience, as –109.

In many respects, a currency forward contract is similar to standard commodity forward contracts. The precise mechanism through which these contracts are fulfilled is unimportant here. What we need to focus on are the terminology and the economics involved in pricing these contracts. In order to understand why forward exchange rates are different from spot exchange rates, we need to pay a brief visit to the well-known interest rate arbitrage conditions that dictate the economics of these transactions. Ignoring the creditworthiness of our counterparty and commission charges, the following two transactions must lead to the same end positions:

1. Purchase one British pound spot for 1.9279 dollars, and place the British pound on 30 days' deposit at the rate of 10.18 percent per annum.
2. Place 1.9279 dollars on 30 days' deposit at the rate of 3.34 percent per annum and purchase British pounds with the proceeds at the 30 days forward exchange rate of 1.9170.

Should either of the two alternatives yield more British pounds than the other 30 days from now, arbitrage will take place in the marketplace. This will drive the component rates—spot exchange rate, 30 days forward exchange rate, the 30 days U.S. and British interest rates—to levels where the two alternative methods of acquiring British pounds 30 days from now result in identical quantities of British pounds, as the current example shows.

1. $1 * (1 + 10.18\% * 30/360) = 1.00848$ British pounds
2. $\{1.9279 * (1 + 3.34\% * 30/360)\}/1.9170 = 1.00848$ British pounds

This type of spot-forward/interest rates relationship is known as *interest rate parity*. It is clear from this example that the forward discount reflects the excess interest earned from immediately acquiring the British currency and placing it on deposit versus placing the lower-yielding U.S. dollars on deposit and purchasing the British pound 30 days from now. In general, *purchasing a higher-yielding currency forward earns a forward discount that precisely reflects the interest rate differential between the two currencies over the term of the forward contract.* Conversely, purchasing a lower-yielding currency forward leads to a forward premium. The forward currency contract can be further compared to a standard commodity forward contract by drawing the analogy between the notion of forward points to cost of carry in trading a physical commodity. Consequently, another commonly encountered term in currency trading is the notion of positive/negative carry. Positive carry refers to forward positions at a discount and negative carry refers to forward positions at a premium when compared to a spot transaction.

To summarize:

Forward Points	Forward Position	Forward Position
Discount	Long Higher-Yielding Ccy	Positive Carry
Premium	Short Higher-Yielding Ccy	Negative Carry

Before returning to the analogy of investing in Treasury bonds, one brief comment on the maturity structure of forward contracts: It is clear from the above example that forward points are simply an arithmetic consequence of interest rate differentials and the term (maturity) of the forward contract. However, interest rates for debt obligations of different maturity tend to vary so that the yield curve may not be flat. This in itself is not sufficient to ensure a term structure in the forward points. Forward points are determined by the difference in the yield curves in the two countries. Therefore, so long as the two yield curves have identical shape, the difference can be constant irrespective of maturity. The key point here is that the income component of the return from a currency position has similar attributes to taking a position on the differential between the two countries' yield curves. In our example, one is investing in British interest rates (or lending pounds) and funding the investment by borrowing U.S. dollars at the U.S. interest rate. The choice of forward contract maturity is dictated by one's investment horizon as well as the relative attractiveness of alternative positions along the yield curve. In this chapter we focus only on normal interbank currency forwards, which tend to be of maturity one year or less. Although one could extend most of the analyses in this chapter to include longer maturities, using the currency swap market, there are additional risk considerations that are beyond the scope of the chapter.

Comparing the income component of the forward currency position to that of a bond investment, we can see the following. Normally, one considers the income component of a bond investment as the coupon payments from the bond. An alternative interpretation is the bond's coupon rate less the short-term interest rate.[2] This amounts to interpreting the opportunity cost of holding a bond as the return from short-term deposits. Therefore, the income return is the interest differential between the bond's coupon payments and the position's short-term funding cost, i.e., the bond's cost of carry. In much the same way as in the case of forward currency contracts, the notion of carry cost is common in fixed-income investing. Positive carry refers to the situation when bonds yield higher than short-term funding rates, and vice versa. Therefore, we can relate the forward points in a currency forward position to the yield differential between bonds and short-term deposits via the concept of carry cost.

The significant difference in the currency case is that frequently one can obtain sizable positive carry between currencies (6.84 percent in the case of the British pound and U.S. dollars) with short-term contracts, whereas individual yield curves are often not steep enough to have such differences. This is an important motivation for holding positive carry currency positions.

Moving on to the capital appreciation (depreciation) component of a currency's total return, the analogy is that of bond price fluctuations. Continuing with the current example of a 30 days forward position in British pounds, at expiration a quantity of British pounds will be delivered at the forward rate of 1.9170. The total return (sometimes also referred to as total excess return—excess in the sense of net of cost) for this position can be computed as follows:

$$
\begin{aligned}
\text{Total Return} &= \text{Capital Return} - \text{Cost of Carry} \\
&= \text{Capital Return} - \text{Forward Points} \\
&= (\text{Ending Spot} - \text{Initial Spot}) - \text{Forward Points}
\end{aligned}
$$

and in percentage terms:

$$
\begin{aligned}
\text{Total} \\
\text{Return} \\
\text{Percent}
\end{aligned}
= \frac{(\text{Ending Spot Rate} - \text{Initial Spot Rate}) - \text{Forward Points}}{\text{Initial Spot Rate}}
$$

The equation above is set up in a format to facilitate comparison between the forward points component of a currency's total (excess) return and that of the net of cost income component of a bond's total (excess) return. The above equation simplifies to:

$$
\begin{aligned}
\text{Total} \\
\text{Return} \\
\text{Percent}
\end{aligned}
= \frac{\text{Ending Spot Rate} - \text{Forward Rate}}{\text{Initial Spot Rate}}
$$

With the current numerical example, the income component of the return is $0.0109/1.9279 = 0.00565$, which annualizes to 6.78 percent return. Note that this is not the same as the interest rate differential of 6.84 percent. This is because the interest rate differential is earned over the horizon of 30 days in GBP. Therefore it is the present value of the differential that matches the income component of the currency's return.[3] The capital return component of the currency's total return is defined in the same way as that of a bond investment, i.e., price change as a percentage of initial price.

It is clear from the current example that the total return component depends on the difference between the final spot rate and the contracted forward rate. In the current example, the total return of investing in British pounds will depend on how much the final spot rate deviates from the forward rate of 1.9170. This shows that the carry return of currency positions dominates the total return of the position when the fluctuation of the ending spot rate around the contracted forward rate is small. Conversely, when potential fluctuation of the final spot rate is large, the carry component of a currency's total return is eclipsed by the behavior of the underlying spot rate. Consequently, currency pairs that are typical candidates for carry positions tend to have tightly bounded variations in spot rates, either via economic conditions or by explicit monetary arrangements such as the ERM adhered to by certain European countries.

From the total return definition of a currency position, one can readily observe the inherent position risk. It is clear that the forward (carry) component of the return is unaffected by the fate of the currency pair at the end of the holding period. Risk, therefore, comes purely from the uncertainty surrounding the terminal spot rate. We can further decompose this risk into two components. The first component deals with the continuous price risk conditional on the current institutional/monetary arrangements between currency pairs prevailing. The second component captures the discrete event risk that reflects a breakdown of currency regimes, such as currency devaluations. The objective of this chapter is to analyze portfolio strategies that capture the carry component of investing in currency pairs while controlling and minimizing the attendant risks. The next two sections present some historical experience of such an approach.

THE FORWARD RISK PREMIUM

In this section we focus on the continuous price risk component of a currency's total return, deferring to the next section analysis of discrete event risk. The central question is whether expected total return from holding currency pairs is different from zero. To answer this question, we examine historical exchange rates of a large sample of currency pairs (both dollar and nondollar crosses). If empirically, average returns are positive then one can interpret this to be a risk premium for bearing continuous price risk.

For illustrative purposes, we continue to refer to the U.S. dollar/British pound (USD/GBP) exchange rate, however the equation structure applies generally to any currency pair. Let S_t denote the spot exchange rate of one British pound in terms of U.S. dollars at time t. Let F_t denote the 1-period forward exchange rate of one pound in terms of dollars. The forward contract is made at time t, while the exchange of currencies will take place at time t + 1.

As a result of interest rate parity, S_t and F_t are related to each other via the 1-period Europound interest rate, i_t, and Eurodollar interest rate, i_t^*:

$$S_t (1 + i_t) = F_t (1 + i_t^*)$$

F_t is greater than S_t if i_t^* is greater than i_t; F_t is less than S_t if i_t^* is less than i_t. In addition, the total rate of return of a forward position is given by

$$[S_{t+1} - F_t]/S_t$$

The question of interest is whether this total return is expected to be different from zero. This question can be reformulated to be whether the forward exchange rate (F_t) is an unbiased predictor of the spot rate at maturity, i.e., S_{t+1}. If so, then the forward risk premium is zero. If not, then the forward risk premium is nonzero.

Numerous academic studies have found that the forward exchange rate is a biased predictor of the spot exchange rate at maturity.[4] This is confirmed in our analysis below. None of the previous studies, however, has convincingly demonstrated that this premium can be profitably exploited. In this section, we demonstrate that a simple trading strategy can be used to capture this risk premium. Furthermore, portfolios of these currency trades have risk characteristics that compare favorably to stock returns.

Data

Our data come from the International Financial Statistics tape of the International Monetary Fund. They consist of end-of-quarter spot exchange rates and 3-month forward exchange rates for 16 countries against the U.S. dollar (USD). These countries (symbols) are: United Kingdom (GBP), Austria (ATS), Belgium (BEF), Denmark (DKK), France (FRF), West Germany (DEM), Italy (ITL), the Netherlands (NLG), Norway (NOK), Sweden (SWE), Switzerland (CHF), Canada (CAD), Japan (JPY), Finland (FIM), Spain (ESP), and Australia (AUD). This provides 136 pairs of currencies. The data begin in 1973:I and ends in 1991:IV, totaling 76 observations.[5]

Measuring the Forward Bias

Columns (1) through (5) in Table 15.1 report the evidence of a forward bias in the 136 currency pairs. Take the first line, which examines the forward bias in the dollar/pound exchange rate. There were 17 quarters when the forward exchange rate, F_t, was above the spot rate, S_t. In seven of those cases, the spot exchange rate in the subsequent quarter, S_{t+1}, was above the forward rate. This number should be 8.5 if F_t is an unbiased predictor of S_{t+1}. In addition, there were 58 quarters in which the forward exchange rate, F_t, was below the spot rate, S_t. In 23 of those cases, the spot exchange rate in the subsequent quarter, S_{t+1}, was below the forward rate. This number should be 29 if F_t is an unbiased predictor of S_{t+1}. In total, the spot exchange rate moved by *less* than the amount predicted by the forward rate in 45 out of the 75 times. We measure the forward bias as

$$(45/75) \times 100 \text{ percent,}$$

or 60 percent. This number should be 50 percent if the forward rate is an unbiased predictor of the spot rate at maturity. Out of 136 pairs of currencies, the forward bias exceeds 50 percent in 130 cases. There is strong evidence that the forward exchange rate overpredicts the movement of the spot exchange rate.

This conclusion is further strengthened by the observation that the current spot rate, S_t, is an unbiased predictor of the future spot rate, S_{t+1}. Column (6) in Table 15.1 reports the spot bias, i.e., the fraction of times that the future spot rate, S_{t+1}, is less than the current spot rate, S_t. In the case of dollar/pound, this turns out to be 46.7 percent, which should be 50 percent if the spot rate is an unbiased predictor of the future spot rate. In total, only 76 of the 136 currency pairs have a spot bias exceeding 50 percent. Thus, there is good evidence that the current spot rate is an unbiased predictor of the future spot rate. Recall that the total return of holding a

TABLE 15.1   Forward Bias and Trading Profits

Currency Pairs	Forward Bias						Trading Profits			
	(1)	(2)	(3)	(4)	(5)	(6)	(7)	(8)	(9)	(10)
USD/GBP	17	7	58	23	60.0%	46.7%	75	45	3.66%	11.43%
USD/ATS	57	29	18	6	53.3	42.7	75	40	1.83	13.18
USD/BEF	28	11	47	16	64.0	46.7	75	48	4.87	12.98
USD/DKK	14	5	61	25	60.0	50.7	75	45	7.37	12.26
USD/FRF	27	12	48	19	58.7	45.3	75	44	3.92	12.33
USD/DEM	67	34	8	3	50.7	44.0	75	38	0.30	13.33
USD/ITL	1	1	60	24	59.0	52.5	61	36	4.91	11.41
USD/NLG	60	30	15	4	54.7	44.0	75	41	3.28	13.31
USD/NOK	14	9	61	26	53.3	50.7	75	40	3.23	10.54
USD/SWE	18	7	57	24	58.7	49.3	75	44	4.83	10.48
USD/CHF	67	32	8	2	54.7	42.7	75	41	1.28	15.03
USD/CAD	23	5	52	19	68.0	53.3	75	51	3.21	4.05
USD/JPY	56	22	19	3	66.7	49.3	75	50	3.59	12.59
USD/FIM	11	4	64	26	60.0	50.7	75	45	6.16	9.34
USD/ESP	18	5	56	17	70.3	52.7	74	52	10.32	11.47
USD/AUD	13	4	50	18	65.1	49.2	63	41	3.08	9.97
GBP/ATS	70	29	5	2	58.7	45.3	75	31	0.66	10.19
GBP/BEF	59	25	16	7	57.3	46.7	75	32	2.19	9.88
GBP/DKK	40	21	35	19	46.7	50.7	75	40	0.11	9.83
GBP/FRF	58	23	17	9	57.3	52.0	75	32	3.02	9.52
GBP/DEM	75	30	0	0	60.0	45.3	75	30	0.40	10.12
GBP/ITL	13	2	48	20	63.9	62.3	61	22	3.90	9.30
GBP/NLG	72	30	3	1	58.7	44.0	75	31	0.79	9.67
GBP/NOK	37	18	38	17	53.3	49.3	75	35	1.48	8.37
GBP/SWE	46	18	29	12	60.0	52.0	75	30	1.19	8.17
GBP/CHF	74	32	1	0	57.3	45.3	75	32	1.09	11.75
GBP/CAD	54	19	21	8	64.0	53.3	75	27	5.34	11.72
GBP/JPY	72	35	3	0	53.3	48.0	75	35	–0.65	11.38
GBP/FIM	35	13	40	17	60.0	52.0	75	30	2.56	7.65
GBP/ESP	22	10	52	21	58.1	55.4	74	31	3.14	9.70
GBP/AUD	16	4	47	17	66.7	55.6	63	21	5.01	12.83
ATS/BEF	11	1	64	23	68.0	68.0	75	24	2.07	2.81
ATS/DKK	2	0	73	25	66.7	68.0	75	25	2.36	3.16
ATS/FRF	13	2	62	23	66.7	68.0	75	25	0.58	5.23
ATS/DEM	59	15	16	9	68.0	48.0	75	24	1.18	2.22
ATS/ITL	2	0	59	13	78.7	72.1	61	13	5.38	4.44
ATS/NLG	38	12	37	14	65.3	53.3	75	26	1.63	2.69
ATS/NOK	3	1	72	27	62.7	58.7	75	28	3.07	6.41
ATS/SWE	7	1	68	25	65.3	62.7	75	26	2.05	7.46
ATS/CHF	66	28	9	5	56.0	46.7	75	33	1.63	7.37
ATS/CAD	13	3	62	30	56.0	61.3	75	33	4.49	13.21
ATS/JPY	48	26	27	10	52.0	42.7	75	36	2.72	10.32
ATS/FIM	3	0	72	25	66.7	54.7	75	25	3.66	6.70

TABLE 15.1   (continued)

Currency	Forward Bias						Trading Profits			
Pairs	(1)	(2)	(3)	(4)	(5)	(6)	(7)	(8)	(9)	(10)
ATS/ESP	10	1	64	22	68.9	63.5	74	23	5.32	9.02
ATS/AUD	5	2	58	28	52.4	63.5	63	30	0.91	13.77
BEF/DKK	17	7	58	24	58.7	58.7	75	31	1.31	2.99
BEF/FRF	28	8	47	22	60.0	60.0	75	30	2.12	5.44
BEF/DEM	71	21	4	0	72.0	29.3	75	21	2.05	3.47
BEF/ITL	2	0	59	20	67.2	65.6	61	20	3.65	4.91
BEF/NLG	66	20	9	0	73.3	41.3	75	20	2.50	3.19
BEF/NOK	15	8	60	24	57.3	56.0	75	32	0.86	6.73
BEF/SWE	18	5	57	26	58.7	57.3	75	31	1.24	7.43
BEF/CHF	71	28	4	1	61.3	41.3	75	29	2.92	7.94
BEF/CAD	31	13	44	24	50.7	58.7	75	37	2.32	13.56
BEF/JPY	65	37	10	6	42.7	36.0	75	43	–0.53	10.67
BEF/FIM	13	6	62	26	57.3	53.3	75	32	1.24	6.91
BEF/ESP	19	6	55	19	66.2	52.7	74	25	5.12	9.20
BEF/AUD	14	5	49	23	55.6	55.6	63	28	2.00	14.14
DKK/FRF	53	17	22	10	64.0	56.0	75	27	2.42	5.20
DKK/DEM	74	24	1	1	66.7	33.3	75	25	2.57	3.97
DKK/ITL	9	4	52	18	63.9	60.7	61	22	2.53	5.11
DKK/NLG	71	23	4	2	66.7	36.0	75	25	2.20	3.64
DKK/NOK	34	14	41	15	61.3	44.0	75	29	1.52	6.14
DKK/SWE	38	12	37	14	65.3	46.7	75	26	3.32	7.03
DKK/CHF	74	26	1	0	65.3	37.3	75	26	3.51	7.93
DKK/CAD	44	14	31	13	64.0	52.0	75	27	7.70	12.63
DKK/JPY	68	34	7	1	53.3	37.3	75	35	1.41	10.26
DKK/FIM	29	14	46	18	57.3	48.0	75	32	1.41	6.55
DKK/ESP	25	7	49	14	71.6	52.7	74	21	6.37	8.55
DKK/AUD	23	11	40	16	57.1	49.2	63	27	3.39	13.78
FRF/DEM	68	26	7	2	62.7	32.0	75	28	–0.22	5.51
FRF/ITL	1	0	60	17	72.1	59.0	61	17	5.30	4.51
FRF/NLG	61	21	14	2	69.3	33.3	75	23	2.73	5.54
FRF/NOK	10	4	65	23	64.0	53.3	75	27	3.50	7.04
FRF/SWE	19	14	56	26	46.7	50.7	75	40	0.20	8.00
FRF/CHF	69	26	6	1	64.0	36.0	75	27	0.76	8.54
FRF/CAD	38	15	37	16	58.7	57.3	75	31	6.20	12.76
FRF/JPY	62	32	13	2	54.7	33.3	75	34	3.62	10.82
FRF/FIM	13	8	62	18	65.3	42.7	75	26	2.55	7.57
FRF/ESP	16	7	58	15	70.3	54.1	74	22	6.23	8.22
FRF/AUD	10	5	53	24	54.0	55.6	63	29	2.13	13.14
DEM/ITL	1	0	60	16	73.8	70.5	61	16	5.34	4.32
DEM/NLG	14	6	61	22	62.7	50.7	75	28	1.33	2.78
DEM/NOK	2	1	73	27	62.7	60.0	75	28	3.46	6.55
DEM/SWE	3	1	72	27	62.7	57.3	75	28	1.32	7.55

TABLE 15.1 (*continued*)

Currency Pairs	\(1\)	\(2\)	Forward Bias \(3\)	\(4\)	\(5\)	\(6\)	Trading Profits \(7\)	\(8\)	\(9\)	\(10\)
DEM/CHF	63	30	12	5	53.3	41.3	75	35	1.50	7.26
DEM/CAD	6	3	69	37	46.7	61.3	75	40	1.04	13.45
DEM/JPY	34	17	41	14	58.7	45.3	75	31	6.72	10.25
DEM/FIM	3	1	72	25	65.3	54.7	75	26	3.90	6.93
DEM/ESP	9	3	65	22	66.2	59.5	74	25	4.09	9.54
DEM/AUD	1	1	62	30	50.8	61.9	63	31	1.75	13.86
ITL/NLG	58	16	3	0	73.8	31.1	61	16	5.33	4.78
ITL/NOK	43	16	18	8	60.7	45.9	61	24	3.07	6.70
ITL/SWE	50	18	11	3	65.6	45.9	61	21	5.18	7.63
ITL/CHF	59	16	2	0	73.8	39.3	61	16	7.78	8.43
ITL/CAD	56	22	5	3	59.0	54.1	61	25	2.93	12.19
ITL/JPY	60	30	1	0	50.8	31.1	61	30	3.68	10.23
ITL/FIM	41	18	20	9	55.7	39.3	61	27	0.70	6.29
ITL/ESP	31	11	30	8	68.9	41.0	61	19	7.39	7.57
ITL/AUD	35	12	26	11	62.3	50.8	61	23	4.76	13.34
NLG/NOK	4	1	71	30	58.7	57.3	75	31	3.29	6.68
NLG/SWE	9	2	66	25	64.0	60.0	75	27	2.49	7.42
NLG/CHF	64	31	11	6	50.7	42.7	75	37	2.69	7.98
NLG/CAD	11	2	64	33	53.3	60.0	75	35	3.29	13.57
NLG/JPY	44	21	31	10	58.7	41.3	75	31	5.95	10.61
NLG/FIM	6	0	69	27	64.0	52.0	75	27	4.06	6.70
NLG/ESP	12	2	62	24	64.9	58.1	74	26	5.17	8.90
NLG/AUD	5	2	58	26	55.6	57.1	63	28	3.17	14.29
NOK/SWE	47	16	28	10	65.3	49.3	75	26	3.04	5.79
NOK/CHF	73	28	2	1	61.3	45.3	75	29	3.78	9.80
NOK/CAD	53	25	22	15	46.7	53.3	75	40	1.84	11.22
NOK/JPY	68	27	7	3	60.0	44.0	75	30	2.04	10.76
NOK/FIM	38	17	37	14	58.7	44.0	75	31	0.62	5.13
NOK/ESP	27	13	47	21	54.1	47.3	74	34	1.25	8.52
NOK/AUD	29	12	34	15	57.1	50.8	63	27	3.75	11.61
SWE/CHF	71	27	4	2	61.3	44.0	75	29	1.64	11.41
SWE/CAD	48	19	27	14	56.0	54.7	75	33	3.68	11.31
SWE/JPY	65	31	10	4	53.3	38.7	75	35	−0.62	11.92
SWE/FIM	25	11	50	15	65.3	40.0	75	26	2.71	5.12
SWE/ESP	18	4	56	18	70.3	55.4	74	22	5.78	7.50
SWE/AUD	21	12	42	20	49.2	55.6	63	32	−1.92	12.50
CHF/CAD	3	1	72	35	52.0	60.0	75	36	1.87	14.60
CHF/JPY	19	7	56	19	65.3	44.0	75	26	5.88	10.31
CHF/FIM	2	1	73	24	66.7	53.3	75	25	4.98	9.33
CHF/ESP	6	2	68	25	63.5	55.4	74	27	5.36	11.89
CHF/AUD	1	0	62	26	58.7	58.7	63	26	4.26	14.65

TABLE 15.1   (*continued*)

Currency Pairs	Forward Bias						Trading Profits			
	(1)	(2)	(3)	(4)	(5)	(6)	(7)	(8)	(9)	(10)
CAD/JPY	67	35	8	2	50.7	46.7	75	37	–0.03	12.97
CAD/FIM	18	8	57	21	61.3	45.3	75	29	6.34	9.77
CAD/ESP	20	4	54	17	71.6	48.6	74	21	12.00	11.86
CAD/AUD	14	3	49	20	63.5	50.8	63	23	3.02	9.32
JPY/FIM	5	2	70	27	61.3	62.7	75	29	3.12	10.25
JPY/ESP	11	3	63	28	58.1	58.1	74	31	6.51	12.80
JPY/AUD	3	1	60	28	54.0	55.6	63	29	1.00	12.31
FIM/ESP	29	9	45	17	64.9	58.1	74	26	5.33	7.51
FIM/AUD	25	11	38	18	54.0	55.6	63	29	2.11	11.67
ESP/AUD	40	15	23	9	61.9	52.4	63	24	6.84	13.98

Notes:

(1) Number of times $F_t > S_t$

(2) Number of times $F_t > S_t$ and $S_{t+1} > F_t$

(3) Number of times $F_t < S_t$

(4) Number of times $F_t < S_t$ and $S_{t+1} < F_t$

(5) $100 \{1 - [(2)+(4)]/[(1)+(3)]\}\%$

(6) Fraction of times $S_{t+1} > S_t$

(7) Number of trades

(8) Number of profitable trades

(9) Mean capital return

(10) Standard deviation of capital return

currency pair can be decomposed into its capital return and carry component, where the capital return component is defined as $(S_{t+1} - S_t)/S_t$. If the current spot rate, S_t, is an unbiased predictor of future spot rate, S_{t+1}, then the expected capital appreciation or depreciation is zero. This leaves us with the conclusion that the expected total return must be equal to the carry. This observation favors high-yielding currencies that offer positive carry relative to low-yielding currencies. Such a conclusion is supported by the earlier evidence that forward exchange rate overpredicts the movement of future spot rate. We shall refer to this as the forward bias.

Trading the Forward Bias: Individual Pairs of Currencies

The tendency of the forward exchange rate to overpredict the movement of the spot exchange rate is evidence that the forward rate is biased. This means that the total return is expected to be different from zero, i.e., that a forward risk premium exists. We now demonstrate how to capture this risk premium systematically, using the following simple trading strategy.

If the forward is at a discount to spot, i.e., $F_t < S_t$, buy one pound forward at time t, and sell it in the spot market at time t + 1. The profit is \$$(S_{t+1} - F_t)$ per pound. The total return is given as $(S_{t+1} - F_t)/S_t$.[6]

With other currency pairs where the forward is at a premium to spot, i.e., $F_t > S_t$, sell the currency forward at time t, and buy it in the spot market at time t + 1. The profit is \$$(F_t - S_{t+1})$ per unit of currency. The total return is given as $(F_t - S_{t+1})/S_t$.

If $F_t = S_t$, we take no position in the forward market.

Columns (7) through (10) in Table 15.1 report the profitability of this simple strategy. In the case of dollar/pound, 75 trades are made, and 45 are profitable. The capital return has a mean of 3.7 percent per annum, and a standard deviation of 11.50 percent per annum.[7]

Out of 136 pairs of currencies, 130 had a positive return![8] On average, the capital return has a mean of 3.15 percent per annum, and a standard deviation of 9.11 percent per annum.

Trading the Forward Bias: Portfolios of Currencies

The standard deviations of the capital returns on the individual currency pairs appear to be quite large. A portfolio of these positions should have much lower return volatility. To form a portfolio of 10 currencies, we randomly selected 10 currency pairs in each quarter, giving each an equal weight.[9] As indicated in Table 15.2, the mean return was 3.35 percent per annum, and the standard deviation was 4.43 percent per annum. Similarly, we construct portfolios of 12, 14, 16, 18, and 20 pairs of currencies. As shown in Table 15.2, when the number of currencies increases, the standard deviations of these currency portfolios tend to decrease, with slight deterioration in the mean return. As expected, these currency portfolios have much smaller standard deviations than those of the individual currency pairs.

To provide a measure of the riskiness of these currency portfolios, we compare their mean/standard deviation ratio to those of the capital return for the Standard and Poor's 500 stock index and

TABLE 15.2   Profitability of Currency Portfolios
1973:I – 1991:IV

Number of Currencies	Mean Return	Standard Deviation	Mean/ Standard Deviation
10	3.34%	4.43%	0.755
12	2.82%	3.35%	0.843
14	2.78%	3.77%	0.738
16	2.39%	3.58%	0.668
18	2.17%	3.56%	0.609
20	2.95%	2.80%	1.054
S&P 500	6.16%	18.11%	0.338
MSCI World Index (in U.S. Dollars)	7.49%	17.67%	0.424

the Morgan Stanley Capital International World Stock Index. In all cases, the currency portfolios have mean/standard deviation ratios that are higher than the stock indices. This comes from the fact that while the mean returns of currency portfolios are lower than stocks, their standard deviations are proportionally even lower. It is clear that currency portfolios are not riskier than stocks, when based on a mean-standard deviation criterion.

In summary, this section documents the phenomenon that the forward exchange rate tends to overpredict the amount of movement in the spot exchange rate. This bias in the forward exchange rate is consistent with the view that there is a forward risk premium in currency prices. Using a simple trading strategy, we demonstrate that this forward risk premium can be profitably extracted, particularly in a portfolio context. Furthermore, the risk appears to be moderate, as the mean/standard deviation ratios of these currency portfolios are higher than those of the capital return components of both the S&P 500 stock index and the MSCI world stock index.

However, the weakness of any empirical analysis is the question of stability or, put simply, "Will history repeat itself?" In one sense, the question is best answered by the passage of time. We do, on the other hand, have strong empirical evidence in support of a profitable carry trading strategy. This simply begs the question "What can go wrong?" To address this question, the next section focuses on the second component of risk—event risk. Just as a closing note to this section, the key to successful applications of such a strategy depends crucially on the management and control of event risk. We therefore elect to focus directly on this issue, bypassing some refinements to the portfolio approach presented here where instead of taking equally weighted positions, one appeals to the techniques of portfolio optimization to enhance efficiency. Readers familiar with this type of technique would no doubt recognize that key inputs to the optimization approach are the cross-correlations between currency pairs. It is hard to see how reliable forecasts of these inputs can be obtained without analyses of event risks. This too leads us to the question to be addressed in the next section.

EVENT RISK IN FORWARD POSITIONS

In this section, we focus on the issue of event risk in the context of forward currency positions. As we have demonstrated, the forward exchange rate is a biased predictor of the future spot rate, which is consistent with the presence of a forward risk premium. In order to extract this forward risk premium, we put on forward positions speculating that the future spot exchange rate will move by less than the amount predicted by the forward exchange rate. On average, the data suggest this to be is a profitable strategy (especially in a portfolio context). Once in a while, however, this strategy will generate large losses, when the spot exchange rate moves significantly more than the amount predicted by the forward exchange rate. This is particularly true when the exchange rate responds to discrete events such as policy shifts. We call such risks *event risks*. The following are examples of events: the realignments in the European Rate Mechanism (ERM) of the European Monetary System (EMS); the dramatic devaluation of the Indonesian rupiah in 1986 (in excess of 40 percent). Other less obvious examples are recent events such as when the authorities of Finland, Norway, and Sweden switched from managing the external value of their currency unit against a weighted basket of currencies in accordance with their foreign trade flows, to the ECU which is a weighted basket according to bilateral trade flows of EC countries only. Yet other examples of policy shifts are that of the Carter intervention in 1979 and the Louvre Accord in 1985. All of these policy shifts resulted in abnormal responses from the currency market with varying degrees of volatility. None of these events lend themselves readily to quantitative analysis. One major difficulty is the lack of homogeneity among these events both in terms of cause and effect. This leads to substantial difficulty in interpreting the evidence presented in the previous section. Since history, as we find it, is a mix of randomly spaced events of this kind, the observations we made in the previous section in fact show that the portfolio strategy is profitable despite event risk. Although the data sample we used in our study is large in the temporal sense, it is limited in the event sense. History simply does not furnish us with sufficient events to afford definitive statistics on the impact of heterogenous event risks.

This leaves us with the central issue of this section: how significant are event risks relative to the forward risk premiums we found in the previous section? How do we measure, even in an approximate sense, the impact of event risk on portfolio performance? Are there early warning indicators to these events? The answer to the first question will provide us with a measure of whether the forward risk premium is (on average) sufficiently high to compensate for the inherent risks (both continuous and event risks) of our trading strategy in a historical setting. The second question leads us to formulate a reasonable measure of event risk that can be used to assess ex-post performance and provide input to answering the third question, while the third question is directed at formulating risk management parameters for such events.

We measure the event risk relative to the forward risk premium by implementing the following trading strategy. At the end of each day, we put on a one-month forward contract based on the trading strategy in the previous section. At the end of the next trading day, we close out this contract by prorating the carry and use the spot rate to settle the capital return. We then open a new one-month forward contract (of the same size) using the same trading strategy. Applying this method to the European currency crosses, we examine the cumulative profit, in percentage terms, for the deutsche mark (DEM) versus each of five European currencies: Belgian franc (BEF), Danish krona (DKK), French franc (FRF), Italian lira (ITL), and Dutch guilder (NLG).

Figures 15.1 through 15.5 graph the cumulative profits for these five cross rates from January 2, 1981, to July 7, 1992. There were nine realignments among these currencies during this peri-

FIGURE 15.1   DEMNLG Forward Bias Results
81/01/05–92/07/07

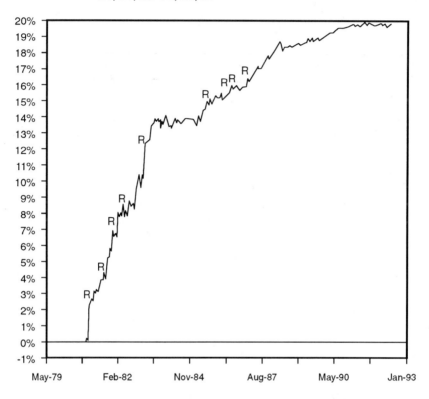

od, marked by an 'R' in the graphs. As a general rule, the cumulative profit rises over time, occasionally interrupted by these realignments. The largest loss was 7.10 percent, which occurred on February 23, 1982, during a realignment of the DEM/BEF. With that exception, however, the realignments appear to have only small interruptions of the cumulative profits, especially in a portfolio context. As Figure 15.6 shows, the interest differential is sufficient to compensate for the realignment risks. Even with a very biased and undiversified portfolio of all currencies that have devalued over the sample period, the cumulative performance of the carry strategy appears to withstand such events. Up to this point, it would be reasonable to conclude that historical evidence support the assertion that the forward bias outweighs the attendant event risks, especially if the portfolio is diversified globally.

FIGURE 15.2   DEMBEF Forward Bias Results
81/01/05–92/07/07

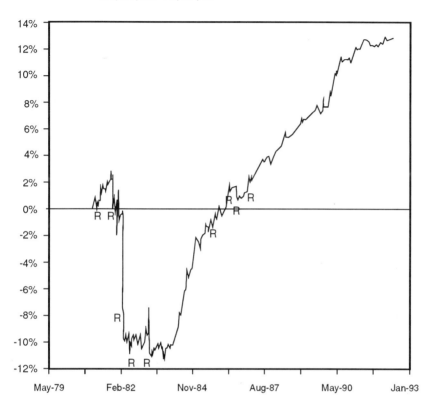

Next we turn to the question of risk measure. A reasonable measure of event risk given the present analytical framework is "the number of days of carry profit lost due to event risk." From this we can think of an event risk ratio as the expected number of carry days lost due to event interruption divided by the expected number of uninterrupted carry days. Ideally, we prefer our event risk ratios to be substantially below unity for a given calendar year. In order to gain insight on this measure, we present some historical experience.

Tables 15.3 and 15.4 provide some comparisons of the size of the realignment losses relative to that of the forward risk premium. In Table 15.3, we ask the question: how many days of cumulative profits prior to the realignment were wiped out by the realignment? In the case of the ERM realignment on March 23,

FIGURE 15.3   DEMFRF Forward Bias Results
81/01/05–92/07/07

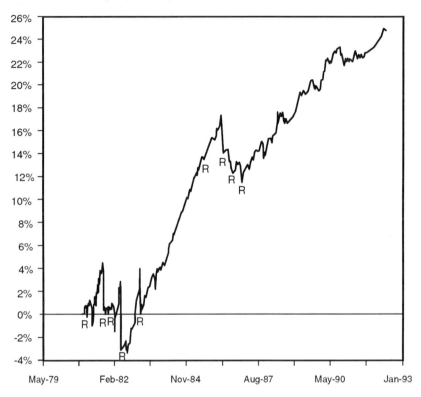

1981, the losses experienced by the DEM/NLG wiped out the cumulative profits of the previous five trading days. This is relatively small. In contrast, the ERM realignment on February 23, 1982, wiped out the entire cumulative profits of the DEM/BEF since the beginning of our sample on January 2, 1981.

To complete the measure, in Table 15.4, we ask the question: how many days of cumulative profits after a realignment were needed to make up for the losses incurred during the realignment? In the case of the ERM realignment on March 23, 1981, the losses experienced by the DEM/NLG were made up after one trading day. This is relatively small. On the other hand, the losses experienced by the DEM/BEF in the ERM realignment on February 23, 1982, were made up only after 1,315 trading days. This is relatively large.

FIGURE 15.4 DEMDKK Forward Bias Results
81/01/05–92/07/07

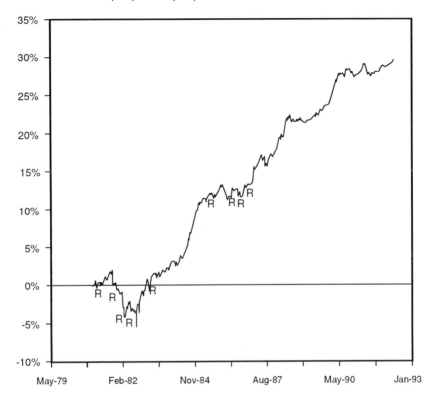

From Tables 15.3 and 15.4, it is obvious that event risk is signifi-cant with individual currency pairs even within a bounded system such as the EMS. In terms of the event risk ratio calculation, con-sider the case of DEM/BEF. If we were to base our expected num-ber of days lost due to event risk from Table 15.3, then it is clear that the ratio would exceed unity for any single calendar year (since it took away more than one year's cumulative profit). If we were to base our expected lost days on Table 15.4, the result is worse since it took well over four years to recover the loss. It is important to examine the expected lost days in both ways. Carry profits can be unusually large just before a potential devaluation. Should the risk subside without any incident, then abnormal carry gains will result. However, if the event is realized, large losses may occur but should be compared to the unusually large risk premium

FIGURE 15.5   DEMITL Forward Bias Results
81/01/05–92/07/07

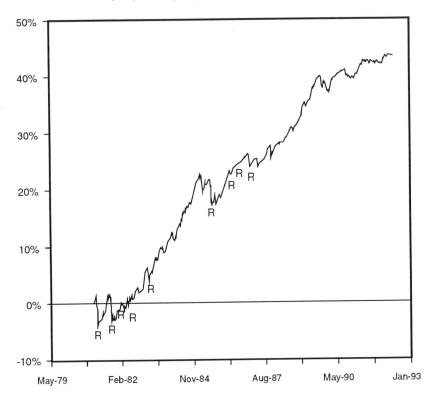

that was offered prior to the event. Therefore the result from Table 15.3 answers the question on expected lost days by showing how long one would have to have been operating this strategy to break even against event risk. The result from Table 15.4 answers the question from a different perspective. It is often the case that after a major devaluation, interest rates fall for the high-yielding currency. This means that post-devaluation, the forward premium declines. Consequently, if post-event carry days were used alone to recoup losses, then the number of lost days due to event risk will proportionally rise. Expected lost days must therefore combine both elements to account for the abnormally large premium prior to, and significantly lower premium subsequent to, the event.

To pursue this concept further, we examine a portfolio made up of equally weighted amounts of BEF, FRF, DKK, and ITL

FIGURE 15.6   Portfolio Forward Bias Results
81/01/05–92/07/07

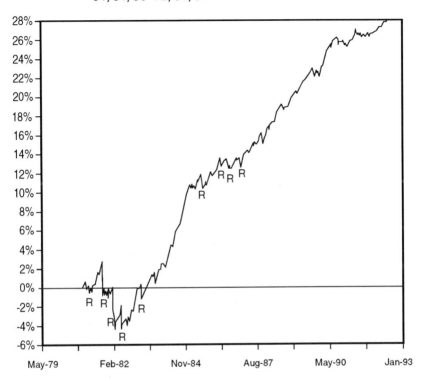

**TABLE 15.3   Number of Previous Trading Days of Cumulative Profits
Wiped Out by a Realignment**

Date	DEM/ NLG	DEM/ BEF	DEM/ FRF	DEM/ DKK	DEM/ ITL	Portfolio of BEP, FRF, DKK, ITL
810323	5	0	11	0	na	na
811005	0	114	80	139	84	90
820223	1	na	13	na	8	na
820614	33	na	na	26	20	52
830322	0	0	54	0	0	5
850722	5	2	3	0	193	52
860408	0	0	150	0	7	20
860804	0	83	0	0	0	0
870112	0	0	0	6	0	0

"na" indicates that the loss exceeds the cumulative profits since January 2, 1981

TABLE 15.4 Number of Subsequent Trading Days of Cumulative Profits Needed to Make Up for a Realignment Loss

Date	DEM/ NLG	DEM/ BEF	DEM/ FRF	DEM/ DKK	DEM/ ITL	Portfolio of BEF, FRF, DKK, ITL
810323	1	0	3	0	60	43
811005	0	1315	351	372	157	544
820223	1	897	44	178	57	227
820614	1	26	175	92	18	125
830322	0	0	91	0	0	2
850722	1	12	24	0	30	34
860408	0	0	533	0	21	147
860804	0	1	0	0	0	0
870112	0	0	0	4	0	0

against the DEM. The NLG was excluded, because it was the most profitable cross rate against the DEM. As of June 14, 1992, the losses of this portfolio due to realignments wiped out no more than 52 trading days of cumulative profits prior to the realignments (in Table 15.3), while these losses required no more than 125 trading days to recoup (in Table 15.4). Clearly, the expected loss ratio drops dramatically below one (between 52/365 and 125/365) even with a small portfolio of European currency pairs, all of which were devalued at least once during our sample period. This is positive evidence for implementing a carry portfolio, especially if one could diversify further by including non-European currency pairs.

Although it is clear that diversification helps, it is also important to assess factors underlying changes in event risk ratios to better manage exposure in individual currency pairs. This takes us to the third question in this section. The recent turmoil in the European currencies is a good case in hand. An immediate observation is that a carry portfolio of European currency pairs only is inadequately diversified against systemic events such as those we recently witnessed in Europe. Both the magnitude, with the Finnish markka losing 32 percent, and the scope of devaluation, involving seven countries at the time of writing, including G7 nations such as Britain and Italy, are unprecedented. It is interesting to examine the behavior of event risk ratios during this period. There is of course no deterministic way of forming expected event risk ratios. However, one could obtain insight from market parameters. Take the case of the Italian lira. Here, we need to appeal to the market's assessment of risk using the currency option market.

Under normal circumstances, one-month DEM/ITL options trade around 3 percent in implied volatility. Just one week before the devaluation, option implied volatility for DEM/ITL has increased to 24 percent. If under normal circumstances, expected lost days is n-days, then the increase in implied volatility must increase our expected lost days proportionately to say 8 times n-days. This is of course an approximation based on the following argument. If normal implied volatility reflects the risk of an adverse event, then an eightfold increase in normal risk level should correspondingly affect our estimate of expected lost days.

Finally, an important factor to consider is that the forward bias strategy is not limited to semi-fixed-rate systems such as the ERM. Rather, it is a general proposition that applies to all currency pairs, albeit with varying degrees of risk. The analyses in the last two sections explored the two sources of risk—continuous price risk and event risk. It is clear that with currencies that are managed within target zones—such as the ERM, Thai Bhat, etc.—the apparent reduction of continuous price risk is obtained at the cost of increases in event risk. The management of these two types of risk is far from being an exact science. We have outlined some of the key issues to be considered in this section. The portfolio tactics and the analytical tools required to manage these risks remain somewhat individualistic to the overall trading style and portfolio structure, of which the forward bias strategy may only be a component. Experience has taught us to go beyond just price statistics (or the purely historical approach) to incorporate economic fundamentals, to make use of derivative products, and to include fixed-income instruments in order to arrive at more efficient portfolio structures. The analysis underlying these portfolio tactics will take us much beyond the scope of this chapter and is perhaps best deferred to another occasion.

CONCLUSION

Based on the historical data and analyses presented in the last two sections, one may view this as evidence that the forward risk premiums (in the form of interest differentials) are sufficiently large to compensate the risks borne by a forward speculator. An alternative interpretation is that our sample is too short to observe the occurrence of very low probability and high risk events, such as a massive realignment, multiple realignments in rapid succession, the introduction of a single European currency, or the dissolution of the ERM. Note that a quick successful conclusion to the push for European Monetary Union is perhaps just as damaging to a carry strategy as devaluations. After all, one may run out of currency pairs to position with. Thus, the apparent profitability in forward speculation is merely reflecting the fact that the speculator is paid a risk premium to compensate risks borne.

Since these low-probability, high-risk events were infrequent in our sample period, we do not know whether the forward risk premium was sufficiently high to compensate for these risks. Such a judgment may be rendered if we can develop a model of the forward risk premium. In terms of ongoing research relevant to this area, we recommend the target zone literature (see, for example, Krugman, 1991) in economics.

To outline the connection, note that in the first place, the continuous risk of the major currencies can be viewed as the movements of a currency inside a very wide target zone. In the second place, the event risk of the European cross currencies can be viewed as realignment risks.

Typically, the target zone literature assumes a known and credible central bank policy of keeping the exchange rate within a band, and proceeds to describe the behavior of the exchange rate inside this band. The assumption is that the target zone is never changed. This is a good description of the ERM in between realignments. The problem is that it does not have realignment or event risk. What is needed is a modification to allow the central bank to change the band or target zone discretely. This would allow us to compare the interest rate differential in relation to the expected loss resulting from a realignment. At the time of writing, the literature in this area is still in its infancy, but it is an interesting and relevant academic field for potential investors in the carry strategy.

NOTES

1. From Reuters financial information services, approximately 11:40 a.m., using midmarket quotes. In practice, adjustments to bid/offer spread need to be made to arrive at executable quotations.
2. This is sometimes referred to as the income component of the "excess" total return of the bond—excess in the sense of return in addition to an assumed opportunity cost of the short-term rate of

funding (or interest). Mathematically, if B_0 is the initial bond price, I denotes the interest income (i.e., coupon receipt plus changes in accrued interest), and B_t denotes the end-of-period bond price, then the total excess return is

$$(B_t - B_0) + (I - i)$$

where i denotes the short-term funding cost. The first term of this expression gives the capital appreciation component of the total return and the second term gives the income component less funding cost. For simplicity, i represents the total interest charge for funding the position B_0 plus accrued interest. The forward price of the bond is $B_0 - I + i$ and the forward premium/discount is $I - i$.

3. Take 6.84%/(1 + 10.18% * 30/360) and we obtain 6.78% as required.
4. Hodrick (1987) provides an excellent summary of the empirical evidence that the forward exchange rate is not an unbiased predictor of the future spot rate.
5. The 3-month forward exchange rates were unavailable for ITL during 1973:I to 1976:II, for ESP during 1973:I, and for AUD during 1973:I to 1976:IV.
6. We have ignored transaction costs because they are trivial for large-scale transactions in the interbank foreign exchange market.
7. A t-test would reject the null hypothesis that the mean capital return is zero at the 5 percent (two-tailed) significance level.
8. Out of the 136 currency pairs, 90 reject the null hypothesis that the mean capital return is zero at the 5 percent (two-tailed) significance level.
9. Previous studies, such as Bilson (1981), Hodrick and Srivastava (1984), and Bilson and Hsieh (1987), have selected portfolio weights to lie on a conditional mean-variance frontier. This procedure tends to create large spread positions between currencies. This problem is avoided by picking a fixed weighting scheme.

References

Bilson, J. F. O., "The 'Speculative Efficiency' Hypothesis," *Journal of Business,* 54, 1981, 435–452.

Bilson, J. F. O., and Hsieh, D. A., "The Profitability of Currency Speculation," *Journal of International Forecasting,* 3, 1987, 115–130.

Cumby, R., and Obstfeld, M., "A Note on Exchange-Rate Expectations and Nominal Interest Differentials: A Test of the Fisher Hypothesis," *Journal of Finance,* 36, 1981, 697–704.

Fama, E., "Forward and Spot Exchange Rates," *Journal of Monetary Economics,* 14, 1984, 319–338.

Geweke, J., and Feige, E. L., "Some Joint Tests of the Efficiency of Markets for Forward Foreign Exchange," *Review of Economics and Statistics,* 61, 1979, 334–341.

Hansen, L. P., and Hodrick, R., "Forward Exchange Rates as Optimal Predictors of Future Spot Rates: An Econometric Analysis of Linear Models," *Journal of Political Economy,* 88, 1980, 829–853.

Hodrick, R., 1987, *Empirical Evidence on the Efficiency of Forward and Futures Foreign Exchange Markets,* New York: Harwood Academic Publishers.

Hodrick, R., and Srivastava, S., "An Investigation of Risk and Return in Forward Foreign Exchange," *Journal of International Money and Finance,* 5, 1987, S5–S22.

Hsieh, D. A., "Tests of Rational Expectations and No Risk Premium in Forward Exchange Markets," *Journal of International Economics,* 17, 1984, 173–184.

Korajczyk, R., "The Pricing of Forward Contracts for Foreign Exchange," *Journal of Political Economy,* 93, 1985, 346–368.

Meese, R., and Rogoff, K., "Empirical Exchange Rate Models of the Seventies: Are Any Fit to Survive?" *Journal of International Economics,* 14, 1983, 3–24.

In the News   16

The Big Casino: How Currency Traders Play for High Stakes against Central Banks

Randall Smith
Staff Reporter, *The Wall Street Journal*
Reprinted from *The Wall Street Journal,* Sept. 18, 1992

INTRODUCTION

This week, the world's currency traders took on Europe's powerful central banks—and got richer.

It was only the latest sign of who is making the really big money on Wall Street these days. It's not hotshot stock pickers or pin-striped investment bankers, but traders who have turned to the currency market for their biggest trades and profits.

Behind the scenes of central banks' efforts to manage their currencies and economies, these traders clash in Wall Street's newest great casino, the largest and least regulated of all the world's markets. "You can move a couple of billion with a couple of phone calls," says Cesar Montemayor, a New York money manager.

Currency traders aren't saying how much they pocketed in the past week as their buying and selling forced first the Finnish, and then in quick succession the Italian, British and Spanish central banks to devalue their currencies. But analysts and bankers estimate that European central banks spent reserves worth 30 billion markkaa to defend the Finnish currency, 24 billion marks to prop up the lira, and as much as 10 billion in support of British sterling.

THREATENED BY TREATY

By launching their attacks against one beleaguered European currency after another, foreign-exchange traders may have helped themselves in more than one way. Not only did they make money against the central banks, but the currency turmoil they caused could influence French voters to reject the Maastricht Treaty when they vote Sunday. The treaty is a threat to the traders, as it would lock the signatory states into a single currency by the end of the century, eliminating European cross-currency trading.

No one is suggesting that the repeated attacks on weak European currencies were premeditated. "Banks in this line of business are hungry for money . . . If opportunities for making money are there, banks will take them," observes David Webb, a professor of finance at the London School of Economics. If the traders' actions put unbearable pressure on the Exchange Rate Mechanism, he says, "that's not the [trading] banks' fault, but the policy makers' fault."

Still, after the Bank of England spent billions Tuesday on a fruitless attempt to prop up the pound, Britain's Chancellor of the Exchequer, Norman Lamont, blamed traders for some of the exchange-rate chaos. "As a result of uncertainties caused by the French referendum," he said, "massive speculative flow [has] continued to disrupt the function of the Exchange Rate Mechanism."

TOP EARNERS

Four of the six highest-paid people on Wall Street in 1991 were traders who deal heavily in currencies, according to *Financial World* magazine. George Soros earned $117 million in 1991 after scoring big with a huge leveraged bet, rumored to have topped $2.6

billion, on the German mark in 1989 and 1990, after the Berlin Wall fell. Paul Tudor Jones, who earned more than $60 million in 1991, made most of his profits in currency trading, traders say.

Then there's the secretive Louis M. Bacon. Six years ago he was just another commodity-futures broker at Shearson Lehman Brothers; these days he rents a vacation home (damaged by Hurricane Andrew, to be sure) on Chub Cay in the Bahamas and has bought a $2.8 million, seven-bedroom mansion in Greenwich, Conn., not far from Diana Ross's house. He manages roughly $800 million, darting in and out of currency and futures markets to grab quick profits and scores of short-term and medium-term trades. Last year, Mr. Bacon had a $20 million paycheck.

Speculators like Messrs. Bacon, Jones and Soros are part of a tidal surge of currency trading, swollen by increased speculative trading by banks, greater foreign investments by U.S. pension funds and the expansion of currency futures and options. Only 5 percent or 10 percent of the trading volume results from routine commercial transactions in which people or companies need to convert one currency to another.

Global currency trading has doubled to $640 billion daily between 1986 and 1989, according to a survey by the Bank for International Settlements. By comparison, daily trading in U.S. Treasury bonds totals about $300 billion, and in U.S. stocks less than $10 billion.

Currency traders can control multibillion-dollar positions with only a few hundred million in capital through massive borrowing, using bank credit lines. (The only limits are set by the credit departments of a trader's bank dealers.) Debt-to-cash levels of 3-to-1 to 6-to-1 are common in the currency market; in stocks, the limit is 1-to-1.

Earlier this year Mr. Soros, for example, reported debts of $7.5 billion, three times the $2.4 billion as he has under management and twice as much debt as R. H. Macy & Co., the troubled retailer. The amount of money run by futures fund managers has doubled in the past three years, topping $20 billion, and currency futures account for the biggest portion of that, according to Managed Account Reports, an industry newsletter. "These funds have a major impact on the day-to-day direction of the foreign-exchange market," says Yale Fisher, head of foreign-exchange trading at BankAmerica.

The leverage, coupled with currencies' frequent sudden moves of 5 percent to 15 percent, makes for volatile results. One leading currency trader, John Henry, scored a gain of 40 percent last December, then suffered a 45 percent loss early this year, then made back all the losses. As one investor in a currency trading fund puts it, "It's like handling nitroglycerin for a living."

TRADING SECRETS

Traders also like the secrecy—and lack of regulation—of the world currency markets. While stock-market trades are instantly made public, currency trades are conducted over telephones and electronic trading systems in the privacy of a network of bank dealers. In theory at least, each trade is known only to the trader and his or her dealer. The lack of regulation has been all the more appealing since last year's Treasury-note auction scandal turned a harsh spotlight and aggressive regulation on the U.S. government bond market.

In this market, big-time currency traders sometimes battle entire governments and central banks. Take famed currency trader Andrew Krieger, who helped Bankers Trust New York rack up 1987 currency trading profits of $513 million.

Mr. Krieger would sometimes seek out smaller markets where he could send currency prices gyrating all by himself. In late 1987, he scored big profits with massive sales of New Zealand dollars, known as kiwis, driving the price down with sales that eventually totaled 14 percent of the country's currency reserves. The kiwi, one trader recalled, fell "like a wounded pigeon." Mr. Krieger hedged his risk of losses by buying an offsetting long-term option allowing him to buy the kiwi.

Angry New Zealand officials decided to play hardball. With New Zealand banks suffering losses on their kiwi holdings, government officials traced the attack on their currency to Mr. Krieger. One former Bankers Trust official says New Zealand's Chancellor of the Exchequer telephoned Bankers Trust chairman Charles Sanford to complain, and the country threatened to raise its interest rates to jack up the kiwi and inflict losses on Mr. Krieger. Mr. Krieger left Bankers Trust soon afterward, and the bank later restated its 1987 financial results. Mr. Krieger says his departure was unrelated to the kiwi trades; Bankers Trust declines to comment.

BUYING STERLING

Mr. Krieger made a similarly hasty exit from his next place of employment, Mr. Soros's Soros Fund Management, only a few months later. He bought more than $1.8 billion worth of British pounds sterling in a single trade through Chemical Bank's London branch, at a time when the Bank of England was trying to drive down the pound. Although Mr. Krieger was merely covering a profitable "short" position (a bet on a decline in the pound), the high-profile trade made it appear that Mr. Soros, who has extensive ties to European power brokers, was tilting against British authorities. Within days, Mr. Krieger left that job. Neither Mr. Soros nor Mr. Krieger will comment on the reasons for his departure.

By the time he left Mr. Soros, Mr. Krieger had such a swashbuckler's reputation that when the central bank of Malaysia, Bank Negara, began roiling the market by taking positions of $5 billion or more against different currencies, rumors spread that Mr. Krieger was recently directing its trades. In November 1990, the bank publicly denied any involvement by Mr. Krieger; he says the rumors were preposterous.

Bank Negara is said to have cooled its frenzied trading since then, but it remains a big player. Mr. Krieger, on the other hand, has turned to a more conservative style of trading, in far smaller amounts other traders deri-

sively call "one-lots"—only $1 million per trade.

RECENT FOCUS

Wall Street traders' focus on currencies is relatively recent. Exchange rates were allowed to float only 21 years ago, in 1971, and currency options and futures didn't proliferate until the mid-1980s. Currency trades are often related to bond trades, because both depend on interest rates prevailing in a given country. For example, the disparity between high German interest rates and low U.S. rates drove down the dollar through much of this year.

Until 1985, central banks of industrialized nations had a laissez-faire policy toward exchange rates. That year, those banks began trying to drive down the dollar to stimulate U.S. exports—making them more affordable to foreigners. Because the pattern persisted for several years, traders who followed that pattern scored consistent profits.

But central-bank intervention doesn't always work, as recent events made abundantly clear. In the past week, traders have "done sensationally well; most grabbed it off the central banks," says one trader. Because the banks were trying to prop up currencies like the pound, the lira and the Swedish krona at unrealistic levels, the banks were "writing checks" to traders who took the other side of the same trades, traders gloat.

GLOBAL MARKET

More than stocks and bonds, currency trading is truly global. The ebb and flow of trading begins in Australia, after the New York market closes around 4:30 p.m., then quickly moves to Tokyo, London and finally back to New York. One bank trader estimates that 30 percent of the volume occurs during the Asian market day, 45 percent during European trading hours, and only 15 percent during the U.S. day. Prices are more volatile in some periods when only a few markets, such as Sydney, are open.

The currency markets are unfettered by the kinds of rules that prevail on a stock exchange. For example, "front-running"—in which a dealer executes a trade for his own account before executing the same trade for a client—is considered acceptable behavior in the currency market, butit is a violation of stock-exchange rules.

Of course, the check on such activities is whether the customer gets a good price on his trade. While some corporate clients monitor currency-market price movements closely, other customers don't, and are thus vulnerable to getting off-market prices that give the dealer a fat profit. "It's a great business for the banks because the customers are so ignorant," says Michael Harkins of Levy Harkins Co., a New York money manager.

The currency market has its own highly evolved, and constantly changing, gamesmanship.

"LINING UP"

Some traders pay close attention to which other big traders are holding big positions in a particular currency, and what market moves would be likely to prompt those trades to unwind those positions. The positions these giant traders take have become important enough to move the market. "We spend a lot of time figuring what will make these guys turn," says one currency trader.

A particularly predatory tactic in this market is called "lining up." As described in *Global Finance* magazine, a trader will call six dealers in quick succession, selling them $50 million apiece and getting another currency in exchange. When the dealers all move to sell the dollars at once, they drive the dollar down and thus strengthen the other currency, producing quick gains for the trader and losses for most of the dealers.

Other traders focus on economic fundamentals, trying to guess what policies central banks will pursue toward their currencies. A lively trade has sprung up in this area as well. Before each "G-7" meeting of finance ministers of the seven industrialized nations, a group called the G-7 Council, organized by former Federal Reserve governor Manuel Johnson, meets to talk about currency issues. The meeting attracts scholars, former politicians, economists—and currency traders.

SOUTHERN EXPOSURE

Some professionals have found ways to limit their losses. One reason Mr. Bacon has attracted so much money to manage is that his draw-downs, or losses, have been relatively minor—a few percentage points at the most—while his gains have been consistent, at times spectacular. In 1990, his Moore Global Investments Ltd. offshore fund scored a return of 86 percent.

Once, while riding the Concorde during a marketing trip to court overseas investors, Mr. Bacon told an associate that one reason he cuts his losses so well is "I'm from the South, and we Southerners are used to losing."

Although few U.S. banks now take the kinds of risks Mr. Krieger did at Bankers Trust, currency trading generates handsome profits for the biggest U.S. banks. Five earned more than $200 million in 1991 foreign-exchange profits, led by Citicorp with $709 million; and such trading produced profits equaling 77 percent of the after-tax profits for the 10 biggest money-center banks. But banks' activity is shrinking because regulators are forcing them to set aside reserves for taking such risks.

Citicorp fields hundreds of salesmen around the globe who grind out thousands of small but high-profit-margin transactions, particularly in exotic currencies such as the Indian rupee. Bankers Trust and J.P. Morgan & Co. both combine dealings with hundreds of corporate clients with trading for the banks' own accounts. Chemical particularly courts trades with the fast-trading hedge funds and futures funds.

17

Foreign Currency Options and the Portfolio Manager

Andrew J. Krieger, KB Currency Advisors, Inc.
Sheri Gorin Baker, KB Currency Advisors, Inc.

INTRODUCTION

Foreign currency options are powerful tools which, unlike the spot, forward, and futures markets, allow portfolio managers to create infinite combinations of asymmetrical risk-reward strategies that reflect very specific market views. The "asymmetrical" feature of options is the characteristic that most profoundly sets options apart from other currency management tools, as they help managers not only make money, but find ways to predetermine maximum losses even when their market assumptions and strategies are completely wrong or when unforeseeable exogenous events cause huge discontinuous price changes.

Foreign currency options can be managed as a separate asset class, in which a portfolio of option "investments" is created that expresses a manager's view on the market. On the other hand, foreign currency options can be used as an overlay tool for protecting the local currency value of a portfolio of international assets. The bottom line is that currency options, regardless of whether they are used as trading or hedging tools, are conservative instruments through which well-thought-out market views can be expressed.

The following chapter will outline some of the unique characteristics of foreign currency options and how they can be used to create risk-controlled investment and hedging strategies in the most liquid and efficient market in the world.

DECISION-MAKING DIALECTIC

Before any portfolio manager can implement a particular currency-based strategy, he or she must first develop a clear view of the market, which, in the world of foreign exchange, means sifting through a vast array of domestic and international factors. The market for foreign currencies is the world's largest, with daily turnover exceeding $1 trillion in the spot market and $60 billion in the currency option market. It is important to understand that no one market player can determine the value of any particular foreign currency—rather, it is the hundreds of thousands of market players, making millions of transactions every day, that determine the relative value of the dollar against the Japanese yen, German deutsche mark, British pound, and other currencies.

In order for a portfolio manager to develop a view on a given foreign currency pair, he or she must first determine and weigh the relevant data. For example, a myriad of fundamental factors exist in the market, including economic, social, political, demographical, and psychological data. Through fundamental analysis, a manager can evaluate the differences that exist between countries in terms of their fiscal, monetary, social, and trade policies, and the investment opportunities that each holds. Such analysis helps the manager develop a scenario of how a changing world will affect the value of each country's currency.

In addition to fundamental analysis, many managers choose to study the market's technical formations. This data can be expressed in a number of different ways, from Elliott Wave analysis to cyclical studies. These data are important not necessarily for their predictive value, but because the majority of players in the currency market look at the same types of technical charts and often expect certain market behavior at "critical" technical levels. The underlying philosophy behind technical analysis is that history tends to repeat itself in similar, if not identical, patterns.

Finally, a good portfolio manager will use a subjective overlay in the decision process. This checkpoint analyzes the substance of dialogues the manager holds with a number of different individuals—including other market participants, economists, and business people—in an attempt to delve more deeply into what is really going on behind the data. This type of discussion also helps a portfolio manager gauge the size and direction of the speculative and investment positions in the market at any one time. For example, if a manager believes that the market is overall long U.S. dollars against the German mark and he expects U.S. dollar weakness, then he will expect that if the dollar falls there will be massive liquidations of dollar holdings, which will further push the dollar to lower levels.

The process of decision making is further complicated by the fact that markets often react perversely when significant news breaks. Furthermore, the market's initial reaction is as likely to prove to be right as wrong, so taking a cue from market behavior can be a very costly procedure. For example, if there were a major earthquake in Tokyo, should a speculator buy or sell Japanese yen? While the speculator's gut reaction may be to sell yen, the yen could actually strengthen significantly if the Japanese were forced to repatriate assets from abroad to pay for the rebuilding of their domestic economy.

Once a trader analyzes those factors which she considers to be relevant to currency market forecasting, she is ready to express her view by taking a position in the market. Proper trading is not wild gambling. Deciding the size of one's trade, determining the allowable loss provisions for every idea, and devising a systematic approach to the process of taking profits requires prudent money and risk management. By designing and following a risk-management system, the manager can relax and focus on the markets because the maximum losses of his or her portfolio are defined, assured, and tolerable. A well-developed risk-management system will further ensure that the psychological and emotional shifts of the trader will not alter the overall risk-reward profile of the entire portfolio. Once a portfolio manager understands the intricacies of options, he can use these tools to create strategies that reflect his market views in a risk-controlled fashion.

BASIC CHARACTERISTICS OF OPTIONS

When someone purchases a currency option, he pays a premium for the right, not the obligation, to buy or sell a fixed amount of some currency in exchange for another at a fixed price on or before a future date. The premium cost represents the maximum

FIGURE 17.1   Spot/Theta Sensitivity DEM/USD Put Option

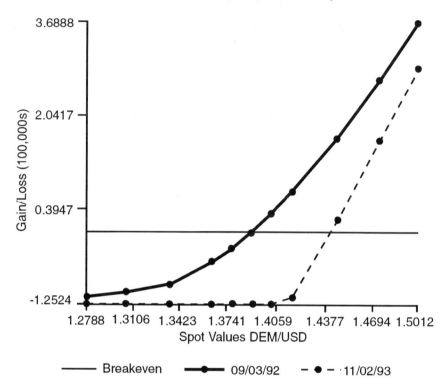

amount that can be lost if the option expires worthless, whereas the potential gains that can be earned through the option are unlimited (Figure 17.1). In contrast, when someone enters into a spot, forward, or futures contract, she is obligated to exchange one currency for another at the contract rate, regardless of whether the contract is in a gain or loss position. As a result, the potential cash losses for a portfolio manager who takes a position or hedges with a forward contract are unlimited (Figure 17.2).

DETERMINING PREMIUM COST

The price of a currency option is determined by several factors, including the current market spot rate, the levels of the respective interest rates, desired strike price, maturity date, and the level of implied volatility. All of the above inputs are entered into an option pricing model that evaluates the distribution of probable

FIGURE 17.2   Spot/Theta Sensitivity DEM/USD Forward Contract

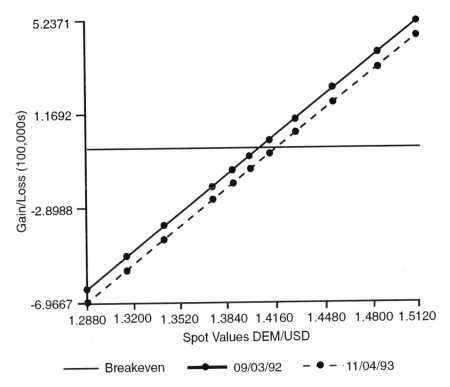

outcomes, given the market's parameters, and then determines an option's theoretical value (premium). The most subjective input to the system is implied volatility, which represents the trading market's estimate as to how much the currency will fluctuate in the foreign exchange market over the life of the option. The greater the expectations of currency fluctuation (the higher the implied volatility), the more expensive an option will be.

In addition, the strike of the option is important in determining the option's premium cost. If, for example, an option's strike price is equal to the actual market rate, the option is considered to be at-the-money and will have a roughly 50 percent probability of finishing in-the-money. The price of this at-the-money option will be greater than the price of an option whose strike price is "worse" than the current market rate and whose probability of finishing in-the-money is less than 50 percent. Such an option is considered to be out-of-the-money.

The risk of loss for out-of-the-money options is less than for at-the-money options, and therefore the *absolute* returns on an out-of-the-money option will be less than for the at-the- money option. In *percentage* terms, however, out-of-the money options can show higher returns than at-the-money options, especially given the leverage that a portfolio manager naturally achieves from an out-of-the-money option investment. Choosing a strike price will depend on the manager's expectations regarding price movements and the amount of premium he or she is willing to risk on a particular idea.

SENSITIVITY/PERFORMANCE MEASURES OF OPTIONS

Delta

The asymmetrical risk-reward characteristic of purchased options affects the way an option increases and decreases in value, given changes in exchange rates. The value of options does not typically change in a 1:1 ratio as spot rates change. Rather, the change in value is only a fraction of the spot change. This percentage change in value for a given change in the market exchange rate is referred to as the option's delta.

Delta can be no lower than zero percent and no greater than 100 percent. An option with a delta of zero percent is essentially worthless, whereas an option with a delta of 100 percent incurs gains and losses in very much the same way as a spot, forward, or futures position. Stated another way, an option's delta approaches 100 percent as it goes deep in-the-money and contracts towards zero percent as it moves far out-of-the-money. As an option moves in-the-money, its delta expands, capturing a greater percentage of a favorable spot move. Conversely, as the spot rate moves against the option holder, the options' delta contracts toward zero percent, limiting losses to the amount of premium paid. For example, if an option has a delta of 25 percent, a 1-pfennig spot move against the option holder decreases the value of the option by only one quarter of 1 pfennig, whereas a forward position would lose 1 pfennig for every 1 pfennig adverse move.

Change in Spot Rate * Delta = Change in Option's Value

OR

$$\text{Delta} = \frac{\text{Change in Option's Value}}{\text{Change in Spot Rate}}$$

Gamma

Gamma defines the rate of change of an option's delta and is an important risk-reward measure in managing a portfolio of options. Because an option's delta is constrained to values between zero percent and 100 percent, its gamma is greatest when the option is at-the-money, and drops toward zero when the option is either very much in-the-money or very much out-of-the-money. In other words, an at-the-money option's 50 percent delta is most responsive, giving it the highest gamma.

Furthermore, an option's gamma typically increases as the time to maturity decreases. This is because any given spot move has more of an impact on an option's final value for a shorter maturity option than for one with a longer maturity. Gamma lets a portfolio manager know how fast the delta of his or her option will change, given a specific market movement, and helps the manager weigh the benefits of holding a long option position versus the potential losses the option will incur if the market remains steady or moves adversely.

Theta

Theta, or time decay, is another critical component of option valuation, as the passage of time reduces the chance for an option to finish in-the-money or make additional gains. Therefore, time decay reduces the value of a long option position. An option's theta is greatest for at-the-money options and declines as the option becomes either very in-the-money or very out-of-the-money. Also, as an option approaches its expiration date, its theta increases—time decay is most rapid near the end of an option's life. Option positions can be managed to help offset the effect of time decay during a market's consolidating phase by "delta hedging." Delta hedging is the "riskless" execution of spot transactions to reduce an option portfolio's sensitivity to spot changes and generally consists of selling market rallies as the delta increases and buying market weakness as the delta decreases. Delta hedging can generate quite positive returns during consolidating, choppy market conditions. A manger can therefore "earn back" some, if not all, of the time decay that may occur during more tranquil market conditions by delta hedging a long option position.

EXPRESSING MARKET VIEWS USING OPTIONS

Structuring option strategies requires a good deal more refinement than does implementing a basic spot or forward transaction. For example, it is not sufficient for someone who uses options to merely determine the direction of the next currency move; he must also figure out the path and duration of the move. Will there be sharp, dramatic changes in direction over a relatively narrow range, or will there be a steady price appreciation or depreciation? If there is a steady, trending price movement, how long will the move take to develop? How far will it go? While the cost of extending an option's maturity by one month, for example, is generally less than the cost of a one-month option, a portfolio manager whose options have too long a maturity for the corresponding market move will see his delta expand too slowly and his options increase too little in value to earn enough money on the position. If the option is too short in duration, the manager will have an insufficient period of time to capture a sustained market move.

There are infinite trading possibilities in options, reflecting a myriad of market opportunities, given a manager's perceptions of future market movements. Once all the questions regarding the direction and path of a currency move are clarified by the portfolio manager, the process of choosing the most cost-effective option strategy begins. First, the manager must consider the market levels of implied volatility that are being used for the options on the currency pair on which he or she has a view. Sometimes the market volatility level is higher than the manager would like to pay, and the break-even on a straight option purchase does not provide an attractive risk-reward profile. At that time, the manager may want to refine his or her view further to implement a spreading strategy wherein the manager buys an option or options of a certain type and maturity and sells others to limit the cost. Such strategies can be developed that maintain a limited loss characteristic for the transaction.

While the premium cost of an option is objectively considered to be the fair market value as determined by the market's level of volatility (and therefore the expected return of that option, if it is dynamically hedged, is the risk-free rate), that cost is subjectively valued by the portfolio manager given his or her views on the market. Ideally, the portfolio manager will purchase assets that she considers to be "cheap," or undervalued by the market, and inventory them until they reach "fair" market value or perhaps even become overvalued.

SAMPLE INVESTMENT STRATEGIES

Starting in June of 1990, the dollar began a sharp descent against the German mark from the DEM 1.7000 level, reaching new all-time lows at the sub-DEM 1.5000 level by October. The dollar began to consolidate and range-trade between DEM 1.46 and DEM 1.52 through Christmastime. This consolidation, which extended for several months, preceded the January 15 deadline that was given to Iraq to leave Kuwait. Implied option volatilities became compressed during this time because of the quiet market conditions, and in fact reached levels of approximately 10 percent—while not a historical low for implied volatilities, certainly a low level given the potential "event risk" on January 15.

At that time, an excellent trade was to purchase a DEM strangle in which one would purchase an out-of-the-money DEM call option and an out-of-the-money DEM put option, expecting a large move in either direction. For example, the cost of purchasing a DEM 1.4500-DEM 1.5300 strangle for three-month maturity would have been 1.80 percent. By the end of March 1991, the DEM was trading at DEM 1.6800, giving the strangle a value of 9.8 percent on this risk-controlled position, or a 444.44 percent profit on the original premium investment! (See Figure 17.3.)

Sometimes implied volatilities are high given a trader's expectations and the maximum loss he is willing to experience. Strategies can be structured, however, that reflect the portfolio manager's underlying view while limiting the cost by both buying and selling options. For example, assume the Japanese yen is trading near its all-time-high level and the portfolio manager believes that a break of that level will result in an acceleration and further substantial strengthening of the yen. The manager wants to limit premium cost, though, because there are a number of negative fundamental conditions that argue for a weaker yen. Also, there are major technical considerations which reduce the probability of the yen accelerating to new all time highs, thereby reducing his willingness to spend much money on the idea.

FIGURE 17.3   Spot/Theta Sensitivity DEM/USD Strangle

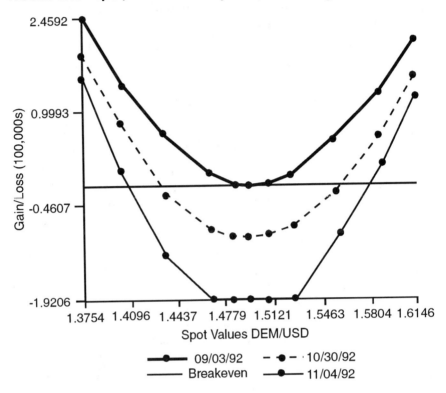

The manager can sell a three-month yen call with a strike of 120.50 and buy twice as many three-month yen calls with a strike price of 118.00 for net zero cost. This strategy will therefore lose no money if the dollar exchange rate stays above the historical lows. If the dollar weakens substantially through the lows, however, the 118.00 yen calls will earn money at twice the rate that the short 120.50 yen call loses money, becoming a net winner. The risk is that the dollar breaks through 120.50 and drifts toward 118.00 by expiry. The maximum loss is yen 2.50 (Figure 17.4).

SAMPLE OVERLAY STRATEGY

Let's assume that a portfolio manager has made a large U.K. money market investment. The sterling holdings are earning approximately 6 percent per annum more than a comparable U.S. Treasury bill investment, but the manager realizes that an adverse

FIGURE 17.4   Spot/Theta Sensitivity JPY/USD

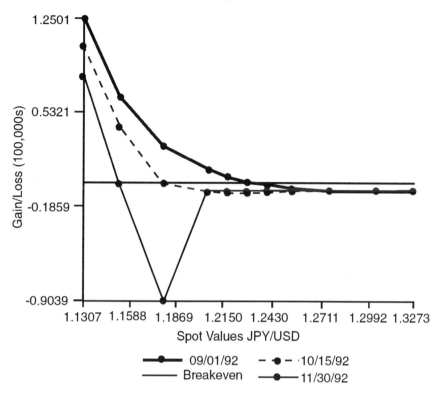

Spot Values JPY/USD

09/01/92   – ● – ·10/15/92
Breakeven   ●——11/30/92

move in the exchange rate between U.S. dollars and British pounds would reduce her overall return—perhaps even make the return negative if the pound weakens by more than 6 percent over the course of the year.

The portfolio manager examines her alternatives with regard to hedging, and considers selling sterling forward to hedge the exchange risk. The imbedded "cost" of hedging one year's exposure in the forward or futures market is 6 percent, however, and that "cost" effectively converts her U.K. investment yield into a U.S. dollar yield. Therefore, the portfolio would only reflect differences in sovereign risk and the potential price appreciation/ depreciation in the underlying money market instruments. Further, if the pound were to strengthen, the forward contract would show losses, effectively preventing the portfolio from benefiting from the favorable currency move and probably forcing the manager to liquidate a portion of her U.K. holdings to cover the losses generated by the forward hedge.

Because of the high cost of hedging (i.e., high interest rate differential), a manager would want to hedge only selectively, for example, when he thought the pound would weaken against the U.S. dollar. Because the manager may be wrong, he should consider selectively purchasing currency options to hedge an expected dollar rise. While the option will have a premium cost associated with it, losses are limited and the gains that arise should the pound weaken will help protect the value of the underlying U.K. money market portfolio.

Let's assume the U.S. dollar is currently trading at $1.8500 per pound. The portfolio manager expects the pound to weaken, so she purchases a $1.8000 sterling put for three months for a cost of $0.0300. Within two months, the pound is at $1.7200 and the manager thinks it is bottoming for the time being. The manager hedges the sterling put option by purchasing pounds at the one-month forward rate of $1.7100, and the pound closes the end of month three at $1.7800. The option is exercised for $0.0200 and the forward earns $0.0700 for a total gain of $0.0900; less the premium cost of $0.0300, the net gain is $0.0600 with a spot rate of $1.7800. The manager has successfully captured $0.0600 of a $0.0700 adverse currency move!

CONCLUSION

Currency options offer tremendous advantages and flexibility for speculation as well as for hedging. While designing the ideal option-based strategy requires a great deal of skill and market experience, the benefits that can be derived through effective option structuring are extremely powerful. Given the desire of today's manager to find conservative approaches to money management, currency option expertise will prove invaluable for achieving success in the 1990s.

18

Quantitative Analysis in the Financial Markets

Grant N. Smith
Millburn Ridgefield Corp.

A BRIEF HISTORY

"It sure beats working for a living" was a favorite phrase of one of the earliest of the breed known as technicians. The "it" was the approach to trading that avoided the usual market analysis of supply and demand, and focused instead on the actions of the market itself. In addition, the above protagonist of leisure had taken the first steps beyond what people normally think of when they hear the term "technical analysis." This entailed two novel ideas: first was the use of computers to assist in the analysis, and second (an outgrowth of the first) was the creation of simulations to analyze trading systems.

These two advances are now old hat. But in the early 1970s they were certainly novel. Recall that there were no PCs, no workstations, no digital data feeds (at least none that mere mortals could afford), and that most "technical analysis" consisted of poring over charts and attempting to divine future price action from the shapes formed by lines drawn on these charts.

Employing computers in the early 1970s meant dispensing with subjective judgment, and formulating firm rules of analysis. These rules could then be applied to historical data to simulate their effectiveness over time. The pioneers doing this made the fortuitous decision to pursue their strategies in the futures markets rather than the equity or fixed-income markets. Their timing could not have been better, coinciding as it did with a series of momentous events whose effects would be felt for the rest of the decade. These were, roughly in order, the failure of the Soviet grain crop, Nixon closing the gold window and thereby ending the Bretton Woods era of fixed exchange rates, fatal experiments with wage/price controls with ensuing inflation, and the Arab-Israeli war, which ushered in an oil embargo against the West, and also the age of the "Oil Weapon."

The resulting turmoil sent prices of most commodities into unheard-of territory. So much so that traditional participants in these markets (the farmers, grain elevator operators, cereal manufacturers, meat packers, etc.) who relied on traditional supply/demand analysis, simply did not believe the prices. Some withdrew from the markets entirely. Others perhaps tried to fight the prices, usually with disastrous results. The "technicians," however, without the intellectual baggage of understanding the fundamental factors that drove the markets in normal times, and coupled with the leverage available in futures trading, made huge profits. And these profits were made so seemingly effortlessly that it hardly qualified as "working for a living."

Such success gets noticed. The techniques used in their analysis were usually simple but effective ways of capturing the observed phenomena, namely, that prices trended, that these trends continued for extended periods of time, and that prices went far beyond what any expert could imagine. Prices did not, however, proceed in a perfectly straight line. Rather, they varied noisily around the underlying trend. But in markets that were so one-directional, the application of virtually any smoothing algorithm (such as simple moving averages) could smother the noise and expose the underlying trend.

THE NEW MARKET PARTICIPANTS

Like the fading sounds of a struck bell, so the vast supply/demand imbalances extant in so many markets began to fade. By the end of the '70s the simple methods employed so profitably throughout the decade began to break down. For many who failed to see the writing on the wall, and failed to adjust their approach, the ensuing losses were as large as their earlier profits. A great many prominent names simply disappeared from the scene.

But, as noted earlier, large profits get noticed, and attract participants to the markets from diverse backgrounds, and with diverse skills. A great many of this new group of people were, and continue to be, people with strong quantitative abilities.

We hear more and more of Wall Street hiring "rocket scientists." Literally, not just figuratively. Scores of Ph.D.s were lured out of their research labs in academia and industry, and into the financial industry. The complexities of analyzing many financial instruments have always required quantitative prowess on Wall Street. This is nothing new, as even well-understood, long-standing financial instruments (such as the diverse group of fixed-income instruments) are mathematical by their very nature. And when one adds in some of the idiosyncrasies of these instruments (like the 360-day year used in U.S. Treasury discount instruments versus the 365-day year in coupon-bearing instruments) a strong quantitative capability is a *sine qua non* for participating in these markets. The old saw about three-star, two-star, and one-star generals is appropriate here. (A three-star general reads and writes; a two-star general reads or writes, but not both; a one-star general can't read or write, but has friends who can.) One has to be at least a 1-star general in most markets.

When one considers some of the many familiar financial instruments, it is very clear that there has always been a need for quantitative analysis on Wall Street. There has always been a need to be able to compare, for example, coupon-paying instruments with discount instruments, or to put a value on an option, or to create a portfolio of assets that meet certain constraints. More recently, in the deregulated world of finance there has grown up a bewildering array of instruments, often tailored to the needs of specific customers. This too requires quantitative skills to engineer instruments with the needed characteristics, to determine how to implement them, and of course, how to price them.

For the most part, the seminal research in these areas was performed in the academic world, and the ideas carried forth by graduates into the wider world. These graduates were usually to be found somewhat outside the mainstream of Wall Street's heavy hitters, and functioned more as in-house consultants to whom the salesmen and traders (the groups that like to think they are the ones that "really make the money") could turn with questions or for research involving quantitative analysis. Their quantitative skills tended to be those current in such fields as financial analysis and econometrics (the branch of economics less concerned with economic theory, and more focused on the quantitative skills required for analyzing data). Such people are still to be found in large numbers, performing many critical analytic functions throughout the financial community, both within Wall Street and in the financial departments of their customers—such as corporate treasuries and pension managers.

However, in the past few years, a quite different group of "quants" has been making waves on Wall Street. These are people that come from rather more exotic fields such as genetics, or from places like the Pentagon (or at least the companies working on Pentagon projects). Their training has typically been far removed from Wall Street, and the application of some of the more esoteric techniques was developed specifically for, and confined to, their specific disciplines. A researcher in genetic algorithms had only one interest in anything to do with finance: to get his or her research funded! And what they were up to in their labs rarely invaded the thoughts of the financial world, with the possible exception of the stock analysts following their companies.

But what has been happening at an increasing pace is that the quants have ceased merely being resources for traders to draw on, and have noticed that they are quite capable of implementing their own ideas rather than simply passing them on to others. This is something comparatively new. The quants have invaded the dealing rooms! As ever, success attracts notice, and news occasionally leaks out about some whiz kid whose income ran into the tens of millions from actually trading on his or her ideas. And Wall Street, always alert to new tools of quantitative analysis, routinely monitors developments in a broad range of scientific disciplines. This is in large measure attributable to the (occasional) demonstrated success of proponents of quantitative analysis. In order to understand the growing power and success of this new breed of people, it is instructive to see how the financial world has changed to accommodate them.

TECHNICAL DEVELOPMENTS

Let us now turn to changes in the financial world (other than the type of people) that have brought quantitative analysis its recognition. To do so, it is easiest to split these changes into various dimensions: communications, the data, computer equipment, the foreign exchange markets, and the analysis techniques. (These developments are summarized in Figures 18.1 and 18.2.)

FIGURE 18.1 Summary of Developments

	1960s	1970s	1980s	1990s
Markets	• Limited access for most to financial markets • Foreign exchange limited to trade-finance	• Growth of financial markets • Growth in popularity of futures	• Explosion in derivatives available • Dis intermediation as debt raised directly in markets • Extensive "Financial Engineering" • Derivatives volumes outstrip volumes in underlying instruments	• Issuers fine-tune ability to offer tailored OTC instruments • Continued growth in derivatives volume • Continued growth in currency trading volume as more countries float their currencies
World Environment	• Relative global stability • Fixed exchange rates • Banks dominate debt markets	• Inflation becomes endemic • Commodities prices explode • Oil prices rise 4000% • Fixed exchange rates disappear in 1st world countries	• Asset inflation continues • Huge cross-border capital flows • Vast increase in size of foreign exchange markets • 3rd World/Latin American debt crises • Growth in financial markets forces pace of financial deregulation • Japan becomes dominant source of international capital • Right-wing (market oriented) politics dominant	• Inflation fears ease, but wariness persists • End of Cold War • More countries float their currencies • Right-wing politics in retreat • Capital more and more global in nature

309

FIGURE 18.1 *(continued)*

	1960s	1970s	1980s	1990s
Communications	• AT&T Monopoly • Expensive • Voice traffic	• Competition begins—MCI • Prices start to decline • Growth in (low-speed) data traffic • Appearance of faster networks	• Array of services available • Much lower prices • Large amounts of data traffic • High-speed networks available (primarily in dense urban areas)	• Multimedia (data) transmissions predominate • Advances in data compresion techniques • Private networks grow • Prices continue to fall
Data	• Few vendors • Limited # of markets • Textual data only • Domestic data predominates	• Growing interest in currencies and financial markets • New exchanges/markets founded • Some graphic display capability • Prices begin to fall • Still primarily domestic data	• Global information available • Extensive graphic presentation of data available • Prices continue to fall • Many more markets and instruments appear	• More value-added data and display software supplied by vendors • Broad coverage of global markets and instruments
Computer Equipment	• Mainframes dominate • Inaccessible to most • Expensive	• Minis increase market share • More accessible • Still expensive • Limited software available - most of it written by users	• Growth of micro's/workstations • Very accessible • Very affordable • Extensive software available	• Explosion in Local Area Networks • Networks re-introduce elements of centralized control • Growth in multimedia computers • Prices stabilize but price/performance improves • Ergonomic/visual interfaces dominate

FIGURE 18.2 Increasing Computational Complexity

Instruments:

Cash Currencies Nonfinancial Futures	Currency Futures	Cash Fixed-Income Swaps	Fixed-Income Futures	Simple Options Derivatives	OTC Tailored Options OTC Derivatives
Quantitative Techniques:					
Simple smoothing	Market Indicators	Higher Order Statistics	Higher Order Linear Techniques	NonLinear Techniques	NonLinear Learning Techniques
E.g.: Moving Av. Exponential Av. Linear Regression	E.g.: Relative Strength Momentum Volatility measures	E.g.: Probability theory Multiple Regression Bayesian Statistics Fourier Analysis	E.g.: Box Jenkins Quadratic Optimization Kalman Filters	E.g.: Higher Order regression Classification/ Separation Chaos Theory Simultaneous Eqns.	E.g.: Neural Nets Genetics Algorithms Artificial Intelligence Expert Systems Fuzzy Logic

Communications

The term "communications revolution" has been cheapened into a
cliché. Living through change day-to-day reveals small steps. But
what is easy to miss are the giant strides made by combining these
small steps. If you call your local phone company today to order
simple residential service, the lists of questions asked and options
offered are bewildering. We forget how recently there was one
class of service, with one type of instrument—the basic
Westinghouse indestructible rotary-dial, probably in basic black.
We forget how recently an international call was the preserve of
the rich and powerful, and space on the (single) transatlantic cable
had often to be reserved days in advance. By contrast, the range of
equipment available now is staggering. And the range of services
offered is equally impressive, ranging from basic (yes, you can still
get basic service by answering no to the dozens of options) all the
way to a private exchange operated and maintained by your
friendly phone company, with more features than any one human
could remember. Remember, too, that we are still talking about
old-fashioned "wired" service. In addition, we are offered digital
cellular pocket-sized phones that already work countrywide, and
will soon work internationally. For higher volume of transmis-
sions we can now buy satellite channels for private use—also once
the preserve of a select few. A mere decade has truly launched us
into an entirely new world. The end of these changes, and indeed
even a slowing in the pace of innovation, is nowhere in sight.

The quantity of information and the type of information
(including voice, data, and video) that courses through the communications networks grows exponentially. Compression techniques squeeze extraordinary amounts of information into existing communications channels (the familiar two- or four-wire
phone line), and the channels themselves are expanding their
capacities at breakneck speed. Coaxial cable and fiber-optic cable
can carry millions of times more information, and the use of digital technologies allows much more "intelligence" into the communications network.

Most critically, the price of both the services and the equipment
available for communications falls steadily, continuously, inex-
orably, and dramatically. Again, although there must eventually
come a time when the pace of technological advance, and coinci-
dent fall in price, starts to slow, there is as yet no evidence of it.

Data

The principal requirement in disseminating data is good communications. For many years, the ticker tape ruled. It gave subscribers no choice over the format, order, or frequency of the data they saw. The quotes were received in the order ordained by the exchanges. Then came quote machines, which gave users a small amount of control over what data appeared on their screens, but provided access only to information pertinent to that day's trading in an instrument. Following in fairly short order came the ability for users to retrieve some limited history of prices, and perhaps the most useful innovation was the ability to display the history in different ways, particularly graphically.

Today we have astonishing quantities of data from a myriad of sources hurtling toward us over faster and faster communications networks. More importantly, we have a plethora of choices in how to retrieve and display that data, as well as facilities for manipulating the data before disseminating and displaying it. Just as in communications, all this comes at continually diminishing cost.

At the upper end of the spectrum, and still rather expensive, is the ability to receive every trade, and even every bid and offer, in every instrument traded anywhere in the world, for 24 hours a day. What was once the preserve of local market participants has now become widely available around the world in a matter of seconds. Needless to say, this has radically altered the make-up of markets, and has given a huge advantage to those who have the technology and the strategies for exploiting this information. The most dramatic recent example of this phenomenon is the success of a few of the New York-based investment banks in their program trading on the Tokyo Stock Exchange. The volume traded on the TSE, all at fixed commissions, was responsible for making the four major Japanese securities houses the largest, most profitable in the world. But when that volume fell in the wake of a falling market, it was a handful of New York investment banks exploiting an arbitrage technology developed for the U.S. equity markets (so-called "program trading") who earned all the profits. There was a lot of screaming and yelling, and attempts to make program trading the scapegoat for the woes of TSE, but the reality was that there were profits to be earned, and it required traders to exploit the available data in order to earn them.

Exploiting the massive quantities of available data requires, in addition to good communications, good data-processing equipment. The human brain is a wonderfully powerful parallel processor, but the sheer volume of financial data flooding the lives of market participants mandates assistance in dealing with it.

Computers

This much-needed help takes the form of computer systems. Few areas of modern life remain untouched by computers, and the above developments in communications and data availability were feasible only with the huge changes in the price-performance characteristics of electronic equipment.

Once there were only mainframe systems. They cost millions of dollars; they were locked away in air-conditioned vaults; they were terribly expensive, inaccessible to most, difficult to use, and temperamental. By and large, their cost, inaccessibility, and need for specialists to use them dictated the type of tasks for which they were used. These were primarily high-volume, relatively straightforward, repetitive tasks involving large quantities of simple, usually identical data. The highly trained specialists who used them were charged with coaxing social behavior out of these unruly beasts. This was usually a difficult task, and always a time-consuming one. (In fact, to this day, the creation of the slick, easily used software to which we have become accustomed, is a labor-intensive, massively time-consuming manual process.) This meant, of course, that only highly automatable, mechanical chores tended to be performed by such machines. It meant also that these machines were made to be good at processing large volumes of data, and also at storing large volumes of data. But it was always extremely difficult to extract any information that was not part of the planned routine. Such a state of affairs was not desirable, but size and cost of computing power, even though declining steadily, prevented any significant advances for more than two decades.

Then began a process of rapid change that was ushered in by the advent of so-called minicomputers toward the end of the '60s. These minis made their appearance first in scientific research labs, and later in commercial applications. Companies like Digital Equipment Corporation (DEC), a company founded by engineers, began producing machines for other engineers to use hands-on in their labs. These scientists had grown impatient with standing in line (usually at the back of the line, too) for a share of a mainframe system. Being natural tinkerers, DEC's "kit" approach appealed to the denizens of the labs. Having a relatively cheap, small machine right under their control more than made up for the fact that mini-computers were quite slow, very limited in capacity, and came with very little software.

The software that did exist was written by the users. One such group of users was working at AT&T's Bell Labs. It is worth remembering just how limited their equipment was. Today most PCs are equipped with several megabytes (millions of bytes) of high-speed memory, and workstations with much more. Eight megabytes is quite common in a PC; 32 is not considered extravagant in a workstation. (Workstations are systems that are built using hardware that sacrifices instruction complexity for speed. The result has been a series of small-sized, blindingly fast computers.) The systems that are now so common in a package that fits on a desk simply did not exist 20 years ago, even in room-sized behemoths. At the time the Bell Labs software scientists were putting their system together, a $1/_4$-megabyte machine was large! Yet somehow, this group managed to shoehorn an operating system with surprising capabilities into a computer with minimal memory.

As in other facets of the information revolution, the price of all this performance proceeds to fall at breakneck speed. The fall in price along with the increase in capacity does not stop at the hardware. Equally great strides have been made in the type and price of software that is available. This is of course the critical factor, since it is the "friendly," easy to learn, ergonomically designed software that we as users see. The hardware is completely hidden from us. But as noted previously, software creation is a labor-intensive, time-consuming process. It would be impossible for someone selling a software package to have to create a version for each type of computer. Instead, what has occurred is that there have arisen de facto standards in operating systems which, in effect, are programs that make any given piece of hardware look like any other hardware running the same operating system. This enables software vendors to create their software to run under a particular operating system, and not worry about the hardware idiosyncrasies of a particular machine. The operating system becomes, for all intents and purposes, the machine.

The de facto standard that has arisen in the financial world centers around the UNIX operating system—the essential design of which was carried out at Bell Labs, and shoehorned into their tiny system. While there are other contenders vying to become the standard, there is one critical advantage offered by UNIX, and that is the fact that it is a "multiprocessing" operating system. Without getting unduly technical, it means that several things can be happening simultaneously in the machine, and only when they compete for a specific resource does the operating system suspend one of them. For example, the eternity (for a computer) between the keystrokes typed by even the fastest typist, is time wasted if the machine is standing idle, and not getting on with some other task. Without the ability to perform useful work during lulls, much of the extraordinary power of modern hardware would be wasted.

This has led to a situation in which a vast array of sophisticated software has been created to run under the UNIX standard. So much for the "supply side."

On the "demand side," the famously impatient people involved in trading complex instruments have been making UNIX their standard. For many years, if you wanted a machine cheap enough to be directly under your control, and small enough to put on your desk, with the ability to run complex algorithms in a flash and with the additional ability to share information with colleagues, you had only one choice: UNIX. (There may be other choices around now, but it is hard to dislodge such a standard.)

The type of software that has become available, and that has been packaged into "solutions" for the financial world, exploits much of what is offered by enhanced communications and the vast array of available data. It provides (relatively) easy to learn capabilities for retrieving, manipulating, and analyzing data and, critically, for providing high-quality visual presentation of the results. If you think for a moment about options (one of the more common financial instruments) you will immediately recognize some of the dimensions they have. Their value varies with time, with the volatility of the underlying instrument, and with the distance of the underlying instrument from the option's strike price. The familiar "dog's leg" diagram shows only one of these dimensions, namely the value at expiration as a function of distance from the strike price. An example of such a static diagram can be found in Figure 18.3, showing the value of a Japanese yen call option at expiration. With better visual presentation, however, one can construct a display of multiple dimensions by creating a surface diagram over which one can mentally "walk." A good display can be a great competitive advantage in the markets. For example, Figure 18.4 is able to demonstrate some of the dynamics

FIGURE 18.3   Yen Option with 118 Strike and ¥2 Premium

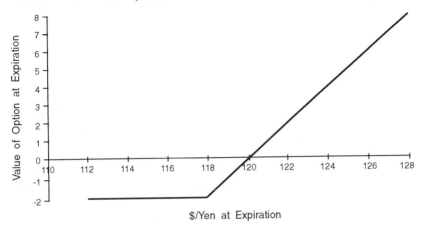

FIGURE 18.4   December 1991 IMM Yen Call Options (Exp. 12/6/91)
Strike Series 750 to 790

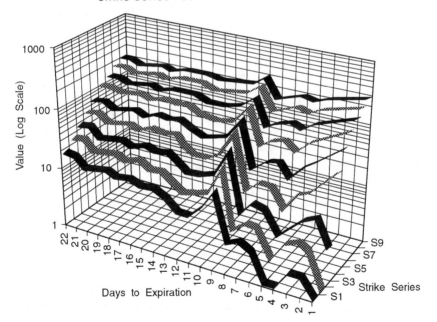

inherent in option values. It shows the behavior of differently struck options as they approach expiration.

The Markets

Such analysis and display capabilities are crucial in understanding the multidimensional risks in complex instruments. The fact that these capabilities exist has contributed in no small way to explosive growth in the types of instruments available. In fact, the growth of the markets has paralleled, and every bit equaled, the growth in the technical capabilities we have touched on above.

For some time, there have been markets in all manner of instruments, from the familiar equities and debt instruments, to the somewhat less familiar instruments of currencies and commodity futures, as well as options on all the aforementioned. Where the growth has come, however, has been in the plethora of derivative financial instruments based on the more traditional ones. It was as late as 1976 that the first futures contract on a debt instrument made its debut as the Treasury bill futures contract traded on the International Money Market (IMM) in Chicago. Today, of course, there is a vast array of futures on interest-rate instruments to be found on futures markets the world over.

In addition, the '70s and '80s was an era of widely divergent interest rates and misshapen yield curves. This meant the end of the dominance of fixed-rate instruments in favor of those whose rates fluctuated with market conditions. This ultimately gave birth to a "swaps market" which has grown to gargantuan proportions. (Simply put, interest rate swaps are arrangements whereby someone who has borrowed at a fixed interest rate "swaps" his interest payment liability with someone who has borrowed at a fluctuating interest rate. A swap can also, of course, be arranged between lenders who wish to swap the type of interest income they receive.) These arrangements are facilitated by middlemen, traditionally banks.

Also in the '80s, Michael Milken—a now infamous, but at the time obscure, employee of Drexel Burnham Lambert—exploited the fact that different companies had to pay very different interest rates for their borrowings. The rates were invariably determined by lending banks, whose analysis of each company's creditworthiness determined the amount and the price of debt it could raise. The banks' credit risk analysis was, for the most part, accurate, which meant that most companies managed to service their debts. Milken's analysis of the situation was that the premiums charged to non-blue-chips for borrowing was a risk premium with very little additional risk. Thus began a huge disinter mediation as second-tier companies bypassed traditional lenders and issued their own debt to be sold through Milken's DBL sales force.

Over this same time period came the continued freeing from regulation of cross-border capital flows. Prior to the mid 1970's, very few countries permitted unrestricted purchases or sales of their currencies. Trade in physical goods was one of the few legitimate reasons to trade in currencies. This functioned adequately during the Bretton Woods era of fixed exchange rates, but Nixon changed all that in 1972. From that point forward, much of the pressure that automatically builds during countries' divergent economic cycles was alleviated through currency realignments. For the first time in years, markets, and not governments, directly determined exchange rates and this gradually made controls on capital flows obsolete. One by one, major western countries (often under protest) made their currencies freely convertible. And so arose the largest market of them all, as people and corporations were freed to invest worldwide. Today the dollar volumes traded in worldwide currency markets dwarf the trading volume in any other financial instrument. It is some 8 times that of the U.S. Treasury debt market, and some 150 times that of the New York Stock Exchange. This volume is not created to finance trade. Rather, it is the result of cross-border capital flows.

Cross-border borrowing and lending is now commonplace, giving rise to another host of financial instruments. These include, to name but a few, a vast market in forward currency transactions (once the preserve of those hedging forward trade-related currency exposure), a swaps market in cross-currency debt, and multidimensional swaps involving fixed-to-floating interest rates across currencies.

The ultimate in financial freedom is the custom-tailored over-the-counter (OTC) instrument. Such instruments are sometimes derivatives of existing ones, but are often tailor-made for a specific investor. A well-known example of the former type is found in the mortgage-backed securities market, where an instrument has its cash flow split into "interest only" and "principal only" components (IO and PO in the jargon). An example of the custom-tailored instrument might be a COD quanto European option on

Euromark deposits. (Translated, it is an option priced in U.S. dollars, whose value will fluctuate with 3-month German interest rates, but will *not* be affected by changes in the U.S. dollar against the D-mark (the "quanto" part). In addition, the buyer can only exercise the option at expiration (the "European" part). And finally, the buyer pays the premium only if the option is in the money at expiration; otherwise it is free (the "COD" part).

Now consider the task of the writers of such an option. Not only must they determine how to implement it (i.e., what instruments need to be bought or sold, and in what quantities) but, vitally, how to price it.

All of this type of innovation in the financial markets would simply not have been possible without the aforementioned advances in communications/data/computer systems. You need, at the very least, to maintain accurate data bases to deal in swaps or currencies, as well as to employ all manner of sophisticated quantitative analysis to monitor, price, and trade such instruments. Without the electronic data feeds, computers and analysis software, calling a trader for a quote would be an exercise in frustration, as well as one of unfathomable risk for the trader.

As we mentioned, quants have always been fixtures on Wall Street. But the big change occurring in the last few years is their appearance on trading desks not merely to serve as programmer/assistants to traders, but to do the trading themselves. They have learned about the markets; they understand the mathematics required for analysis; and, having grown up with computers, they understand and can use them to best advantage. They handle the job from soup to nuts, analyzing the markets and selecting the data feeds, hardware, and software they need. What software can't be bought off the shelf, they create themselves.

As also mentioned earlier, the people now found performing quantitative analysis in financial markets often come from distinctly nonfinancial backgrounds, where they have gained familiarity with a host of techniques developed originally for nonfinancial applications.

The Quantitative Techniques

The original proponents of quantitative analysis in financial markets used primarily straightforward linear techniques. Luck perhaps played a large part in their early success—luck in timing, as well as luck in selecting the futures markets as their vehicle.

The techniques they used are probably best summarized in existing books, especially *Kaufman*. It is probably best to refer to those books for details of any techniques mentioned here. For our purposes, we will go into only as much detail as is merited by the discussion.

A host of early quants (and probably quite a few still today) made extensive use of the familiar moving average (MA). Most often, they would have used crossover systems, in which two MAs calculated over different time periods, generated a signal to trade when they crossed. The data was invariably a single price for each day in the time window (usually the exchange-posted "settlement price"), and the time periods chosen were determined partly by folklore, and partly for expediency of calculation. Most often, calculations were performed on the equivalent of an old-fashioned adding machine. The unfortunates who had to manually plod through calculations in various markets every day tended to choose MA s that involved less rather than more data.

It did not take long for people to realize the advantages of "exponential smoothing" for ease of calculation. In order to calculate and exponential average, the technique requires only two pieces of data: yesterday's exponential average (EA), and today's price. Depending on how heavily you weight today's price relative to the weight of yesterday's EA determines how "short" your equivalent MA would be. A simple rule of thumb gives the weighting of today's price that would be (reasonably) equivalent to an N-day MA as

$$\text{Weight} = W = 2/(N + 1)$$

The weighting for yesterday's EA would then be

$$1 - W$$

All very simple computationally.

And then of course came a host of variations in which "envelopes" were placed around one or both of the averages in a crossover system, which had the effect of retarding the signals. At that stage of the game, rules were most often the result of folklore, or perhaps human observation of a system's behavior in a market. (For example, if the crossover system being used seemed to generate too many false signals, it could be slowed down by changing the time window in an MA (or weighting factor in an EA), or perhaps by placing a 1 percent envelope around the slower average.)

One of the great advances came not in the quantitative techniques themselves, but in the idea of using computers and historical data to simulate the trading system. For the first time, there was a way to answer questions about which MAs really were best, or which envelope worked best. It involved finding someone to let you use their computer, finding (or more likely creating) the historical data, and finding a programmer to write the programs.

Recall that computers were, at that time, expensive luxuries that most traders could not afford. The most likely source of computer time was a brokerage house where the quant did his or her trading. Of course the brokerage house would not let just any trader use its systems; the trader had to be a major commission generator. But supplying computer time was about all the brokerage houses were able to do. They had no historical data, and their programmers were employed to write and maintain accounting and order-processing software. The traders were left to their own devices in finding data and hiring programmers. The few traders who did sufficient volume to afford such luxuries had few places to turn to find people with the requisite computer skills combined with at least some notion of what a market was, and how markets worked. Somehow such people were dredged up, and so began the era of computerized, historical data-collection and analysis.

And off to work they went. They simulated hundreds of variations of MA crossover systems, employing different time periods and different tests of existing folklore. Compared with those traders who were stuck with folklore, the competitive advantage was immense for traders who had reliable information as to which time periods and/or rules worked best in the different markets. A further advantage was being freed from the constraints that manual calculations imposed. Longer time periods and more complex envelopes could be examined without the trader having to sit up with a calculator all night.

From that point forward, those with access to the still-expensive data and computer equipment could use their market skills and imagination in devising ever more clever and convoluted trading systems. For the most part, the mathematics was still quite simple, and the techniques exclusively linear. But the imaginative combinations and arrangements of data and techniques gave rise to all manner of trading systems that implemented particular peoples' ideas of how markets worked. For the reader interested in the forms that these ideas took, an illustrative book is *Wilder.*

There one can get a sense of the types of market observations quantitative traders made, and the techniques they used to formalize them. There are a couple of interesting points to note in that book. First is the fact that those trading systems were very definitely geared to the assumption that the trader had no access to computers or electronic data. The worksheets make plain that the calculations were manual, and often time-consuming. The second point is that there was an implicit assumption that someone (the author?) had examined those systems using historical data and had selected the suggested parameters from the simulations. It is not clear from the book whether this was in fact the case. But the principal point in recommending readers to this book is to illustrate how traders approached formalizing their ideas using quantitative techniques, as opposed to nontrader quantitative types applying their (nonmarket) techniques to the markets.

For quite some time, many people did very well trading using this type of approach. But, as we saw earlier, their success could, in large measure, be attributed to the fact that they were analyzing markets that were in an exceptional phase. Almost everything appeared to generate profits!

As the markets eventually settled back into a more normal mode, these traders began to experience difficulty. There were some who were exceptions to this generality, and two major factors distinguished them. First, the successful traders had access to continually expanding data sources and computer power. Second, they focused their efforts and attentions on the foreign exchange markets, as well as the other financially oriented markets that were appearing.

The computer power grew in importance because it soon became clear that the "right" trading system in a market was only one dimension of success. At least as important, and possibly more so, was the portfolio of markets that one traded; not only which markets were in your portfolio, but also their relative weights. Simulating an entire portfolio of markets in which simulated quantitative systems are used is definitely a job for a computer. It is inconceivable that this could be undertaken manually in any detail. Even with computers, people often resort to using aggregated information (such as monthly returns rather than daily, or even daily rather than minute-to-minute returns) to make the simulation more manageable. There are all manner of pitfalls in aggregating data, but if it comes down to a choice of no simulation at all, or one using aggregated data, the choice is clear. But it is important to recognize what could be hiding in the simulations. For example, a simulation showing a perfectly acceptable 2 percent return for a portfolio from January 1 to February 1 could be obscuring the fact some time during January the portfolio might have experienced an unacceptable interim loss of 10 percent!

Even so, more extensive abilities to simulate portfolios of markets is a major advantage, whatever their shortcomings. Nowadays, of course, much more detailed simulations are the norm among more successful traders.

On the issue of emphasizing currency markets in the portfolio, there was something more than luck involved. There was the observation of two critical aspects of currency markets. First, there are extremely varied ways to implement a trade in these markets, and second, they exhibit serial correlation (i.e., they trend) more often than not.

On the first point, it is worth comparing foreign exchange markets with other markets. Most markets offer a limited number of ways to trade. In the more liquid, widely followed markets, there is the ability to trade the actual instrument (the "cash" market), often a futures contract on the instrument, and often an option on the instrument.

For those market participants not actually "in the trade," the cash markets frequently present idiosyncrasies that can trap the unwary. Futures markets offer the ability to trade in an instrument closely related to the cash market, but with very precise rules and regulations governing quality, quantity, and delivery. This is both an advantage in that it is easier to understand what you are getting into, and a disadvantage in that they must be designed to appeal to the widest possible audience, and so may not precisely meet your particular needs. For example, there have long been futures on various U.S. Treasury debt instruments, but not on corporate debt. And so if it is corporate debt you are trying to trade (which might be for any number of reasons, from hedging a liability or income stream, to outright speculation), you would have had to make do with a proxy in the form of a futures contract on Treasuries. Similarly, there are exchange-traded futures on a half-dozen of the major currencies, but not on most currencies, and only recently against anything but the U.S. dollar. Exchange-traded options have similar limitations. These days, of course, off-exchange (OTC) options are available in almost any form one might desire, but not usually to anyone needing to trade small quantities.

All of these choices also exist in the foreign exchange markets. But the great difference is the existence of the inter-bank (IBK) market. Again, the IBK is not generally accessible to any but the largest traders, but it is where 95 percent of the trading in currencies occurs. It is also the market where anything other than the major currencies can be traded, and where there exists an active forward market. It is the market where it is possible to operate with relative anonymity. Rumors fly around continually as to who's doing what in the IBK market, but for the most part it is impossible to confirm such rumors. No IBK market-maker is likely to risk the wrath of a customer by letting the market know what that customer is up to.

But, primarily, it is the market where it is possible to trade billions of dollars in a matter of minutes. The importance of that ability will become clearer when we look at some of the quantitative strategies currently being explored.

While this is still very much a "person at the end of a phone line" market, it is fiercely competitive, meaning that accurate, timely information is a priceless commodity. This has been made possible with the advent of low-priced computing power and communications. They also allow market-makers to offer customers information and fast executions at narrow bid/offer spreads in a wide variety of instruments. If this is such a private, counter-party market, what data reaches the outside world?

Not surprisingly, the market-makers advertise and publicize many of their prices and transactions over various electronic wire services, such as Reuters and Knight-Ridder. Unlike centralized markets, however, there is no regulation requiring simultaneous publication of transactions to all participants. To a large extent, the IBK market-makers control the information flow, and tend to offer their data primarily through a single vendor. This makes the quant's choice of data-provider a critical decision. In the foreign exchange world, Reuters is far and away the dominant service in carrying most of the pertinent information. This data does not come cheap, and can easily run to $10,000 per month for comprehensive coverage. This—as with computer power, communications facilities, and people—means that the more sophisticated quantitative analysis remains the preserve of larger and wealthier organizations. We are turning here from the massive communications and computer investments required by the market-makers, to that required in quantitative analysis.

THE INVESTMENT IN QUANTITATIVE ANALYSIS

This is a point that is often overlooked. In an age in which a powerful PC system can be had for $5,000 and PC software for quantitative analysis is available for $2,000–$5,000 (and some of it, like "System Writer," very well thought out and presented), one could be forgiven for wondering why anyone would invest vastly larger sums.

The answer hinges primarily on the type of quantitative analysis that is being explored on Wall Street. You can do a lot with the PC-based packages, but they have their limitations. They tend to include a menu of the more familiar quantitative techniques, such as moving averages, relative-strength indicators, stochastics, linear regressions, etc. And with imagination, a student of markets can devise quantitative trading systems that address his or her ideas of how markets work. The mathematics is almost exclusively linear.

The larger quantitative organizations, however, have the resources to go much further. They have the capability to receive and store more data (right down to every reported transaction), and to manipulate that data in a variety of creative ways.

The type of analysis dictates the type of data required. The type of quantitative analysis that is being found more and more often in foreign exchange markets is nonlinear, and draws on such fields as genetic algorithms, neural networks, nonlinear dynamics (which includes the use of fractals and chaos theory) and artificial intelligence (which includes expert systems). There is much common ground covered by these approaches, but there are also some important distinctions to be drawn among them.

What tends to be common is the use of very granular data rather than aggregated data. For the most part that entails every reported transaction, or at least a detailed sampling every, say, 60 seconds. This contrasts with what most PC-based analytics can manage, namely once-per-day data. In addition, data is monitored and sampled for most of the 24-hour day, rather than the more common single time zone. There are two principal reasons for this detail of data. First is the fact that most of the techniques we will discuss require copious quantities of data, and second is the fact that many of the quantitative analysts are attempting to design systems that react very rapidly to changes in the market. (As mentioned above, this rapid reaction to events requires access to a marketplace in which massive transactions can be completed efficiently and cheaply.)

Also common to these techniques is the use of (again, very granular) data from *related* markets in the analysis. Many traditional quantitative analyses of a market will focus exclusively on that market. The techniques we are discussing here inherently allow, and even require, a much broader base of data from other related markets in order to derive robust trading systems.

These four areas split neatly into two camps: a group in which the technique "learns" from the data, and the "nonlearning camp," which makes use of tools for representing the analyst's knowledge. The first group encompasses genetic algorithms, neural networks, and subsets of artificial intelligence and nonlinear dynamics. Briefly, in all these techniques the analyst selects the data he or she considers important, splits it into a "learning set" and a "confirmation set," establishes "goals," which are used to judge how good a particular decision was, and then finally turns the software loose to see what it can discover from the data in the "learning set."

The learning is done in different ways in each technique, but the common thread is that the analyst tells the technique what the "perfect outcome" is (if there is such a thing), and then tells it to search for common threads in the data that can be used to predict such a perfect outcome.

In genetic algorithms, the learning occurs, as suggested by the name, in an evolutionary manner. Originally developed to simulate populations of living organisms, the idea was that the most successful individuals would displace the less successful and thereby grow to be a majority, much as the human race has managed on earth. The system starts out with some arbitrary set of genes (which represent the rules for generating a trading signal), and in each subsequent "generation" there is a random "mutation" applied to some of the genes. By looking into the future (which, in the learning set, is a known quantity) at the outcome of the trades made by each gene, the technique can determine how well that gene is performing in reaching the goals that were set. Those genes that are making the best trades in each generation are allowed to propagate and become part of the next generation.

Some subset of those genes that are doing poorly will "die" and so be forced out of the "gene pool" in the next generation. Figure 18.5 outlines the various steps that are inherent in setting up a genetic algorithm experiment, and Figure 18.6 illustrates the way these techniques might be employed in a specific example. You can see here how much of an art the analysis is. The analyst is required to select appropriate data, determine realistic goals, specify all sorts of rules on how many mutations occur in each generation and how fast a gene can propagate, etc. As in all quantitative analysis, it is important to recognize that the techniques are tools, and tools used by competent artisans will turn out better products than the same tools in the hands of a neophyte.

The same comments hold for neural nets. Although the scope here for the unskilled to do harm is much greater. Neural nets "learn" in an approach that mimics the way researchers think the

FIGURE 18.5   Genetic Algorithms

The process is intended to mimic natural selection in populations. It is an itera-tive procedure in which one creates a new generation from the prior one. The rules of pro generation determine the ultimate outcome.

The basic steps are as follows:

1. **INITIALIZE**
   Randomly create an initial population of individuals (each with randomly selected characteristics), consisting of, say, 200 individuals.

2. **EVALUATE**
   Determine how successful each individual was in the past generation. (The criteria for success are determined by the problem. For example, in a world of tall trees, the most successful leaf-eaters will be the ones of similar height to the trees, or that can fly.)

3. **PROPAGATE**
   Set up rules by which individuals propagate. For example, allow the most successful 20% of the population to clone 2 copies of themselves; the next most successful 20% clone 1 copy of themselves, and the worst 60% would be eliminated. (The population size remains the same.)

4. **MUTATE**
   Create some simulated "genetic diversity" by (i) randomly mutating the genes of a few individuals, and (ii) randomly swapping random parts of the genes of a few pairs of individuals.

5. **ITERATE**
   Return to step (2).

Figure 18.6

A simple genetic algorithm example might be as follows:

Objective:
Predict the direction of price change at
12 noon tomorrow, based on hourly price
changes over the past 5 days.

Representation

State problem in binary string form	E.G.: +move represented by 1 −move represented by 0	Past 5 days might be a string such as 11010001101....1 120-bits long (5 days * 24 hours)
	Individuals would be represented as: 11010001101....1 0.....1011 1 Past 5 days 120 bits Next day 12 bits	last bit is the one being predicted

Initialize	Create population of, say, 200 randomly generated strings
Evaluate	From sample of known outcomes, determine which individuals contained the correct last bit.
Propogate	Eliminate those individuals with the incorrect last bit, and generate copies of the remaining ones until you reach the correct population size.
Mutate	Select a few individuals; select a few bits in those individuals, and flip them (i.e., a 0 becomes a 1, and vice versa). Select a few pairs of individuals; randomly select a piece of their bit-strings, and swap them.
Iterate	Return to 'Evaluate' step.
Terminate	Stop the iterations when certain conditions are met E.g.: All the individuals are identical, or after, say, 5000 iterations

329

physical brain works. Namely, that learning consists of creating links between adjacent nerve cells. In the brain, the strength of a link is determined chemically and/or by physical size. In a neural net, it is a simulated connection between adjacent electronic "cells." As the system learns, the most successful "rules" for reaching the stated goal will be those which the most and/or strongest "links."

There has always been one major drawback to this approach, and that is the need for the analyst to accept the output of a trained net largely on faith. It is difficult, if not impossible, to ask the system why a net evolved as it did. Assuming the analyst wants to ask why, it is his or her job to devise tests that give clues to the answer. For example, you first train the net on a single data series, say each transaction in a currency. You then retrain the net with the original data, but now add in the transactions of a second currency. If there is no difference in what the trained net tells you to do, you can infer that there was no information in the second data series that the neural net found to be valuable. You then have to satisfy yourself that your test would yield the same conclusion if you changed the learning set. Carefully constructed, such tests give a guide to what is important information, but offer no guarantees.

Neural nets have proven to be very successful in dealing with data containing little "noise." An example of such data might be typed script. Each letter produced by a typewriter (or printer) will be consistent except for minor variations that could crop up when, say, the printer is low on ink, making an area of the page faint or partly obscured. But for the most part, this is data containing little noise. Handwritten text, on the other hand, is entirely another story. And market data, consisting as it does of the aggregated behavior of a diverse group of people with diverse objectives, is noisier still. The level of noise in the raw information is such that mindless application of the technique may still manage to generate a trained net, but it would yield a system in which a skilled analyst could have little confidence. This means that judicious preprocessing of the data—a very subjective human skill—is a necessity.

Some forms of artificial intelligence follow a similar "learning" approach by building up a set of "rules of inference" and modifying them by trial and error. And in the nonlinear dynamics field, there are techniques that attempt to classify the probable outcome of a decision, given some known inputs. There are several approaches to doing this, but they all entail attempting to obtain the maximum "separation" between desirable and undesirable outcomes. Some attempt to create several "bins" into which the trades will be separated (such as auto regressive trees), and others attempt to minimize the distance in N-dimensional space between members of one group, but maximize the distance between groups. (The "dimensions" here are what the analyst considers pertinent data series.)

In the second camp—the "nonlearning" camp—fall techniques in which it is up to the analyst to observe the functioning of the markets and to establish a set of criteria under which trades are most likely to succeed. The key difference in these techniques is in who is doing the "learning." In the prior group of techniques, the learning process is inherent to the technique; here it is external to the technique itself. Here the techniques become tools for implementing the (human) analyst's learning. (It is worth noting here that the amount of data, and the combinations of that data which are possible, is often mind-boggling. In addition, there are often subtleties in data that a human might overlook. In both cases, non-human learning of the type found in the above techniques is a necessity. What we are cautioning against here is the careless use of such tools.)

In a subset of artificial intelligence known as expert systems, the analyst's role is played by a "knowledge engineer." The knowledge engineer's function is to understand the thought process of the trader or system designer, and to codify it into a series of "if-then-else" rules. The role played by the expert system is found in the "rule manager" component of the system, in which arbitration among seemingly conflicting rules occurs. The resolution of conflict attempts to use the context of a decision to determine the best rule to apply. Techniques such as "fuzzy logic" are employed here.

Just as with expert systems, most nonlinear techniques are a means of implementing a human's ideas. On Wall Street, the trendiest subset of nonlinear dynamics are the fields of fractals and chaos theory. In a nutshell, this group of techniques is one in which the analyst hypothesizes that the market is a type of nonlinear mathematical process. The market can be thought of as a machine stamping out parts. In this case, the market is the machine, and the parts are prices. If you can correctly identify which machine the market is, then you can correctly identify the next part (price) that the machine will generate. In practice, using such techniques is somewhat akin to a "super heterodyne" radar detector. The radar detector internally generates a "perfect" radar signal, and then compares it with what comes in over its antenna. If the signals match—and "match" is a statistical measure of how similar they are—the machine beeps. In a similar way, chaos equations can be shown a stream of prices, and determine whether they follow some sort of order—or in the parlance of chaos theory, whether there is a price "attractor" present. Figures 18.7, 18.8, and

FIGURE 18.7

Starting Value: 0.5

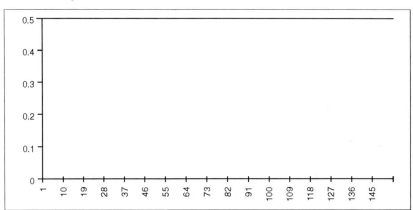

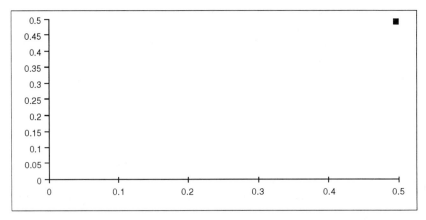

Attractor Generated By: $A(t) = 4 \times S \times A(t-1) \times (1 - A(t-1))$

Where: $A(t)$ = Attractor on day t
S   = Starting value

FIGURE 18.8

Starting Value: 0.8

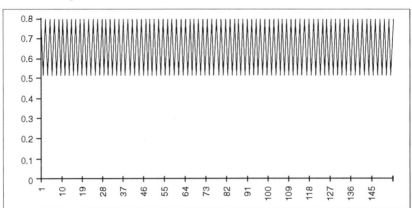

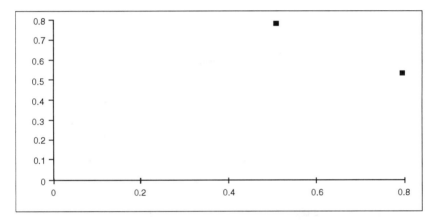

Attractor Generated By: A(t) = 4 x S x A(t-1) x (1 - A(t-1))

Where: A(t) = Attractor on day t
           S   = Starting value

18.9 illustrate this by using an equation known to generate an attractor. In Figure 18.7 the starting input value of 0.5 will result in a single output of 0.5—the straight line in the upper chart. The "attractor" is thus a single point (shown in the lower chart). If the starting input is changed to 0.8 as in Figure 18.8, the system generates an oscillating output. Looking at the upper chart, even the human eye can see that the output oscillates between two points— and these two points appear in the lower chart. However, things start to get interesting with, for example, a starting value of 0.975,

FIGURE 18.9

Starting Value: 0.975

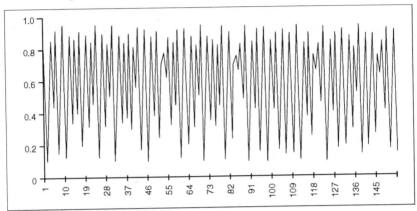

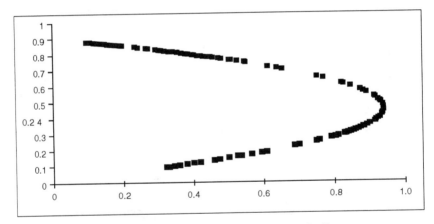

Attractor Generated By: A(t) = 4 x S x A(t-1) x (1 - A(t-1))

Where: A(t) = Attractor on day t
S   = Starting value

as shown in Figure 18.9. If a person looks at the upper chart, it appears to be bouncing all over the place, much as a chart of prices might. But in fact, there really is an order to the system in the sense that the points all lie on a parabolic-shaped line shown in the lower chart. So what might appear at first blush to be random, is not random at all. Of course, this is all probabilistic, but that is the basis of all such techniques. They are not far-removed in spirit from the linear techniques that are commonly used in quantitative analysis. But they do offer ways to cope with data series that are often (or even usually) distinctly nonlinear. They invariably require mathematical skills far beyond those of linear techniques, but the human skills in understanding the markets and selecting the appropriate mathematics remain the same.

CONCLUSION

And so we find we have come full circle. Fifteen or twenty years ago, better human understanding of markets, and observation of their behavior, led people to the successful use of quantitative analysis. While their techniques were often mathematically simple and invariably linear, there was no limit to their imaginative use of those tools. Their success was in large measure a result of their market skills, rather than their quantitative skills.

More recently, Wall Street has become aware of the more modern, exotic quantitative techniques in the world, and has imported hundreds (thousands ?) of nonfinancial people who happened to be familiar with those techniques, and asked them to apply their knowledge to the financial markets. The nature of some of the quantitative techniques (such as the group that is able to "learn") meant that trading systems could be devised purely from the data, without any real understanding of markets. Many a tear was shed over the results.

But, as with most things, it is the combination of the quantitative skills with the domain-knowledge of market participants, and coupled with the advances in the markets, communications, and computer power, that has yielded, and will continue to yield, results. The human brain is still the best analyzer of a noisy world, but it needs help in dealing with the extraordinary quantity of information. Quantitative techniques have been an invaluable and very profitable source of that help.

Rigorous, careful, and sophisticated quantitative analysis does not come cheap. It requires expensive people, powerful computing, and costly data. But when the mix is right, the results can be astonishing.

The Significance of Technical Trading-Rule Profits in the Foreign Exchange Market: A Bootstrap Approach

Richard M. Levich, New York University, Stern School of
    Business, and National Bureau of Economic Research
Lee R. Thomas, Investcorp Bank E.C., Bahrain

TECHNICAL TRADING-RULE PROFITS

Since the advent of floating exchange rates in the early 1970s, numerous empirical studies have investigated the time series behavior of exchange rates and the empirical distribution of exchange rates. A null hypothesis that features prominently in these studies is whether exchange rates can be characterized as serially independent drawings from a stationary distribution. Alongside these studies, tests of foreign exchange market efficiency have examined the profitability of various trading rules. A null hypothesis in these studies has been that mechanical rules for generating trading signals should not result in unusual (risk-adjusted) profits.

A variety of empirical studies support the notion that mechanical trading rules are often profitable when applied in the spot foreign exchange market. A drawback to these studies is that most do not measure the statistical significance of their results, while others measure statistical significance assuming that the volatility of exchange rates is constant. The latter assumption is questionable, since recent evidence rejects the hypothesis that exchange rates can be described as random, independent drawings from a stationary distribution. Evidence is more consistent with the view that exchange rates are drawn from nonstationary distributions.

The purpose of this chapter is to undertake new tests of the random behavior of exchange rates and the profitability of mechanical trading rules. Our tests do not rely on assumptions regarding the distribution of the process underlying exchange rate changes. Our approach involves the application of bootstrap methods—i.e., the generation of thousands of new series of pseudo exchange rates, each new series constructed from random reordering of the original series. We measure the profitability of the mechanical trading rules for each new series. The significance of the results from the original series can be assessed by comparison to the empirical distribution of results derived from the thousands of randomly generated series.

Overall, our empirical results suggest that mechanical trading rules have very often led to profits that are highly unusual relative to the profits earned by the same rules when applied to the randomly generated time series of exchange rates. Based on a sample of five currencies over the period January 1, 1976, to December 31, 1990, and nine trading rules, we find that in 27 cases the original exchange rate series produced profits in the top 1% of all times series, in 12 cases the original series produced profits in the top 5% of all time series, and the remaining six cases produced profits that were positive but less significant. Splitting the entire 15-year sample period into three 5-year periods revealed that on average the profitability of mechanical trading rules has declined in the 1986–1990 period, although profits remained positive (on average) and significant in many cases.

The plan for the remainder of this chapter is first to review some of the earlier research on spot exchange rates and market efficiency. Then, we present our own methodology and data sources. Our empirical results are presented next. A summary and conclusions follow at the end of the chapter.

PREVIOUS RESEARCH

Efficient Market Theory

There are now a substantial number of empirical studies testing the efficiency of the foreign exchange market. Surveys of this literature have been prepared by Levich (1985, 1989) and Hodrick

(1987). A critical point in the formulation of these studies is that all tests of market efficiency are tests of a joint hypothesis—first, the hypothesis that defines market equilibrium returns as some function of the available information set, and second, the hypothesis that market participants set actual prices or returns to conform to their expected values.

To be more specific, if we define $r_{j,t+1}$ as the actual one-period rate of return on asset j in the period ending at time $t + 1$, and $E(r_{j,t+1} \mid I_t)$ as the expected value of that return conditional on the information set available at time t, then the excess market return can be written as

(1) $$Z_{j,t+1} = r_{j,t+1} - E(r_{j,t+1} \mid I_t).$$

The market is efficient if the expectational errors follow a fair game process such that $E(Z_{j,t+1} \mid I_t) = 0$ and $Z_{j,t}$ is uncorrelated with $Z_{j,t+k}$ for any value of k. In words, the market is efficient if, on average, expectational errors are zero, and these errors follow no pattern that might be exploited to produce profits.

In the case of speculative trading in spot or forward foreign exchange markets, risk is present but a risk premium may or may not be characteristic of equilibrium pricing and returns.[1] For example, in the monetary model of exchange rates, domestic and foreign currency bonds are assumed to be perfect substitutes once the interest differential between foreign and domestic assets offsets the foreign exchange rate change. In this case, there is no foreign exchange risk premium—any sustained speculative trading profits would be deemed unusual and a violation of market efficiency. However, in the portfolio balance model of exchange rates, domestic and foreign currency bonds are assumed to be imperfect substitutes, and in equilibrium investors require a risk premium (which could vary over time) in addition to the expected exchange rate change to compensate them for the uncertainty of exchange rate changes. In this case, some positive level of profits from trading rules would be consistent with an equilibrium. Since the equilibrium expected return in foreign exchange speculation could be zero or positive and time varying, it has been difficult to gauge what constitutes unusual or excessive profits, as would be characteristic of an inefficient market.

The primary technique for testing spot market efficiency has been to compute the profitability of various mechanical trading strategies. One popular technique for generating buy and sell signals is the *filter rule*.[2] To illustrate the operation of a filter rule, assume that the speculator initially holds no currency positions, neither foreign nor domestic currency, neither long nor short. However, our speculator does have an initial stock of wealth that provides him with the necessary credit to trade foreign exchange contracts with a commercial bank, or the necessary collateral to trade foreign currency futures contracts on an exchange. An x percent filter rule leads to the following strategy for speculating in the spot $/FC exchange market:

- Whenever FC rises by x percent above its most recent trough (a buy signal), borrow $ and by converting the proceeds into FC at the spot exchange rate, take a long position in FC;
- Whenever FC falls x percent below its most recent peak (a sell signal), sell any long FC position and take a short FC position by borrowing FC and converting the proceeds into $ at the spot exchange rate.

The flexibility to take both long FC positions (following buy signals) and short FC positions (following sell signals) is commonplace for currency traders and speculators in currency futures markets.[3] In addition, the strategy could be followed by American speculators whose wealth is denominated in dollars, as well as by foreign speculators with wealth denominated in FC. As we will show, the returns from the strategy would be added to the risk-free rate of return on the speculator's initial wealth.

In the spot foreign exchange market, the return (R) from a *long* foreign currency (FC) position over the period $(t, t+1)$ is measured by

(2L) $$R_{t,t+1} = \ln(S_{t+1}/S_t) - (i_\$ - i_{FC})$$

where i_{FC} represents the interest earned on the long FC position, $i_\$$ is the interest expense of the short $ position and S is the spot exchange rate in $/FC.[4] By analogy, the return from a *short* foreign currency position over the period $(t, t+1)$ is measured by

(2S) $$R_{t,t+1} = -\{\ln(S_{t+1}/S_t) - (i_\$ - i_{FC})\}.$$

The reader will recognize equations (2L) and (2S) as the uncovered interest parity condition, also known as the Fisher Open effect.

Accordingly, under the joint null hypothesis of market efficiency and no foreign exchange risk premium, the expected return from following the trading strategy is zero.

Spot speculation of the sort described can be conducted using lines of credit or explicit margin secured by our speculator's initial wealth. With his or her wealth invested in Treasury bills that earn interest for the speculator, it follows that the *entire* realized return from following a mechanical signal

$$(3) \qquad R_{t,t+1} = d_t \left[\ln(S_{t+1}/S_t) - (i_\$ - i_{FC}) \right]$$

where d_t is a dummy variable (defined $d_t = +1$ for long positions and $d_t = -1$ for short positions) should be interpreted as an unusual return—a risk premium, over and above the risk-free rate of interest. However, under the joint null hypothesis of market efficiency and a time-varying exchange risk premium (RP_t), expected returns from currency speculation will be positive. In this case, only the *excess* return

$$(4) \qquad \pi_{t,t+1} = R_{t,t+1} - RP_t$$

should conform to the conditions of a fair game if the market is efficient. The conundrum, then, in interpreting the empirical series of returns as in equation (3) is that occasional profits may be the result of chance, but sustained profits could either be indicative of market inefficiency or fair compensation for an exchange risk premium. The empirical support for a nontrivial exchange risk premium is mixed.[5] In practice, most empirical studies of spot market efficiency have not taken an exchange risk premium explicitly into account. One exception is Sweeney (1986) who measures the profitability of filter rules relative to a constant risk premium. In this chapter we examine the effect of including a constant risk premium and find that there is no material effect on our results.

Empirical Evidence on Exchange Markets

Studies by Dooley and Shafer (1976, 1983) report the filter rule trading profits for nine currencies using daily spot rates over the 1973–1981 period. Their calculations are adjusted to reflect the interest expense and interest income of long and short positions (as in equation [3]) and transaction costs are incorporated by using bid and asked foreign exchange quotations. Their results indicate that small filters ($x = 1\%$, 3%, or 5%) would have been profitable for all currencies over the entire sample period. The authors also reported results for 10%, 15%, 20% and 25% filters. These filters were profitable in more than one-half of the sub-periods, but the results were more variable than for the smaller filters. However, even with the small filters there appears to be some element of riskiness in these trading rules, since each filter would have generated losses in at least one currency during at least one sub-period. Even so, for three currencies (yen, guilder, and pound sterling) every small filter was profitable in every sub-period. The authors did not report any measures of statistical or economic significance of these profits.

A study by Sweeney (1986) used a similar filter rule technique on daily exchange rates for ten currencies over the April 1973 to December 1980 sample period and reached similar conclusions.[6] Filters of 0.5%, 1%, 2%, 3%, 4%, 5%, and 10% led to trading profits in more than 80% of the cases. The results for the smaller filters (0.5%, 1%, and 2%) were again superior. Sweeney divided his sample into a 2.5-year estimation period followed by a 5-year post-sample period. Filter rules that were profitable in the first period tended to be profitable in the second. Under the assumption of constant exchange rate volatility, Sweeney calculated that in about one-third of the cases, the profits from filter trading were statistically significant. Again, the results were more pronounced for the smaller filters.

Schulmeister (1987, 1988) conducted an in-depth analysis of the $/DM rate over the April 1973 to September 1986 period, using several technical models in addition to the simple filter model.[7] In particular, Schulmeister tested a popular moving average rule that generates signals based on a crossover between short-term and long-term moving averages of past exchange rate. According to this rule, when the short-term moving average penetrates the long-term moving average from below (above) a buy (sell) signal is generated. Results for the 3-day to 10-day, 5-day to 10-day, and 4-day to 16-day combinations are reported.

Schulmeister's results suggest that most of these technical models would have resulted in profitable trading strategies even after adjusting for interest expense and transaction costs. In particular, the moving average rules are profitable in each of the 10 sub-periods analyzed. Schulmeister suggests that the reason for his results is that exchange rate changes and speculative profits appear to be non-normally distributed. There are too many small exchange rate changes (relative to a normal distribution) but also too many large exchange rate swings (also relative to the normal). The implication from the latter is that once an exchange rate move has started, it is likely to proceed more or less uninterrupted, which allows market technicians time to identify a profitable investment opportunity.[8]

Two papers that analyze the statistical properties of exchange rates are also worth noting. In an analysis of daily spot exchange rates over the period 1974–1983, Hsieh (1988) rejects the hypothesis that exchange rates are independently drawn from a fat-tailed distribution that remains fixed over time. While the usual tests do reveal the presence of serial correlation in exchange rates, Hsieh argues that this may be the result of heteroskedasticity. Once heteroskedasticity is removed from the data, very little serial correlation remains. Exchange rates appear more accurately characterized as drawings from distributions that vary over time with changing means and variances.[9]

Engel and Hamilton (1990) model the time-varying nature of exchange rate distributions as a Markov switching process between state 1 and state 2 where exchange rate movements are drawn from distributions

$N(\mu_1, \sigma_1^2)$ in state 1, and

$N(\mu_2, \sigma_2^2)$ in state 2.

Assume that these states evolve so that

$$\Pr(s_t = 1 | s_{t-1} = 1) = p_{11}$$
$$\Pr(s_t = 2 | s_{t-1} = 1) = 1 - p_{11}$$
$$\Pr(s_t = 1 | s_{t-1} = 2) = 1 - p_{22}$$
$$\Pr(s_t = 2 | s_{t-1} = 2) = p_{22}.$$

If p_{11} and p_{22} are high, and μ_1 and μ_2 have opposite signs, then there will be "long swings" (i.e., uninterrupted trends) in exchange rates—the sort that might be susceptible to mechanical trading rules. Analyzing quarterly data for the period 1973:4 to 1988:1, Engel and Hamilton conclude that the long swings hypothesis (p_{11} and p_{22} high, and μ_1 and μ_2 with opposite signs) fits the data significantly better than a state independent model of a single distribution.

DATA AND METHODOLOGY

A characteristic of exchange rates is that while it might be possible to model a series from one period as drawings from a fixed distribution, it is not possible to "turn the clock back" and draw additional samples from the same time period. Instead, researchers typically "turn the clock forward" and draw additional observations from an extended sample period. This technique may confound the analysis if the sampling distribution itself varies over time.

In classical statistics, statistical statements about population parameters are based only on the sample of data actually drawn in the context of an assumption about the distribution function that generated the sample. An alternative is the *bootstrap* approach, which assumes nothing about the distribution generating function.[10] The distribution generating function is determined empirically using numerical simulation. By drawing numerous random samples (with replacement) of size n from the original data itself, these new samples generate an empirical distribution. Probability statements regarding the original data (for example, the mean, standard deviation, or other moments) can now be made with reference to the empirical distribution.

In this chapter, we have collected data on futures prices for five currencies (British pound [BP], Canadian dollar [CD], German mark [DM], Japanese yen [JY], and Swiss franc [SF]) for the period January 1, 1976, through December 31, 1990, or approximately 3800 daily observations. Our data source is I.P. Sharpe & Co., now a part of Reuters. Quotations are on closing settlement prices from the International Monetary Market of the Chicago Mercantile Exchange. A single time series is assembled by bringing together quotations on successive near-term contracts. For example, futures prices in January and February of 1976 reflect the March 1976 contract; futures prices in March, April, and May of 1976 reflect the June 1976 contract; and so forth.[11] Since futures prices reflect the contemporaneous interest differential between the foreign currency and the U.S. dollar, price trends and returns can be measured simply by

$$(5) \qquad R_{t,t+1} = \ln (F_{t+1}/F_t)$$

where F_t is the currency futures price at time t.[12]

By the use of futures contracts, we eliminate the need for overnight interest rates on spot interbank deposits and we also obtain a reliable and consistent data set. However, each individual futures contract displays a deterministic decline in maturity from roughly 110 days to 20 days as we follow its price movements. Samuelson (1976) has proved that "near futures contracts show more variability than (sufficiently far) distant ones," so there is some possibility that return variances may be rising as our contracts move toward maturity and then falling abruptly as we roll into the next futures contract. However, Samuelson (1976) also shows that for some stationary price generating processes, variance may rise over some intervals as time to maturity (T) rises, even though in the limit, variance of futures price changes is zero as T→∞. Thus, whether variance rises as our futures contracts move from T = 110 to 20 days to maturity remains an empirical question. As a practical matter, however, volatility in futures price changes, $\sigma^2(R_{t,t+1})$, will be heavily dominated by spot price changes (see Appendix). Our analysis of futures price changes reveals that there is no significant difference between volatility for "far" maturities ($80 \leq T_f \leq 110$) and "near" maturities ($20 \leq T_n \leq 50$).

In order to generate a vector of buy and sell trading signals, we utilize filter rules of size $x = 0.5\%, 1\%, 2\%, 3\%, 4\%$, and 5% and three moving average crossover rules: 1-day/5-day, 5-day/20-day, and 1-day/200-day. Each vector of signals is then applied to the original series of currency futures prices to measure the actual profitability of using these mechanical rules on the original sequence of price changes given in equation (5). The total return (TR) from following a trading strategy is measured by

$$(6) \qquad TR_{1,N+1} = \sum_{t=1}^{N} R_{t,t+1} = \sum_{t=1}^{N} d_t \ln(F_{t+1}/F_t)$$

where $d_t = +1$ is a long FC position and $d_t = -1$ is a short FC position.[13] Under the hypothesis of no currency risk premium, TR should not be significantly different from zero.

If a risk premium is present, however, TR will overstate the true excess return from following the trading rule, especially if there is a prolonged trend in the currency over the sample period. To correct for this effect, we follow Sweeney (1986) and estimate the risk premium as a constant over the sample period and equal to the returns from a buy-and-hold strategy, or

$$(7) \qquad RP_{1,N+1} = \sum_{t=1}^{N} \ln(F_{t+1}/F_t)$$

The benchmark for assessing unusual performance over a period is then the constant RP. Since our trading rules earn the RP over the fraction of days $(1 - f)$ long FC, and give up the RP over the fraction of days (f) short FC, the benchmark expected profit from the trading rule can be written as

$$(8) \qquad\qquad R^* = (1 - f)\,RP - f\,RP$$

If the fraction of days long FC is near 50% or RP is small, R^* will approach zero. In our analysis, both conditions hold. Consequently the total return can be viewed again as an excess return.

As noted earlier, technical models employing filter rules and moving averages are popular models that have been analyzed in earlier studies. The filter sizes and moving average lengths are selected as they have been applied in earlier studies. Other filter sizes and moving average lengths—along with other technical models—could, of course, be analyzed. Data-mining exercises of this sort must be avoided. Rather than torture the data until a profitable rule materializes, we will report our empirical results for all of the popular models that we test.

We now describe our simulation technique. Each series of futures prices of length $N + 1$ corresponds to a series of log price changes of length N. These N observations could be arranged in $M = N!$ separate sequences, each sequence $(m = 1, \ldots M)$ corresponding to a unique profit measure $(X[m,r])$ under trading rule r for $r = 1, \ldots R$.[14] For each currency, we generate a new comparison series (a shuffled series), by making a random rearrangement of price changes in the original series. By operating on the sequence of price *changes*, the starting and ending price *levels* of the new series are constrained to be exactly as their values in the original data. And by randomly rearranging the original data, the new series is constrained to have identical distributional properties as the original series. However, the time series properties of the new data are made random. Our simulation, therefore, generates one of the many paths that the exchange rate might have followed from its level on the starting day of the sample until the ending day, holding constant the original distribution of price changes.

This process of randomly shuffling the series of returns is repeated 10,000 times for each currency, thereby generating 10,000 i.i.d. drawings from all $m = 1, \ldots M$ possible sequences. Each of the 10,000 notional paths bears the same distributional properties as the original series, but the time series properties have been scrambled with each path, by construction, drawn independently of the other notional paths. Each technical rule (all filters and moving averages) is then applied to each of the 10,000 random series and the profits, X[m,r], are measured. This procedure generates an *empirical distribution* of profits. The profits of the original series can then be compared to the profits from the randomly generated, shuffled series. Under the null hypothesis, if there is no information in the original sequence of data, then the profits obtained from trading in the original series should not be significantly different from the profits available in the shuffled series. The null hypothesis that there is no information in the original time series of data is rejected at the α percent level if the profits obtained in the original series are greater than the α percent cutoff level of the empirical distribution.

EMPIRICAL RESULTS

In Table 19.1, we present descriptive statistics on the original times series of futures price returns. The mean daily return for all currencies is small and averages near zero. The largest (absolute) mean return was negative 4 basis points per day for the BP in the second sub-period, or roughly 10% per annum. The daily standard deviation in the full sample varies from 0.27% for the CD to 0.79% for the SF. For the CD and the JY, the standard deviation of returns is fairly constant across the three sub-periods. However, for the other three currencies, volatility rises sharply in the second sub-period.

Estimates of the skewness and kurtosis of daily returns are also reported in Table 19.1. In the full sample, four currencies display significant positive skewness while the CD reveals significant negative skewness. In the three sub-periods, however, there are many instances where skewness becomes insignificant, or as is the case for the BP, changes signs from negative to positive skewness and back to negative skewness—each one being significant. By comparison, positive kurtosis (measured against a value of 3.0 under the null hypothesis) is apparent for every currency during every sample period.

The autocorrelation of daily returns for lags 1–10 is reported in Table 19.2.[15] The estimates reveal a considerable amount of signifi-

TABLE 19.1 Sample Statistics of Daily Returns: Foreign Exchange Futures

	Currency & Variable	Full Sample	1976–80	1981–85	1986–90
DM	N	3786	1258	1264	1264
	Mu	0.000012	0.000073	–0.000338	0.000302
	Sigma	0.006740	0.005170	0.007579	0.007204
	T-value	0.11	0.50	–1.58	1.49
	Skewness	0.22	–0.09	0.52	–0.01
	s.e.	0.04	0.07	0.07	0.07
	Kurtosis	5.50	7.02	4.99	4.77
	s.e.	0.08	0.14	0.14	0.14
BP	N	3786	1258	1264	1264
	Mu	0.000077	0.000273	–0.000418	0.000377
	Sigma	0.007065	0.005626	0.008170	0.007137
	T-value	0.67	1.72	–1.82	1.88
	Skewness	0.82	–0.33	0.46	–0.20
	s.e.	0.04	0.07	0.07	0.07
	Kurtosis	6.22	7.19	6.08	4.89
	s.e.	0.08	0.14	0.14	0.14
CD	N	3785	1257	1264	1264
	Mu	0.000019	–0.000100	–0.000090	0.000246
	Sigma	0.002696	0.002512	0.002571	0.002968
	T-value	0.43	–1.40	–1.25	2.95
	Skewness	–0.21	–0.13	0.02	–0.47
	s.e.	0.04	0.07	0.07	0.07
	Kurtosis	7.33	4.33	6.66	9.07
	s.e.	0.08	0.14	0.14	0.14
JY	N	3533	1006	1263	1264
	Mu	0.000072	0.000230	–0.000190	0.000208
	Sigma	0.006964	0.007113	0.006532	0.007248
	T-value	0.61	1.02	–1.03	1.02
	Skewness	0.31	0.16	0.85	0.02
	s.e.	0.04	0.07	0.07	0.07
	Kurtosis	5.70	4.09	7.97	5.34
	s.e.	0.08	0.15	0.14	0.14
SF	N	3786	1258	1264	1264
	Mu	–0.000007	0.000045	–0.000345	0.000280
	Sigma	0.007856	0.006778	0.008517	0.008153
	T-value	–0.05	0.24	–1.44	1.22
	Skewness	0.16	–0.03	0.41	–0.01
	s.e.	0.04	0.07	0.07	0.07
	Kurtosis	4.86	5.48	4.80	4.28
	s.e.	0.08	0.14	0.14	0.14

Note: N = number of logarithmic returns

Sample period for JY is 1977–1990

TABLE 19.2 Autocorrelation Functions of Daily Returns - Foreign Exchange

	1	2	3	4	5	6	7	8	9	10	Sample Size
DM											
Full Sample	-0.0044	0.0270	0.0205	-0.0304	0.0113	0.0254	0.0039	0.0383a	0.0137	0.0028	3786
1976–1980	0.0478	0.0644a	-0.0375	-0.0420	0.0058	0.0434	0.0103	0.0511	0.0248	0.0658a	1258
1981–1985	-0.0266	0.0724b	0.0429	-0.0386	0.0029	0.0464	-0.0116	0.0430	0.0132	-0.0266	1264
1986–1990	-0.0107	-0.0430	0.0208	-0.0155	0.0153	-0.0138	0.0138	0.0170	0.0097	-0.0071	1264
BP											
Full Sample	0.0282	-0.0074	-0.0148	-0.0055	-0.0113	0.0183	-0.0027	0.0136	0.0288	-0.0180	3786
1976–1980	0.0292	-0.0176	-0.0143	-0.0212	-0.0227	0.0196	0.0157	0.0112	0.0544	0.0242	1258
1981–1985	0.0156	0.0351	-0.0016	-0.0222	-0.0418	0.0346	-0.0009	0.0160	0.0187	-0.0637a	1264
1986–1990	0.0368	-0.0628b	-0.0440	0.0238	0.0282	-0.0134	-0.0209	-0.0012	0.0266	0.0036	1264
CD											
Full Sample	0.0665b	-0.0310a	-0.0209	0.0196	0.0317a	0.0170	0.0183	0.0156	0.0149	-0.0215	3785
1976–1980	0.0449	-0.0176	0.0498	0.0237	0.0450	0.0099	0.0750b	0.0393	0.0194	0.0047	1257
1981–1985	0.1044b	-0.0296	-0.0656a	-0.0014	0.0447a	0.0551	0.0017	0.0454	0.0230	-0.0432	1264
1986–1990	0.0451	-0.0508	-0.0436	0.0245	0.0025	-0.0157	-0.0179	-0.0345	-0.0062	-0.0361	1264
JY											
Full Sample	0.0087	-0.0032	0.0324a	0.0078	0.0123	0.0215	-0.0044	0.0424b	0.0421b	0.0332a	3533
1976–1980	0.0184	-0.0401	0.0172	0.0072	0.0108	0.0137	-0.0210	0.0206	0.9839b	0.1083b	1006
1981–1985	-0.0207	0.0266	0.0485	0.0417	0.0108	0.0575a	-0.0051	0.0459	0.0419	-0.0382	1263
1986–1990	0.0230	-0.0019	0.0263	-0.0225	0.0166	-0.0025	0.0076	0.0550a	0.0113	0.0290	1264
SF											
Full Sample	0.0112	0.0234	0.0102	-0.0181	0.0033	0.0061	0.0025	0.0128	0.0225	0.0016	3786
1976–1980	0.0921b	0.0719a	-0.0018	-0.0055	-0.0113	0.0063	0.0188	-0.0060	0.0495	0.0516	1258
1981–1985	-0.0322	0.0620a	0.0127	-0.0273	0.0080	0.0272	-0.0115	0.0291	0.0120	-0.0310	1264
1986–1990	0.0007	-0.0581	0.0124	-0.0177	0.0037	-0.0206	0.0039	-0.0001	0.0155	-0.0050	1264

TABLE 19.2 (continued)

| | Original Autocorrelations | | | | Heteroskedasticity Consistent Autocorrelations | | | |
| | No. Significant in 30 Lags | Box-Pierce | | | No. significant in 30 Labs | Box-Pierce | | |
		Q(10)	Q(20)	Q(30)		Q(10)	Q(20)	Q(30)
DM								
Full Sample	4	17.21	37.97	52.19	3	11.46	26.91	38.55
1976–1980	5	24.13	31.96	52.13	3	12.44	18.54	35.20
1981–1985	3	18.07	26.92	40.18	3	12.64	19.54	30.96
1986–1990	2	4.66	21.33	36.06	2	4.09	18.94	33.57
BP								
Full Sample	1	10.99	29.21	41.97	1	7.22	20.25	30.08
1976–1980	0	8.33	17.32	22.57	0	6.23	13.31	18.10
1981–1985	2	12.11	21.14	40.41	1	7.27	13.87	28.76
1986–1990	3	12.56	31.40	37.32	3	11.58	27.41	32.83
CD								
Full Sample	3	33.17	48.46	63.25	2	18.78	29.59	42.96
1976–1980	3	18.92	29.81	45.45	3	14.20	24.23	39.88
1981–1985	4	32.31	52.59	62.77	1	15.19	27.89	35.94
1986–1990	1	12.92	26.43	33.42	1	8.79	19.38	25.73
JY								
Full Sample	3	22.96	32.70	38.87	2	17.30	25.82	31.32
1976–1980	3	22.36	34.22	45.02	2	16.40	25.93	34.81
1981–1985	1	17.68	25.31	33.33	0	12.65	20.12	26.77
1986–1990	0	7.67	16.62	25.05	0	5.85	14.00	22.64
SF								
Full Sample	1	6.94	25.95	37.00	1	5.14	19.49	28.66
1976–1980	4	24.35	34.71	59.65	2	11.64	18.49	35.76
1981–1985	2	10.96	19.09	30.35	1	8.13	14.59	24.25
1986–1990	2	4.89	20.54	33.59	2	4.46	18.73	32.23

Note: $Q(10) \sim X^2(10)$ with critical values 25.2, 20.5 and 18.3 at the 1%, 5% and 10% significance levels
$Q(20) \sim X^2(20)$ with critical values 40.0, 34.2 and 31.4 at the 1%, 5% and 10% significance levels
$Q(30) \sim X^2(30)$ with critical values 53.7, 47.0 and 43.8 at the 1%, 5% and 10% significance levels

a: significant at 5% level with standard error = $1/\sqrt{N}$

b: significant as above and with heteroskedasticity consistent standard error

349

cant autocorrelation. For the DM, SF, and CD we find evidence of significant positive autocorrelation at lags 1 and/or 2. In more general tests for autocorrelation, we find significant Box-Pierce Q statistics for the DM and CD (over the full sample) and the JY and SF over the 1976–1980 sub-period.[16] No Q statistics are significant for the BP, or for any currency in the final 1986–1990 sub-period.

Sample autocorrelation may be spurious in the presence of heteroskedasticity.[17] Given the empirical evidence reviewed earlier on heteroskedasticity in currency movements, we follow the methodology of Hsieh (1988) and compute heteroskedasticity-consistent estimates of the standard error for each autocorrelation coefficient, $s(k) = \sqrt{(1/n)(1 + \gamma(x^2,k)/\sigma^4)}$, where n is the sample size, $\gamma(x^2,k)$ is the sample autocovariance of the squared data at lag k, and σ is the sample standard deviation of the original data. As expected, this adjustment reduces the number of significant autocorrelation coefficients (only those noted by the letter "b" in Table 19.2). None of the adjusted Box-Pierce Q statistics are significant at the 5% level.[18]

The profits associated with the generation of buy and sell signals using filter rules and moving average rules are reported in Tables 19.3A and 19.3B, respectively. Over the entire 15-year sample period, every size filter results in positive profits for every currency. Average profit in the Canadian dollar across all filters is 1.8%, substantially less than the average for other currencies where results range between 6.6% and 8.1%. The results are much the same for the moving average rules, which led to average profits of 2.6% for the CD, and between 6.9% and 9.0% for the other currencies.

As expected, small filters and trading rules based on short-term moving averages result in considerably more trading signals than larger filters and rules embodying long-term moving averages. The 0.5% filter rule for the SF traded 907 times in 15 years, or about 60 trades per year; the 1/5 moving average rule for the SF produced 975 trades, or 65 trades per year. We calculate that the likely cost of transacting in the currency futures market is about 2.5 basis points (0.025%) per transaction for a large institution. A more conservative estimate would be roughly 4.0 basis points.[19] At 65 trades per year, a speculator would have his or her trading profits reduced by 1.62% per year, or 2.60% per year if we take our more conservative measure. Transaction costs of this magnitude would nearly decimate the 3.1% annual return for the 1/5 moving

TABLE 19.3A   Profitability of Filter Rules, Percent Per Annum (Sample Period, January 1976–December 1990)

Currency Sample Size	Filter Size (in %)						Average Profit
	0.5	1.0	2.0	3.0	4.0	5.0	
DM (N=3786)							
Actual Profit	1.9	8.9	5.6	7.7	7.8	7.9	6.6
No. of Trades	833	411	193	99	62	41	
Rank in 10,000	7652	9998	9808	9975	9981	9991	
BP (N=3786)							
Actual Profit	10.0	6.6	6.2	7.8	6.7	4.9	7.0
No. of Trades	793	432	192	108	69	53	
Rank in 10,000	9994	9852	9850	9961	9907	9609	
CD (N=3785)							
Actual Profit	2.9	3.5	1.4	0.7	1.5	1.0	1.8
No. of Trades	309	119	51	28	15	11	
Rank in 10,000	9969	9989	9089	7845	9317	8672	
JY (N=3533)							
Actual Profit	6.7	7.8	8.0	7.3	10.2	8.5	8.1
No. of Trades	777	412	170	98	60	44	
Rank in 10,000	9883	9965	9973	9945	9997	9987	
SF (N=3786)							
Actual Profit	7.2	6.5	3.4	7.1	9.8	5.8	6.6
No. of Trades	907	541	253	127	78	64	
Rank in 10,000	9873	9808	9680	9872	9991	9702	

average rule in the Canadian dollar and take a considerable bite out of the other transaction generating rules. For the other trading rules we consider, the volume of trading is considerably smaller, and transaction costs do not significantly affect profits.

The rank of the filter rule profits for the actual series in comparison to the 10,000 randomly generated series is also reported in Table 19.3A. The results are quite striking. In fifteen of the cases, the profits of the actual series rank in the top 1% (9900 and above) of all the simulated series. In ten further cases, the rank is in the top 5% (9500–9899). The remaining five cases rank lower, but in no case lower than the top 24% of the simulated series (rank 7600 and above). Thus in 25 of our 30 cases, we can reject the hypothesis that there is no information in the original series that can be exploited for profit by our filter rules.

TABLE 19.3B **Profitability of Moving Average Rules, Percent Per Annum (Sample Period, January 1976–December 1990)**

Currency Sample Size	Moving Average: Short-term (days)/Long-term(days)			Average Profit
	1/5	5/20	1/200	
DM (N=3786)				
Actual Profit	5.6	11.1	7.6	8.1
No. of Trades	950	212	79	
Rank in 10,000	9786	10000	9990	
BP (N=3786)				
Actual Profit	8.1	8.8	9.4	8.8
No. of Trades	935	192	42	
Rank in 10,000	9975	9987	9993	
CD (N=3785)				
Actual Profit	3.1	2.6	2.1	2.6
No. of Trades	957	190	91	
Rank in 10,000	9977	9917	9804	
JY (N=3533)				
Actual Profit	7.8	10.5	8.7	9.0
No. of Trades	866	190	87	
Rank in 10,000	9957	10000	9994	
SF (N=3786)				
Actual Profit	7.5	4.4	8.7	6.9
No. of Trades	975	213	71	
Rank in 10,000	9912	9235	9987	

The results are much the same for the moving average rules. We find twelve cases in which the profits of the actual series rank in the top 1% of all of the simulated series and two additional cases that are significant at the 5% level. The remaining case ranks lower, but still in the top 8% of the simulated series (rank 9200 and above). Again, these results imply a strong rejection of the hypothesis that there is no information in the original series that can be exploited for profit by our moving average rules.

Summary statistics on profitability for the simulated series are shown in Table 19.4A for the filter rule trading strategies and in Table 19.4B for the moving average rules. In all cases, the average profit in the simulated series is very small and insignificantly dif-

TABLE19.4A   Statistics on the Profitability of Filter Rules Over 10,000 Simulated Samples, 1976–1990 Period, Profits in Percent Per Annum

Currency	Filter Size (in %)					
	0.5	1.0	2.0	3.0	4.0	5.0
DM						
Average Profit	−0.008	−0.012	−0.022	−0.026	−0.034	−0.039
Median Profit	−0.009	−0.015	−0.027	−0.021	−0.034	−0.038
Standard Dev.	0.413	0.410	0.414	0.411	0.409	0.409
BP						
Average Profit	0.003	−0.002	−0.011	−0.017	−0.012	−0.008
Median Profit	−0.004	0.000	−0.012	−0.010	−0.013	−0.011
Standard Dev.	0.433	0.435	0.431	0.436	0.430	0.425
CD						
Average Profit	−0.005	−0.008	−0.010	−0.014	−0.021	−0.026
Median Profit	−0.004	−0.010	−0.011	−0.016	−0.023	−0.026
Standard Dev.	0.164	0.165	0.163	0.159	0.156	0.153
JY[a]						
Average Profit	−0.014	−0.014	−0.011	−0.014	−0.011	−0.016
Median Profit	−0.011	−0.009	−0.007	−0.013	−0.008	−0.017
Standard Dev.	0.417	0.414	0.414	0.412	0.411	0.409
SF						
Average Profit	0.000	−0.004	−0.019	−0.025	−0.032	−0.044
Median Profit	−0.001	−0.013	−0.012	−0.028	−0.037	−0.047
Standard Dev.	0.480	0.476	0.483	0.483	0.481	0.480

[a]JY data is for 1977-1990 period.

ferent from zero. The average profit is positive for a sample of 10,000 simulated series in only three cases. The other sample statistics for the simulated series suggest that average profits are normally distributed without skewness or kurtosis.

These results strongly suggest that the actual exchange rate series contained significant departures from serial independence that allowed technical trading rules to be profitable. If the actual series had been generated randomly, our simulations suggest that average profits would be close to zero. Gauged against these simulations, the actual path of exchange rates is seen to embody a significant degree of serial dependence.

To measure the stability of these results over time, we split the sample period into three five-year sub-periods and repeated our analysis. We decided to split the sample in this arbitrary way

TABLE 19.4B   Statistics on the Profitability of Moving Average Rules Over 10,000 Simulated Samples, 1976–1990 Period, Profits in Percent Per Annum

Currency	Moving Average: Short-term (days)/Long–term(days)		
	1/5	5/20	1/200
DM			
Average Profit	–0.005	–0.022	–0.064
Median Profit	–0.005	–0.018	–0.062
Standard Dev.	0.415	0.411	0.403
BP			
Average Profit	–0.002	–0.016	–0.035
Median Profit	–0.006	–0.016	–0.036
Standard Dev.	0.435	0.434	0.416
CD			
Average Profit	–0.004	–0.005	–0.020
Median Profit	–0.006	–0.007	–0.019
Standard Dev.	0.164	0.165	0.160
JY*			
Average Profit	–0.009	–0.017	–0.043
Median Profit	–0.008	–0.018	–0.045
Standard Dev.	0.410	0.413	0.401
SF			
Average Profit	0.000	–0.024	–0.074
Median Profit	0.003	–0.021	–0.076
Standard Dev.	0.478	0.482	0.468

*JY data is for 1977–1990 period.

rather than based on foreign currency strength and weakness, since the latter might exaggerate the profitability of trend-following rules. Our results for filter rules (in Table 19.5A) show that out of ninety cases (5 currencies × 6 filter rules × 3 periods) the application of filter rules to the original data resulted in profits in 78 cases and losses in the remaining 12 cases. Across all currencies, the average profitability of filter rules fell from 7.2% in 1976–1980 to 6.6% in 1981–1985, and fell again to 3.9% in 1986–1990. Smaller filters appeared to be most profitable in the first two sub-periods, while in the final sub-period, the 3%, 4%, and 5% filters appeared to be more profitable on average. The recent decline in profitability is most apparent for the DM and SF, for which 0.5%, 1%, and 2% filters generally would have produced losses. Of the ninety cases in Table 19.5A, profits significant at the 10% level were found in more

TABLE 19.5A   Profitability of Filter Rules, Percent Per Annum. Three Sample Sub-Periods

Currency	Filter Size (in %)						Average Over All Filters
	0.5	1.0	2.0	3.0	4.0	5.0	
DM							
1976–1980	5.2c	7.7b	4.9c	4.3c	4.8c	4.4c	5.2
1981–1985	6.1	18.1a	13.6a	12.2b	7.1	8.1c	10.9
1986–1990	–5.4	1.4	–2.5	5.9	9.8b	8.9c	3.0
BP							
1976–1980	8.1b	10.0a	7.3b	9.6b	10.8a	6.9c	8.8
1981–1985	13.1b	7.5	5.1	6.8c	5.6	5.7	7.3
1986–1990	9.1c	2.2	6.4	8.2c	1.7	1.3	4.8
CD							
1976–1980	3.7b	5.9a	0.2	–0.9	–1.8	–0.0	1.2
1981–1985	2.4	2.5c	3.2b	0.3	–0.3	–1.2	1.1
1986–1990	2.5	2.3	–0.1	1.6	5.4	5.3	2.8
JY							
1977–1980	7.4c	5.2	13.5a	14.2a	9.7b	8.2c	9.7
1981–1985	3.2	9.0b	4.4	2.0	10.2b	10.6a	6.6
1986–1990	9.4b	8.6b	7.3c	6.4	9.8b	6.0	7.9
SF							
1976–1980	16.5a	11.1a	7.9b	13.6a	12.4a	5.0	11.1
1981–1985	6.0	12.3b	5.1	6.8	` 7.4	6.3	7.3
1986–1990	–0.7	–3.8	–1.6	–0.0	7.8c	4.0	0.9
All Currencies							
1976–1980	8.2	8.0	6.8	8.2	7.2	4.9	7.2
1981–1985	6.2	9.9	6.3	5.6	6.0	5.9	6.6
1986–1990	3.0	2.1	1.9	4.4	6.9	5.1	3.9

Note: a – Significant at 1% level, rank > 9900:   11 entries
      b – Significant at 5% level, rank > 9500:   18 entries
      c – Significant at 10% level, rank > 9000:   15 entries
      not significant at 10% level, rank < 9000:   46 entries

                     90 entries total

nearly half of the cases. However, the number of cases with significant profits declined from 24 to 12 to 8 across the three sub-periods.

A similar set of results for moving average rules during the three sub-periods is reported in Table 19.5B. All 45 cases (5 currencies × 3 rules × 3 periods) result in positive profits. On average, there is some deterioration over time in the profitability of these rules, but the overall decline is small. The most pronounced

TABLE 19.5B   **Profitability of Moving Average Rules, Percent Per Annum. Three Sample Sub-Periods**

Currency	Moving Average: Short-term (days)/Long-term(days)			Average Over All MA Rules
	1/5	5/20	1/200	
DM				
1976–1980	6.1b	9.3a	5.2b	6.9
1981–1985	9.9b	11.4b	5.0	8.8
1986–1990	2.1	10.8b	5.5	6.1
BP				
1976–1980	6.8c	11.0a	4.6	7.5
1981–1985	9.8c	2.5	9.4c	7.2
1986–1990	8.8c	13.8a	8.7c	10.4
CD				
1976–1980	3.2b	5.1a	1.8	3.4
1981–1985	3.2b	1.4	0.4	1.7
1986–1990	2.6	1.5	5.4c	3.2
JY				
1977–1980	6.2	16.5a	12.6a	11.8
1981–1985	9.0b	6.7c	4.5	6.7
1986–1990	8.0c	9.9b	3.5	7.1
SF				
1976–1980	9.8b	1.7	6.2c	5.9
1981–1985	12.0b	5.8	6.2	8.0
1986–1990	0.9	6.1c	7.4	4.8
All Currencies				
1976–1980	6.4	8.7	6.1	7.1
1981–1985	8.8	5.6	5.1	6.5
1986–1990	4.5	8.4	6.1	6.3

Note: a – Significant at 1% level, rank > 9900:   6 entries
       b – Significant at 5% level, rank > 9500:   11 entries
       c – Significant at 10% level, rank > 9000:   10 entries
       not significant at 10% level, rank < 9000:   18 entries

                                 45 entries total

decline was for the 1-day/5-day rule in the third sub-period for DM and SF. Despite this, more than half of the cases held significant profits at the 10% level. And in the case of moving average rules, the number of cases with significant profits was fairly constant at 11, 8, and 8 across the three sub-periods.

These results for five-year sub-periods illustrate some of the risks that are entailed in technical trading, although it appears that some of these risks can be diversified by not operating in a single currency with a single technical rule.

The aforementioned results are unadjusted for a possible currency risk premium. Using equation (7) to estimate a constant risk premium for each currency over the 15-year period leads to the results in Table 19.6. The average per annum risk premium is negative for DM and SF and positive for the other three currencies. The estimated risk premiums are small relative to the size of trading rule profits and none are significant.

In equation (8), we noted that the risk premium should be adjusted further for days long FC and days short FC. These calculations are reported in Table 19.7. In nearly all of the cases, the percentage of days long and short is in the 45%–55% range.[20] As a consequence, the expected return (R*) from trading rules that permit both long and short positions is nearly zero. These results suggest that the adjustment needed for a constant risk premium would be small (a few basis points) and that our earlier results are unaffected by including a risk premium.

The methodology in Sweeney (1986) permits us to compute a significance level for excess returns (actual returns less the risk premium) under the assumption that both the risk premium and the standard deviation of returns are constant over the period. In Table 19.7, the t-values for excess returns are significant in 35 cases. It is interesting to note that the pattern and magnitude of t-values corresponds roughly to the pattern of significance values reported in Tables 19.3A and 19.3B, using the bootstrap simulation approach.

TABLE 19.6   Estimate of the Currency Risk Premium, Percent Per Annum (Sample Period, January 1976–December 1990)

Currency	Risk Premium	T-Value
DM	−0.32	−0.11
BP	2.03	0.68
CD	0.49	0.49
JY	1.93	0.66
SF	−0.17	−0.17

Note: Risk premium estimated as the average return from a buy-and-hold strategy over the sample period. See equation (7) in text.

TABLE 19.7 Excess Returns from Trading Rules Adjusting for a Risk Premium, Days Long and Days Short

Currency		Filter Size						Moving Average		
		0.5	1.0	2.0	3.0	4.0	5.0	1/5	5/20	1/200
DM	Total Return	1.9	8.9	5.6	7.7	7.8	7.9	5.6	11.1	7.6
	Risk Premium	-0.32	-0.32	-0.32	-0.32	-0.32	-0.32	-0.32	-0.32	-0.32
	Days Long	1810	1747	1846	1881	2011	2093	1910	1893	1824
	% Days Long	47.81%	46.14%	48.76%	49.68%	53.12%	55.28%	50.45%	50.00%	48.18%
	Days Short	1975	2018	1914	1877	1596	1505	1857	1694	1943
	% Days Short	52.17%	53.30%	50.55%	49.58%	42.16%	39.75%	49.05%	44.74%	51.32%
	R*	0.01	0.02	0.01	-0.00	-0.04	-0.05	-0.00	-0.02	0.01
	T-Value	0.65	3.05	1.92	2.65	2.69	2.73	1.93	3.82	2.61
BP	Total Return	10.0	6.6	6.2	7.8	6.7	4.9	8.1	8.8	9.4
	Risk Premium	2.03	2.03	2.03	2.03	2.03	2.03	2.03	2.03	2.03
	Days Long	2074	2048	2046	1888	1998	2057	1971	2063	1985
	% Days Long	54.78%	54.09%	54.04%	49.87%	52.77%	54.33%	52.06%	54.49%	52.43%
	Days Short	1711	1694	1696	1853	1741	1678	1796	1524	1774
	% Days Short	45.19%	44.74%	44.80%	48.94%	45.99%	44.32%	47.44%	40.25%	46.86%
	R*	0.19	0.19	0.19	0.02	0.14	0.20	0.09	0.29	0.11
	T-Value	3.28	2.15	2.01	2.61	2.20	1.57	2.68	2.85	3.11
CD	Total Return	2.9	3.5	1.4	0.7	1.5	1.0	3.1	2.6	2.1
	Risk Premium	0.49	0.49	0.49	0.49	0.49	0.49	0.49	0.49	0.49
	Days Long	2133	2209	2117	2352	2448	2279	2033	1861	1951
	% Days Long	56.35%	58.36%	55.93%	62.14%	64.68%	60.21%	53.71%	49.17%	51.55%
	Days Short	1645	1568	1646	1400	1271	1403	1730	1725	1820
	% Days Short	43.46%	41.43%	43.49%	36.99%	33.58%	37.07%	45.71%	45.57%	48.08%
	RR*	0.06	0.08	0.06	0.12	0.15	0.11	0.04	0.02	0.02
	T-Value	2.49	3.00	1.18	0.51	1.18	0.78	2.69	2.27	1.83

TABLE 19.7 (continued)

Currency		Filter Size						Moving Average		
		0.5	1.0	2.0	3.0	4.0	5.0	1/5	5/20	1/200
JY	Total Return	6.7	7.8	8.0	7.3	10.2	8.5	7.8	10.5	8.7
	Risk Premium	1.93	1.93	1.93	1.93	1.93	1.93	1.93	1.93	1.93
	Days Long	1643	1598	1622	1758	1825	1905	1629	1690	1683
	% Days Long	46.50%	45.23%	45.91%	49.76%	51.66%	53.92%	46.11%	47.83%	47.64%
	Days Short	1880	1923	1886	1746	1678	1574	1884	1644	1837
	% Days Short	53.21%	54.43%	53.38%	49.42%	47.50%	44.55%	53.33%	46.53%	52.00%
	R*	-0.13	-0.18	-0.14	0.01	0.08	0.18	-0.14	0.03	-0.08
	T-Value	2.34	2.73	2.79	2.49	3.46	2.84	2.71	3.58	3.00
SF	Total Return	7.2	6.5	3.4	7.1	9.8	5.8	7.5	4.4	8.7
	Risk Premium	-0.17	-0.17	-0.17	-0.17	-0.17	-0.17	-0.17	-0.17	-0.17
	Days Long	1761	1789	1799	1564	1634	1660	1828	1660	1779
	% Days Long	46.51%	47.25%	47.52%	41.31%	43.16%	43.85%	48.28%	43.85%	46.99%
	Days Short	2024	1996	1959	2159	2066	2023	1938	1987	1994
	% Days Short	54.46%	52.72%	51.74%	57.03%	54.57%	53.43%	51.19%	52.48%	52.67%
	R*	0.01	0.01	0.01	0.03	0.02	0.02	0.00	0.01	0.01
	T-Value	2.11	1.91	1.00	2.08	2.88	1.70	2.20	1.29	2.56

Note: R* is adjusted risk premium as in equation (8). T-Value is for excess return measured by total return minus R*.

SUMMARY AND CONCLUSIONS

The purpose of this chapter is to update earlier evidence on the profitability of simple technical trading rules and to extend these results using a new statistical test. Our results show that the profitability of simple technical models that was documented on data from the 1970s continued on into the 1980s. Moreover, our statistical tests suggest that the profitability of these technical rules is highly significant in comparison to the empirical distribution of profits generated by thousands of bootstrap simulations.

The profitability of trend-following rules strongly suggests some form of serial dependency in the data, but the nature of that dependency remains unclear.[21] Oddly, the BP series does not reveal any significant autocorrelation, yet the trading profits in the BP are consistently positive across all trading rules and sub-periods, broadly similar to the results for other currencies. Our technical rules for the DM, CD, and SF are most profitable during sub-periods when there is no significant autocorrelation, rather than in other sub-periods when serial correlation is present. Only the JY has its most profitable sub-period when its autocorrelation is significant. Still the technical rules produced consistently positive and significant results for the JY in the 1986–1990 sub-period, when there is virtually no autocorrelation in daily returns. Thus the link between serial dependency in the data and the profitability of the technical rules is also an open question.

The persistence of trading profits over the 15-year sample period is itself a striking result. However, we also found evidence that these profits have declined somewhat over the most recent five-year sub-period. This decline was more pronounced for smaller filter rules (0.5%, 1.0%, and 2.0%), the returns from moving average rules being more consistent over time. A possible explanation for the persistence of trading profits is the presence of central bank intervention that tends to lean against the wind and retard exchange rate movements. The Federal Reserve Board has recently made available data on its historic daily intervention activity making possible a test of this hypothesis.[22] The profitability of trend-following rules may instead be the result of excessive private speculation that causes prices to follow, at least temporarily, a speculative bubble path away from their fundamental equilibrium values. It is also, of course, possible that too little capital is committed to currency speculation, making market prices slow to adjust to their equilibrium values. While commercial banks are exceedingly active in interbank market trading and intra-day positions may be large, far less capital is committed to overnight and longer-term currency positions.

The results presented here could be extended in several worthwhile directions. One would be to specify alternative models for generating exchange rates, such as a univariate ARIMA time series model, a Markov switching model, or a GARCH model. Each specification could itself be taken as the null model, and we could then generate numerous simulated series using bootstrap techniques. Comparing the profitability of the original series with the empirical distribution of profits (and distributions of other sample statistics) would determine whether we can reject any null model.[23] While this technique could clarify which statistical model (or models) was consistent with the generation of currency prices, because these null models are not necessarily equilibrium economic models, they would not necessarily tell us whether the profits earned by technical trading rules were unusual in an economic, risk-adjusted sense.

APPENDIX

Using the notation from the text, we can write the interest rate parity relation with continuous compounding as

(A1) $$F_t = S_t \exp[i_{\$,t} - i_{FC,t}] = S_t \exp[D_t]$$

At time $(t-1)$, equation (A1) can be re-written as

(A2) $$F_{t-1} = S_{t-1} \exp[D_{t-1}]$$

Dividing A1 by A2 and taking logarithms, we have

(A3) $$\ln(F_t/F_{t-1}) = \ln(S_t/S_{t-1}) + (D_t - D_{t-1})$$

or

(A4) $$f_t = s_t + d_t$$

where f_t is the price trend or the daily profit as defined in equation (5) in the text. The variance of f_t is

(A5) $$\sigma^2(f_t) = \sigma^2(s_t) + \sigma^2(d_t) + 2 \, Cov(s_t, d_t)$$

As an empirical matter, it is well documented (see Levich [1989]) that the volatility of the interest differential, d_t, is far less than the volatility of the spot rate. Practically speaking, then, volatility in futures contracts will tend to be dominated by contemporaneous volatility in spot contracts rather than by changes in interest rates as the contract matures.

References

Alexander, Sydney S. "Price Movements in Speculative Markets: Trends or Random Walks," *Industrial Management Review*, May 1961, 2: 7–26.

Bilson, John F.O. "Technical Currency Trading," in L. Thomas, ed., *The Currency Hedging Debate*, London: International Financing Review, 1990.

Black, Fischer. "Equilibrium Exchange Rate Hedging," *Journal of Finance*, July 1990, 45, No. 3: 899–907.

Branson, William H., and Dale Henderson. "The Specification and Influence of Asset Markets," in R. Jones and P. Kenen, eds., *Handbook of International Economics* (Amsterdam: North-Holland Publishing), 1985.

Brock, William, Josef Lakonishok, and Blake Lebaron. "Simple Technical Rules and the Stochastic Properties of Stock Returns," University of Wisconsin, Social Science Research Institute, Working Paper #9022, January 1991.

Cornell, W. Bradford, and J. Kimball Dietrich. "The Efficiency of the Market for Foreign Exchange Under Floating Exchange Rates," *Review of Economics and Statistics*, February 1978, 60, No. 1: 111–20.

Dominguez, Kathryn M. "Does Central Bank Intervention Increase Exchange Rate Volatility?" working paper, Harvard University, April 1992.

Dooley, Michael P., and Jeffrey Shafer. "Analysis of Short-Run Exchange Rate Behavior: March 1973–September 1975," International Finance Discussion Papers, No. 76. Washington, D.C., Federal Reserve System, 1976.

Dooley, Michael P., and Jeffrey Shafer. "Analysis of Short-Run Exchange Rate Behavior: March 1973–November 1981," in D. Bigman and T. Taya, eds., *Exchange Rate and Trade Instability* (Cambridge, Mass.: Ballinger Publishing), 1983.

Efron, B. "Bootstrap Methods: Another Look at the Jackknife," *The Annals of Statistics*, 1979, 7, No. 1: 1–26.

Efron, B. *The Jackknife, the Bootstrap and Other Resampling Plans* (Philadelphia: Society for Industrial and Applied Mathematics), 1982.

Engel, Charles, and James D. Hamilton. "Long Swings in the Dollar: Are They in the Data and Do Markets Know It?" *American Economic Review*, September 1990, *80*, No. 4: 689–713.

Fama, Eugene F., and Marshall Blume. "Filter Rules and Stock Market Trading Profits," *Journal of Business*, January 1966, *39*: 226–41.

Froot, Kenneth A., and Richard H. Thaler. "Anomalies: Foreign Exchange," *Journal of Economic Perspectives*, Summer 1990, *4*, No. 3: 179–92.

Frenkel, Jacob A., and Richard M. Levich. "Foreign Exchange Markets: Spot and Forward," in the *New Palgrave: A Dictionary of Economic Thought and Doctrine* (London: Macmillan), 1988.

Hinkley, David V. "Bootstrap Methods," *Journal of the Royal Statistical Society*, 1988, *50*, No. 3: 321–37.

Hodrick, Robert. *The Empirical Evidence of the Efficiency of Forward and Futures Foreign Exchange Markets* (Chur, Switzerland: Harwood Academic Publishers), 1987.

Hsieh, David A. "The Statistical Properties of Daily Foreign Exchange Rates: 1974–1983," *Journal of International Economics*, 1988, *24*: 129–45.

Levich, Richard M. "Empirical Studies of Exchange Rates: Price Behavior, Rate Determination and Market Efficiency," in R. Jones and P. Kenen, eds., *Handbook of International Economics* (Amsterdam: North-Holland Publishing), 1985.

Levich, Richard M. "Is the Foreign Exchange Market Efficient?" *Oxford Review of Economic Policy*, Fall 1989, *5*, No. 3: 40–60.

Maddala, G.S. *Introduction to Econometrics* (New York: Macmillan), 1988.

Samuelson, Paul A. "Is Real-World Price a Tale Told by the Idiot of Chance?" *Review of Economics and Statistics*, February 1976: 120–24.

Schulmeister, Stephan. "An Essay on Exchange Rate Dynamics," unpublished working paper, Austrian Institute of Economic Research, 1987.

Schulmeister, Stephan. "Currency Speculation and Dollar Fluctuations," *Quarterly Review*, Banca Nazionale del Lavoro, December 1988, No. 167: 343–65.

Sweeney, Richard. "Beating the Foreign Exchange Market," *Journal of Finance*, March 1986, *41*: 163–82.

NOTES

1. Asset models of exchange rates are discussed in Levich (1985) and Branson and Henderson (1985).
2. Filter rules were used by Alexander (1961) to test for trading profits in American equity markets. Follow-up tests by Fama and Blume

(1966) found that no profits were available after adjusting for trans-action costs, dividends paid during short sales, and pricing disconti-nuities.

3. By comparison, portfolio managers may often face restrictions on their ability to execute short sales. For example, an American manag-er of a foreign currency bond fund might be allowed to hedge the currency risk in his foreign bonds, but not allowed to then short the currency. See Sweeney (1986) for an example of a currency filter rule with short sale restrictions.

4. For convenience, we follow the traditional practice in this field and measure the returns in logarithmic form. Returns could also be mea-sured assuming simple interest, geometric compounding, or some other convention.

5. See Froot and Thaler (1990) for a discussion of the evidence on the foreign exchange risk premium.

6. Sweeney imposes a restriction on short FC positions. From an initial position in $, a buy signal triggers a move into FC while a sell signal results in a move back into $. Profits from this trading rule are evalu-ated vis-à-vis the benchmark of buying and holding the FC. The same methodology was used by Cornell and Dietrich (1978) in an analysis of five currencies over the March 1973 to September 1975 period.

7. He also tested a momentum model, based on the rate of change in past exchange rate, and a combination model involving both moving average and momentum models.

8. A trend-following rule in which the investor buys more as the cur-rency goes up and sells more as the currency goes down is a dynam-ic call-replicating strategy. As the strategy produces a synthetic currency call option, the profits from this strategy should be skewed. By comparison, the trading rules here entail a fixed position that is held until the next signal of opposite sign appears.

9. This result underlies the generalized autoregressive conditional het-eroskedasticity (GARCH) model that includes the specification of a time-varying and serially correlated error term. An autoregressive integrated moving average (ARIMA) process is a more restricted representation of a time series process with constant variance and time invariant parameters.

10. For more on the bootstrap method, see Efron (1979, 1982) and Hinkley (1988). For an application of bootstrap techniques to techni-cal trading rules in the stock market, see Brock, Lakonishok, and LeBaron (1991).

11. The June 1976 Japanese yen contract had extremely light trading vol-ume and so there are no observations for yen during the months of March, April, and May 1976. Data for the yen begin in June 1976 with prices for the September contract.

12. In this assumption, we rely on the interest rate parity relationship that is well established in the empirical literature. See Frenkel and Levich (1988).
13. In our calculations, d_t may also equal zero during the initial observations of a sample before a trend has developed.
14. In our case with N approximately 3800, M is, conservatively speaking, a huge number. With N = 50, for example, $M = 3.04 \times 10^{64}$.
15. Autocorrelations at lags 11–30 were computed but they are not reported here.
16. The Box-Pierce Q(k) statistic tests the joint hypothesis that the first k autocorrelation coefficients are zero. We also computed Ljung-Box Q* statistics, which gave nearly identical results.
17. See Maddala (1988, pp. 218–219).
18. The adjusted Box-Pierce Q(K) statistic reported in Table 19.2 is calculated as $\Sigma_{k=1}^{K}[\rho(k)/s(k)]^2$, which is asymptotically distributed as X^2 with K degrees of freedom.
19. We consider two elements in the cost of transacting: first, the bid/ask spread, which we take as $0.0002 or $0.0001 per transaction, and second, the brokerage commission, estimated at $11.00 per round-trip transaction. Since the sizes of currency futures contracts, are fixed and futures prices are variable, the percentage cost of transacting varies somewhat across currencies and over time. Our likely estimate reflects an average across these dimensions.
20. The Canadian dollar results for the 3.0%, 4.0%, and 5.0% filters are an exception.
21. Bilson (1990) models the relationship between past and future exchange rate changes as a nonlinear function of observable variables.
22. See Dominguez (1992) for a description of this data and a test of the impact of intervention on exchange rate volatility in the 1985–1991 period.
23. Brock, Lakonishok, and LeBaron use technical models in concert with bootstrap simulation techniques to test the adequacy of alternative null models for the generation of stock market prices.

20

Value, Yield, and Trend:
A Composite Forecasting
Approach to Foreign
Exchange Trading

John F. O. Bilson
Trading Development Corporation

INTRODUCTION

In this chapter, three approaches to strategic currency investing
are examined. The three approaches are based upon considerations of value, yield, and trend. Value-oriented currency investments are based on the value of the exchange rate relative to the
relative purchasing power of the two currencies. The yield strategy invests in high yielding currencies and borrows in low-
yielding currencies. The trend strategy is based on a nonlinear
autoregressive model, which purchases currencies as their prices
rise and sells currencies as their prices fall. All of the approaches
are implemented through the development of forecasts of expected returns and volatilities based on the underlying model. These
forecasts are then translated into recommended positions through
a mean-variance portfolio optimization framework. The perfor-

---

*The factual statements herein have been taken from sources that we believe to
be reliable, but such statements are made without any representation as to accuracy, completeness or otherwise. The opinions expressed are solely the responsibility of the author. From time to time, Trading Development Corporation or one
or more of its officers may buy or sell, as principal or agent, the securities
referred to herein or options relating hereto, and may have a long or short position in such securities or options. This report should not be taken as a solicitation
or offer of the purchase or sale of securities. Prices shown are approximate.

mance of the strategies is then examined, using monthly data over the 1976 to 1992 time horizon. The results demonstrate that each of the approaches would have been profitable over the entire sample but that a two- to three-year time horizon is necessary before the returns pass standard tests of statistical significance. The approaches are then combined into an integrated strategy. Because the realized returns from the particular strategy are either uncorrelated or negatively correlated, the integrated strategy generates higher returns without a corresponding increase in risk. This chapter also includes a test for in-sample bias and demonstrates that in-sample bias is not a major cause of the profitability of the strategy.

Traditional equity investors have long been familiar with the delineation of investment strategies into categories such as growth, value, small cap, and international. This segmentation of investment strategies provides several advantages for the purchaser of investment services. First, performance can be evaluated relative to the strategy peer group rather than to the market as a whole. Second, investors may utilize the categories to either diversify across investment styles or to overweight a particular style which the investor may feel should outperform the market. In this chapter, I shall attempt to develop a similar segmentation approach to investing in foreign currencies. The three styles of investment that I shall consider are based on considerations of value, yield, and trend. The value-oriented approach invests in currencies that are undervalued relative to the purchasing power of the currency over goods and services. During the floating-rate period, exchange rates have deviated greatly from the values predicted by relative prices in the short run, but they have tended to move toward purchasing power values over the longer term. The yield-oriented approach invests in high-yielding currencies and borrows low-yielding currencies. If the foreign exchange market is efficient and risk neutral, high-yielding currencies should depreciate against low-yielding currencies at the rate of the interest rate differential. However, it has often been the case that high-yielding currencies tend to appreciate relative to low-yielding currencies, so that the yield-oriented strategy captures not only the interest rate differential but also a capital gain on the investment. Finally, the trend-oriented investor invests in currencies that have appreciated and sells currencies that have depreciated. If the exchange rates evolve as a random walk, the trend-related strategies will have a zero or negative expected present value. Many investors believe, however, that currencies prices do exhibit sustained trends and a number of currency managers do sell programs based on trend-following approaches.

While each of these investment styles has been profitable over the floating-rate period, it is also the case that there have been periods in which each of them has performed poorly. Poor performance can be attributed to one of two circumstances. First, the approach used is not forecasting large expected returns because the currency is not over- or under-valued, the yield differential is not large, or the currency is not trending. Under these circumstances, the approach will not take large positions and the volatility of returns will be low. Second, an approach will underperform because the approach fails to predict market returns. For example, a value-oriented investor may begin to invest in a currency when it becomes undervalued on a purchasing power parity basis by 20 percent. However, undervaluations of 40 percent have not been uncommon in the foreign exchange market and the approach will have negative returns if this outcome occurs. A disciplined value approach would extend the position as the currency continues to depreciate so that the profitability will be restored when the currency finally recovers, but there can be a long period of time before profitability is achieved. Investors who rely on a yield-oriented approach will experience losses when a currency moves sharply against the interest rate differential. For example, the devaluation of the peripheral currencies against the core in the European Monetary System following the failure of the Danish vote on the Maastricht treaty created large losses for systems trading on interest rate differentials. Finally, trend-following approaches can be hurt by choppy, trendless markets.

One of the points that I will emphasize in this chapter is that a combination of the three approaches considerably reduces underperformance due to the two factors mentioned in the previous paragraph. While it is likely that any single approach will go through extended periods of low anticipated profitability, the probability that all three approaches cannot find positions with anticipated profitability is substantially smaller. Combined approaches also reduce losses due to forecast errors. For example, in a choppy market, trend followers will tend to be hurt, but value and yield investors will be profitable. The value strategy will be profitable because of its buy low, sell high, feature, while the yield strategy will be profitable if the final change in the exchange rate is small. On the other hand, a trending market will be profitable for the trend-following approach, but it could be unprofitable for the value approach if the trend is against the purchasing power parity value or if it is against the interest rate differential.

I would like to stress the limitations of this study before getting into the details of the approach. First, the approach taken to value, yield, and trend investing relies on specific models of these approaches that may differ substantially from other models of these approaches. One should consequently not view the simulated returns discussed in this chapter as indicative of the type of returns achieved in practice by investment advisors utilizing these approaches. In addition, the results presented herein are simulated and are designed with the benefit of hindsight and should not be considered as indicative of future performance. Second, while value, yield, and trend constitute three important approaches to foreign currency investing, they are by no means the only approaches taken to the market. Other important approaches include market making, discretionary trading, and options volatility trading. I do not cover these approaches because they are extremely difficult to simulate and because of data limitations. For both of these reasons, the results reported herein should not be considered as indicative of the actual returns possible from currency trading.

The approach that is taken to the formulation of the trading strategy is taken from Bilson (1981). The profit or loss on a forward contract is defined in equation (1):

(1) $$\text{Profit} = (S_{t+1} - F_t)^* Q_t$$

where S_{t+1} is the realized spot rate at the maturity of the contract, measured in terms of dollars per unit of foreign currency, F_t is the forward rate for the maturity of the contract, and Q_t is the quantity of foreign currency purchased or sold. Multiplying and dividing by the forward rate converts this relationship into the following:

(2) $$\text{Profit} = r_{t+1} q_t$$

where $r_{t+1} = (S_{t+1} - F_t)/F_t$ is defined as the return on the forward contract, and $q_t = Q_t F_t$ is the dollar value of the forward position. The trader's problem is to choose q_t on the basis of expectations of the realized value of r_{t+1}, $E(r_{t+1})$, expectations of the volatility of

r_{t+1}, $V(r_{t+1})$, and expectations of the correlation of r_{t+1} with other potential investments.

I will summarize this decision process in a simple mean-variance optimization process. The expected utility function is described in equation (3):

(3) $$E(U) = E(r)'q - (1/2a)\, q'Vq$$

where $E(r)$ is an $n \times 1$ vector of expected returns, q is an $n \times 1$ vector of positions, a is a scalar representing the investor's degree of risk aversion, and V is an $n \times n$ covariance matrix representing both the absolute volatility and the correlations of the returns. $E(r)'q$ is the expected profit on the position, and $q'Vq$ is the prior variance of the profit. The investor's expected utility is positively related to expected profitability and negatively related to the expected volatility of profit with the degree of risk aversion represented by the parameter a. Maximizing $E(U)$ with respect to q leads to the following expression for the vector of positions:

(4) $$q = a\, V^{-1}\, E(r)$$

According to equation (4), the investor requires three pieces of information to determine the desired set of positions. The first element is the risk aversion parameter, a. Assume that the expected return and variance are such that the prior Sharpe ratio, the expected return divided by its standard deviation, is unity. Then equation (4) implies that

(5) $$E(r)'q = a$$

In other words, the parameter, a, represents the expected profit that the investor would like to make on a risk investment with a Sharpe ratio of unity. More generally, equation (4) can be written as:

(6) $$E(r)'q = a\, E(r)'V^{-1}\, E(r)$$

In equation (6), $E(r)'V^{-1}\, E(r)$ is the square of the prior Sharpe ratio. Assume, for example, that the investor expects to make $1 million when the Sharpe ratio is 1. Then he would attempt to make $4 million in a situation where the Sharpe ratio is 2. Consider a situation in which the monthly standard deviation of the return is 1 percent and that all variation in the Sharpe ratio is due to the variation in the expected return. We would then have the following situation:

Expected Return	Sharpe Ratio	Position	Expected Profit
0.0%	0.0	0	0
0.5%	0.5	50	0.25
1.0%	1.0	100	1.00
1.5%	1.5	150	2.25
2.0%	2.0	200	4.00
2.5%	2.5	250	6.25

The table demonstrates that the size of the position is proportional to the expected return. As a consequence, there may be extended periods of time in which a particular strategy is absent from the market because its forecasts of expected returns are low. This timing feature of the model constitutes an important difference between foreign exchange investments and traditional equity models. In the traditional equity version of the mean variance framework, the investor is typically constrained to fully allocate capital across the range of permissible investments. Since forward contracts do not require the placement of capital, the neutral position for a currency investor is a zero investment. As expected returns increase in absolute size, then either long or short positions will be taken. With constant variance, the size of the position taken is proportional to the expected return. Once the scale of the position is determined, the allocation across currencies is designed to maximize the expected profit for a given level of risk.

In the following simulations, the risk aversion parameter is set equal to 10 percent of the presumed client capital. This implies that when faced with an investment with a Sharpe ratio of unity, the client will attempt to make a 10 percent return over the holding period. The two standard deviation range for this investment varies from a loss of 10 percent to a gain of 30 percent. In simulation experiments, setting the risk aversion parameter equal to this value has resulted in a risk-return trade-off that is comparable to that from holding a passive portfolio of U.S. equities.

Having determined the investment strategy, the investor's problem is to formulate expectations of expected returns, variances, and correlations. In the following sections, I will approach this problem from the perspective of value, yield, or trend investing. However, before proceeding to the formulation of expected returns, I will first develop a simple model of the volatility of returns. The correct modeling of volatility is essential in the implementation of mean variance portfolio programs.

A SIMPLE MODEL OF VOLATILITY[1]

With the development of options markets in the major currencies, market-determined estimates of volatility are now widely available. However, implied volatilities from options prices are not available for the beginning of the floating rate period. In its place, I shall develop a model of implied volatilities based on short-term interest rate differentials. The idea behind this measure is straightforward. If the exchange rate was fixed, then short-term interest rate differentials on different currencies would have to be the same. Any difference in yields would create a risk-free arbitrage opportunity, which would rapidly be eliminated. More generally, market participants engaged in uncovered interest rate arbitrage must balance the expected return from the interest rate differential with the volatility of the exchange rate. Equation (4) above may be used to formalize this notion.

$$(4) \qquad\qquad q = a\,V^{-1}\,E(r)$$

Under the assumption that the exchange rate evolves as a random walk, the expected return will be equal to the interest rate differential. Assuming that the market clears holding the exogenously determined quantity of assets, q, equation (4) implies that the variance is proportional to the absolute value of the interest rate differential.

$$(7) \qquad\qquad V = a\,q\,(i - i^*)$$

where $(i - i^*)$ is the short-term nominal interest rate differential.

The hypothesis embodied in equation (4) will be tested by regressing the square of the ex post return on the absolute value of the interest rate differential. The equation is estimated using monthly data over the period from January 1976 to November 1992. The regression is estimated by OLS for each currency individually and by Zellner's seemingly unrelated regression procedure with cross equation restrictions on the slope co efficient. T-statistics are provided in parentheses beneath the coefficients.

Currency	Constant	Slope	R-SQ	S.E.	D.W.
Sterling	0.0011	0.0788	0.004	0.0025	1.93
	(3.60)	(0.94)			
Mark	0.0004	0.2882	0.062	0.0018	1.81
	(1.62)	(3.66)			
Yen	0.0009	0.1330	0.024	0.0018	1.91
	(4.32)	(2.24)			
Pooled	0.0008	0.1446			
	(6.02)	(4.01)			

With the exception of sterling, these results support the contention that the volatility of the return is positively related to the absolute value of the interest rate differential. If one is prepared to accept the contention that absolute volatility is an appropriate measure of risk, the results offer support to the contention that interest rate differentials reflect a time-varying risk premium rather than a forecast of the expected change in the value of the exchange rate. The problem with this approach, as we shall see below, is that the volatility of currency returns appears to be diversifiable in a larger portfolio of assets.

Figure 20.1 describes the relationship between the yield differential and the implied volatility of the currency returns. When two currencies have similar one-month Eurocurrency deposit rates, the implied volatility is approximately 10 percent on an annualized basis. On the other hand, when the annualized one-month differential is 15 percent, the implied volatility is approximately 18 per-

FIGURE 20.1   Volatility and Yield

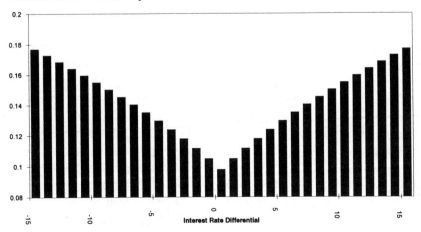

FIGURE 20.2 Implied Volatilities

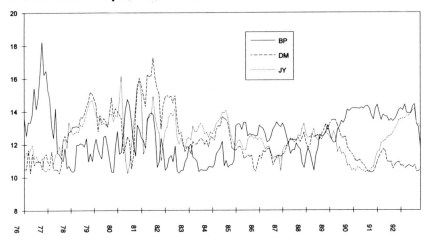

cent on an annualized basis. In Figure 20.2, the implied volatilities are plotted over the sample period. Figure 20.2 demonstrates that implied volatilities have varied substantially over the floating rate period.

VALUE INVESTING IN FOREIGN CURRENCIES[2]

The purchasing power parity theory of the foreign exchange rate is based on the theory of international commodity arbitrage. The absolute version of the PPP relationship predicts that arbitrage will equalize the prices of commodities denominated in the two currencies.

(8) $$P = S P^*$$

In equation (8), P represents the prices of domestic commodities in dollars, and P^* represents the price of foreign commodities denominated in the foreign currency. S is the exchange rate, expressed in dollars per unit of foreign currency. If domestic prices are above foreign prices on an exchange rate adjusted basis, the theory predicts that the domestic economy will experience a current account deficit and a domestic recession. Both factors will tend to lower domestic prices, raise foreign prices, and depreciate the exchange rate, thereby bringing the arbitrage condition into balance.

There are many factors that operate to prevent free commodity arbitrage. In addition to tariffs, taxes, and transportation costs, higher prices may reflect higher rents and wages. On the assumption that these factors are relatively stable, the relative version of the PPP doctrine posits that the inflation rate differential should equal the rate of depreciation of the exchange rate.

$$(9) \qquad\qquad dP = dS + dP^*$$

In equation (9), dP represents the domestic rate of inflation, dP^* represents the foreign rate of inflation, and dS represents the rate of depreciation of the exchange rate. In contrast to equation (8), equation (9) allows for a constant difference in relative prices to reflect differential cost structures.

The theory of value investing that we will use combines elements of both the absolute and relative versions of the purchasing power parity relationship. The expected return from value investing is defined in equation (10).

$$(10) \quad E(Rv) = b_0 + b_1 ((dP - i) - (dP^* - i^*)) + b_2 \ln(P/(S\ P^*))$$

The first term in this expression represents the differential inflation rate minus the difference in short-term interest rates. The differential inflation rate is represented by the actual difference in wholesale price inflation over the past twelve months. If the difference in inflation rates is already discounted in the interest rate differential, then the value-oriented investor would not predict a change in the exchange rate greater than the interest rate differential. However, if the inflation rate differential exceeds the interest rate differential, then the value-oriented investor predicts a depreciation in excess of the interest rate differential. The second term in the equation represents the absolute deviation from purchasing power parity. The theory predicts that if a currency is overvalued on an absolute purchasing power parity basis, then part of the adjustment will occur through an adjustment of the exchange rate. The constant term in the regression is included to provide a base for the price series and to allow for long-term differences in relative prices due to structural factors.

Equation (10) was estimated subject to the constraint that the slope coefficients are the same for each currency. The SUR estimates are provided below.

	b_1	b_2
Estimated Coefficient	−2.2356	0.0414
Standard Error	0.4561	0.0110
T-Statistic	4.90	3.74

The b_1 coefficient measures the sensitivity of the expected return to the inflation rate differential relative to the interest rate differential. The negative coefficient estimated value of 2.2356 implies that a 1 percent increase in the foreign inflation rate, all else held equal, will result in a 2.23 percent depreciation of the foreign currency relative to the dollar. The estimated value is over 4 standard deviations from zero. The b_2 coefficient measures the sensitivity of the expected return to the over- or under-valuation of the foreign currency prices relative to the dollar. In September 1992, the estimated PPP values were 1.38 $/BP, 0.5235 $/DM (1.9102 DM/$), and 0.006735 $/JY (148.47 JY/$). Based on these estimates and the beginning of period exchange rates of 1.7843 $/BP, 0.7080 $/DM and 0.8346 $/JY, the foreign currencies were overvalued relative to the dollar by 25.59 percent for sterling, 30.17 percent for marks, and 21.44 percent for yen. The b_2 coefficient of 0.0414 suggests that 4.14 percent of the overvaluation will be eliminated by a depreciation of the currency over a period of one month. In the following table, I provide a stylized spreadsheet for calculating the position for the value-orientated investor. The investment period is from the end of September to the end of October 1992.

	BP	DM	JY	US
Exchange Rate	1.7843	0.7080	0.8346	
WPI	1971	1300	889	1251
WPI(-12)	1878	1271	901	1291
Euro 1	8.28%	8.31%	3.54%	3.42%
Inflation	4.83%	2.25%	-1.14%	-3.14%
Over/Under	-25.93	-30.17	-21.44	
E(R)	-1.66%	-1.36%	-1.21%	
Std.Dev.	3.82%	3.82%	2.99%	
Position	($706)	$254	($1144)	
EOP XR	1.556	0.6489	0.8106	
P&L	$85	($20)	$32	$98

Notes:

XR = Beginning of period spot rate ($/*)

WPI = IMF Producer Price Index

WPI(-12) = WPI twelve months previously

Euro 1 = One-Month Eurocurrency Deposit Rate

Inflation = Rate of Change in WPI over previous twelve months

Over/Under = Estimated over/under valuation on a PPP basis

E(R) = Expected Return for month from forecasting equation

Std.Dev. = estimated standard deviation from volatility model

Position = $ value of position in $'000 per $ million in assets

EOP XR = End of period spot rate

P&L = Profit or Loss on position in $'000 per $ million in assets.

At the end of September 1992, the value approach predicts negative expected returns for all of the currencies in the portfolio. (A negative expected return represents a positive expected return on a short position in the currency or a positive return on a long dollar position.) This recommendation was based on the assessment that all of the currencies were overvalued on a purchasing power parity basis and because U.S. inflation was lower than the inflation rates of the other currencies. (Our estimates of the real inflation rate differential are 2.66 percent for the U.K., 0.50 percent for Germany, and 1.88 percent for Japan.) Because the interest rate differentials are larger for the European currencies than for the yen, the estimated volatility for the European currencies is almost twice as large as the estimated volatility for the yen. These two considerations, expected return and volatility, provide the inputs for the mean variance optimizer. The output from the optimization procedure leads to a net short position of $450,000 per million in assets for the European currencies and $1,144,000 per million in assets for the yen. The yen position is larger primarily because of the lower forecast of volatility. In this particular period, the value approach resulted in a profit of $98,000 per million in assets.

In Figure 20.3, the history of the expected returns from the value-oriented strategy is presented. As one would expect, the expected returns follow long cycles corresponding to the period of over- and under-valuation of the dollar. The positive returns peaked in 1985 with the overvaluation of the dollar and then declined rapidly with the dollar's fall in 1986 and 1987. The period

FIGURE 20.3   Expected Returns from Value Investing

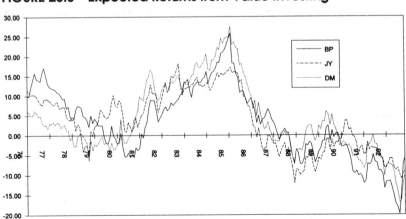

FIGURE 20.4   Index from Value Investing

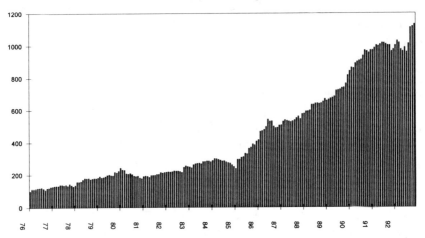

from 1988 to 1991 offered relatively few opportunities for this approach, but the fall in the dollar in 1992, particularly against the European currencies, resulted in expected returns in the 15 percent to 20 percent range.

In Figure 20.4, the index value of a $100 initial investment in the value approach is plotted. Over the 17-year period, the $100 investment grew to approximately $1131, representing a compound return of $15.23 percent in excess of any interest return on the funds. This average, however, fails to describe the variability of the returns during the period. The value strategy experienced two periods in which the returns over the previous year amounted to a loss of approximately 20 percent. An investor in the value-oriented strategy must be prepared to wait for an extended period of time before realizing positive expected returns. The average monthly return is 1.28 percent with a standard deviation of 3.93 percent. These statistics can be used to create the following prospective return analysis.[3]

Horizon	Return	Std. Dev.	R − 2SD	R + 2SD	T-Stat
1 Month	1.28	3.93	−6.59	9.14	0.32
3 Months	3.88	6.81	−9.75	17.50	0.56
6 Months	7.90	9.64	−11.37	27.16	0.82
1 Year	16.43	13.63	−10.82	43.69	1.20
2 Years	35.57	19.27	−2.98	74.11	1.84
3 Years	57.85	23.60	10.64	105.05	2.45
4 Years	83.79	27.26	29.28	138.30	3.07
5 Years	113.99	30.47	53.04	174.93	3.74

FIGURE 20.5   Annual Returns from Value

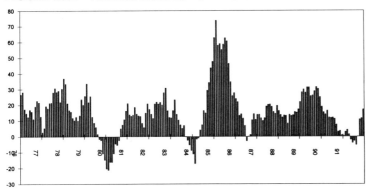

In this table, the return is the forecasted return over the holding period and Std.Dev. is the estimated standard deviation of the return. The next two columns estimate the average return plus or minus 2 standard deviations and are an estimate of the probable range in the returns over the holding period. The final column estimates the T-statistic, or Sharpe ratio, of the returns. The table demonstrates that there is a reasonable probability of loss from the value strategy through the two-year investment horizon. However, if the approach is followed for five years, the negative two standard deviation return is 53 percent, which represents a compound return of 8.5 percent per annum in addition to any interest earned on funds invested.

In Figure 20.5, the annual returns from value investing are plotted. According to the projections in the table, these annual returns should range between a loss of 10.82 percent and a positive return of 43.69. The actual returns over a one-year horizon range from a loss of 21 percent to a gain of 74 percent. Clearly the two standard deviation range only provides a rough guide to the actual outcome over a given time horizon. In part, this is due to the fact that the strategy itself does not embody a constant degree of risk because positions will be scaled up when expected returns are high or when expected volatility is low. However, over time, the value-oriented strategy has provided positive returns, and these returns do not appear to have substantially diminished with time.

YIELD INVESTING IN FOREIGN CURRENCIES[4]

In Figure 20.6, the one-month Eurocurrency deposit rates are plotted for the major currencies. The chart demonstrates that there

FIGURE 20.6   One Month EuroDeposit Rates

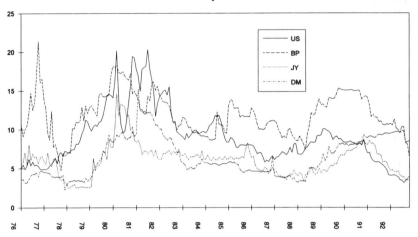

have been large differences in short-term rates between the major currencies during the floating rate period. The divergences were greatest in the period from 1979 to 1982. From 1983 to 1991, there was a gradual convergence of short-term interest rates between the major currencies. At the beginning of 1991, short-term rates on marks, yen, and dollars were all essentially the same. Since that time, however, the divergences have expanded as rates have fallen in Japan and the United States and risen in Europe.

There are basically two approaches to explaining these divergences. In a world dominated by risk-neutral investors, the difference in yield between two currencies must be equal to the expected capital gain from the appreciation or depreciation of the currency. If dollars pay a 10 percent yield and marks pay a 5 percent yield, then the dollar must be expected to depreciate against the mark by 5 percent over the year in order for the return on the two investments to be equivalent. The difficulty with this argument is that short-term cross-currency investments embody a high degree of absolute risk. For example, the 5 percent differential between marks and dollars amounts to a yield of a little over 0.4 percent over a month. The monthly standard deviation of the exchange rate is approximately 3.5 percent. On the assumption that the exchange rate evolves as a random walk, the one standard deviation range from investing in dollars by borrowing marks is negative 3.1 percent to positive 3.9 percent, and the two standard deviation range is negative 6.6 percent to 7.4 percent. As we have demonstrated, the volatility of the return increases with the interest rate differential. Under these circumstances, it is not entirely unexpected that the floating exchange rate period has segmented international short-term capital markets so that short-term interest rates are primarily related to domestic developments and are basically independent of exchange rate expectations. The large amounts of capital that would be required to bring interest rates in line with exchange rate expectations are simply not available for an investment with these risk/return characteristics.

The inadequate supply of capital for uncovered short-term interest arbitrage does provide an opportunity for the marginal yield-oriented investor. The fundamental motive behind yield investing is the assumption that changes in the exchange rate are either unrelated to interest rate differentials or that they are, in fact, positively related in the sense that high-yielding currencies have demonstrated a tendency to appreciate against low-yielding currencies. Thus by investing in high-yielding currencies and borrowing in low-yielding currencies, the investor captures the yield differential and has the possibility of a capital gain as well. Although the risk of this strategy in the short term is high, over time unanticipated profits and losses will tend to cancel out and the risk/reward ratio will improve.

The link between yield investing and foreign currency trading is the interest rate parity condition, which links spot and forward exchange rates with short-term interest rate differentials.

$$(11) \qquad F = S(1+i)/(1+i^*)$$

In equation (11), F is the forward rate ($/*), S is the spot rate ($/*), i is the U.S. interest rate and i^* is the foreign interest rate. Equation (11) is a minimum risk arbitrage condition that can be expected to hold very closely under normal conditions. The condition states that if the foreign interest rate is above the U.S. rate, then the forward rate will be at a discount to the spot rate. The purchase of a forward contract is financially equivalent to borrowing in the U.S. and investing in the foreign currency. Thus a yield-oriented investor could implement the strategy by buying forward contracts when the forward price is at a discount to the spot and sell forward contracts when the forward price is at a premium to the spot. For example, at the end of September 1992, short-term rates were 3.42 percent in the U.S. and 8.28 percent in the U.K.. At the same time, the spot rate was 1.7843 and the one-month forward rate was 1.7771. An investor who borrowed in dollars at 3.42 percent and invested in sterling at 8.28 percent would realize an annualized return of 4.86 percent if the exchange rate remained unchanged. Alternatively, the investor could implement the strategy by purchasing a forward contract at 1.7771. If the spot rate remained at 1.7843 at the maturity of the contract, the investor would realize a profit of 72 ticks, which represents a return of 4.84 percent on an annualized basis.

Statistically, the issue with yield investing is whether the ex-post return from currency investing is related to the interest rate differential. Equation (12) provides a framework for testing this hypothesis:

$$(12) \qquad E(R_y) = c_0 + c_1 \ln((1 + i)/(1 + i^*))$$

In this equation, $\ln((1 + i)/(1 + i^*))$ is equal to the interest rate differential or the forward premium or discount on the currency. If the coefficient c_1 is zero, then the interest rate differential is exactly offset by the anticipated change in the exchange rate and there is no expected return from yield investing. If c_1 is equal to minus one, then the change in the exchange rate is unrelated to the interest rate differential and the expected return from yield investing is exactly equal to the interest rate differential. Finally, if c_1 is less than minus one, then high-yielding currencies tend to appreciate relative to low-yielding currencies, and the yield investor will capture both the interest rate differential and the capital gain from the appreciation of the currency. Equation (12) was estimated using the SUR technique, using monthly data over the period from January 1976 to November 1992.

	c_1
Estimated Coefficient	−3.1937
Standard Error	0.5626
T-Statistic	5.67

The coefficient on the interest rate differential is −3.19. This implies that the expected return from yield investing is approximately three times the interest rate differential. In the example given above, an investor who is long sterling at a rate of 8.28 percent against the dollar at 3.42 percent would have, on average, earned a return of 15.50 percent p.a. This return is comprised of 4.86 percent from the yield differential itself and 10.64 percent from the appreciation of sterling against the dollar.

The constant terms in equation (12) represent a constant rate hurdle from which to start the yield differential strategy. The hurdle rates are 2.31 percent for sterling, –3.86 percent for marks, and –2.85 percent for yen. In other words, if U.K. rates are 2.31 percent above U.S. rates, then the expected return from yield investing is zero. As the U.K. rate differential moves above the hurdle rate, the expected return becomes positive. On the other hand, rates in Germany and Japan have to be 3.86 percent and 2.85 percent below U.S. rates before there is a positive expected return from borrowing in these currencies. The hurdle rates may be considered as a reflection of the long-term inflation rate differentials between the respective currencies.

Although the expected return is proportional to the interest rate differential, the positions taken by the mean-variance optimizer are not, because the implied volatility is also influenced by the interest rate differential. The following table illustrates the construction of the position in the case of the British pound.

Rate Differential	Expected Return	Standard Deviation	Position ($'000 per $m)
0.00%	–7.37%	9.80%	($767)
5.00%	8.60%	12.97%	$510
10.00%	24.57%	15.51%	$1021
15.00%	40.54%	17.69%	$1295
20.00%	56.51%	19.63%	$1466

At a zero interest rate differential, the expected return from yield investing is negative 7.37 percent because of the positive rate differential required for sterling/dollar positions. As the interest rate differential increases, both the expected return and the estimated standard deviation increases. The fourth column contains the recommended positions for a $1 million investment. The position reaches a leverage of 1 at an interest rate differential of 10 percent p.a. The degree of leverage does continue to increase from this point, but at a more gradual rate. For example, a doubling of the differential from 10 percent to 20 percent results in a 50 percent increase in the size of the position.

The following table provides a stylized spreadsheet for the yield strategy. The numbers are for a position taken at the end of September 1992 realized at the end of October.

	BP	DM	JY	US
Spot	1.7843	0.7080	0.8346	
1 Mnth Forward	1.7771	0.7051	0.8345	
Euro-1	8.28%	8.31%	3.54%	3.42%
E(R)	0.67%	2.05%	1.06%	
Std.Dev.	3.82%	3.83%	2.99%	
Position				
($'000 per $m)	($1072)	$1696	$716	
EOP Spot	1.5560	.6489	.8106	
P&L	$133	($135)	($20)	($22)

The position in this example is equivalent to the following cash positions:

	Borrow/Invest ($m per $m)	Interest Rate	Revenue/Cost ($'000)
BP	($1072)	8.28%	($88)
DM	$1696	8.31%	$141
JY	$716	3.54%	$25
US	($340)	3.42%	($11)
			$65

In this table, the revenue/cost calculations are annualized for purposes of comparison with the interest rates. In addition to the initial $1 million in capital, the investor borrows $340,000 in dollars and $1,072,000 in sterling. Then $1,696,000 of these funds is invested in marks and $716,000 is invested in yen. If the exchange rates do not change over the investment period, the resulting portfolio will yield 6.58 percent on an annualized basis, relative to a 3.42 percent yield if the original funds are held in dollars. Of course the assumption that the exchange rates will not change is unwarranted. As the previous table demonstrates, the rise in the dollar over the investment period resulted in a loss of 2.22 percent for the month.

Let us now examine the performance of the yield investment strategy over the sample period. Figure 20.7 plots the expected returns from the strategy for each of the currencies. For most of the sample period, the expected returns from yield investing have fluctuated in a range of plus or minus 10 percent. (A negative return should be interpreted as a positive return on a short position.) Unlike the value-oriented strategy, the yield strategy typically does not exhibit large swings in expected return. The exception to this rule is the gradual increase in the expected returns on the

FIGURE 20.7   Expected Return from Yield Investing

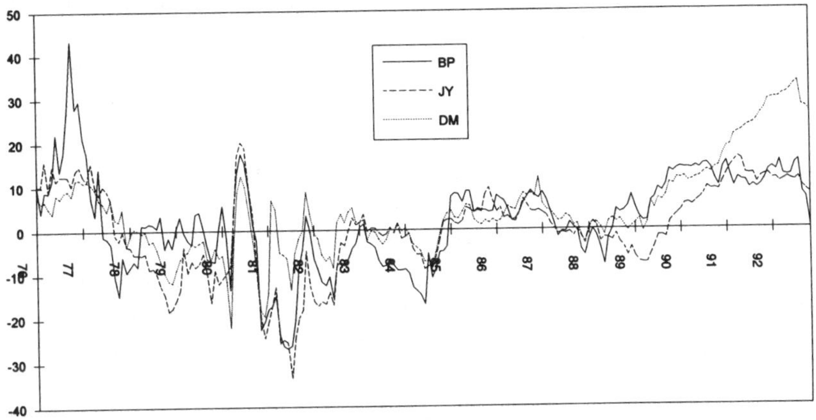

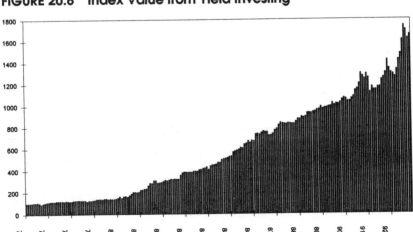

D-mark during 1991 to 1992 as German interest rose in response to the financing costs of Eastern Germany. More typically, the yield-oriented approach is concerned with relatively short-term divergences in interest rates, which permit high-yielding cross-currency spreads to be placed.

In Figure 20.8, the index value of an initial $100 investment in the yield strategy is plotted. The end of period value of the index is $1657, representing an average annual compound return of approximately 18 percent. While the monthly returns exhibit approximately the same volatility as the value strategy, the yield

FIGURE 20.8   Index Value from Yield Investing

returns are less correlated and the path of the index exhibits less volatility. When the value strategy experiences a loss, it will tend to expand the size of the position since the over- or under-valuation of the currency has typically increased. For the yield strategy, the only role for the exchange rate is to determine the quantity of foreign currency to be purchased or sold. For example, suppose the program called for an investment of $1 million in sterling. At an exchange rate of $2, BP 500,000 would be purchased. If in the subsequent period, the exchange rate fell to 1.5 with the interest rate differential unchanged, the yield strategy would now want to be long BP 660,000 in order to maintain the same dollar value of the investment. Hence while both value and yield exhibit a tendency to buy when the currency is falling, this tendency is far more pronounced for the value strategy than it is for the yield strategy.

The following table performs a horizon analysis for the yield strategy:

Horizon	Average	Std. Dev.	R − 2SD	R + 2SD	T-Stat
1 Month	1.45	3.54	−5.62	8.53	0.41
3 Months	4.43	6.13	−7.83	16.69	0.72
6 Months	9.05	8.67	−8.29	26.38	1.04
1 Year	18.91	12.26	−5.61	43.43	1.54
2 Years	41.40	17.34	6.73	76.08	2.38
3 Years	68.15	21.23	25.68	110.62	3.20
4 Years	99.95	24.52	50.91	148.99	4.07
5 Years	137.77	27.41	82.94	192.59	5.02

Because of a higher average return, the yield strategy reaches a positive two standard deviation lower band in two years. Over a one-year horizon, the strategy offers an average return of 18.91 percent with a two standard deviation range from −5.61 percent to 43.43 percent. The actual annual returns are plotted in Figure 20.9. The actual average annual return was 18.79 percent and the two standard deviation range was −2.78 to 79.44. The peak in the annual returns occurred in 1980, when there was a great deal of variation in short-term interest rates. In Figure 20.7, we saw that the expected return from yield investing went from negative 20 percent to positive 20 percent to negative 20 percent in 1980. The large movements in short-term rates, and the associated movements in currency values, were largely responsible for the large returns during this period.

FIGURE 20.9   Annual Return from Yield Investing

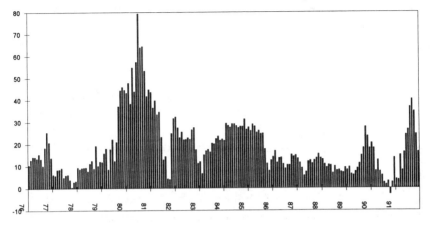

TREND INVESTING IN FOREIGN CURRENCIES[5]

Figure 20.10 describes the evolution of exchange rates during the floating rate period. The issue that will be addressed in this section is whether there are sustainable trends in these exchange rates. The literature on this issue is somewhat mixed. The conventional econometric approach based on vector autoregressions has tended to conclude that exchange rates do not exhibit predictable trends. On the other hand, studies employing filter rule methodologies have found that these rules tend to result in statistically

FIGURE 20.10   Exchange Rate Indices

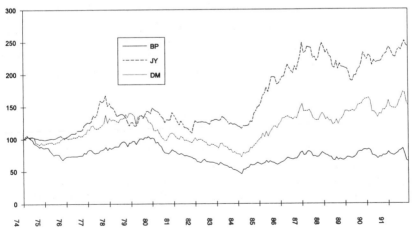

significant profits. Since both types of study use the same data, the different conclusions must be attributed to the different methodologies employed. In this section, we will explore this issue and develop an investment methodology based on trend-following principles.

Let us begin with the autoregressive approach. Define the past trend as the rate of change in the exchange rate over the past three months. In the following regressions, we relate the past trend to the observed change in the exchange rate over the following month. The regression relation is described in equation (13)

$$(13) \qquad\qquad DS_t = d_0 + d_1 \text{ Trend} + u$$

where DS_t is the range of change in the exchange rate, Trend is the past trend, and u is a residual. Estimating this equation for the three major currencies resulted in the following estimates of the coefficients:

	d_0	d_1	R_SQ	Std Error
BP	−0.0013	0.0019	0.003	0.03
	(0.51)	(0.86)		
DM	0.0021	0.0022	0.004	0.03
	(0.85)	(0.91)		
JY	0.0039	0.0022	0.004	0.03
	(1.55)	(0.92)		

(T-Statistics in parentheses beneath the coefficients)

These results certainly support the contention that there are no predictable trends in foreign exchange rates. The R-squared statistics are extremely low and none of the coefficients are significantly different from zero at standard significance levels.

The problem with the autoregressive approach is with the implied assumption that the future trend is proportional to the past trend. In other words, the model assumes that the larger the past trend is, the greater the future trend will be. The regression model rejects this assumption by setting the slope coefficients close to zero. On the other hand, filter rule studies typically adopt a nonlinear methodology. For example, a simple filter rule model would be to buy if the trend is positive and sell if the trend is negative. The important difference between the methodologies is that the size of the position is related only to the sign, and not the size, of the trend.

In Figure 20.11, the actual relationship between the past trend and the future trend is explored. The three-month trend has a standard deviation of approximately 6 percent. In Figure 20.11, the standardized trend is calculated as the trend over the past three months divided by its standard deviation. These observations are then divided into standard deviation blocks. For example, the negative 2 standard deviation block includes all values that are less than negative 1.75 standard deviations. The –1.5 block includes all observations between –1.5 and –1.75 standard deviations. For each block, the subsequently observed rate of depreciation is computed. The results shown in Figure 20.11 clearly reject the assumption of a linear relationship between the past trend and the future rate of depreciation. The positive correlation is strongest at 0.5 standard deviation and then declines toward zero at two standard deviations.

In equation (14), I propose a simple nonlinear formulation of the trend following relation.

(14) $$E(R_t) = d_0 + d_1 X4 + d_2 X5$$

where X4 is the past trend, and $X5 = X4 \exp(-abs(X4)/std(X4))$ is the discounted trend. In this formulation, $abs(X4)$ is the absolute value and $std(X4)$ is the standard deviation. Using the volatility model developed on page 372, the standard deviation of the three-month trend is equal to the implied volatility of the one-month trend multiplied by the square root of 3. This feature of the model

FIGURE 20.11   Trend Related Expected Returns

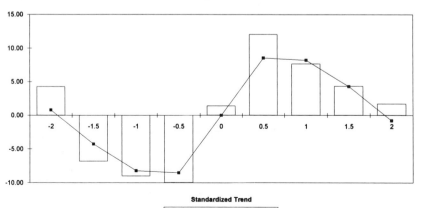

implies that the size of the potential trend depends on the absolute value of the interest rate differential.

The following table provides estimates of equation (14):

	d_1	d_2
Estimated Coefficient	−0.0752	0.5147
Standard Error	0.0348	0.1126
T-Statistic	2.15	4.56

Both coefficients are statistically significant at standard levels. The nonlinear relationship implied by the coefficients is described by the continuous function in Figure 20.11. It is obvious from the figure that the nonlinear function closely matches the block function approach to modeling the relationship between past trends and future returns. The constant terms in the regression provide estimates of the long term trends in the return. The estimated constant terms are 0.1254 percent per month for sterling, 0.0437 percent per month for marks, and 0.0024 percent per month for yen. All of these estimates are not significantly different from zero.

The following table provides a stylized spreadsheet for calculating the positions from the trend model. All of the numbers are for positions taken at the end of September 1992.

	BP	DM	JY	US
Spot(t)	1.7843	0.7080	0.8346	
Spot(t–3)	1.9045	0.6562	0.7962	
Forward(t)	1.7771	0.7051	0.8345	
Euro-1	8.28	8.31	3.54	3.42
Std.Dev.1	3.82%	3.83%	2.99%	
Std.Dev.2	6.62%	6.63%	5.18%	
Trend	−6.52%	7.60%	4.71%	
D.Trend	−2.43%	2.42%	1.90%	
E(R)	−7.65%	8.60%	10.39%	
Position				
($'000 per $m)	−1699	788	1388	
Spot(t+1)	1.5560	0.6489	0.8106	
P&L				
($'000)	211	−62	−39	108

In this table, Std.Dev.1 is the estimated standard deviation of the monthly return and Std.Dev.2 is the estimated standard deviation of the trend. Since U.K. and German rates are large relative to U.S. rates, the standard deviation of the trend is larger than it is for Japan, where interest rates are closer to U.S. rates. Over the previous three months, sterling had declined by 6.52 percent against the dollar while the mark had rallied 7.60 percent and the yen had rallied 4.71 percent. All of these trends are in the normal range where the model would expect the trend to continue. As a result, the trend system predicts an annualized return of –7.65 percent for sterling, 8.60 percent for marks, and 10.39 percent for yen. The expected returns, in conjunction with the estimates of the standard deviations and correlations, are used as inputs by the mean variance portfolio optimizer. The recommended positions are short $1,699 million sterling, long $0.788 million in marks, and long $1.388 million in yen. Over the subsequent month, all of the currencies fell sharply. Profits of $211,000 on sterling offset losses of $62,000 on marks and $39,000 in yen. Overall the program generated a profit of $108,000 per million invested, for a 10 percent return for the month.

In Figure 20.12, the value of a $100 initial investment in the trend program is plotted. Over the entire period, the $100 would have grown to $2523, representing a compound annual rate of return of 20.84 percent. This rate of return is considerably higher than the 15 percent return from the value strategy and is also superior to the 18 percent return from the yield strategy. The prospective returns from the strategy are described in the following horizon analysis:

Horizon	Return	Std. Dev.	R–2SD	R+2SD	T-Stat
1 Month	1.24	3.69	–6.15	8.63	0.33
3 Months	3.78	6.40	–9.02	16.57	0.59
6 Months	7.69	9.05	–10.40	25.79	0.85
1 Year	15.98	12.80	–9.61	41.57	1.24
2 Years	34.51	18.10	–1.68	70.71	1.90
3 Years	56.01	22.16	11.68	100.33	2.52
4 Years	80.93	25.59	29.75	132.12	3.16
5 Years	109.85	28.61	52.62	167.07	3.83

As with the value and yield approaches, a two-year time horizon is required before the trend strategy exhibits a reasonable probability of profit. Over a one-year horizon, the two standard deviation range is from –9.61 percent to 41.57 percent. The actual range of annualized returns, as described in Figure 20.13, is from a loss of 13.29 percent to a gain of 70.15 percent.

FIGURE 20.12   Index Value from Trend Investing

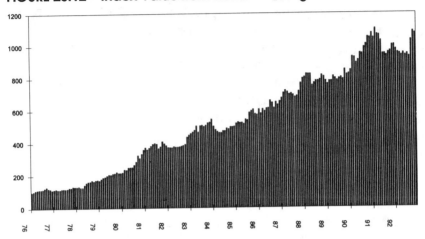

FIGURE 20.13   Annual Returns from Trend Investing

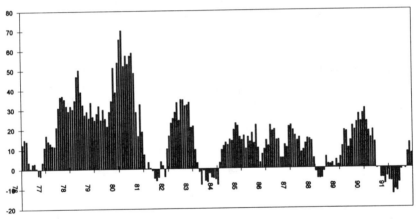

COMBINED TRADING STRATEGIES

In the preceding section, it was demonstrated that trading strategies based on considerations of value, yield, and trend have been profitable during the floating rate period. We now turn to the issue of combining the strategies into an integrated approach to the markets. The primary factor determining the gains from integration is the correlation between the expected and actual returns. If the returns are highly correlated, then the different strategies are all capturing the same movements in the exchange rate. Under these conditions, any one of the strategies will be sufficient and the gains from integration will be small. On the other hand, integration will be most beneficial when the returns are uncorrelated. If the actual returns are uncorrelated, then risk will be reduced because forecast errors will tend to cancel. If the expected returns are uncorrelated, then periods with low expected returns for one strategy will be compensated by periods of higher expected returns for another. In the following table, we examine the correlations of expected returns, actual returns and the normalized return forecast errors for each of the strategies.

	Value	Yield	Trend
Value	1.00	+0.31	−0.06
	1.00	+0.29	+0.03
	1.00	+0.38	−0.02
Yield		1.00	−0.02
		1.00	+0.13
		1.00	−0.18
Trend			1.00
			1.00
			1.00

In this table, the first row provides estimates of the correlation between the actual returns, the second row provides the correlation between the expected returns, and the third row provides estimates of the correlation between the forecast errors. The value and yield strategies exhibit a correlation of approximately 30 percent. These strategies are expected to be positively correlated because both employ interest rate differentials in their forecasting equations. The correlation is certainly not high enough, however, for the two approaches to be considered as substitutes for each other. On the other hand, the trend strategy is basically uncorrelated with both the value and the yield strategies. The lack of correlation occurs with both actual returns and expected returns.

The integration of the approaches begins with the specification of a composite forecasting equation:

(15) $E(R) = b_0 + b_1 X1 + b_2 X2 + b_3 X3 + b_4 X4 + b_5 X5$

In equation (15),

X1 = the deviation of the exchange rate from its PPP value

X2 = the inflation rate differential minus the interest
    rate differential
X3 = the nominal interest rate differential
X4 = the trend in the exchange rate
X5 = the "discounted" trend

Equation (15) was estimated using Zellner's seemingly unrelated regression procedure, using monthly data over the period from January 1976 to November 1992. The following estimates were obtained:

Coefficient	Initial	Integrated
X1	0.0415	0.0416
	(3.74)	(3.63)
X2	−2.2356	−1.3075
	(4.90)	(2.66)
X3	−3.1937	−2.2816
	(5.67)	(3.71)
X4	−0.0751	−0.0769
	(2.15)	(2.26)
X5	0.5147	0.5245
	(4.56)	(4.80)

In this table, the initial parameter estimates are taken from the forecasting equations for each strategy presented earlier. The integrated parameter estimates are taken from the estimation of equation (15). The primary difference between the two sets of estimates is in the parameter estimates of the coefficients on X2, the real interest rate differential, and X3, the nominal interest rate differential. Since these two variables are correlated, the initial estimates "double count" their influence when the strategies forecasting equations are estimated separately. In the integrated approach, the parameters suggest a weight of 1 on the real interest rate differential and a weight of 2 on the nominal interest rate differential. In effect, the integrated estimates allow the value approach to specialize on the value indicators while leaving the yield considerations to that strategy. The parameter estimates relating to the valuation of the currency relative to PPP and the parameter estimates of the trend model are largely unaffected by the introduction of trend estimation. All of the parameter estimates are statistically significantly different from zero at standard significance levels.

The constant terms in the regression are attributed to the base for the PPP calculations. In effect, the PPP values also reflect longer-term differences in interest rate differentials. The estimated PPP values at the end of the sample period are 1.1973 $/BP, 0.5684 $/DM (1.7593 DM/$), and 0.7666 $/JY (130.44 JY/$). Based on these estimates, sterling was overvalued by 40 percent, marks by 21 percent, and yen by 8 percent at the end of September 1992. Combining the approaches led to the following position analysis at this time. The table provides the expected returns generated by each strategy and the position recommended by the mean variance optimization framework.

	BP	DM	JY
Value	–23.98%	–11.61%	–6.70%
Yield	+11.08%	+11.15%	+0.22%
Trend	–9.27%	+8.21%	+7.61%
Total	–22.17%	+7.75%	+1.14%
Position ($'000 per $m)	–3061	2311	327

In the case of sterling, the value approach predicts that the currency is overvalued and the trend approach confirms that sterling is falling against the dollar. On the other hand, the yield strategy is positive on sterling because U.K. rates are higher than U.S. rates. In the case of the mark, the value approach also suggests that this currency is overvalued, but the yield and trend strategies are positive. The combined model suggests a modest 7.75 percent expected return on long D-mark positions. Finally, in the case of the yen, the yield strategy has no opinion because of the parity of U.S. and Japanese rates while the value and trend strategies tend to offset each other. Based on all of these considerations, the recommended position is short $3 million in sterling, long $2.3 million in marks, and long $0.3 million in yen. This position generated a return of approximately 10 percent in October 1992.

We now compare the performance of the strategies based on the initial and integrated parameter estimates:

	Initial	Integrated
Value	1.28%	1.06%
	(3.93%)	(5.35%)
Yield	1.45%	0.08%
	(3.54%)	(4.55%)
Trend	1.24%	1.16%
	(3.69%)	(3.57%)

This table describes the average monthly return and the standard deviation of the monthly returns for each of the strategies. The most noticeable feature of the table is the increase in the standard deviation of the value and yield strategies when the integrated parameter estimates are employed. This finding suggests the paradoxical result that the use of the integrated system increases the risk of the trading strategy. This cannot be the case because the integrated estimates minimize the variance of the sum of the forecast errors. By recognizing the interaction between the strategies, the integrated system actually lowers the variance. The reduction in variance arises from the correlation matrix rather than the absolute risk of the strategy. The correlations between the strategies are presented below.

	Value	Yield	Trend
Value	1.000	-0.586	-0.039
Yield		1.000	-0.090
Trend			1.000

By removing the common nominal yield component from the value and yield strategies, the integrated model provides a negative -0.586 correlation between the returns. This high negative correlation reflects the fact that overvalued currencies have often been associated with high interest rates relative to the dollar. The value and yield strategies are also nominally negatively correlated with the trend model. In Figure 20.14, the index values for the three strategies, based on the integrated parameter estimates, are

FIGURE 20.14   Index Values for Integrated Strategy

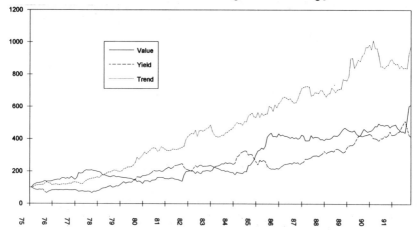

plotted. The figure demonstrates the negative correlation between the value and yield strategies.

In Figure 20.15, the index value for the integrated strategy is presented. A $100 investment in December 1975 would have grown to over $31,000 over the 17-year period. This represents a compound annual return of 39.85 percent over the period, or 2.8 percent per month. The returns from the integrated strategy are substantially higher than the returns from the separate strategies for two reasons. First, because the strategy returns are negatively correlated, the mean variance optimizer can allocate a greater degree of leverage to the integrated strategy than it can to any individual strategy. Earlier in this chapter, we saw that the mean variance model employed in this chapter has the feature that the expected profits are proportional to the square of the prior Sharpe ratio. (The prior Sharpe ratio is the ratio of the expected return on the portfolio to the expected risk.) Since the integrated model has a higher expected return and lower risk, the degree of leverage is increased. The other important reason why the returns on the integrated strategy are much higher than the returns on the individual strategies is because of rebalancing. In each period, the "capital" available to trade is equal to the preceding period's capital plus the previous periods trading profits. This capital is then allocated across the strategies based on the expected returns and expected risks. It is important to note that the capital allocation is in no way dependent on prior profitability. In fact, strategies that have previously lost money are likely to receive a larger allocation from the profits generated by

FIGURE 20.15   Index Value of $100 Initial Investment

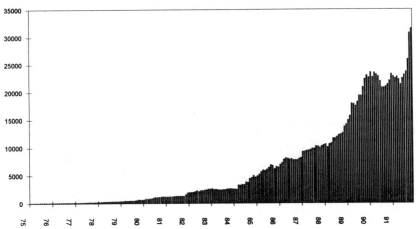

other strategies. This capital allocation model can be compared with the alternative model of not rebalancing. In the alternative model, the capital allocations are set at the beginning of the period and are not revised over time. Compared to the rebalancing model's compound return of 39.85 percent, a non-rebalancing model using the same forecasting equations would have had a compound annual return of 18.48 percent. Rebalancing clearly plays an important part in determining the returns of the integrated model.

The following table contains a horizon analysis of the integrated model:

Horizon	Average	Std. Dev.	R–2SD	R+2SD	T-Stat
1 Month	2.83%	5.39%	–7.95%	13.61%	0.52
3 Months	8.73%	9.34%	–9.94%	27.40%	0.93
6 Months	18.23%	13.20%	–8.18%	44.63%	1.38
1 Year	39.78%	18.67%	2.43%	77.12%	2.13
2 Years	95.38%	26.41%	42.57%	148.19%	3.61
3 Years	173.10%	32.34%	108.42%	237.78%	5.35
4 Years	281.73%	37.34%	207.04%	356.61%	7.54
5 Years	433.57%	41.75%	350.07%	517.07%	10.38

While each of the individual strategies required a two-year time horizon before generating statistically significant expected profits, the integrated strategy achieves statistical significance after one year. After two years, the 2 standard deviation lower band has increased to 42 percent. An annual return above 20 percent over two years is clearly superior to most conventional estimates. In Figure 20.16, the annual returns from the integrated strategy are

FIGURE 20.16   Annual Returns from Integrated Strategy

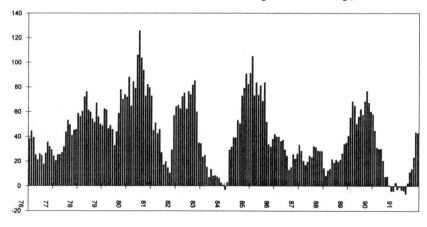

plotted. The actual annual range from a –6.25 percent to 125.84 percent.

THE ISSUE OF IN-SAMPLE BIAS

One of the common criticisms of econometric forecasting models and simulated trading strategies is that these studies are subject to in-sample bias. In developing the strategy, the researcher is working with the benefit of hindsight and will clearly avoid indicators that have not worked well during the sample period. In addition, the seemingly unrelated regression technique chooses the parameters of the forecasting equation to maximize the expected utility from the strategy. The simulated results consequently always provide the most optimistic assessment of the strategy. Furthermore, there is no fundamental reason why these strategies should have been profitable in the past and no reason why the past profitability should provide any indication of future profitability. All the results are actually saying is that if an investor had known the parameters of a model estimated over the 1976 to 1992 period in 1976, then utilizing the strategy over the time period would have been profitable. While these criticisms should be taken seriously, a number of factors suggest that the issue of in-sample bias may not be too serious. First, the models discussed in this chapter have all been previously published in a similar form to that presented here. The value approach was originally published in 1984, the yield approach in 1981, and the trend approach in 1990. Second, the actual number of parameters estimated—8 in the integrated model—is small relative to the 203 observations on 3 currencies. In-sample bias is likely to be most serious when there are large number of parameters relative to the number of observations.

To explore the issue of in-sample bias, the sample data is split into two subsamples, the first running from January 1976 to December 1983 and the second running from January 1984 to November 1992. I will first estimate the integrated model for the two sub-samples and then use the first sample parameter estimates to determine positions in the second sample and vice versa. I then compare the performance of this model with the performance of the in-sample model.

	Full Sample	76–83	84–92
X1	0.0416	0.0142	0.0654
	(3.63)	(0.53)	(4.12)
X2	–1.3075	–0.5056	–2.0124
	(2.66)	(0.67)	(2.34)
X3	–2.2816	–2.2228	–2.7550
	(3.71)	(2.10)	(2.47)
X4	–0.0769	–0.1829	–0.0276
	(2.26)	(3.05)	(0.67)
X5	0.5245	0.8135	0.2953
	(4.80)	(4.79)	(2.04)

The value approach parameters are not significantly different from zero in the first period, but they are highly significant in the second period. Offsetting this feature of the results, the trend parameters are both larger and more significant in the first period than in the second. The yield parameter is virtually the same across the two subperiods. More importantly, all of the coefficients have the same sign over the two periods, and at least two of the strategies are successful in each subsample.

In the second stage of the test for in-sample bias, the 76–83 parameters are used to implement the integrated strategy over the 84–92 period and the 84–92 parameters are used to implement the strategy over the 76–83 period. The returns from the split sample approach are then compared with the returns from the in-sample version of the model.

	Average	StdDev
In-Sample	3.04%	5.39%
Split-Sample	2.72%	6.18%
Difference	0.32	2.67%

The in-sample strategy had an average return of 3.04 percent per month and a monthly standard deviation of 5.39. When the sample is split, the average return declines to 2.72 percent per month and the monthly standard deviation increases to 6.18 percent. The difference due to in-sample bias amounts to 0.3 percent per month. This difference is not statistically different from zero at standard significance levels. In order to examine the relationship between the two series more closely, the split-sample returns are regressed on the in-sample returns.

(15) $R1 = -0.4170 + 1.0329 \ R2 + u$
              (1.93)   (29.65)
          $R\text{-}SQ = 0.8139 \ S.D. = 2.67$

According to this regression, the in-sample returns, R2, account for 80 percent of the variation in the split-sample returns. This evidence suggests that while the issue of in-sample bias is present, it is not a major determinant of the results reported in this chapter.

CONCLUSION

In this chapter, I have compared three approaches to foreign exchange trading. Each of the approaches was found to have value in its own right, but the results clearly demonstrate that an integrated combination of the approaches results in higher average returns and lower risk. The integrated approach invests in under-valued, high-yielding, upward-trending currencies and borrows overvalued, low-yielding, downward-trending currencies. These concepts are relatively simple to explain to a non-technical audience and result in a disciplined and consistent approach to directional trading.

There are a number of advantages from combining a variety of trading approaches. This chapter demonstrates that the value-oriented strategy, when traded in isolation, included a relatively large yield component. However, when integrated, the approach was able to concentrate more directly on the issues relating to valuation. We also demonstrated that rebalancing of capital across the strategies resulted in a substantial improvement of average returns. Finally, one further advantage that is not stressed in this chapter is the value of netting across the strategies. If each approach is implemented separately, it is extremely likely that the approaches will partially take offsetting positions. By integrating the approaches, transactions costs are saved by not implementing offsetting positions.

During the period of floating exchange rates, the approach outlined in this chapter has presented an extremely attractive risk/return trade-off relative to other investments. As in all studies of market efficiency, there can be no presumption that this trade-off will continue to exist in the future. If more capital is invested in this approach, it is likely that situations of extreme over- and under-valuation will be eliminated and that international differences in short-term interest rates will be small. Under these circumstances, the expected returns from the model described here will decrease and the size of the positions will be reduced. It is also the case that losses could be incurred by the program if the expected returns failed to forecast actual returns. The results have demonstrated that at least one year of trading is required before there is a reasonable expectation of profit. Over shorter horizons, the expected returns are small relative to the expected risk.

REFERENCES

Abuaf, Niso, and Philippe Jorion, "Purchasing Power Parity in the Long Run," *Journal of Finance* (1990, Vol. 45).

Alexander, S. S., "Price Movements in Speculative Markets: Trends or Random Walks?" *Industrial Management Review* (1961, Vol. 2).

Bailey, Richard T., and Tim Bollerslev, "The Message in Daily Exchange Rates: A Conditional Variance Tale," *Journal of Business and Economic Statistics* (1989, Vol. 7).

Bilson, John F. O., "The Speculative Efficiency Hypothesis," *Journal of Business* (1981, Vol 54).

Bilson, John F. O., "Technical Currency Trading," in Lee Thomas (ed.), *The Currency Hedging Debate* (IFR, 1990).

Bilson, John F. O., "Purchasing Power Parity as a Trading Strategy," *Journal of Finance* (1984).

Bilson, John F. O., "Hedging Currency Risk," in Sumner Levine (ed.), *Handbook of Global Investing* (HarperCollins, 1992).

Cumby, Robert E., and John Huizinga, "The Predictability of Real Exchange Rate Changes in the Short and Long Run," NBER Working Paper # 3468, 1990.

Domowitz, Ian, and Craig S. Hakkio, "Conditional Variance and the Risk Premium in the Foreign Exchange Market," *Journal of International Economics* (1985, Vol. 19).

Dooley, Michael, and Jeffrey Schafer, "Analysis of Short Run Exchange Rate Behavior: March, 1973–November, 1981," in *Exchange Rates and Trade Instability* (Ballinger, 1983).

Engel, Charles M., and James D. Hamilton, "Long Swings in the Dollar: Are They in the Data and Do Markets Know It?" *American Economic Review* (1990, Vol. 80).

Fama, Eugene F., "Forward and Spot Exchange Rates," *Journal of Monetary Economics* (1984, Vol 14).

Fama, Eugene F., and Kenneth R. French, "Dividend Yields and Expected Stock Returns," *Journal of Financial Economics* (1988, Vol. 22).

Hodrick, Robert, *The Empirical Evidence on the Efficiency of Forward and Futures Foreign Exchange Markets* (Harwood Academic Publishers, 1987).

Hsieh, David, "Testing for Non-Linear Dynamics in Daily Foreign Exchange Rate Changes," *Journal of Business* (1989, Vol. 62).

Kim, Yoonbai, "Purchasing Power Parity in the Long Run: A Cointegration Approach," *Journal of Money, Credit and Banking* (1990, Vol. 20).

Koedijk, Kees G., and Peter Schotman, "How to Beat the Random Walk: An Empirical Model of Real Exchange Rates," *Journal of International Economics* (1990, Vol 29).

Levich, Richard M., and Lee R. Thomas, "The Significance of Technical Trading Rule Profits in the Foreign Exchange Market: A Bootstrap Approach," *Journal of International Money and Finance* (1993 forthcoming).

Mark, Nelson C., "Exchange Rates and Fundamentals: Evidence on Long-Horizon Predictability and Overshooting," Working Paper, Ohio State University, August 1992.

Sweeney, R. J., "Beating the Foreign Exchange Market," *Journal of Finance* (1986, Vol. 41).

Sweeney, R. J., "Some New Filter Rule Tests: Methods and Results," *Journal of Financial and Quantitative Analysis* (1988, Vol 23).

Taylor, S. J., "Profitable Currency Futures Trading: A Comparison of Technical and Time Series Rules," in Lee Thomas (ed.), *The Currency Hedging Debate* (IFR, 1990).

NOTES

1. A number of recent studies have examined the volatility of exchange rates using more sophisticated techniques than those used in this chapter. See, for example, Bailey and Bollerslev (1989), Domowitz and Hakkio (1985), and Hsieh (1989).
2. The trading model developed in this section was first described in Bilson (1984). For research on the topics discussed in this section, see Abuaf and Jorion (1990), Engel and Hamilton (1990), Cumby and Huizinga (1990), Kim (1990), and Koedijk and Schotman (1990).
3. Horizon analysis is related to the literature on forecasting asset returns developed by Fama and French (1988), where it is demonstrated that asset returns become more predictable over longer time horizons. See Mark (1992) for an application of this approach to the foreign exchange market.
4. The trading model discussed in this section is based upon Bilson (1981). There is a very large literature on the relationship between exchange rates and interest rates. See Hodrick (1987) for a survey.
5. Related literature for this section includes Alexander (1961), Bilson (1990, 1992), Dooley and Schafer (1983), Levich and Thomas (1993), Sweeney (1986, 1988), and Taylor (1990).

21

Informational Portfolio Strategies™ and Dynamic Asset Allocation of Currencies

Dr. Sanford J. Grossman
Quantitative Financial Strategies, Inc.

INTRODUCTION

International currencies make up an asset class that is distinct from international equities or international bonds. The currencies have risk-return profiles that differ from those of equities and bonds and that are substantially uncorrelated with those assets. In the same way that international equities and international bonds have added important diversification to many institutional portfolios, international currencies may provide yet another opportunity to add diversification. Throughout this chapter, when we refer to a foreign currency asset class, we mean an investment in a short-term money market instrument of a foreign country, financed at the U.S. interest rate.

GLOBAL ASSET ALLOCATION

Dynamic Asset Allocation

The chief benefit of portfolio diversification is that, by adding financial instruments to a portfolio, one can raise the average return achievable for a given level of risk. While diversification can benefit even a fixed, or static, portfolio allocation, the benefits of global diversification are greatly enhanced through dynamic asset allocation. Static asset allocation—also called strategic asset allocation—allocates a portfolio based on an investor's long-run desired mix; the allocation is fixed over time. Dynamic asset allocation—also called tactical asset allocation—changes the asset mix based upon changes in the expected risk and returns of each asset class. Dynamic asset allocation is built upon the premise that it is possible to identify changes in expected returns and risk.

Modern Portfolio Theory

Figure 21.1 shows a mean-standard deviation efficient frontier and preference diagram. The efficient frontier of what is attainable is plotted by taking combinations of cash, bonds, and stocks. The horizontal axis represents the standard deviation, and the vertical axis shows the average return. Cash has a low expected return and a low standard deviation. Stocks have a high expected return and a high standard deviation. Bonds are somewhere in between. By forming different portfolios—that is, various combinations of stock, cash, and bonds—we could attain anything on this frontier. The upper line on the diagram is a statement of the investor's risk preferences. This investor, like most of us, requires higher expected return to bear more risk. With these risk preferences and this feasible frontier of attainable risk and reward, the optimal portfolio for this investor is 50 percent stock, 40 percent bond, and 10 percent cash, and it is occurring at the tangency between his or her preferences and the efficient frontier.

FIGURE 21.1   Efficient Frontier A

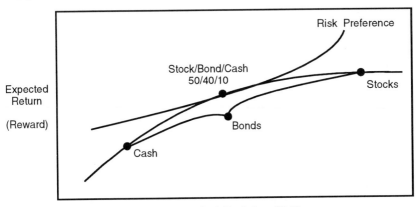

Static asset allocation is based upon the idea that none of these curves ever move. If none of these curves ever move, the investor's allocation should not change. Dynamic (or tactical) asset allocation, on the other hand, is based upon the idea that expected returns and volatilities change, and therefore the optimal allocation should change. Sometimes the average return to cash changes, or the average return and risk of stocks change. Once he recognizes that the efficient frontier can move around, the investor whose preferences are constant will naturally change his asset allocation between stocks, bonds, and cash.

Figure 21.2 illustrates this point. It shows a lower expected return for stocks and a higher expected return for cash than was shown in Figure 21.1. In this situation, it is now optimal for the investor to be investing 10 percent in stocks, zero percent in bonds, and 90 percent in cash.

The market presents an investor with variable investment opportunities. For example, if a particular asset is in great favor, then the market may price it high and may offer a low expected return. Dynamic asset allocation is based upon the idea that the investment opportunity set changes in a measurable way. The optimal mix should change as the investment opportunity set changes.

Later sections of this chapter will discuss how Informational Price Theory™ provides a theory to explain why it is that the efficient frontier changes its position. This chapter will also explain how Informational Portfolio Strategies™ incorporates insights

FIGURE 21.2 Efficient Frontier B

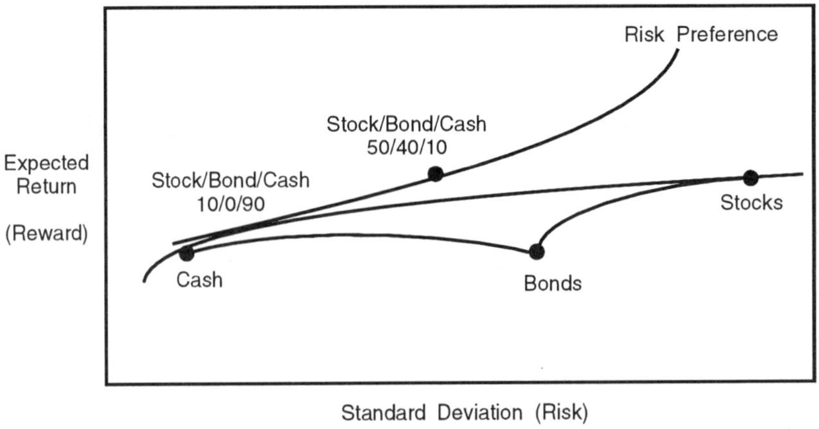

Standard Deviation (Risk)

from Informational Price Theory™ to develop a quantitative model of the relationships between price movements, expected returns, and risk, which is used to dynamically adjust allocations as the efficient frontier moves.

Benefits of Global Dynamic Asset Allocation

The benefits of incorporating international currencies into a global dynamic asset allocation strategy are demonstrated in Figure 21.3, which compares the simulated performance of three hypothetical portfolios dynamically allocated according to Informational Portfolio Strategies™: (a) U.S. stocks, U.S. government bonds; (b) U.S. stocks, U.S. government bonds, treasury bills, eurodollars, and the following international government bonds—German, French, British, Japanese, and Canadian; (c) the same portfolio as (b) with the addition of the following international currencies— German, Swiss, British, Japanese, and Canadian. The results for the portfolios shown in Figure 21.3 were achieved by using the Informational Portfolio Strategies™ model to compute a new expected return for each asset every time market conditions change (instead of using one estimate of expected return based on the historical average return—which is how a static optimal allocation would be selected). Each time the mean return changes, a new portfolio allocation is then selected to maximize the expected return per unit of risk, based on achieving the highest return subject to a 3.5 percent per month level of risk (equivalent to the

FIGURE 21.3   Benefits of Global Dynamic Asset Allocation
Average Monthly Return over T-bills, 1976–1991
(Simulated Results)

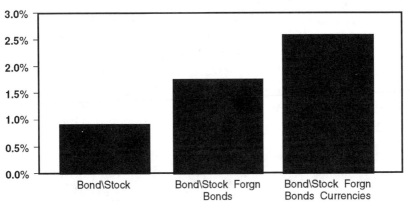

monthly risk of a fixed 60 percent stock/40 percent bond portfolio). All portfolio allocations are implemented (hypothetically) by taking futures positions. By holding positions in foreign bond futures (as opposed to cash bonds), there is no currency return (no exchange rate risk) included in the foreign bond allocations. Short positions may be held, as well as long positions, so that, for example, the portfolio can earn a positive return from correctly anticipating that a particular currency will depreciate against the dollar.

As Figure 21.3 shows, the diversification provided by including currencies in the portfolio generates a higher expected return for the same level of risk.

CURRENCIES AS AN ASSET CLASS

The preceding discussion has focused on the benefits of dynamic global asset allocation and the enhanced risk-adjusted expected returns that are associated with the inclusion of currencies in such a strategy. The discussion that follows will focus on currencies as a distinct asset class and explain how currencies can be incorporated into an international multi-asset-class portfolio that is dynamically allocated to optimize risk adjusted return.

At least two objections have been raised to the consideration of currencies (i.e., dollar-financed investment in foreign money market instruments) as an independent asset class. The first objection questions whether currency risk and return are uncorrelated with equity or bond risk and return. The second objection contends that currency investments do not have a positive expected return.

Currencies as an Independent Source of Risk and Return

An argument that is sometimes used against including currencies in a portfolio is that foreign equity and foreign bond investments already have currency risk built into them. In fact, from the perspective of a U.S. investor, an investment in foreign equities or foreign bonds can be considered to have two components: an equity risk component (in the case of equities) or an interest rate risk component (in the case of bonds) and a currency (exchange rate) risk component.

For a U.S. investor holding a portfolio of foreign equities and/or bonds, the risk and expected return of that portfolio have two components. One component is the risk and return of the foreign instruments denominated in the foreign currency, and the other component is the risk and return associated with fluctuations in the foreign currency exchange rates (the foreign currency component). An investor, having selected a portfolio of international equities and bonds in order to attain an attractive risk-adjusted equity and bond return, has, in consequence, also assumed a portfolio of currency positions. The allocations within the currency portfolio, however, have not been selected to optimize the risk-adjusted return of the currency portfolio, but are merely a by-product of the allocations of the equities and bonds in the portfolio.

The return to foreign equity can be decomposed into: (a) the excess of the equity return over the foreign money market rate, plus (b) the foreign money market rate. In other words, a foreign equity position can be decomposed into (a) an equity position financed by borrowing at the foreign market rate, plus (b) an investment in the foreign money market instrument. This decomposition is convenient because part (a) has no currency risk and part (b) has all the currency risk. In other words, the currency risk of a foreign equity position is equivalent to the currency risk of the foreign money market investment of the same size as the equity investment. The foreign currency component of the return is the difference between the foreign money market rate and the U.S. money market rate, adjusted by the exchange rate.

The above decomposition is illustrated by the following example. Consider an investor with $100 worth of German equities. Over a short period of time, his or her return will be composed of the rate of return on the equities in excess of the German short-term interest rate plus the dollar return from a $100 investment in German short-term money market instruments. If S_1 is the spot exchange rate (in $/DM), and the U.S. interest rate is 7 percent, and the DM interest rate is 8 percent, then borrowing $100, converting it at the current exchange rate S_1 ($/DM), and lending at the deutsche mark interest rate will yield $1.08(100/S_1)$ deutsche marks in one year or $S_2(1.08(100/S_1))$ dollars (where S_2 is the exchange rate at the end of the year). Thus, by creating $100(1.07) liability, the investor obtains an asset worth $S_2(1.08(100/S1))$ dollars. The dollar return from holding a deutsche mark deposit instead of a U.S. deposit can therefore be expressed as: $100[(1.08)(S_2/S_1) - 1.07]$. This example shows that the return to holding a foreign currency depends on the relationship of the future movement in the exchange rate relative to the current interest rate differential. The return will be positive, so long as the deutsche mark does not depreciate relative to the dollar by enough to cancel out the interest rate differential (i.e., it will be positive if $S_2/S_1 > 1.07/1.08$).

A similar decomposition can be applied to foreign bond return: (a) the excess of the foreign bond return over the foreign money market rate, plus (b) the foreign money market rate. The currency risk of the foreign bond investment is equivalent to the currency risk of the foreign money market investment of the same size as the bond investment. The foreign currency component of the return is, here again, the difference between the foreign money market rate and the U.S. money market rate, adjusted by the exchange rate.

Numerous empirical studies have shown that, among the major currencies, foreign exchange risk has a very low correlation with foreign equity risk and it also has a low correlation with foreign bond risk. This means that the optimal allocation among international currencies is not likely to be the same as the optimal allocation among international equities or bonds. It is therefore desirable to decompose the currency component from an international portfolio and allocate it separately. This may be accomplished by overlaying a strategic dynamic currency hedging program on a portfolio of equities and/or bond holdings or by holding: (i) equities index futures, (ii) foreign bond futures, and (iii) currency futures or forward contracts. In such a way we can optimally allocate a portfolio to both international equities, bonds, and currencies, rather than creating an optimal stock and bond allocation that automatically generates a (not necessarily optimal) currency allocation.

SOURCES OF POSITIVE EXPECTED RETURNS IN CURRENCY FUTURES: THE INFORMATIONAL PORTFOLIO STRATEGIES™ APPROACH

The second objection that is given against the inclusion of currencies in a diversified international portfolio is that a portfolio of currencies will not have a positive expected return. In this section it will be explained how a dynamic asset allocation strategy may earn a positive expected return from currency positions (i.e., from positions in international money market instruments). As will be explained further below, the return from holding a foreign currency is related to the interest rate differential between the foreign currency and the U.S. dollar. Investing in a foreign currency will have a positive return to the extent that the exchange rate of the foreign currency does not depreciate by as much as the difference between the foreign and U.S. money market rates.

Exchange Rates and Interest Rate Differentials

Holding a portfolio of foreign currency futures serves as a way of lending in high interest rate currencies and borrowing in low interest rate currencies. The investor can choose to lend in currencies with interest rates above the U.S. rate by holding long positions in the futures of such currencies, and borrow in currencies with interest rates below the U.S. rate by holding short positions in the futures of such currencies. The forward premium (the percent difference between the spot price and the futures price of a foreign currency) must be a function of the difference in interest rates for borrowing in that currency versus the interest rate for borrowing in dollars, because one can effect a futures position in a currency by borrowing dollars, converting those dollars to the currency, and lending in the currency.

For example, suppose that the interest rate in yen is 4 percent and the interest rate in dollars is 7 percent, then borrowing one yen and converting it at the current exchange rate S (dollars per yen) will yield S*1.07 dollars at the end of the year at a cost of 1.04 yen. This makes the forward exchange rate S*1.07 dollars per 1.04 yen, or 1.07/1.04 times the current exchange rate S. The ratio of the two interest rate factors (which is approximately equal to 1 plus the difference between the two interest rates; i.e., 1 + (.07 − .04)) determines the ratio of the spot and the forward exchange rate. Since a short forward position in yen is equivalent to borrowing in yen and lending in dollars, the yield on that forward position is the interest rate differential between dollars and yen.

The sale of a yen forward has a *net return* composed of (a) the interest rate differential (of the dollar interest rate above the yen interest rate), plus (b) the rate of actual appreciation of the dollar relative to the yen.

The difference in interest rates between dollars and yen is determined by the relative demand for borrowing yen versus dollars. From the perspective of Informational Price Theory™ this relative demand has two components: an informational component and a noninformational component. It is the noninformational component of the relative demand for currencies that is the source of positive expected returns.

Efficient Market Theory—The Traditional Approach

According to the traditional view of efficient market theory, there is no relationship between price moves and expected returns. The price of an asset changes only because new information is received about the payoff investors will get from holding the asset. Since any price changes perfectly reflect changes in future payoffs, the expected returns from a given asset (expected payoffs divided by price) remain constant.

Suppose, for example that the price of a stock is $500 and its expected payoff is $50. If information is released that the payoff will increase to $100, the price will rise to $1000, so that the expected return remains 10 percent.

According to efficient market theory, a price move might be a signal that an asset was *previously* under- or overpriced, but it can never be a signal that the asset is *currently* mispriced. Efficient market theory provides no way to use price moves to identify buying or selling opportunities.

Informational Price Theory™

Informational Price Theory™ [1] asserts that certain price moves provide signals about expected returns. Informational Price Theory distinguishes two different types of price movement: informational price moves and noninformational price moves.

Noninformational price movements occur when certain investors change their risk or liquidity preferences. These preference changes may cause those investors to want to reduce (or increase) their holdings in an asset class for reasons other than a change in information about future payoffs. For example, a mutual fund anticipating a large redemption may sell equities and increase its holdings of cash-equivalent instruments. Investors with an increase in wealth may feel a desire to take greater risk, and this will increase the demand for equities.

Changes in risk or liquidity preferences produce trading activity, which causes price moves that are not related to a change in expected payoffs. Price moves that occur without corresponding changes in payoffs result in changes in expected rates of return (payoff divided by price). Investors who do not share the same risk or liquidity preferences that produced the noninformational price move have an opportunity to earn excess risk-adjusted returns by taking the other side of those trades.

Informational and Noninformational Components of Interest Rate Differentials and Foreign Currency Expected Returns

Efficient markets proponents would argue that the difference in interest rates between two currencies reflects an expected change in the exchange rate. For example, if the interest rate in Germany is higher than the U.S. interest rate, the interest rate differential between the two currencies reflects an anticipated depreciation of the deutsche mark versus the dollar.

Informational Price Theory™ suggests (and statistical analysis confirms) that the interest rate differential has two components: an informational and a noninformational component. It is the second component, described below, which provides a source of positive expected returns to holding positions in foreign currencies.

The difference in interest rates between dollars and deutsche marks is determined by the relative demand for borrowing in deutsche marks versus borrowing in dollars, compared to the supply of reserves to the German and U.S. banking systems.

The informational component of the interest rate differential (and of the relative demand) consists of information about the future exchange rate of deutsche marks versus dollars. For those borrowers (or lenders) who are indifferent between borrowing in deutsche marks or in dollars, the interest rate differential should match the differential between the current exchange rate and the expected future exchange rate, otherwise they will shift their borrowing to the currency with the lower "real" interest rate. If all borrowers and lenders are indifferent about the currencies they borrow or lend, a currency with a high interest rate relative to the dollar interest rate will on average depreciate relative to the dollar. Thus, it may be that the deutsche mark interest rate is higher exactly because the currency is expected to depreciate relative to the dollar. The informational component in the interest rate differential is thus the expected change in the exchange rate.

However, there are many borrowers and lenders who are not indifferent about whether they borrow or lend in deutsche marks or in dollars and for these borrowers, other considerations may affect the interest rates they are willing to accept on deposits for loans in a particular currency. For example, in the U.S., as in many other economies, most domestic deposit holders prefer to hold deposits in dollars rather than in other currencies. For individuals or businesses that do not import or export, foreign deposits (which are subject to exchange rate fluctuations) are more risky than domestic deposits. Indeed, for most investors, deposits serve as a risk-free asset, and they prefer to minimize risk on that portion of their investments.

The risk aversion of domestic depositors creates a segmented market for domestic deposits. The consequence of segmented markets is that central banks are able to effect changes in interest rates in order to implement monetary policy—changes that are not related to information about exchange rates.

For example, the central bank in Germany may seek to control inflation by raising interest rates in order to decrease the demand for credit. This strategy may be successful because many domestic borrowers, being risk-averse about assuming obligations denominated in a foreign currency, will not go outside Germany to borrow at a lower foreign interest rate. If the central bank in this way succeeds in reducing inflation, the deutsche mark may actually appreciate relative to other currencies with lower interest rates.

Noninformational changes in interest rate differentials may occur when central banks effect changes in domestic interest rates in order to implement monetary policy. These changes are noninformational because they are effected by the central bank *in order to cause a change* in the net demand for loans in the currency, rather than *resulting* from a change in the net demand for loans caused by a change in information about future exchange rates.

An increase in the relative demand for borrowing in one currency rather than another will tend to raise the relative interest rate in that currency. Since this shift in relative interest rates occurs independently of information about future exchange rates, it is a noninformational price change. Movements in interest rates that are due to noninformational factors (and therefore are not offset by subsequent changes in spot exchange rates) create an opportunity for investors to hold a portfolio of forward positions in foreign currencies with a positive risk-adjusted expected return.

INFORMATIONAL PORTFOLIO STRATEGIES™ AND DYNAMIC ASSET ALLOCATION OF CURRENCIES

The selection of the optimal currency portfolio is a dynamic process. As the pattern of interest rate differentials changes, the expected returns associated with any particular portfolio change, and thus the optimal portfolio changes.

Dynamically Adjusting the Optimal Portfolio

The key to the performance of Informational Portfolio Strategies™ lies in how the allocations to each asset are dynamically adjusted, i.e., in the ability to accurately estimate changes in the mean return of each asset. In the case of the currencies, a change in the mean return is related to predicted changes in the exchange rate relative to the interest rate differential. The objective of IPS™ is to identify when exchange rates will depreciate or appreciate relative to the interest rate differential, and (everything else held constant) to take long positions in currencies whose exchange rate can be expected to appreciate and short positions in those whose exchange rate will depreciate.

To accomplish this objective, IPS™ uses insights from Informational Price Theory™ to construct a quantitative statistical model to analyze the pattern of short-term interest rate differentials among different countries. The model identifies interest rate differentials that have noninformational components and thus offer a positive risk-adjusted expected return. IPS™ takes positions in those interest rate differentials by dynamically adjusting a portfolio of currency futures or forwards.

Statistical Technology

IPS™ identifies optimal currency portfolios through a statistical analysis of the simultaneous covariations among interest rate differentials and ensuing changes in exchange rates. Roughly speaking, when the interest rate of one currency is high relative to its typical position among the interest rates of other currencies, the model forecasts that the forward price will rise (bringing its interest rate relationship back to its typical relative position). In this case, a long position in that currency forward contract is likely to have a positive return. Similarly, an unusually low interest rate predicts a forward price fall, suggesting that a long position will not be profitable. The statistical analysis shows that forward price moves that result in atypical relative interest rate positions tend to be followed by forward price reversals, resulting in nonzero returns. In this way, the model indicates which price moves are noninformational and thus offer opportunities to earn positive returns.

SUMMARY

The Informational Portfolio Strategies™ approach to dynamic global asset allocation treats currencies as a distinct asset class. By using futures or forwards to isolate the currency risk/return component of an international portfolio, IPS™ is able to dynamically optimize the currency allocations in an international portfolio instead of bearing currency risk as a by-product of other asset class allocations or hedging it away. The lack of correlation between currency risk and other asset classes makes currencies a good source of portfolio diversification. The insights of Informational Price Theory™ regarding the noninformational aspects of exchange rate fluctuations enable IPS™ to incorporate currencies into a dynamic global asset allocation strategy as a significant source of positive expected return.

NOTE

1. Informational Price Theory™ is discussed in my book, entitled *The Informational Role of Prices*, MIT Press, 1989.

Appendix

The Cash Foreign Exchange Market: An Overview

I. WHAT IS FOREX?

Long before the former USSR opened the door even a crack to capitalism or free market thinking, some of the more aggressive traders in the world's most active free market could be found in Moscow. In fact, many of the former hard-line communist countries harbored small outposts of pure capitalism known as Foreign Exchange (Forex) dealing rooms. Tucked neatly out of sight, squirreled away behind the camouflage of centrally planned economic policies, there were Forex traders gazing at currency prices on a quote screen.

Since 1971, when floating exchange rates began to materialize, the cash Foreign Exchange market has grown into the world's largest financial market. According to a survey by the Bank for International Settlements (BIS), global currency trading volume doubled between 1986 and 1989 to reach an average of $640 billion per day. A survey conducted by the Federal Reserve Bank of New York in April 1992 estimated the average daily turnover in the United States alone at $192 billion, an increase of 49% over its 1989 estimate of $129 billion. Similar growth in worldwide trading between 1989 and 1992, applied to BIS's 1989 estimates, would put the current market size at over $950 billion. Not surprisingly, in September 1992 *The Wall Street Journal* described

417

anecdotal trading volume estimates of $1 trillion per day. In comparison, daily trading volume averages $300 billion in the U.S. Treasury Bond market, and less than $10 billion in the U.S. stock markets.

The Forex market is a cash interbank or interdealer market. The market is both highly differentiated from, yet intrinsically linked to, the currency futures market. Forex is not a "market" in the traditional sense. There is no centralized location for trading activity as there is in currency futures. Trading occurs over the telephone and through computer terminals at hundreds of locations worldwide. The direct interbank market consists of dealers with currency settlement capabilities trading as principals.

It is this dealer segment of the market that is responsible for generating a large portion of the overall Forex volumes. That is, trading between dealers, not volume generated by customers, creates the largest turnover in the market. There is a tremendous value created by this dealer-to-dealer activity since it provides most of the liquidity in the market, much as locals provide liquidity in a futures pit.

II. CASH FOREX VERSUS CURRENCY FUTURES

It is useful here to highlight differences between cash Forex and currency futures.

Contract size is predetermined in futures. In Forex, one million dollars worth of a currency is generally accepted as a minimum round lot, but any smaller size is possible. Single orders larger than a million dollars are regularly traded in the Forex market. On large-size trades, however, time of day can have a direct impact on the liquidity available for the trade. For example, it is more difficult to obtain liquidity in British pounds in the afternoon in New York, after London business hours are over. Overall, the Forex market remains the preferred choice for liquidity on large trades.

There are distinct differences in liquidity between the cash and futures markets. These differences can have a large impact on the quality of executions one receives in each market. It is rarely possible to execute a large trade on the futures exchange at only one price. Slippage, which represents the difference between the best price or fill and the worst fill, can be considerable. In Forex, it is typical to execute an entire large-size trade at one price. However, the futures market is usually considered more efficient than the cash market at executing smaller trades below one million dollars.

Futures trading results in transaction costs. Brokerage, clearing and exchange fees are generally required in addition to the bid/offer spread paid away in the trading pit. There is also a bid/offer spread in the Forex market but there are normally no additional costs, such as brokerage, if a customer trades directly with a principal dealer. A customer who has unique needs in areas such as reporting or credit usage may incur specific charges.

Forex is a continuous market. There are dealers in every major time zone, in every major dealing center (i.e., London, New York, Tokyo, Hong Kong, Sydney, etc.) willing to quote two-way markets. Unlike the futures markets, this provides 24-hour market access to participants. An "Exchange for Physical" or EFP provides traders with the ability to exchange a cash Forex position for a futures position.

A substantial difference between the cash Forex and futures markets involves the number of traded currencies available. The futures market offers a limited number of actively traded currencies. The cash Forex market by definition provides access to all exchangeable currencies. In practice, many "exotic" currencies are either tightly regulated or simply too illiquid to trade.

III. IMPORTANCE OF CREDIT AND DELIVERY IN THE FOREX MARKET

What truly defines the core structure of the cash Forex market is the settlement and delivery process. Convention has been built around the actual delivery of one currency against another, so even the "spot" market is for two-day settlement. This reflects the difference in time zones between nations as well as the actual time it once took, before the high-speed computer era, to wire money over oceanic cables. The forward market is generally considered to be any delivery time beyond the typical two-day spot period.

Since this is a delivery-based market, cash has to flow between counterparties at a point in time. However, most nations are not in the same time zone, and therefore currency deliveries cannot occur simultaneously. This creates a risk for the entity that must send out a payment before receiving its payment in return. Delivery risk becomes a very real factor in Forex—a risk that is not a fundamental part of the futures market. The futures clearing-house assures each party to a transaction of proper delivery. In Forex, the decision to do business with a counterparty is a credit decision.

Unlike the futures market, where the exchange reduces most credit concerns, counterparty creditworthiness is crucial to the cash Forex market. The willingness of one party to trade Forex with another depends on an analysis of the ability and commitment of each party to meet mutual delivery obligations. As a result, Forex dealers with higher credit ratings, such as "AAA" rated firms, are more attractive to their counterparties in the markets. This type of credit analysis often drives trading relationships. The willingness of one party to execute Forex with another is determined by the amount of credit line available for the counterparty as well as by overall relationship factors such as information flow and execution quality.

IV. SPOT AND FORWARD TRADING

Around 90% of Forex trading volume is generated by spot and forward and swap trades (see Figure 1). The spot market, for normal two-day delivery, is the most actively traded, and represents the current "cash" value of a currency. A large portion of the daily volume is generated by spot dealers trading among themselves to cover transactions made with clients or other dealing counterparties. Spot dealers also often "job" the market, seeking to profit by holding a position intraday for small market moves.

Forward trading is basically any Forex trade with a delivery or value date more than two days away. In general, forward trading represents the trading of differentials between outright forward (future) settlement prices and the spot price. In some respects this differential, or "the forward," is akin to the basis in futures. Forwards are added to or subtracted from the spot price and are traded independently of spot. The premium or discount represents the carrying cost or value of a forward delivery and is calculated directly from the difference in interest rates between currencies. Currencies may also be "swapped" whereby a currency is simultaneously bought (or sold) for a future value date and sold (or bought) for another date in equivalent amounts.

FIGURE 1   Distribution of Daily FX Turnover in the U.S.

Transaction Segment	1992	1989
Spot	50.5%	60.5%
Forwards and Swaps	37.7%	32.9%
Options (OTC)	8.4%	3.9%
Exchange Traded Derivatives	3.4%	2.7%

Source: The Federal Reserve Bank of New York, April 1992 Survey

Dealers who trade forwards operate in a substantially different environment than spot traders. Forward trading is generally not as volatile as spot trading since forwards are largely comprised of interest rate differentials. The forward dealer also concerns himself primarily with positioning his book to take advantage of incremental shifts in global interest rates rather than the rapid movements of the spot market.

A forward trade often begins as a spot transaction. A client needing to execute a Forex transaction might call a dealer who has established a credit line, which may include a futures-like margin account for the client. At the dealing firm, the client will typically speak with a salesperson who will obtain a price for the client from a spot trader in the dealing room assigned to a particular currency. Since the spot price is the actively moving price, this is executed first. Later in the day, the salesperson will obtain the forward points from the forward trader. These points, added to or subtracted from the spot price, result in the outright forward price.

Over-the-counter (OTC) currency options and exchange-traded options on futures contracts currently represent around 12% of the U.S. daily FX turnover. This segment, especially the OTC options area, has grown rapidly since 1989. Several OTC options dealers now offer average rate, barrier and other customized option contracts in addition to the traditional European- and American-style option contracts.

V. SETTLEMENT AND MARGINING

The cash effect of a Forex trade (the settlement process) is a major consideration for most market participants. In an outright forward transaction no cash flows between counterparties until the actual settlement date. In fact, no cash will be realized until the settlement date, even if the position is offset and no market risk remains.

In a swap transaction, in which an equivalent amount of currency is bought or sold from one date to another to meet specific delivery requirements, a cash settlement occurs on each leg of the swap as that leg reaches maturity. As a result, moving a position forward to a new date may still create a cash settlement when the nearer date matures. However, appropriately structured swaps can manage the cash flow consequence of forward trading.

The cash market settlement process differs markedly from the futures market, in which daily cash settlements are the norm. Open positions in the futures markets are marked-to-market at their closing prices, and any unrealized profits or losses are adjusted to the customer's margin account daily. As a result, the amount of margin deposit has a direct impact on the volume of allowed trading for each customer.

Currency dealers have been slow to fully embrace the notion of margin trading in the Forex market. This may be the result of several factors, including the notion that Forex dealers, thriving in a business based on cash settlements and credit lines, do not see themselves as brokers in the traditional sense. They tend to associate margin trading facilities with a type of retail activity perceived as peripheral to their main business. As investment pools and funds have dramatically expanded their trading activities in currencies and moved into the cash markets, currency trading has in fact come virtually full circle. While these funds do have large asset bases, most of their balance sheet capital is subject to speculative exposure and credit lines are difficult to rationalize. To capture business from this decidedly professional and non-retail sector, Forex dealers have been pushed, sometimes reluctantly, to offer margin facilities to these fund managers.

The reluctance of Forex market participants to expand into a margined trading environment is often related to operations and systems concerns. While most major cash Forex dealers posses sophisticated computer systems and operational capabilities to monitor credit exposure, process Forex trades, and handle daily settlements in a large variety of currencies, they have traditionally lacked systems capable of managing margin balances, making and tracking margin calls, producing clear, concise daily customer statements, and, if necessary, holding customer funds in appropriate segregated accounts.

Leverage is another concept not historically present in cash Forex. While it is a natural tool for trading on margin, it is also anathema to many institutional Forex dealers such as banks. Ultimately, one could argue that a Forex dealer should be in a position to offer the same degree of gearing found in the futures market. However, this again presumes that a Forex dealer has the operational capability to monitor a margin account closely, particularly one trading at a high leverage ratio. Since most dealers do not have this type of infrastructure, dealers have found it prudent, given the position sizes traded in Forex, to offer leverage multiples that are more conservative than those found in the futures market.

VI. WHO ARE THE MARKET PLAYERS

Central Banks

If there exists any governing influence over the Forex market, it is the central banks. Each central bank attempts to control the relative value of its currency through indirect methods, such as interest rate adjustments carried out by raising or lowering bank borrowing rates, or by tightening or loosening money supply.

The central bank action that can throw the most frenzied excitement into a Forex trading room is the sudden appearance of intervention, in which central banks are seen buying or selling large amounts of currency or dollars in a generally concerted manner through dealers in the interbank market. This attempt to adjust and control the level of exchange rates can have a direct impact on the overall direction of the market for an extended period, or it may be meant only as a warning to the market that central bankers, through the G-7 or any other clandestine gathering committee, are becoming concerned with the level and direction of exchange rates.

The skill with which central banks carry out Forex market intervention has been the fodder for after-hours cocktail conversations among currency dealers for years. In the early years of central bank intervention, following the introduction of free-floating exchange rates, it was widely agreed (among Forex dealers at least) that the central banks were unsophisticated currency traders.

Attempts through intervention to alter the market-determined prices of the dollar, however, often served only to throw temporary volatility into the market and enrich speculators and dealers. For interbank dealers, intervention means large intraday swings in prices which could result in huge profits or losses. In any event, traders were provided with excellent opportunities to buy or sell dollars in anticipation of a continuation of the dollar's original trend.

Recently, only through huge trade size and dealing several points off the market were the central banks able to adjust market direction, even temporarily. The difficulty is that attempting to change the course of a trading market becomes futile unless larger and larger sums are thrown against it.

By the middle of the 1980s, the use of technical analysis had made its way into the Forex market. Although it had been used for many years in the futures markets, Forex spot traders had long relied on instinct instead. Forex speculators had been using "charts" for years but interbank dealers had resisted the tool as an infringement upon a business seen more as art than science. But over the years the market adopted the technique on a broad basis. This is not an appropriate moment to argue the merits of technical analysis save one basic point: If every major market player is looking at the same support and resistance levels (fearing that everyone else is anyhow), then such price levels indeed become significant.

Ultimately the central banks learned this as well, and began looking at these support and resistance levels as the perfect opportunities for intervention. With much less muscle than before, the market could be moved in the desired direction by "lifting offers" at the resistance level and "hitting bids" at support levels. By thus timing their efforts, central banks have become, from time to time, more effective in enforcing market adherence to their desired exchange rate comfort zones. The market has advanced one step further by anticipating the levels that concern the central banks and, in many instances, reacting before actual intervention is sighted.

Corporations

Corporate participants were for many years the major market segment responsible for customer-driven volume in Forex. Initially, these clients utilized the Forex markets largely to execute transactions related to cross-border payments or receipts. The repatriation of a foreign dividend or the payment for plant and equipment overseas were the type of corporate transactions that accounted for much of the corporate volume.

Corporations, guided by corporate FX salespeople working at cash Forex dealers, soon saw the value in hedging risk in various foreign exposures. Buying forward contracts became a well accepted and conservative response to foreign currency exposure. This market segment has grown tremendously over the years as hedging techniques have become increasingly sophisticated. Through the use of options and timing models, professional currency managers have turned hedging currency exposure into a rapidly growing professionally managed business.

Institutions with underlying foreign exposure in their portfolios are willing to allow currency managers to actively manage currency risk. Recognizing that exchange rates can have a profound effect on the performance of a foreign denominated portfolio, institutional investment managers have been allowing currency managers to manage currency exposure based upon an agreed benchmark. This style of hedging, known generally as "Currency Overlay," has brought substantial volume to the Forex market lately.

Currency overlay managers are many and varied. They include commercial banks, investment banks, and boutique shops specializing in managing currency exposure through a multitude of methods. There are two components generally included in effective currency management. First, the currency manager reviews the underlying exposure of the client and determines what currencies need to be hedged and in what proportions a basket of currencies should be managed to properly reflect the underlying holdings.

The second step is the actual decision process utilized by the manager. A manager may use fundamental economic analysis to determine appropriate moments to put on or take off a hedge, or technical, quantitative or systematic methods to determine appropriate hedging opportunities.

Speculators

Without a doubt, speculators have become major market participants. As a group, they are widely different. They can range in size from a wealthy individual to a huge investment company.

High-net-worth individuals recently have been able to obtain margin trading facilities and have been active in the markets. A number of extremely wealthy individuals worldwide have chosen to speculate in the Forex markets, deploying substantial amounts of capital in the endeavor with varying degrees of success. As in any investment market, a part-time attempt to succeed can prove quite difficult.

As a market force speculators have a substantial role in determining the true value of currencies. Regardless of style or methodology, speculators sell to extremes until they believe the appropriate value for that moment has been determined. While most speculators add their impact to the market simply by putting on positions that increase the total size of market long or shorts and then wait for the general market direction to move as anticipated, some speculators have tried to trade positions large enough to move the market or even change its direction at least briefly. Without overall market consensus, this is a difficult undertaking. Those few speculators successful enough to alter the desired direction have made huge market bets which are often met with stiff admonishment from central bankers.

Consider the equity markets of twenty years ago and the impact of mutual funds managed by professional equity managers. Certainly the growth of the equity market is directly attributable to the professional investor. If the currency markets gain just a small portion of the acceptance that equities currently enjoy, the market volume will grow dramatically and the impact of professional currency managers will become even more profound.

VII. WHAT MOVES THE MARKET?

Many things influence the direction of prices simultaneously.

The ebb and flow of capital between nations effects a concomitant adjustment of currency prices. Known as Purchasing Power Parity, (PPP), this theory suggests that over time, exchange rates would reflect the relative cost of acquiring identical goods between two nations. This theory is fine as long as all holders of a particular currency have equal faith in the value of such currency and that no future expectations are considered in the valuation process.

Relative value is a factor in the global currency price adjustment process, and fundamental economic forces such as inflation and interest rates will serve to drive currency prices. Economic factors such as inflation, interest rates and trade patterns all influence currency prices. Faith in a government's ability to stand behind its currency will also impact currency price.

Any of these broad-based economic conditions can cause sudden and dramatic currency price swings if such conditions are seen to be changing. This is a key concept because, in many cases, what drives the currency market is the anticipation of an economic condition rather than the condition itself.

Buying or selling currencies in response to economic or political events which occur is reactive. Buying or selling currencies based on anticipated events is speculative. This latter activity is largely what drives the market. The vast bulk of currency activity is generated by market participants anticipating the direction of currency prices.

Activities by professional currency managers, generally on behalf of a pool or fund, have also become a factor moving the market. While professional managers may behave independently and view the market from a unique perspective, most if not all are at least aware of important technical chart points in each major currency. As major support or resistance levels approach, the behavior of the market becomes more technically oriented and the reactions of many managers are often predictable and similar. These market periods may result in sudden and dramatic price swings as substantial amounts if capital are invested in similar positions.

For example, in September of 1992, a number of major currency speculators sold massive amounts of British pounds, forcing a major drop in that currency's value and ultimately forcing the UK to pull out of the ERM. Often after such dramatic events, the market resumes a more normal pattern as each currency settles into its new market-determined range and professionals manage their positions independently.

VIII. HOW IS THE FOREX MARKET ACCESSED?

At the most basic retail level, one can access the Forex market at any airport currency booth. For a service fee (and a price mark-up that can be as much as 5% to 10%), one can buy or sell currencies. In fact, for many Americans a trip to the currency exchange booth overseas is the first introduction to how much direct impact the Forex market can have on their life. This is a contrast to Europeans who have long been familiar with the impact of foreign currencies on their lives.

To directly participate in the Forex market on a wholesale or institutional level, there are a number of possible modes of access. High-net-worth individuals with private banking relationships should be able to access the cash market Forex operation of their bank. Typically, private banking groups have an established process for credit lines or margining of accounts. In this situation, individuals may be able to participate in the market on a limited basis, typically without the ability to take or make currency delivery. This is known as a netting account, in which profit and loss are calculated between an opening and closing trade and only dollar settlements take place.

Certain large investment firms also operate Forex operations for high-net-worth clients sometimes as Agents only. In these instances the investment firm, for a fee, may seek a price on behalf of a client for a specific Forex trade from principal Forex dealers.

High-net-worth individuals with either substantial balance sheets or the ability to post substantial sums as margin may be able to obtain trading accounts with principal Forex dealing desks. This has an advantage over private banking relationships, which often require the client to call a special private banking Forex desk, which may mark up the Forex price.

At a principal Forex dealing desk, market convention holds that customers call a customer desk, not the currency trader directly. This is because the currency trader is actively dealing with other principal currency dealers on a continuous basis in order to manage his currency position on behalf of the firm.

The customer desk is normally situated next to the Forex traders and the advisors who work on this desk will shout out to the traders seeking a quote on behalf of the customer. This customer advisor is a crucial part of a Forex dealing operation, responsible for handling customer trade executions in the spot market and then helping the customer "roll" the position forward. Customer people are also a crucial link for market information and outlook. The customer desk will also assist in setting up the account and handle any reports required by the customer. Customer advisors are often an important source of help in managing currency exposures.

Corporate clients requiring actual currency delivery will need a credit relationship with a Forex dealer. In the case of delivery accounts, which include nearly all corporate clients, there are payments against delivery, hence risk, to both counterparties. Thus, there are strong reasons for customers to trade with a counterparty with the highest credit rating possible, just as the Forex dealer is concerned with the ability of his customer to make good on a payment or delivery.

Investors seeking to participate in the cash currency markets may be unable or unwilling to make investment decisions themselves or trade directly with a principal Forex dealer. An alternative would be to hire a professional currency manager who provides the investor with advice which the investor may or may not act on. Or, an investor may hire a currency professional and give the professional discretion over the account. This is a superior way to work with a professional manager as the manager is likely to have the most experience and skill executing currency trades. The downside of this approach is that a single advisor may not provide the broadest access to different currency management techniques.

As in any market, there are Forex managers devoted to a particular style or specialization. There are professional managers in the Forex market with highly evolved approaches to investing and equally sophisticated risk management techniques. As in other markets, it may be more appropriate to hire a group of managers considering the potential benefit gained from diversification of style and philosophy. Although an investor can accomplish this directly, the administrative and operational burdens may be high. One alternative may be through a currency fund or other pooled type of vehicle which provides all the support services and control mechanisms.

IX. WHY IS THE FOREX MARKET ATTRACTIVE TO INVESTORS?

Professional investors have dramatically increased their level of participation in the cash Forex markets in recent years. The daily volume of activity driven by investment managers working for individual accounts or currency funds has grown astronomically. Add to this the growing use of cash Forex by individual investors and you have a rapidly growing investment arena. An appropriate way to close this chapter and summarize what has been dis-

cussed is to touch on the many reasons professional investors
have flocked to this market.

Liquidity

Without a doubt, the cash Forex market is the most liquid market.
This market can absorb trading volumes and per-trade sizes that
dwarf the capacity of any other market (see Section I). On the simplest level, liquidity is a powerful attraction to any investor as it
suggests the freedom to open or close a position at will.

The pool of professionally managed assets, including pension
and other trust funds as well as market-specific investment vehicles, has grown exponentially over the last twenty years. These
collective investment vehicles, including large "Hedge Funds,"
have seen huge increases in assets under management. A mounting problem regarding the management of these assets includes
finding a place to deploy such assets prudently. As the pool of
professionally managed assets grows (a by-product of an investment world that has become too complex for the average individual investor), the market allocation problem worsens. Markets
with limited opportunities, such as equity markets with only a
finite number of listed companies, become overburdened with
professional managers.

The cash Forex market is well equipped to handle this volume.
It is also able to absorb trading volume over time as well as in
brief bursts of activity. Investment professionals who are increasingly responsible for larger and larger size accounts need market
outlets that can absorb these higher trading volumes. Cash Forex
has become a natural alternative.

Access

Cash Forex is a continuous global market. The only breaks in trading occur during a brief period over the weekend. Naturally, in the
modern interconnected financial world, events at any hour, in any
part of the globe can affect some or all parts of the investment
community. A substantial attraction for participants in the Forex
market is the 24-hour nature of the market. A trader is able to put
on a trade in London, follow it in New York and close the trade in
the middle of the following day in Tokyo. This type of market
access is invaluable to a market participant who needs to react

quickly to global events. In Forex, a participant need not wait to react to an unfavorable event as is the case in many markets.

Flexible Settlement

Many professional investment managers have a particular time horizon in mind when they establish positions. In the Forex market, a position can be established for that specific period. Trades can be established for any date the investor desires. There are limits, of course. While it is possible to trade forwards out five or even, in rare cases, ten years or more, most market participants acting as investors may find it harder to put on positions beyond six months because of credit considerations.

Execution Costs

One can measure execution costs in two general ways. Obviously, any hard brokerage or other fees represent one type of cost. The other relates to the quality of the execution or the "fill." The cash Forex market traditionally has no brokerage charges, only a natural market bid-offer spread. One caveat is that the growth of cash market margin trading and the increasing demand for reports and other operational services by professional investment managers may force many principal Forex dealers to begin charging some type of fee to cover the cost of these extraordinary needs.

Execution Quality

In providing a fill, the cash Forex market is normally very efficient. Because the market is highly liquid, most trades can be executed at a single market price. This avoids the problem of slippage found in futures and other exchange-traded instruments where limited quantities can be traded at one time at a given price. However, the efficiency of fills in Forex does not normally extend to very small-size trades, which may be better filled on an exchange.

Trendiness

Over long historical periods currencies have shown substantial and identifiable trends. Trending markets are typically an attraction for investment professionals as they can provide longer-term position-taking opportunities. Each individual currency offers a unique historical pattern of trends providing investment managers diversification opportunities within the Forex market.

Non-regulated

In many respects, the cash Forex market is a pure unencumbered free market. It is a virtually unregulated market. Individual players may be regulated for reasons relating to their overall business or because of the way their entity is structured, or because of local country constraints. But the market itself is free and open. There are no exams, and no licenses are required to participate. This is a market based on convention and credibility. If a participant lives up to its commitments, it earns credibility. If it operates within accepted convention, a participant will be accepted.

This free-market nature means that participants operate and compete in an environment where there are no hard rules. In this market information is king and there is no "inside information." All information is fair game. Participants with the best contacts and connections may have the edge. In this market, there are no formal reporting requirements for large-size trades. Huge trades which defy a central bank's wishes may be tremendously profitable for the speculator "unnamed." The cash Forex market, this last bastion of pure unbridled capitalism, appeals to the professional investor for all of these reasons today, and is growing rapidly because of them.

Index